WITNESS TO
TREASON

How the GOP, Trump, & Greed Betrayed America

ROBERT N. McLAUGHLIN

Cloud9 Publishing Company
Philadelphia, PA

Also by Robert N McLaughlin

Danny and Mickey, Ordinary Heroes
The true story of boyhood friends, baseball, the Great Depression,
WWII, and the World Series
Go to dannyandmickey.com

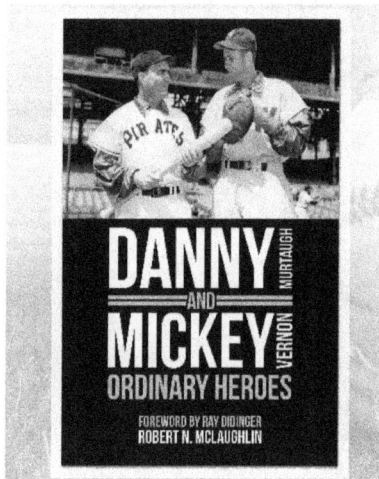

Retail bookshop owners can order this author's books on
http.www.ingramcontent.com/retailers/ordering

Dedication

This book is dedicated to the men and women who see and hear the truth and champion it, and to those who see and hear lies and speak and act against them.

Witness to Treason

Treason

Whoever, owing allegiance to the United States, levies war against them or adheres to their enemies, giving them aid and comfort within the United States or elsewhere, is guilty of treason and shall suffer death, or shall be imprisoned not less than five years and fined under this title but not less than $10,000; and shall be incapable of holding any office under the United States.

United States Constitution, Article III, Section 3,
18 U.S. Code § 2381 – Treason

Acknowledgements

There are many people who contributed to this book. I want to express my thanks to all my friends who took time to look at the early drafts of this work and who provided enthusiasm for the book and for me. Thanks for your faith in me.

My biggest fan and cheerleader is my wife Dorothy. Her 'eagle-eyes on the prize' confirmed for me that the book was ready to be given its final wings.

I am especially pleased to have my daughter-in-law, Helene McKelvey-McLaughlin join me in creating this cover design for my second book. The cover is truly an example of a picture being worth a thousand words.

Additionally, and most importantly, were the various readers – Ed Donnelly, III, Dr. Michael Milone, John King, Mike Blair, Gary and Jo-Rene Queensberry - a diverse team who read the book one chapter at a time, providing important feedback on content and grammar, and questioned passages and phrases that seemed clouded and needed clarification.

I continue to learn how research is endless on every project, how one fact can lead to the discovery of so many other facts. I am thankful for the many news articles, op-ed features, news broadcasts, photos, political cartoons, and wide assortment of books from which so many words and ideas are presented here. I have attempted to ensure that the references within the chapters and the bibliography at the end of the book fully credit the authors of the works referenced herein. I acknowledge the accuracy and dependability I receive from my local newspapers, the Philadelphia Inquirer, and the Delaware County Daily Times. I value the immediacy of the electronic media and the vigilance of the journalists and publishers who stand ready 24/7, 365 as watchdogs of factual reporting, and who stand above the fog of lies and confusion that oftentimes obscure what really happened or what was really said. Thank you, all. No previous period in our American history has been in more need for an abundance of truth to be showered on us.

Preface

Oftentimes when I see our 45th President on television, in the
newspaper, or on the cover of a magazine, I recall sitting in a darkened
neighborhood movie theater a long time ago, inside the Apollo theatre
in Chester, PA. It is Saturday afternoon somewhere between noon and
three PM. I know this because the Saturday movie matinees always
started and ended within those three hours when I was a kid. In this
memory I am always eight years old and I am wedged in a narrow seat
between my brothers Mickey and Ritchie, and all around me are more
friends who either live in the same WWII-era housing project, or close
by. Yes, girls are there too, but they are sitting with their girlfriends.
Boys with boys, girls with girls, at least until junior high school. So
there I am staring towards the front of the theater at a larger than life
white screen hanging from the ceiling over the center of the stage.
There is a rousing action-packed scene in flaming Technicolor of
firefighters responding to a fire emergency in a small town somewhere
in America. All of us are enthralled in the drama that unfolds on the
screen.

On the screen, the firehouse doors open and fire engines scream their
way out and onto the street as several figures in firemen clothing hop
onto the moving vehicles, pushing their way securely onto every inch
of the racing fire truck. The uniformed firemen flutter their wings and
a few balance themselves with one leg on the ladders. The fire trucks
move swiftly, winding around streets, and swerving to avoid startled
motorists who suddenly find themselves in the way of these wild 'hell-
bent for rescue' platoons of firefighters.

When the firetrucks reach the burning building some of their
occupants immediately hop off the truck and begin using their beaks to

Witness to Treason

drag water hoses toward the building, while others literally fly to watering stations to prepare to spray the raging fire. It was a breathtaking sequence. Eventually, lives are saved and the fire is extinguished. The firemen and their engines return to the fire station. All of the town's residents go back to their lives, some perching on tree branches, others grooming their beaks or ruffling their neighbors' feathers. The closing credits for "Bill and Coo", an hour-long feature film* starring only parakeets, fades and another feature begins.

Yes. Parakeets. I never forgot the trained parakeets in the film and how skilled they were. Like my young friends in that long ago time, I was impressed that parakeets were able to do so much so well. I've never forgotten the cleverness of the film-makers who produced it but neither I nor my friends were fooled. We knew it was a fantasy. The point of my sharing this memory is plain and simple. The nature of things animate or inanimate is not easily changed nor disguised. These birds though cleverly disguised were not real firemen, they were always birds. They will not one day magically become firemen. They will remain birds. Even as kids, we understood you can dress up a parakeet in anything but it is still a parakeet. You can put a monkey in a suit, it is still a monkey. No one can make a silk purse out of a sow's ear. If you could do any of these things, it would be unprecedented. These old adages apply here in 2018.

On January 20, 2017, Donald J. Trump was sworn in as the 45th President of the United States of America. He wears the cloak and mantle of the highest office of our country but he is like the monkey in a suit, and like the parakeet who is not a fireman. He is still Donald J. Trump, a former NYC real estate salesman, a former New Jersey casino developer, and a former reality TV host. He also happens to be an accused sexual predator, a federal tax evader, and a suspected traitor to America. He can wear a suit and sit in the Oval Office but neither the suit nor the office will transform him. On the contrary, in these unprecedented times, he is diabolically Un-Presidented.

I am hopeful that this book will help you to see clearly who it was (and who it still is) that stood alongside, marched with, and cheered for Donald Trump. I hope you will see and remember who supported his insatiable greed and benefited with him, who it was who refused to confront him forcefully about the numerous allegations of his sexual assaults on women, and who embraced and encouraged his hateful disdain for America's truest values of freedom, liberty, and justice for all Americans.

This book is my personal record of the unimaginable events that have occurred since Donald Trump scarred our nation's image when he began his campaign to run for President of the United States of America. The pages that follow here will not divulge secrets nor provide new information not previously reported elsewhere. What is offered here is an orderly account of what happened in America in the last two years, and who allowed it to happen. Most importantly, it is a written account of the truth, in my words and in the words of numerous journalists who reported on all of it. In the recounting, many of the Presidents own words, and his senior aides' own words, tell the most damning parts of the nightmare we have all shared. All of us have been witnesses to the truth. When this nightmare is over, and it cannot come a day too soon, you and I will move forward, having dodged a near-fatal blow to our nation's integrity and to our individual liberties. This book will then be lingering proof for me that the nightmare did happen. America was in danger. It was not a dream. I will keep my journal as a touchstone. It will serve to remind me on occasion that losing our inalienable rights of liberty and the pursuit of happiness can happen here in America.

If I begin to worry or doubt that it can ever happen here again, I will open the book and read it again. It is a cautionary tale that bears remembering.

* "Bill and Coo" was produced by Ken Murray in 1948.
https://www.youtube.com/watch?v=KvdpUrhhcrY)

WITNESS TO TREASON
How the GOP, Trump & Greed Betrayed America

Table of Contents

Like no other, Who is Donald Trump?, Business bankruptcies,
Trump University, Trump Foundation, Outrageous personal attacks,
"Birther", 2016 GOP Primary Campaign.......................................

More of the Same, Presidential Campaign, In his own words, Russia,
if you are listening, The Russians are here, Stalking Hillary,
The Access Hollywood Tape, Aftermath from Access Hollywood
tape, Eighteen women, The Enemy Within..

Worse than ever, Whose is bigger?, Repeal and Replace, A Gathering
of Generals, Never too early, Trump's first week, The Muslim Ban,
The Media Is the Enemy, Trump's Wiretap Tweet, March 4, 2017,
Foxes in the Hen House, Healthcare, Protecting the Rich, Unleashing
the Kraken, Neil Gorsuch, Brett Kavanaugh

Trump's Wall, Mexican Immigration, DACA Dreamers, ICE
Roundup Patrols, "Zero Tolerance", An American first, Selling off
National Parks, Drilling Alaska & Grand Canyon, Bears Ears and
Grand Staircase Parks, Drilling and Mining in the Grand Canyon,
Alaska's Arctic National Wildlife Refuge, Offshore Drilling

A Russian Cloud, Comey and "the fake Russian probe.", Stormy
Daniels, Puerto Rico,Charlottesville, Trump's Responses, Parkland,
FL, The Company He Keeps, Who Betrayed America?

SNAFU, The Party of No, All for Nothing, A Check on the President?
the New GOP?, Southern Democrats and New Republicans,
Dixiecrats, The GOP Today, McConnell and Ryan,Party Over
Country, The Misogynist, The Mueller Investigation, Trump's Voter
Fraud, Gerrymandering, GOP Voter Suppression, the National
Census, Stepford Guys and Boys from Brazil, Whose Side Are They
On?, Profiles in Courage? Abandoning ship. When needed most,
Away all boats!, Conclusion

Quid Pro Quo, Apalachin, NY and Indian Wells, What is Dark
Money?, What Makes Dark Money "Dark"?, Dark Money vs PACs
and Super PACs,

Introduction

A single candle stands vigilant on my living-room window sill in my home in a small suburban community in Pennsylvania. It faces the world outside and shines its small light boldly every minute of every day, 24/7 as they say, since the 45th President of the United States was inaugurated on January 20, 2017. It may appear to be an over-dramatic display of concern to some neighbors who know why it remains lit day and night. But a passing traveler or an unfamiliar visitor to my home might not even notice it. Most often it provokes neither notice nor comment.

The candle was conscripted by me to be a sacred sentry to stand in solitary defiance to the darkness that has fallen over our country. Its tireless ray of Hope is purposed in its place to shine constantly for 365 days a year, 366 during leap years, to give added light to every day until the 45th President of the United States has permanently left the White House.

This small sentry announces my hope for America's quickest return to the truest intent of the Founding Fathers, a return to the rule of law solemnly enacted for the benefit of its citizens who consent to liberty and justice for all. Presently, America's leadership and the supporters of that faulty leadership have declared a divorce from justice and liberty for all.

On Tuesday, November 8, 2016, the dark side of America the Beautiful reared its ugly, mottled head and fully displayed its deep prejudices and its primal adherence to the violent voices of hate. We were not expecting such denunciation of American core values from within America. Most Americans on both political sides were not aware of the hidden deeds being carried out by others who wanted to detour America from its centuries-old path of safekeeping the promises of liberty in our homeland.

This book is presented as a guidebook to the reader who seeks clarity and understanding about how such an awful fate has fallen like a biblical plague upon our land of the free and the home of the brave. Within the book's chapters you will discover "the enemy within", the people and institutions who are responsible for this blitzkrieg attack on America. You will see the powerful forces who combined to use their own billions of dollars to feed hate, to produce lies, and to breed a mindless strain of political candidates who owe allegiance only to the powers that cloned them.

The crowning insult to the American nation and to its people of goodwill and good judgement is amplified by the election of this 45th President. The nightmare we find ourselves in seems to have come to us out of an aberrant storm with no warning signs, or quickly brought on by a bad meal, or possibly the remnant of a horror film viewed immediately before going to sleep for the evening. How did it happen? Why didn't we see it coming?

In fact it did not happen overnight. This nightmare is the culmination of much planning begun in bold earnest in 1992. Inside these pages you will read about some of the planning and understand the power that money, lots of money, buys in any political campaign and how the use of that money corrupts democracy. You will see how a wide swath of communities across America were tricked into voting against their own interests and how they continue to support a President who will steal their pennies to add to his fortune and to his friends own billions of dollars: a President of the United States who respects no man or woman and who has no decent moral code of conduct.

The assault on American fundamental principles is real. In this present time, the tightening restrictions on liberty and justice began immediately after the 2017 Inauguration and will continue to be pursued and enforced by the present White House administration, and not at a slower pace but at an alarmingly increasing pace. Presently the chaos in the halls of government is deafening. The dangers to our freedoms are real. Those men and women, accepting the new President's flawed script with its false mission, echo the hatred and actions which should make us mindful of the Taliban and ISIS, those violent bands of radicals who prefer to be blinded by their ignorance and hate.

The causes for America's present shame resides in several places and with several people. You will feel their presence in this book. You will be a silent witness to the deceitful actions undertaken by the powerful persons and institutions who financed disruptive actions at campaign functions, and who supported treason by enabling foreign enemies to shape American opinions and subsequently usurp their votes. Fortunately, the antidotes for tyranny in America are still a free press, and the ballot box (or any computerized version of it.)

America is now forever stripped of its innocent belief that, because we are powerful and protected by oceans and great distances, we are safe from harm. Unexpectedly, the harm that was done came from those within America, rich and greedy donors with a selfish interpretation of liberty and justice, who feverishly supported the 45th President: a pretender whose words, actions and ideas harm and shame America. After discovering who the men guilty of selling America for power and money are, the final chapter in the book discusses what you and I can do to help to rescue America. Ideas and actions are provided to show you how to support a restoration of a citizen democracy in America, a cause that until this current crisis, has never been of major concern inside our homeland. Most importantly, "VOTE" in 2018 against the GOP, the Republican Party of chaos. Speak out, go out and canvas your neighborhood, and energize as many voters as you can. You will be proud that you did your part to save America in 2018, and beyond.

Chapter One
Unprecedented

"As democracy is perfected, the office of president represents, more and more closely, the inner soul of the people. On some great and glorious day the plain folks of the land will reach their heart's desire at last and the White House will be adorned by a downright moron."   H.L. Mencken

Like no other

No single word was given more prominence in the American political discourse in 2016, 2017 and 2018 than the word unprecedented. Unprecedented is listed in the dictionary as an adjective used to describe an out-of-the ordinary or never-before-occurring event or accomplishment. It is specifically used to modify its intended subject as "having no precedent", such as never having been seen before. For example, an athlete or a team may be described as having won a specific championship for an unprecedented sixth time in a row. It is a dual purpose word as it can be used to announce an occurrence which can either be a wonderful one or a disastrous one such as the afore-mentioned team losing an unprecedented thirty-one games in a row in the following season. Both are unprecedented, one is good and the other one is bad.

Donald Trump's actions and behavior as both a candidate and as the elected US President are unarguably unprecedented and bad. News print, internet reports, television news, and casual neighborhood discussions about Trump were prefaced with an avalanched usage of this word. His campaign to secure the Republican Party's nomination for President of the United States was a brutal display of crass mud-slinging politics rarely seen in America's election history. Trump's lack

1

of respect for his opponents, even for his own supporters, matched his lack of respect for anything resembling the truth. He randomly attacked the most defenseless persons in our country: the poor, minorities, immigrants, the disabled, women, the disadvantaged, a gold star family, and most offensively, Senator John McCain AZ-R who was a prisoner of war for five years in the notorious Hanoi Hilton prison camp in North Vietnam. In July 2015, Trump said, "He's not a war hero. He's a war hero because he was captured. I like people that weren't captured." At a campaign rally in August 2016, he sent a thinly-veiled suggestion to right-wing gun advocates that 'they may be able to stop' Hillary from taking away their Second Amendment rights. Trump told the large crowd and millions of his supporters watching on television, "If she gets to pick her judges, nothing you can do, folks," As the crowd began to boo, he quickly added: "Although the Second Amendment people - maybe there is, I don't know." Oblique as it was, Mr. Trump's remark received a wave of condemnation from Democrats, gun control advocates and others, who accused him of suggesting violence against Clinton. Bernice A. King, daughter of the Rev. Dr. Martin Luther King Jr.., called Mr. Trump's words "distasteful, disturbing, and dangerous."

As the election neared, he incited his audiences at repeated campaign rallies to chant "Lock Her Up", a mob-like behavior shamefully led by a US Army General and a US Senator (Michael Flynn and Jeff Sessions) who within months would be appointed to cabinet positions in the Trump administration. The jail reference chant was in response to GOP's bogus charge of Clinton's improper use of an email account. The FBI dutifully investigated and found the incident to be minor and ended the investigation, but the US Army General was indicted for lying to the FBI about meeting with Russian diplomats before the election. (He is still waiting to see if he will be locked up.) Trump continued to be combatant and lashed out at all of the news media except his loyalists at Fox News. His communication at his campaign appearances was loud and discordant. He avoided serious criticism of his governing policies because he was not knowledgeable on the issues of governance. His campaign was a firestorm where he would figuratively set fire to his opponent's plans and often figuratively burn his own ass.

Still he lumbered onward because the GOP was devoid of moral character and any leadership to stop him. The GOP leaders in the Senate and in the House were desperate to win this election and readily became subservient on Trump's runaway train fueled by Trump supporters who listened only to him because he mimicked their voices and amplified their blind rage against the disappointment with their own lives. Trump promised his voters whatever they wanted even if keeping those same promises would destroy them and their children's futures. Additionally, Trump knew he would not need to keep his promises once he was elected. His words and actions were not formed from honesty or with any design in mind for anything other than clearing obstacles in his path to the Presidency. In his spoiled rich kid persona, he was going to be the first person to find his way to Uncle Wiggly's house and win the game even if he had to send everyone else backwards into oblivion.

Regardless of the crude manner and inappropriate slanders Trump voiced and despite each succeeding offense being more offensive than the previous one, neither the rube GOP Party nor Trump's voter base were deterred from advancing Trump unashamedly onto Election Day and enabling Trump's sinister goal of becoming America's 45th President.

Trump's comments and behavior were described as unprecedented for a political candidate when scandalous was a more accurate word. During his campaigns for President, hundreds of millions of men, women, and children viewed and listened to repeated videos and recordings showing Trump expressing his opinions on many topics leaving millions to recall in their minds his past offenses that included raucous careers as a bankrupted real estate salesman and a reality TV personality. His true character was displayed for public viewing, usually at his own insistence for being in the public eye. Mr. Trump was proud of, in fact he reveled in, his un-precendented behavior. Incredibly, it did not deter his voting base from praising his candidacy.

Who is Donald Trump?

"Mr. Trump has spent his career in the company of developers and celebrities, and also of grifters, cons, sharks, goons and crooks. He cuts corners, he lies, he cheats, and he brags about it, and for the most part, he's gotten away with it, protected by threats of litigation, hush money and his own bravado. Those methods may be proving to have their limits when they are applied from the Oval Office." NY Times Editorial, April 11, 2018

A blind person on first meeting Donald Trump cannot tell you the color of his hair, or the color of his eyes, or whether his nose is large or small, but he can see Donald Trump 's character very clearly, possibly clearer than most of us. How? Because Donald Trump likes to speak, a lot, and after he speaks more than ten seconds, and says anything beyond "Good morning" or "Hey", the blind man can hear, and thereby see what kind of person is standing in front of him. The basis for a conversation with Trump is simple; the discussion must always be on his terms and must center on him, and the standards for the truth can be low. Here are a few facts.

Donald John Trump was born in NYC. His grandparents were immigrants from Germany and Scotland. He was raised in the Queens section of the city where his parents owned a real estate business. As a teenager, Trump was sent off to military school after it was discovered he often left his high school classes and went into Manhattan. He attended Fordham University then transferred to the University of Pennsylvania to complete business courses specializing in real estate. Upon graduation, he grabbed a million dollar loan from his father and returned to Manhattan. Here is a brief personal biography after college.

- Three marriages, two ended because of his infidelity.
- Five children. Three with his first wife, one each with his second and third wife.
- A minimum of six major bankruptcies, 1992-2009. <u>See list below.</u>
- A plethora of extra-marital affairs throughout his married life and varied business careers.
- Settled three lawsuits with out-of-court payments to Trump University students immediately after 2016 Presidential election.
- Rumored to have conducted numerous undocumented real estate business dealings and money laundering with Russian mobsters and billionaires (oligarchs).

Business bankruptcies

Billionaire or scam-artist? Donald Trump's recklessness and inability to manage led some of his companies into bankruptcy. He says his use of federal law to protect his interests illustrates his good business skills. "I have used the laws of this country just like the greatest people that you read about every day in business have used the laws of this country, the chapter laws, to do a great job for my company, my employees, myself and my family," Trump said in August 2015.

The New York Times reported in 2016 that Trump "put up little of his own money, shifted personal debts to the casinos and collected millions of dollars in salary, bonuses and other payments." "The burden of his failures," according to the newspaper, "fell on investors and others who had bet on his business acumen."

List of recorded Trump bankruptcies

Trump Taj Mahal opened April 1990.

A $1.2 billion Taj Mahal Casino Resort in Atlantic City. In the summer of 1991, it sought Chapter 11 bankruptcy protection. Trump relinquished half of his ownership in the casino and sold off his yacht and his airline. The <u>bondholders were awarded lower interest payments</u>. The Taj Mahal emerged from bankruptcy within weeks of its filing but was later closed.

Trump Castle Hotel & Casino opened in 1985.

Entered bankruptcy in March 1992. The Trump Organization relinquished half of its holdings in the Castle to the bondholders. The casino remains in operation under new ownership and a new name, the Golden Nugget.

Trump Plaza Casino, opened May 1984.

Entered bankruptcy in March 1992. Trump Plaza closed in September 2014, putting more than 1,000 people out of work.

Trump Plaza Hotel, Manhattan, NYC, bought for $407M in 1988.

Sought bankruptcy protection in 1992, was more than $550 million in debt when it entered Chapter 11 bankruptcy. Trump gave up a 49 percent stake in the company to lenders, as well as his salary and his day-to-day role in its operations. He later sold a controlling stake in the property, which remains in operation.

Trump Hotels & Casino Resorts, a holding company for Trump's three casinos.

Entered Chapter 11 in November 2004 to restructure $1.8 billion of debt. The holding company emerged from bankruptcy less than a year later, in May 2005, with a new name: Trump Entertainment Resorts Inc. The Chapter 11 restructuring reduced the company's debt by about $600 million and cut interest payments by $102 million annually. Trump relinquished the majority control to bondholders and gave up his title of chief executive officer.

Trump Entertainment Resorts, casino holding company.

Entered Chapter 11 in February 2009. Emerged from bankruptcy in February 2016, now a subsidiary of Icahn Enterprises.

Trump University

Trump University was initially presented to Donald Trump as a business plan for a real-estate training program. The person who created the plan was hopeful that Trump would agree to be paid a flat fee for the use of the Trump name on the course. Trump agreed but characteristically, instead of just selling his name, he decided he wanted to be the principal owner. In 2004, Trump University was incorporated in New York and Trump owned 93% of the company. The focus of the instruction was real estate investing. The course tuition ranged from $1,495 seminars to a $35,000 "Gold Elite" program. Just like many Trump projects, the first few years were successful and more than 7,000 courses were sold, at least 15% were for the "Gold Elite" program. Between 2004 and 2010, student complaints about the university began to increase and several formal lawsuits were filed against the university and Trump. Trump denied all allegations but in 2010 the Trump University ended its operations.

On August 24, 2013, the State of New York filed a $40 million civil suit against Trump University alleging illegal business practices and false claims made by the company. Trump denied the allegations, and said New York Attorney General Eric Schneiderman was "a political hack looking to get publicity". Trump filed a complaint alleging that the state Attorney General's investigation was accompanied by a campaign donation shakedown; the complaint was investigated by a New York ethics board and dismissed in August 2015. During fact gathering, New York State described Trump University as a bait-and-switch scheme and said the organization was not a university. The Trump University lawsuits were among the many legal challenges Trump faced during the 2016 Presidential campaign.

Unprecedented

During primary campaign speeches, Trump repeatedly called the presiding judge on the Trump University case, U.S. District Judge Gonzalo P. Curiel, a "hater". The judge came under attack by Trump at campaign rallies when Trump mentioned in several campaign speeches that the judge was a "hater" and described the judge as "Spanish" or "Mexican". Trump added Curiel should recuse himself saying the judge could not be impartial in the case due to his Mexican heritage. Judge Curiel parents emigrated from Mexico and he was born and raised in Indiana.

Trump's references to Curiel's ethnicity, as well as his comments that "someone ought to look into" the judge, alarmed legal experts, who expressed concern about the effects of Trump's comments on judicial independence. On June 7, 2016, Trump issued a lengthy statement saying that his criticism of the judge had been "misconstrued" and that his concerns about Curiel's impartiality were not based upon ethnicity alone, but also upon rulings in the case. On November 18, 2016, only a few weeks after the election, it was reported Trump agreed to pay $25 million to settle the two class-action lawsuits and the New York suit. The plaintiff's attorneys agreed to forgo their fees and work pro bono so the amount will go to the many former Trump University students who are part of the case. New York Attorney General Eric Schneiderman, whose office filed one of the three lawsuits, said of the final settlement: "This settlement marked a stunning reversal by President Trump, who for years refused to compensate the victims of his sham university."

On April 11, 2018, the $25 million dollar settlement in the Trump University class action lawsuit was finalized paving the way for thousands of former students who paid for classes at the now-defunct real estate seminar to get some of their money back. The settlement was delayed because one woman wanted to opt out and sue Donald Trump separately. The final decision confirmed the real estate school featured false advertisements and empty promises. *CNN's Patricia DiCarlo and Curt Devine contributed to this report.*

Trump Foundation

On July 17, 2018, two New York state officials confirmed that the state of New York formally opened an investigation into whether President Trump and his charitable foundation violated state law. The NY state tax department probe, which has been ongoing for more than a month, is looking into whether the Donald J. Trump Foundation – and Trump himself – violated state law by transferring assets or making certain misrepresentations to the state with respect to tax liability and tax assignment, the officials said. "Gov. Cuomo believes there is one set of rules for everyone – no matter who you are or how much power you have," one Cuomo aide said. "This matter will be investigated to the fullest possible extent, and if appropriate, referred for criminal prosecution." Cuomo counsel Alphonso David said the governor would be willing to give the attorney general's office a referral to launch a criminal probe into President Trump's charitable foundation. NY state Attorney General Barbara Underwood had previously filed a bombshell civil lawsuit in Manhattan Supreme Court this past June accusing the commander-in chief and his three oldest children of operating a bogus namesake charity "in persistent violation" of federal and state laws for more than a decade. Reportedly, the lawsuit charged that $2.8 million was spent to promote Trump's presidential campaign, along with supposed charitable funds used instead to "pay off the legal obligations of entities (Trump) controlled, to promote Trump hotels, (and) to purchase personal items." The attorney general's office referred apparent violations of federal law to the IRS and Federal

Elections Commission. The suits say the Trump Foundation "was little more than a checkbook for payments to not-for-profits from Mr. Trump or the Trump Organization." The impetus for New York State's investigation into the Trump Foundation's operations was provided by facts uncovered in a 2016 investigative reporting article published in The Washington Post by David A. Fahrenthold.

The chart below shows source of annual donations to Trump Foundation charity, 1987-2014

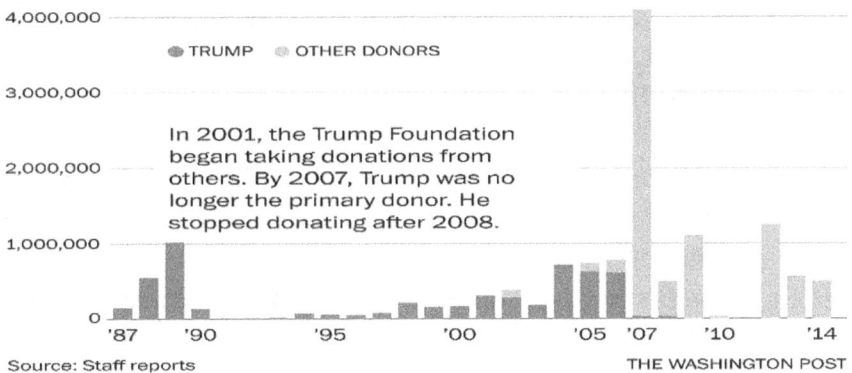

In 2001, the Trump Foundation began taking donations from others. By 2007, Trump was no longer the primary donor. He stopped donating after 2008.

Source: Staff reports

THE WASHINGTON POST

Here are a few of the allegations regarding how the charity misappropriated its funds:

- $5,000 was used to advertise Trump Hotels
- $10,000 was spent on a six-foot tall portrait of the president, later found on display at the sports bar at Trump's Doral golf resort
- $25,000 donation in 2013 to a political group connected to Florida Attorney General Pamela Bondi, (R), who at the time

was considering whether to open a fraud investigation against Trump University. (Sarah Parnass/the Washington Post). Bondi did not investigate the Trump University. The Washington Post reported that Trump paid a penalty in 2018 for that 2013 donation

- $100,000 was allegedly used to settle a legal dispute with the city of Palm Beach, which Trump resolved by contributing the amount to the Fisher House Foundation
- $258,000 was allegedly used to settle lawsuits against Trump and his businesses including $158,000 paid to a man who sued the Trump National Golf Club after it failed to pay him a promised $1 million for scoring a hole-in-one at a charity golf tournament
- In 2009, Donald Trump asked the Charles Evans Foundation in New Jersey for a donation. Trump said he was raising money for the Palm Beach Police Foundation. The Evans Foundation said yes and it gave a total of $150,000 to the Donald J. Trump Foundation. Then, Trump's foundation turned around and made donations in 2009 and 2010 to the police group in South Florida. In those years, the Trump Foundation's gifts totaled $150,000. Trump turned the Evans Foundation's gifts into his own gifts, without adding any money of his own. On the night that he won the Palm Tree Award for his philanthropy, Trump may have actually made money. The gala was held at his Mar-a-Lago Club in Palm Beach and the police foundation paid to rent the room. It's unclear how much was paid in 2010, but the police foundation reported in its tax filings that it rented Mar-a-Lago in 2014 for $276,463

To learn more about the Trump Foundation, go to this link
https://www.washingtonpost.com/politics/how-donald-trump-retooled-his-charity-to-

spend-other-peoples-money/2016/09/10/da8cce64-75df-11e6-8149-
b8d05321db62_story.html?utm_term=.e4bba8141ed0.

Underwood also charges that the foundation, whose board members include Trump siblings Don, Jr.., Ivanka, and Eric, violated campaign-finance laws by "illegally providing extensive support" to the then-candidate's 2016 campaign, despite being explicitly prohibited from "participating or intervening in any political campaign on behalf of a candidate." E-mails show campaign manager Corey Lewandowski dictating charitable expenditures be dedicated to helping Trump get elected. Lewandowski wrote to a staffer shortly before the Iowa caucuses, "Is there any way we can make some disbursements this week while in Iowa?" An added note of interest, the Trump Foundation had no employees. If, as reported, foundation money was spent for a painting, a charity, a campaign, etc., the money would have been authorized by a family member, and no one else.

Outrageous personal attacks

Trump's vile moral character and bankrupted business record did not prevent his rise in American politics. He was neither shamed nor embarrassed by his private and public disgraces. So, it was not surprising to decent Americans that Trump would careen like a stumbling drunk through a narrow alley, and noisily knock over metal trash cans, their garbage spilling onto worn cobblestones and damaged pavements. He bred chaos! His campaign headquarters and staff resembled feral kittens scampering in all directions when the dogs are let loose. His campaign style was a page taken from conservative party campaigning, always smearing his opponents with a fuselage of outrageous lies and personal ridicule.

Witness to Treason

During the Presidential campaign there were many grievous incidents highlighted in political campaign ads shown on television (see reference list below) where his own words and actions were proof of his unfitness for any public office including one where he shamelessly entertained his audience at a campaign rally by mocking the physical motions and movements of a disabled journalist. In another campaign speech he bragged he could shoot someone on Fifth Avenue and get away with it. Prior to seeking political office, he added insult to injury to women in general when he announced in a radio interview with Howard Stern that he respects women but he doesn't think a flat-chested girl could ever be a "10". In a television interview he boasted about his preference for nuclear weapons and shared how much he likes all war, even nuclear war.

Later as President, he flirted with nuclear war when he engaged in a months-long kindergarten tweeter debate with North Korea's own juvenile dictator Kim Jung-Un. Trump casually and with crude bravado promised that he, not America, would rain "fire and fury" on Korea. Does that sound familiar? It was an echo of a not-too-distant dictator who no longer scares anyone. Hopefully, Trump's own "Mother of all wars" will never come. Playfully seeking to agitate the madman, our President placed millions of people in the path of imminent destruction. In his school-yard spat with a crazy man, Trump proved to the world that no one is crazier and madder than himself.

"Birther"

Donald Trump began his political career based on a single outrageous lie promoted by far-right conservative fringe theorists (referred to as "birthers") who wanted to remove Obama as President of the United

States of America. Mainstream political commentators correctly and firmly identified the "birther" belief as a racist response to Obama's status as the first African American President of the United States.

Trump began his public "birther" attacks in an interview on Good Morning America in March 2011. Trump said he was planning to run for president and he added that he believed then-President Barack Obama was not a citizen of the United States of America. He said Obama was born in Kenya and was not born in Hawaii, thus aligning himself with the lunatic fringe. In the same interview he admonished the interviewer and the viewing public that someone who shares his same view should not be so quickly dismissed as an "idiot". It is likely that he knew how he sounded because he was correct in reading the minds of everyone who heard him say it. Yes, the viewers who heard him immediately thought he was an idiot. This 'fact' was served to a community of 'idiots' and was subsequently ingested by Trump. On his own initiative in the same interview Trump added as proof a short unsupported one-liner, "Growing up no one knew him". This was another tidbit provided by the lunatic fringe, an old claim ranked as a lie, aka Pants-on-Fire by Politifact. Thus began Trump's noble race to save America, a task he has since assured us many times that only he could perform all by himself.

Trump later appeared on The View repeating several times that he wanted Obama to show his birth certificate. He speculated "there's something on that birth certificate that Obama doesn't like". The View's host Whoopi Goldberg described Trump's 'news flash' as "the biggest pile of dog mess I've heard in ages." On a follow-up interview on March 30, 2011's edition of CNN Newsroom, anchor Suzanne Malveaux commented on Trump's 'nobody knew him' statement and pointed out that she had made a documentary for which she had gone to Hawaii and spoken with people who knew Obama as a child. Nevertheless, Trump continued his attack on the President on April 7, 2011 in a NBC TV interview broadcast when he said he was not satisfied that Obama had proved his citizenship. Thereafter, Joseph Farah of WorldNetDaily described as a "fringe" and far right website known for promoting falsehoods and conspiracy theories, contacted Trump and was reportedly on the phone with Trump every day for a week assisting Trump with a "birther primer", providing answers to questions, and giving advice.

On April 27, 2011, the White House released the President's long-form birth certificate. Trump crowed "I am really honored and I am really proud, that I was able to do something that nobody else could do." But Trump's silence was short-lived. The 2016 candidate-in-waiting struck again. On October 24, 2012, Trump offered to donate five million dollars to the charity of Obama's choice if Obama would publish his college and passport applications before October 31, 2012. The President correctly dismissed Trump's latest lunacy and no documents were published. Obama continued his successful campaign and was re-elected to a second-term as President. Trump went to Moscow for the Trump Miss Universe pageant.

But the 'birther' issue did rise again. On September 16, during the 2016 Presidential campaign, Trump was badgered by journalists to address his previous claims about Obama's birth certificate. He still refused to publicly admit the legitimacy of Barack Obama's Presidency. Finally, on September 16, 2016, as the Republican Party presidential nominee was surrounded by news journalists and viewed on television and the internet by hundreds of millions of Americans and people throughout the world, Trump conceded after five years that "President Barack Obama was born in the United States. Period." With this short sentence, Donald Trump publicly stepped away from his friends in the Ku Klu Klan and his like-minded White Brotherhood and White Supremists, but he did not completely abandon them. Shockingly, Trump as President in 2017 again showed the world where he stands on race in America when a quiet college town in Virginia took center-stage in American politics.

In the end, the facts had never changed. President Barack Obama had always been born on August 4, 1961, at Kapi'olani Maternity & Gynecological Hospital (now called Kapi'olani Medical Center for Women & Children) in Honolulu, Hawaii. His parents were Ann Dunham from Wichita, Kansas and her husband Barack Obama Sr., a Luo from Nyang'oma Kogelo, Nyanza Province (Kenya) who was attending the University of Hawaii. Birth notices for Barack Obama were published in The Honolulu Advertiser on August 13, 1961 and the Honolulu Star-Bulletin on August 14, 1961. Those are the facts, and nothing but the facts. *Barack Obama citizenship conspiracy theories, From Wikipedia, the free encyclopedia*

2016 GOP Primary Campaign

Trump was one of the eighteen Republicans who were seeking to become the Republican Party's nominee for the 2016 Presidential election. The campaign began in earnest in 2015 and the candidates in alphabetical order who eventually finished behind Trump were Jeb Bush, Ben Carson, Chris Christie, Ted Cruz, Carly Fiorina, Jim Gilmore, Lindsey Graham, Mike Huckabee, Bobby Jindal, John Kasich, George Pataki, Rand Paul, Rick Perry, Marco Rubio, Rick Santorum, and Scott Walker. The campaign trail was pockmarked with an almost-equal number of candidate debates. On the evening of March 16, 2016 the twelfth and final debate was held between the nominees seeking to represent the Republican Party in the 2016 Presidential election. The debate was broadcast on the CNN cable network and the four remaining candidates were John Kaisch, Ohio Governor, Marco Rubio, Florida Senator, Ted Cruz, Texas Senator and Donald Trump, Real Estate Developer. These four survived a year-long nasty version of 'King of the Mountain', the juvenile game of rough and tumble where the last person standing wins. Trump's bloody, chaotic march through America's red states was nearing its end. The candidates were singularly vilified and eviscerated by Trump and his rigid and unmovable base of followers. Trump employed a juvenile, low-brow name-calling attack on his opponents using scurrilous names such as like Little Marco, Lyin' Ted, Low Energy' Jeb, '1 for 38 Kasich', and other daily insults and threats, even referring to Carly Forina's face, and Ted Cruz' wife's, photo coupled with a threat of "spilling the beans" about Mrs. Cruz. All of these verbal attacks landed like nuclear weapons on Trumps 'fellow' candidates, disintegrating them, and resulted incredibly with his nomination as the Republican Party candidate for the President of the United States in 2016.

The combination of blistering name calling and the constant ridicule of his components served as entertainment to Trump's base. The frenzy increased and the inability of the Republican Party's factions of libertarian, moderates, and conservatives to find common ground to stop this tsunami combined to loosen a 'black swan' on the American political stage. When the sun set on July 20, 2018, Trump was standing as the Republican Party's proud choice to represent their party and values on the stage in the Quicken Loans Arena in Cleveland, Ohio. Though not visible, a messy pile of bruised and battered Republican Party loyalists lay at his feet. He was now the king of the hill and was reminiscent of a sailor who had barreled his way through both the denizens of the Barbary Coast and the lower Bowery, both in a single day. The Republican Party, the Grand Old Party (GOP), nominated Donald Trump to be its candidate to be the next President of the United States. Trump's crude circus of denigrating and maligned insults sullied the political process beyond easy repair. Those of us outside the GOP were glad to see the GOP suffer through its détente with Trump. We were not expecting the chaos that would ensue in the general election campaign to follow. We were deaf to the faint voice of a distant carnival barker warning the passing crowd, "You ain't seen nothing yet."

While all of this was unfolding, the Democratic Party's primary campaign blandly chugged its way to completion. Its cross-country journey to select a nominee for the 2016 Presidential election was much quieter. It was predictably quieter than the GOP debacle because there were six candidates instead of eighteen and it was mercifully quieter simply because Donald Trump wasn't involved in it. Not directly, anyhow.

As early as Inauguration Day in 2013, the political buzz within the Democratic Party was that Hillary Clinton, former First Lady, former New York Senator, and former Secretary of State, was the leading choice of the senior members of the Party for succession to President Obama. She had been narrowly defeated in the 2008 Democratic primary for President and was now embraced by the Party. The five major candidates on the Democratic primary ticket for President were Bernie Sanders, Vermont senator; Martin O' Malley, former Maryland governor; Jim Webb, former Virginia senator; Lincoln Chafee, former Rhode Island governor; and Lawrence Lessig, Harvard Law Professor. The debates were not as contentious nor as personally nasty as the GOP's debates had been. The competition was swiftly pared down and when the Democratic Party's ninth and final primary debate for the

Witness to Treason

2016 U.S. presidential election was held on April 14, 2016 at the Duggal Greenhouse in Brooklyn Navy Yard, only Hillary Clinton and Bernie Sanders remained. There was a tenth debate scheduled to be held in San Francisco in the final week before the primary elections but Hillary Clinton declined to participate in the tenth debate and it was cancelled. Shortly after the tenth debate was cancelled, Donald Trump who was not yet the formal nominee of the GOP offered to debate Bernie Sanders just ahead of the June 7th primary. The only condition for the Trump-Sanders debate was for the profits to be donated to a charity which the candidates would agree on. Bernie Sanders accepted the offer but Trump did an about-face and declined to participate, stating there was no need for him to debate a candidate who would not win the Democratic nomination. It proved to just be another photo-op opportunity for Trump to bait an opponent or adversary, then switch lanes and insult them. This was a learned real estate strategy which Donald Trump would continue to use through his candidacy and into his eventual presidency.

After the final Democratic debate was completed, the two Democratic candidates campaigned in relative silence when compared with the GOP Trump circus. They chased each other across America seeking to gain more voters and delegates to secure the nomination at the Democratic National Convention to be held in Philadelphia during the final week of July. The Democratic Party signaled their readiness to start serious political fisticuffs on July 26 when they nominated Hillary Clinton to be their candidate in the 2016 Presidential election. Soon the Clinton campaign would meet the Trump train-wreck head-on.

Chapter Two
Forewarned

"Will people ever be wise enough to refuse to follow bad leaders"   Eleanor
Roosevelt.

More of the Same

At the end of July 2016, both of the major political parties in America
had completed their national conventions and selected their candidates
for President. The focus now shifted totally onto Donald Trump and
Hillary Clinton. There was no doubt that the forthcoming campaign
would be loud and boisterous. Trump was no gentleman and Hillary
Clinton was not a woman who backed away from conflict. During her
service as US Secretary of State from 2009-2013, she stood bold and
strong for America's principles against Russia's President and ruthless,
Napoleon-sized bully, Vladimir Putin. She and all Americans
witnessed Trump's disregard for truth, any truth, and his disrespect
for any and nearly all persons during his frenzied climb to the top of
an undisciplined Republican Party. It was clear that Truth was going to
be the primary victim in the 2016 Presidential campaign. Yet, no one
was prepared for the next three months to come.

There is a phrase traced back into the 16th century which fits the lesson
to be gathered from reviewing Trump's earlier history, and from
witnessing his recent two years in the public arena. The phrase is
"Forewarned is forearmed", or today we modernize it to, "forewarned
is fair warned." The idiom says if we are given advance warning of
danger, we can hopefully expect to be able to arm ourselves against
that danger and thus protect ourselves. In the fall of 2016, we should

have been prepared for what was to come. Indeed, if the campaign had lasted longer, it would have been worse. America was already shocked almost daily by the ugly and brazenly offensive tone which Trump paraded onto the campaign circuit across America and into its homes. Though forewarned, and after numerous standards had been trampled, there was even worse to come.

2016 Presidential Campaign

August 2016 ushered in the most disturbing national election campaign in American history. Most of the credit for this infamous accomplishment must be given to Republican Presidential candidate Donald Trump but there is much messy credit to be assigned to the two most powerful leaders of the 2016 GOP Party, Mitch McConnell of Kentucky and Paul Ryan of Wisconsin. They did nothing to interfere with the Trumpmania that rampaged through the Republican Party. Additionally, all of the GOP representatives in the Senate and the House of Representatives were equally complicit through their insistence in standing their ground for themselves and their special interests and doing nothing to protect America.

There was no illusion within both parties as to the truest measure of Trump's personal character. His P.T. Barnum circus-like behavior was always visible in his personal life and business career, and his lack of genuine interest in any political ideology emphasized that his vision for America was single-minded. He would be king and rule accordingly, and everyone would love him and his new set of clothes. In the fall, the barrage of campaign advertisements from both parties began with much regularity and great energy, exploding on viewing screens on televisions, computers, phones, and on radio broadcasts, in newspapers and on electronic and digital billboards. It is reasonable to suppose even sky-writers were enlisted in the campaign somewhere in the skies above us.

In his own words

Donald J. Trump is on record in every social media –print, radio, television, and campaign events - saying publicly what he really thinks about race, women, religion, business, government, and sports. He comments on everything and he is never fearful of speaking his thoughts. He just will not be held responsible for them unless he is being lauded for them. In the incidents and on the videos noted below, Trump tells us in his own words who he is and how proud he is of himself, to the extent that he would encourage every young man and woman to 'be like Trump'. He has faced criticism over the years for saying sexist things about women, referring to them as pigs or worse. His disrespect for women was highlighted during his public feud with former Fox News's TV journalist, Megyn Kelly, which culminated with him suggesting that the journalist had blood coming out of her eyes and "blood coming out of her wherever".

Another prime example is an impromptu moment during the GOP primary in 2016. The GOP primary included one woman among its eighteen candidates, Carly Fiorina, a former Hewlett-Packard CEO. In an interview in Rolling Stone magazine, writer Paul Solotaroff said he was sitting with Trump who was watching a newscast when a video clip zoomed in on Fiorina, one of Trump's opponents in the Republican primary. Here is what Trump said at that moment, referencing his impression of Mrs. Fiorina's appearance as less than flattering. "Look at that face!" he said at a conference table with his staff as Mrs. Fiorina took a question about him on television. "Would anyone vote for that? Can you imagine that, the face of our next president?!"

Witness to Treason

Trump later added to his assessment of Ms. Fiorina when he said, "I mean, she's a woman, and I'm not supposed to say bad things, but really, folks, come on," he said, according to the report. "Are we serious?" Later when Fiorina spoke to the afore-mentioned Fox News journalist Megyn Kelly about Trump's remarks, Fiorina suggested that Trump was getting nervous that she was gaining ground on him. "Maybe, just maybe, I'm getting under his skin a little bit because I am climbing in the polls." Trump in his own interview with Fox later dismissed his remarks as merely a jocular moment and he said he was referring to Mrs. Fiorina's persona, not her face. Would you believe him? Would his own mother have believed him? Among his many faults, he is a misogynist. Here below, in his own words, Trump told America and the world who he really is.

A number of Donald Trump's statements leading up to the 2016 Presidential election. In the past, any one of these would have been fatal—but somehow none were.

1. On Mexican immigrants. "When Mexico sends its people, they're not sending their best. They're sending people that have lots of problems. They're bringing drugs. They're bringing crime. They're rapists." June 16, 2015, candidacy announcement speech.
2. On Republican Senator John McCain's war record as a POW in Vietnam. "He's not a war hero. He was a war hero because he was captured. I like people who weren't captured." *July 17, 2015, Family Leadership Summit in Iowa.*
3. On Megyn Kelly, a Fox News analyst and one of the moderators. In an August 7, 2015, CNN interview, "You could see there was blood coming out of her eyes, blood coming out of her wherever."

4. On Republican Presidential candidate Carly Fiorina. "Look at that face! Would anyone vote for that? Can you imagine that, the face of our next president?!" *September 9, 2015, in Rolling Stone*

5. New York Times reporter Serge Kovaleski, "Now the poor guy, you ought to see this guy. 'Ah, I don't know what I said! I don't remember!'" *November 24, 2015 campaign rally,* Trump physically mocks Kovaleski who has a congenital condition called arthrogryposis that affects his joints.

6. On nuclear weapons. "I think, for me, nuclear is just the power, the devastation is very important to me." December 15, 2015. Trump answers a debate question about his priority use of the "nuclear triad," the three ways (air, land and sea) that nuclear missiles can be launched.

7. On terrorists. "The other thing with the terrorists is you have to take out their families, when you get these terrorists, you have to take out their families. When they say they don't care about their lives, you have to take out their families," *December 2, 2015, interview on "Fox & Friends."*

8. On Muslim ban. "Donald J. Trump is calling for a total and complete shutdown of Muslims entering the United States until our country's representatives can figure out what is going on." *December 7, 2015. Trump reads from a statement by the Trump campaign.*

9. On campaign violence. "So if you see somebody getting ready to throw a tomato, knock the crap out of 'em, would you? Seriously. Okay? Just knock the hell — I promise you, I will pay for the legal fees. I promise. I promise." *February 1, 2016, rally in Cedar Rapids, Iowa.*

10. On the Ku Klux Klan "Well, just so you understand, I don't know anything about David Duke, okay? I don't know

anything about what you're even talking about with white supremacy or white supremacists. So, I don't know." *February 28, 2016 on CNN,* when asked if he'll disavow the endorsement of former Ku Klux Klan leader David Duke.

11. On women and abortion. "The answer is that there has to be some form of punishment." March 30, 2016, at an MSNBC town hall meeting in Green Bay, Wisconsin, discussing what should happen to women who procure illegal abortions.

12. On US Federal Judge Curiel. "The judge was appointed by Barack Obama, federal judge. Frankly, he should recuse himself because he's given us ruling after ruling after ruling, negative, negative, negative. What happens is the judge, who happens to be, we believe, Mexican, which is great. I think that's fine." *May 27, 2016, rally in San Diego,* in which he criticizes Indiana-born Judge Gonzalo Curiel, who, on the basis of his Mexican ancestry, Trump alleges Curiel cannot judge fairly in a lawsuit related to Trump University in which Trump settled April 2018 by paying students $25 million.

13. On black Americans. "Look at my African American over here!" June 3, 2016, Trump at a campaign rally in Redding, California.

14. "Russia, if you're listening, I hope you're able to find the 30,000 emails that are missing. I think you will probably be rewarded mightily by our press. Let's see if that happens." *July 27, 2016, at news conference in Doral, Florida,* encouraging Russia to hack into Hillary Clinton's emails.

15. On Khizr Kahn. "If you look at his wife, she was standing there. She had nothing to say. She probably—maybe she wasn't allowed to have anything to say." *July 30, 2016, Trump interview with ABC News,* referring to Khizr Khan and his wife Ghazala, parents of a Muslim U.S. soldier killed in Iraq. At the

Democratic National Convention, Khizr Khan previously criticized Trump for his anti-constitutional ban on Muslims.

16. On Putin and the Ukraine. "He's not going into Ukraine, OK? Just so you understand. He's not going to go into Ukraine, alright? You can mark it down and you can put it down, you can take it anywhere you want." *July 30, 2016, Trump interview on ABC,* referring to Russian President Vladimir Putin, whose 2014 annexation of Crimea proved that he was already in Ukraine.

17. On receiving a Purple Heart. "I always wanted to get the Purple Heart. This was much easier." August 2, 2016, Trump speaking at a rally in Ashburn, Virginia where a supporter presented him with a copy of a medal the veteran had been awarded in Iraq. The Purple Heart is awarded to members of U.S. military who are injured or killed while serving.

18. On Hillary and the Second Amendment. "If [Hillary Clinton] gets to pick her judges, nothing you can do folks. Although the Second Amendment people, maybe there is, I don't know." *August 9, 2016, at a rally in Wilmington, North Carolina.* Many read his remark as a suggestion that opponents of Clinton should take up arms against her if she's elected president.

19. Who founded ISIS? "ISIS is honoring President Obama. He is the founder of ISIS. He founded ISIS. And I would say the co-founder would be crooked Hillary Clinton." *August 10, 2016, Trump interview on ABC News.*

20. On seeking black American voters. "You're living in poverty, your schools are no good, you have no jobs, 58 percent of your youth is unemployed. What the hell do you have to lose?" *August 19, 2016, Trump at a rally in Dimondale, Michigan,* explaining why African Americans should vote for him.

Witness to Treason

Michael Kruse is a senior staff writer for POLITICO, Taylor Gee is a researcher with POLITICO Magazine

Trump – In his own words

Trump's words on a Woman's place in his world.
"Putting a wife to work is a very dangerous thing.", "and when I come home from work, if dinner's not ready, I go through the roof.", "I'd look at that fat ugly face of hers…"

Trump's words on girls and women,
"Asked if he treats women with respect?" "I can't say that either."
"A person who is flat-chested is very hard to be a 10."

Trump's frequent use of MF**k, etc. curses at campaign speeches
https://www.youtube.com/watch?v=dTh-1hto9wU

Trump mocks reporter's disability at campaign rally,
"He stands there and he's shaking and he's saying, I don't remember what I said. I don't recall"
https://youtu.be/PX9reO3QnUA

Trump's impression on children, Tots watching Trump's foul language. Author file 0715
"I could stand in the middle of Fifth Avenue and shoot somebody and I wouldn't lose any votes."
"And I say to them, you can go f**k yourself…"
http://www.businessinsider.com/hillary-clinton-donald-trump-advertisement-children-2016-7,
Source: Role Models, Hillary campaign Trump incites violence during several campaign appearances

---

"Knock the shit out of them." "I'd like to smash him. Yes, smash him good."
https://www.facebook.com/AC360/videos/10158589481890533/

"My son Max can't live in Trump world", Mother of autistic teen
https://adage.com/article/campaign-trail/son-live-trumpworld-republican-mom/306235/

Trump on nuclear threat and self-control of nuclear red button.
"I love war." "I would bomb the shit out of them."

Here is a link to a 10 minute stroll down memory lane narrated by Trump: https://www.youtube.com/watch?v=KR6ByvuJYMU - Trump's "from the gutter" philosophy on a wide range of topic.

"Russia, if you are listening"

Trailing miserably in the major polls and desperately seeking any lifeline to save his sinking campaign, Trump appeared to make a pact with the devil. On July 27, 2016, Trump broadcasted a public plea to the leader of Russia, America's primary foreign adversary, to find information recently stolen from the Democratic National Committee and provide the information to the American media. The stolen information was reportedly thousands of emails that Trump said would embarrass Clinton and support him during the Presidential campaign. His words on national television were, "Russia, if you're listening, I hope you're able to find the 30,000 emails that are missing," Mr. Trump added, "I think you will probably be rewarded mightily by our press." **Video link**
https://www.youtube.com/watch?v=3kxG8uJUsWU, CSPAN@cspan.

Witness to Treason

Trump's comment above was given in response to reporters' questions
about the hacking of the Democratic National Committee's (DNC)
computer servers which was announced a few weeks earlier by
American intelligence agencies who believed with "high confidence"
was the work of the Russian government. Mr. Trump's plea to Russia
was another bizarre moment in the on-going mystery of whether
Vladimir V. Putin's government had been seeking to influence the
United States' presidential race.

 The leaked documents published by a hacker who called himself
"Guccifer 2.0" and who is now confirmed to be a character created by
Russian intelligence, portrayed some DNC committee officials as
favoring Mrs. Clinton's candidacy while being negative about her
opponent, Senator Bernie Sanders. The release of the internal party
emails and documents led to a change of leadership in the Democratic
Party in the critical months just before the party's final campaign
efforts to elect Clinton as President in the November election. Trump
added in his comments that the uproar over whether Russia was
meddling in the election was a "total deflection" from the
embarrassing content of the emails. He stated "I don't know if it was
the Russians. It could've been anybody."

The Russians are here

On July 13, 2018, two years after Donald Trump's campaign staff's
daily claims of no Russian collusion, and nineteen months after
President Trump's solitary insistence that there was no Russian
meddling in the 2016 presidential election, the US Department of
Justice's Special Counsel headed by former FBI Director, Robert
Mueller issued indictments against Russian military officers, whereby
the Grand Jury for the District of Columbia charged "twelve Russian

military officers with Count One, Conspiracy to Commit an Offense Against the United States involving a Russian Federation ("Russia") operation to be engaged in cyber operations that involved the staged releases of documents stolen through computer intrusions. These Russian military-based units conducted large scale cyber operations to interfere with the 2016 U.S. presidential election. Viktor Borisovich Netyksho was the Russian military officer in command of Unit 26165, located at 20 Komsomolskiy Prospekt, Moscow, Russia. Unit 26165 had primary responsibility for hacking the DCCC and DNC."

We know now, aided by subsequent news releases and information gathered through a number of investigations, Trump's personal televised plea to Russia to "find the 30,000 emails" had its origins in a series of emails and meetings that occurred a few weeks earlier in June 2016. These emails and meetings occurred between June 3 and June 9, 2016 and involved key members of the Trump campaign team and five Russian nationals but the meeting was never disclosed until months after the general election was over. The events began on June 3, 2016 when Donald, Jr. received an email from Rob Goldstone, a Russian national and long-term acquaintance of Trump Sr. In the email, Goldstone told Donald, Jr. that he could introduce him to sources from the Russian government who could provide negative facts about Hillary Clinton which would be helpful to Trump's election campaign. The email mentioned the information was coming from sources connected to the Russian government because the Russian government was hopeful to support Trump Sr.'s election.

Donald Jr. replied to Goldstone that he was away for a few days but he was interested. It is not clear if any other action was taken by Donald Jr. on that day but it may be more than coincidence that less than five hours later, Trump, Sr., announced excitedly in an interview that he would be making a major speech the following Wednesday which would interest the nation's voters.

Donald Jr. gleefully replied to Goldstone on June 7, and after exchanging several more phone calls, a meeting was arranged two days later. On June 9, Donald Jr. hosted the meeting with Russian nationals in Trump Tower. The attendees representing the Trump team in this meeting were Donald Trump, Jr..; Trump's son-in-law, Jared Kushner; and Paul Manafort, Trump's campaign manager. The Russian attendees included Goldstone; Natalia Veselnitskaya, a Russian lawyer; Anatoli Samochornov, a translator; Rinat Akhmetshin, a Russian-American lobbyist and former Soviet counterintelligence officer; Ike Kaveladze, a Georgian-American, US-based senior vice president at Crocus Group, the real estate development company. Note: This meeting was uncovered when Kushner filed a revised version of his security clearance form to US Security officials on April 6, 2017. The first security clearance form he submitted did not include this meeting with the Russian nationals.

On July 8, 2017, more than a year after the Russian meeting took place, the New York Times published a story on the June 9, 2016 meeting. Donald Jr. released his emails hours later when he was informed the New York Times was printing the story about the undisclosed meeting. . After the meeting became public, Donald Jr. said the meeting lasted a few hours, that it was not noteworthy, and that no future meetings were planned. He told the press on July 8, 2017 the meeting was held to discuss adoptions of Russian children by Americans. But shortly afterward, he tweeted a correction. He agreed to the meeting with the understanding he would receive damaging information about Hillary Clinton from the Russians. Coincidentally, only four hours after the June 9, 2016 meeting was adjourned, Trump Sr. tweeted a question to

Hillary Clinton asking her if she knew where her missing emails were, similar to when he made a public announcement on June 3 the day the Goldstone email was received.

In a general press interview following the meeting's disclosure, Trump Sr. was asked if he was aware the meeting took place in Trump Tower. He said he didn't know about the meeting. It was later confirmed that while the meeting was taking place in Trump Tower, Trump Sr. was in his office one floor above the meeting room.

Less than a week later after the June 9 meeting, national news networks reported the Democratic National Committee's computers were hacked and Russian agents were suspected. This major interruption affected the country's election process throughout the remainder of the Presidential campaign and seriously impacted the election. There was much discussion and concern as to who hacked the DNC and what information was taken. Then on July 22, Trump answered a reporter's question and said he didn't know anything about who had the leaked the emails but maybe our enemies know, and if they did, they possibly would then know everything. Within hours, WikiLeaks, a Russian ally, posted 20,000 of the reported 50,000 emails stolen from the DNC.

Then on July 27, the June 3 Russian email invitation to Donald Jr. comes full circle when Trump voices his "plea" to Russia to find Hillary's missing 30,000 emails. A coincidence? Not likely. The plea to Russia, and the almost immediate publication of emails by WikiLeaks later becomes a subject for extensive investigation by a special counsel ordered by the US Department of Justice... It is most likely to be fully determined in the future. Was it another example of Trump's indiscreet manner and poor decision-making or was it more than that? It was a treasonous action to invite any outside government, and above all, our strongest adversary, to interfere in our democratic processes, and certainly, to the extent that doing so weakens our national integrity. Coincidence? It is commonly found in many investigations that when coincidences pile up, a plan emerges.

In the following year, as more details were discovered, the Trump Tower meeting became a major focus of the government's investigation into collusion between Russia and the Trump campaign, and that focus remains through 2018. There is more information on that meeting and the participants in Chapter 11, Russian Collusion.

Hillary

Intimidation - the hallmark of Trump's approach to social and business relations, and now governmental relations, is his insistence on dominating all of his relationships. He is the elephant in the room, the bull in the china shop, the bully in the playground. It works for him because he is careful to surround himself with people who fear him, who are paid by him, who drink his poison, and who are trampled by his aggressiveness. He burrows himself inside situations and environments where a weakness is exposed and left unprotected. Additionally, he is shameless as to his tolerance for his own rude, crude, and hateful behaviors. He proudly applauds his own infamous actions and words captured on video, radio, tape, and now his tweets. It is possible the Steele Dossier revelations may yet provide him with more such infamy for him to celebrate.

A grievous example of Trump's intimidation technique was displayed on national television and across the world during the 2016 Presidential debates. There were three debates broadcast on varying networks. In summary, these debates offered the voters in America an opportunity to witness on television the character and knowledge of both candidates. A reasonable person with eyes and ears could see Trump's lack of respect for his opponent, for women in general. His misogyny was on full view for the entire viewing audience on October 9 at the site for the second Presidential debate at Washington University in St. Louis, MO. During this second debate, Trump unleashed his single-most effective tool that he likes to uses against women: he decided to intimidate his female opponent, Hillary Clinton, with his dominant male presence. Whenever Hillary Clinton moved about on the stage while answering moderator questions, Trump creepily stalked her across the stage, crowding her movements, and peering menacingly over her shoulder.

His behavior on the video is expressive of a misogynist, a woman hater, a person who, though disguised in a man's clothing, is a predatory animal who is about to pounce on its prey. In a triumphant display of courage and control, Clinton did not falter and did not runaway. In fact she was a runaway-victor in this debate and in the other two debates. The truth of Trump's character was visible once again to the tens of millions of voters across America. Shamefully for

America, it was not enough to convince many voters to reject Trump. Why not?

YouTube video (lostcub) Trump stalking Hillary
https://www.youtube.com/watch?v=T2yvMB_y0kk

The Access Hollywood Tape

In previous elections, any one of the events already discussed in this book would have doomed a candidate who was running in a primary election for anything. Not one of these stopped Trump. However, on October 7, a month before the general election and just two days before the above-referenced debate, a sledgehammer exposé hit the proverbial fan. A death knell and a scandal beyond imagining occurred when the Washington Post published a video and a news article about Donald Trump. The video spread like a wild-fire onto every television and cable network in the US. It was likely to be the final nail in Trump's coffin. Featuring Trump himself and in his own words, the video was described colloquially as, 'a real humdinger.'

The Presidential election was only four weeks away when the notorious "Access Hollywood tape" was released to the world. There had already been a plethora of scandalous behaviors by Republican Presidential candidate Donald Trump caught on camera. This one was colossal. On October 7, 2016, The Washington Post published a news article with an accompanying video from 2005 which depicted Donald Trump and television host Billy Bush sequestered on a studio lot bus having "an extremely lewd conversation about women". Billy Bush, co-host of Access Hollywood, and Trump then host for a TV reality program titled The Apprentice were going to a scheduled taping of a segment of the soap opera, "Days of Our Lives" where Trump would

36

make a guest appearance. There were several other persons on the bus but only Trump and Bush were wearing microphones. Trump was reportedly aware at the time that he was being recorded. In the casual conversation between Trump and Bush, both men can be heard discussing women. This is not altogether an unusual topic between men in Hollywood or anywhere else around the world. What was shocking to the viewers were Donald Trump's comments and his attitudes toward women including a now-infamous statement where he provided unsolicited details of his Neanderthal approach to women.

In the video,* Trump described his attempt to seduce a married woman and indicated he might start kissing the woman that he and Bush were about to meet, Arianne Zucker, who portrayed Nicole Walker on the soap opera and who would appear alongside Trump in the episode in which he was a guest star. Trump added, "I don't even wait. And when you're a star, they let you do it, you can do anything... grab them by the pussy." The transcript and the audio and video portions of the event flooded the newsprint, internet, and television networks at a rapid pace, seemingly far beyond Mach speed. Public reaction was swift. The Democratic Presidential candidate, Hillary Clinton, was among the first political figures to respond to the tape, tweeting shortly after its release, "This is horrific. We cannot allow this man to become President."

Many attorneys and media commentators characterized Trump's statements as describing acts of sexual assault. Touching a person's genitals without consent (also known as groping) is considered sexual assault in most jurisdictions in the United States. Lisa Bloom, a sexual harassment expert and civil rights lawyer, stated: "Let's be very clear, he is talking about sexual assault. He is talking about grabbing a woman's genitals without her consent." John Banzhaf, a George

Witness to Treason

Washington University public interest law professor, stated, "if Trump suddenly and without any warning reached out and grabbed a woman's crotch or breast, it would rather clearly constitute sexual assault," as was emphasized so brutally in Trump's own statement "I don't even wait."

Trump's initial soft apology stated that "This was locker room banter, a private conversation that took place many years ago." He further emphasized the insincerity of his apology by adding off-handedly, "I apologize if anyone was offended." Trump apologized a second time for the video's content after the recording provoked strong reactions by media figures and politicians across the political spectrum. Media comments further highlighted Trump's history of criticizing women for their looks as sexist. On October 8, CNN aired segments from multiple interviews Trump gave on the Howard Stern Show prior to his political career in which he made comments similar to those on the Access Hollywood tape. In September 2004, Trump commented on his daughter Ivanka's body and when asked, he tells Stern that it is okay for Stern to call his daughter "a piece of ass".

Nevertheless none of these missteps by Trump prompted serious condemnation from Republican officials. Their lukewarm responses were varied. Trump's vice-presidential running mate Mike Pence, Senate Majority Leader Mitch McConnell, and Republican National Committee Chairman Reince Priebus, indicated their disapproval of Trump's words but they did not renounce their support or call for his resignation from the ticket. A few Republicans, most prominently former presidential nominee John McCain, stated they would no longer support Trump's presidential campaign but very few GOP members of Congress called for Trump's withdrawal from the ticket. House Speaker Paul Ryan, Republican from Wisconsin, announced he

would no longer defend or support Trump's campaign but he
continued endorsing Trump through the election.

Uncensored full video of Access Hollywood Tape
Donald Trump's Access Hollywood Tape uncensored - commander in
chief of the United States of America,
https://www.youtube.com/watch?v=K2xGvXugrpM

Aftermath from Access Hollywood tape

There was an outcry from a large segment of American voters, but too
many voters and the conservative news outlets meekly looked the
other way and continued their blind allegiance to Trump. There was
some action related to the scandalous tape. Billy Bush was immediately
forced to resign from his position as co-host on Access Hollywood and
host on NBC's Today show. His future in the entertainment industry
was seriously jeopardized. Trump was not adversely affected by the
tape's repeated airing on TV and the outrage it caused across the
country. He was not censured by the GOP nor was he abandoned by
his hardy ban of loyalists. He eventually received sixty three million
votes, three million votes less than Hillary Clinton's sixty-six million
votes. Shockingly though, he was elected President of the United States
on November 8 because he received the highest number of electoral
votes 304 to Clinton's electoral 227 votes.

*Note: There were four other Presidents who were elected with less votes than the
person ahead of them: John Quincy Adams 1824, Rutherford B. Hayes 1876,
Benjamin Harrison 1888, George W. Bush, 2000, and Trump. Donald Trump lost the
popular vote by a bigger margin than any other US president in history. He lost the
popular vote by 2.8 million votes which is five times more than the 544,000 votes
by which George W. Bush lost to Al Gore in 2000.*

Witness to Treason

It was later disclosed the publication of this Access Hollywood (AH) video tape was prompted by Trump himself. "Mr. Trump's denial of claims contained in an earlier Associated Press story in which twenty former employees on his TV reality show, "The Apprentice" had described Mr. Trump's behavior toward women as lewd and inappropriate." When the existence of this 2005 Access Hollywood tape first became known, the NBC network refused to release the 2005 video but then did so only after the Washington Post received a copy elsewhere and proceeded to print the story on October 7, filed by its Post reporter, David Fahrenthold. In the video, Trump tells Billy Bush about a failed attempt to seduce Nancy O'Dell, who was Bush's co-host at the time of the recording:

Full transcript of the Access Hollywood tape

"I moved on her, and I failed. I'll admit it. I did try and fuck her. She was married. And I moved on her very heavily. In fact, I took her out furniture shopping. She wanted to get some furniture. I said, "I'll show you where they have some nice furniture." I took her out for furniture—I moved on her like a bitch. But I couldn't get there. And she was married. Then all of a sudden I see her, she's now got the big phony tits and everything. She's totally changed her look. Later, referring to Arianne Zucker (a Hollywood actress whom they were waiting to meet), Trump said, "I better use some Tic Tacs just in case I start kissing her. You know I'm automatically attracted to beautiful women—I just start kissing them. It's like a magnet. Just kiss. I don't even wait. And when you're a star, they let you do it. You can do anything. Grab 'em by the pussy. You can do anything."

Eighteen women

Shortly after the Access Hollywood video went viral, fifteen more
women filed accusations of sexual misconduct by Trump for sexual
assaults occurring between 1990 and 2015 on airplanes, in lounges, and
in elevators. These assault claims were added to three sexual assault
suits previously filed and existing as a matter of public record. Trump
denied all of the assaults telling the nation all eighteen women were
lying, adding he would sue them all.

In December 2017 a year after the Access Hollywood tape was released
and the eighteen additional charges above were ignored by GOP party
leaders, Democratic Senator Al Franken, Minnesota, was accused of an
improper advance while traveling on a USO Tour in 2006 with a female
actress. He was quickly suspended from Congress within weeks of the
accusation and the righteous GOP Congress scheduled hearings on the
charges of sexual assault immediately. Franken resigned his senate seat
on December 7, 2017. In response to Congress' actions regarding
Franken, bi-partisan attorneys and commentators renewed a call for a
similar investigation into the October 2016 sexual assault charges filed
against the President. Senator Kristen Gillibrand (D) New York,
publicly called on Trump to resign from holding office as President of
the United States. When Sarah Huckabee Sanders, the White House's
current press secretary, was asked about the numerous accusations and
about the eighteen women's decisions to come forward again, she
ignored the charges of sexual assault against the President. Sanders
said, "The people of this country in a decisive election supported
President Trump."

Witness to Treason

As of this book's publication,

- No investigation of the sexual assault charges against Trump has been authorized nor conducted by the GOP dominated Senate and House of Representatives.
- No Republican has supported any inquiry into any of Trump's accused behavior.
- The GOP has never given his accusers any voice nor semblance of credence in the halls of justice within the US Capitol.

The Enemy Within

In October 2016, I wanted to express my concern about Trump and engage with voters the need to vote against him, even though I refused to believe he could ever win the election. I was certain the great majority of American voters were too savvy to be fooled by him. I was horribly mistaken.

Here below is a reprint of a Letter to the Editor submitted by me to my local newspaper, The Delaware County Daily Times, which serves as a critical news source in one of the most populated counties in southeastern PA just below Philadelphia, PA. The newspaper editorial staff selected the title, **Why is Trump our 'enemy within'**. It was published on October 4, 2016.

Dear Editor,

It has been a long and noisy presidential election campaign. Many people have scoffed and joked at the campaign rhetoric for more than a year, but now it is time to be serious about who you will cast your vote for in early November. More-so than ever before, you must Stop, Look, and Listen at what has been said during these past 12-18 months.

Our nation has never been closer to a desecration of its American values from an 'enemy within' then it is today. The Republican candidate for President freely spews hateful invectives and it is inconceivable that in January he can suddenly become a calm statesman who can broker peace and cooperation in our national and world community.

A vote for this Republican candidate for President is a shameful smear on the fundamental promise of America's freedoms for all its citizens, and it is a betrayal to the millions of men and women who have fought for America's principles, specifically to the many thousands who have died in past wars, and to those who are still dying in wars being fought around the world. He said, "I like wars." But he has never served in the US Armed Services. The world has heard so many heartless words from him. He has not withdrawn them. So, it is important to recall his words and his actions over his lifetime of self-service to himself.

Your own life's experiences tells you repeatedly that a wolf in sheep's clothing is still a wolf, a demagogue in a suit is still a despot, and a person who demeans women, the disabled, and heroes is not fit to lead America. Clearly, such a man is not fit to stand beside Americans. It is always unwise and unsafe to invite evil into your home, regardless of your reason. The lame silvery promises of every tyrant echoes down the halls of history to us. It is a familiar refrain. "I am great. I alone can make you great. I alone can fix it. Here have a bite of this apple".

Soon, Wednesday, November 9th will arrive and it will be a momentous and joyful day when this man is sent home to his gilded mansions and his tall office towers empty-handed. Plan on sharing that day with me. Please think before you cast your vote on November 8th

It did not stop him. Why not?

Every word Trump said and every action he took in his past careers and his 2015 and 2016 campaigns should have convinced reasonable people to reject him and to never look back. Anyone of his many missteps would have dive-bombed any other candidate's bid for election for any local, state, or federal office. Yet incredibly all of it was accepted by GOP party leaders and GOP legislators at every level of office in America. The GOP senators, congressmen and congresswomen swallowed Trump's poison willingly and silently? An enormous part of American voters accepted his dark vision of how to improve America and became willing soldiers who filled his campaign rallies with a cacophonous circus tent atmosphere of hatred and ugly chants – all created to drive themselves into a mindless frenzy. His unprecedented bad behavior was limitless.

How was Trump able to survive his attacks on American values? How was he able to cross the lines of decency openly and unapologetically in full view of American men, women, and children? How was he ever elected? More importantly, what kind of President would Donald J. Trump become? Will he transform himself into a man befitting the office he holds? Or will he fail to become a silk purse, and become more like the parakeet in a fireman's clothing, or worse, just a monkey in a suit?

Chapter Three
UnPresidented

A horse's ass by any other name is still a horse's ass.   *Anonymous*

Worse than ever

What came to my mind at dawn's first light on November 9, 2018, was a phrase that an attending physician might solemnly announce to his patient's loved ones when something goes terribly wrong for the patient. The words I kept hearing inside my head were, "I'm afraid America has taken a turn for the worse."

Yes, move over Harry Truman. On that morning of infamy, Donald J. Trump became the biggest upset-winner in American Presidential elections and he, not Hillary Clinton, was going to be America's 45th President. Not only were Clinton and Trump and more than half of American voters shocked but tens of millions of people in nations around the world were shocked. In the swiftly passing eighteen or so months of political campaigning that swept America's social landscape, and after many subsequent expert analysis and puzzled brows, there is still wonderment in understanding and mystery in uncovering all of the reasons for the election outcome. I began this chapter with a medical reference and I will continue another medicine adage assuring us that "time heals all things." I sincerely hope so. I will leave the work of discovery to others who follow me. For now, let me tell you some of the things America has witnessed during the first 100 days of the Trump presidency. I will begin on Trump's Inauguration Day.

Witness to Treason

According to reports in early December 2017 that were denied by opposing parties shortly thereafter, Michael Flynn, the soon-to-be appointed National Security Advisor, was seated at Trump's inauguration speech while he texted a former business partner that the Obama administration's US sanctions on Russia which included blocking a private Russian-backed plan to build nuclear plants in the Middle East will now be 'ripped up', and that the plan backed by Flynn and Trump was now, "good to go."
"https://en.wikipedia.org/wiki/Timeline_of_the_Trump_presidency,_2017_Q1 - cite_note-6

Although the "Flynn Inauguration Day texting" report has been publicly denied and was forwarded to several congressional committees for review, it is indicative of the rumors and facts that have flourished around the Trump White House almost every day since Trump's election. The festive pomp and circumstance of the inauguration of a new President normally calms the tempest air and unites the country. America celebrates its democracy with the peaceful change of leadership in America from one leader to another but this would not happen with the inauguration of the 45th President of the United States. This unification never came. America's ritual so sacred to good people all over the world was fractured. This freedom to choose, never exercised in Russia and China, appeared to be off its wheels. The new President was No. 45, but he was the first of his kind, and not a good kind. General Flynn's inauguration text, the moment that may never have happened, was a precursor of so many events that did or didn't happen. Chaos would come to dominate the Trump presidency.

Whose is bigger?

On Inauguration Day, Trump addressed the nation with repeated promises of greatness to come but on the following morning in typical Trump-form he tweeted false information (lies) informing America and the world that his crowd of attendees at his Inauguration in Washington, DC was the largest number of people to ever attend a US Presidential Inauguration. He "tweeted" publicly the morning after the Inauguration that the crowd attendance was much larger than the actual smaller number reported in news reports. It was in keeping with his continuing juvenile and obsessive focus that size matters to him in all things personal, always emphasizing that his bank account, possessions, personal features and relationships are certainly larger and greater than anyone else's. On the very next day, setting a pattern that the Trump White House would repeat as often as the sun rises over the Trump White House administration, Sean Spicer, the White House Press Secretary, was dispatched to the White House press conference to criticize the media for inaccurately presenting the presidential inauguration attendance. As punishment for disrespecting the President's mathematical calculations, there were no questions taken from the press. Thus began the inevitable transference of "newspeak" from Orwellian literature to Trump pronouncements.

Trump Inauguration Day crowd. The biggest ever? Not at all. Not close

Repeal and Replace

Later on Inauguration Day, after Flynn and everyone else put away the cell phones, and the crowds undeniably decreased in size, Trump could not resist his opportunity to display his petty personality as well as showing his propensity "to put the cart before the horse" when he and the GOP leadership wrapped themselves in a spiteful moment. Trump and the GOP gathered together in the Oval Office on Day 1 of the Trump presidency to trumpet their new power to begin the immediate end to the 2015 Affordable Care Act (Obamacare). Smiling broadly, President Trump issued Executive Order 13765 as his first official order designed to scale back parts of the Affordable Care Act. This first official step would signal his intention to repeal and replace his predecessor's greatest victory. Derisively christened by the GOP as Obamacare, the crowning moment had come for Trump and the GOP.

He was joined this Day 1 to fulfill a promise he tweeted on February 9, 2016, "We will immediately repeal and replace Obamacare - and nobody can do that like me. We will save $'s and have much better healthcare!" 6:15 PM - Feb 9, 2016. Trump and the GOP Party of No were giddy with battle glory ringing in their ears and ready to victory dance in their bare feet. After seven years of complaining, and detracting, and seething, the GOP, the Party of No, was going to finally succeed at something, even though they were going to do something negative. They would repeal the first universal healthcare legislation ever passed in America and replace it with a new healthcare bill, the American Health Care Act, aka Trumpcare.

The Party of No, so named during the eight years of President Barack Obama's presidency when Republican Senator Mitch McConnell of Kentucky brazenly boasted "I will gladly spend my entire remaining years in Congress hoping to ensure only one goal for me, to never let Barack Obama be successful". He did just that as the hate-filled leader of a GOP unwilling to say yes even for their constituents benefit. McConnell's position is hauntingly familiar to Alabama Governor George Wallace standing in the doorway of the University of Alabama in 1963 to deny access to black Americans who wanted to attend a state school in a free American nation. Wallace moved after President John Kennedy sent troops from Alabama's own National Guard to protect federal officials and black students as they entered the building. McConnell's self-damning stand to deny healthcare to fellow Americans who pay for his bountiful healthcare cries out to those outside Kentucky that one old-time southern legislator's time has passed. As John McCain may have been signaling to McConnell with his final vote in the Senate, "thumbs down" on pettiness and ugly politics, "We must be better than that."

Witness to Treason

Trump and his GOP Party of No were greatly embarrassed in late March when the Speaker of the House Paul Ryan had to cancel the full Congressional vote on a bill to replace the Affordable Care Act because the GOP with a majority in both houses did not have enough votes to successfully pass their replacement healthcare bill. The GOP poorly constructed Trumpcare Bill is never presented for a vote in Congress. The GOP decides to save political face and avoid the public humiliation of witnessing its failure to pass, especially after spending seven years vowing to repeal and replace the Affordable Care Act as their first piece of legislation.

Obamacare, hated by Trump and the GOP, was still triumphantly standing as the law of the land for healthcare. Now two years later, it is growing greater in popularity despite the GOP meanness in trying to sabotage its success. Obamacare is affectionately embraced by tens of millions of Americans (Republicans and Democrats) who now have healthcare for the first time in their lives.

A Gathering of Generals

There were several other orders issued from Trump's desk before he moved on to the Inaugural Balls in the evening, He signed another bill waiving a rule that requires military personnel to wait seven years after retiring before serving in a civilian post. His signature will allow him to begin hiring a slew of "his generals" into his administration. His stable of generals included General Flynn, General "Mad Dog" Mattis, General Kelly, and General Mc Master. Two of "Trump's generals" are no longer in the administration and a third has changed positions from Homeland Security to White House Chief of Staff.

Never too early

Always being consumed with himself but nevertheless feeling insecure in his position as every budding dictator is likely to be, Trump filed a form with the Federal Elections Commission (FEC) within hours of his swearing in ceremony, declaring his eligibility to run for re-election in 2020. Then he held his first campaign rally for the 2020 Presidential campaign near Orlando, Florida, on February 18, 2017. It was the earliest such event by any incumbent President in US history. Though unprecedented, this made sense for Trump because his approval rate at the beginning of his term was 41%, lower than any person previously elected President in America's 242 years of existence. Each succeeding month through March 2018, his approval rate sunk even lower. Then, adding insult to the administration's fabrication of Trump's inaugural crowd size was the appearance of record crowds of people on the National Mall on the very next day. Massive crowds attended Women's March events in many cities across America and around the world, and the largest crowd was in Washington, DC. Altogether, it was estimated that four million people attended Women's March events protesting the Trump inaugural and his new administration. The protest also highlighted the list of sexual charges filed against him by a minimum of eighteen women during the Presidential campaign. Overall, it was the largest single-day protest in U.S. history, and women all across the world, in seven continents, marched against Donald Trump and his misogynist attitude and his lack of respect for women worldwide.

https://en.wikipedia.org/wiki/First_100_days_of_Donald_Trump%27s_presidency - cite_note-theatlantic_T100_Treelection-602

Trump's first week

The traditional first milestone for viewing a President's performance is the period including the initial three months of governing the country, commonly referred to as the First 100 Days. In Trump's administration it was clear one week or so would be sufficient to take the measure of the President and his friends. One day, one week, one year, it didn't take long to see that Donald Trump the candidate, now as the 45th President, was not likely to change his stripes. The first full week of Trump's presidency began with a showcase of busy work where he rushed to hammer home to his 35% base of election-day voters that he will keep his promises.

On Monday, he signed a memorandum withdrawing the United States from the Trans-Pacific Partnership, an international trade agreement he will consider rejoining sixteen months later after he fails to win his personal 'thirty-day trade war' with China in April 2018. In a private meeting with congressional leaders, he announced that 3–5 million illegal votes prevented him from winning the popular vote. This unsubstantiated charge of voter fraud is repeated often but it is never proven despite many efforts to do so by Trump advocates. As a counterpoint, on the same day, a federal-court lawsuit is filed against the President accusing him of violating the Constitution's Foreign Emoluments Clause which states no sitting President can own properties and services which produce income to him from foreign countries. Trump unlike previous Presidents did not step away from ownership of his public business holdings.
https://en.wikipedia.org/wiki/Timeline_of_the_Trump_presidency,_2017_Q1 - cite_note-35

On Tuesday, Trump began his attack on America's environment. The many years of restoring and safeguarding rivers, oceans, and forests from runaway industrial pollution were wiped out by his single pen-stroke when he signed Executive Order 13766, which expedites environmental reviews and approvals for future infrastructure projects. The order denies the necessary time required to study impact of projects in order to safeguard the public interest. Instead, land developers, coal barons, and corporate entities can quickly bypass reasonable inspections and avoid regulations that restricted these interests from destroying America's environment. Trump's administration is filled with the largest concentration of business and financial executives in federal government since 1919. On this same day, to the delight of the oil and gas energy interests , he signed a Presidential memoranda to reverse the Obama administration's halt on the Keystone XL and Dakota Access oil pipelines, the latter of which has been the subject of protests by the Standing Rock tribe. In a small nod to steel workers, he required the pipelines to use domestic steel, and called for "expedited reviews of and approvals for" manufacturing facilities and "reductions in regulatory burdens". This latter directive favors large businesses by removing safety features and reducing regulations that protect workers in factories. It is noteworthy that the former directive to use domestic steel was withdrawn by Trump after Keystone informed the White House it will use less expensive foreign steel and not domestic steel.

This day will not end until yet another action occurs pertaining to Trump's 'Lock Her Up' cheer-leading buddy, Michael Flynn. It is announced in news reports that Flynn is interviewed by the FBI about prior conversations with Russian Ambassador Sergey Kislyak. A few days later Acting Attorney General Sally Yates informs White House Counsel Don McGahn that Michael Flynn's public account of his interactions with Russian officials during the transition were untruthful, making him vulnerable to blackmail. Trump accepts the

55

information but does nothing. Within two months, Michael Flynn seeks immunity from Congress in exchange for testimony on White House links to Russia. Nearly a year later on December 1, 2017, General Flynn pled guilty to lying to the FBI, and in August 2018, he was still awaiting final sentencing in a Washington, DC courtroom.

By Wednesday in his first week, Trump must've been giddy with self-satisfaction. How else can anyone explain why he awoke that day and issued Executive Order 13767 directing the Department of Homeland Security to begin construction of a wall on the Mexico–United States border. This announcement failed to please Mexico's President Enrique Peña Nieto who immediately rejected the idea to pay for any border wall between the United States and his country. In an early preview of Trump's 'disciplined' negotiating style, Trump issued at the same time, Executive Order 13768 to cut federal funding for sanctuary cities in America. These are cities with large Mexican-immigrant populations who planned to refuse to comply with the Trump administration's harsh immigration (ICE) enforcement measures. Trump's Orwellian order increases the number of border patrol and immigration officers and deportation standards become tougher. The southwestern United States would soon resemble a number of armed military posts, much too reminiscent of border crossings formerly seen in East Germany and still existing in North Korea. Also, in keeping with his obsession to refuse to admit he lost the popular vote to Hillary Clinton, he announces publicly that he will appoint persons to investigate alleged voter fraud from the 2016 presidential election. He suggests convening a national panel to investigate voter fraud on a massive scale. He needs desperately to convince himself and his 35% voter base that more than 3-5 million votes were stolen from him. Trump increased the low end of the vote range from 3 million to 3.5 million because 3.5 million is the minimum number of votes he needs to find in order to have more votes than Clinton.

On, Thursday, January 26, Press Secretary Sean Spicer announces that Trump's latest plan is to have the US-Mexico border wall funded by a 20% tax on imports from Mexico. Not surprisingly, Mexican President Enrique Peña Nieto does not leap for joy, he abruptly cancels a proposed meeting with Trump. For anyone keeping score, its Mexico 2, Trump 0.

During a visit to the Pentagon on Friday, the 27th, President Trump signs Executive Order 13769, suspending the Refugee Admissions Program for 120 days and denying entry to citizens of Iraq, Iran, Libya, Somalia, Sudan, Syria, and Yemen for 90 days. This is a precursor to Trump's edict later referred to as "The Muslim Ban."

Keeping track of the early grumblings of an FBI investigation into Russian interference in America's recent election is relatively simple to do during the first week of the Trump administration. But it will soon become almost impossible for the suspects to keep their lies coordinated. Two more pieces of news reported later occur on this day. Trump advisor George Papadopoulos is interviewed by the FBI concerning Russian meetings in 2016, and President Trump invites FBI Director James Comey to a private dinner at the White House. It is reported later that after dinner, Trump asks Comey to pledge loyalty to Trump, and Comey demurs. This is not insignificant because soon Trump will ask Comey to "let go of Flynn." Regarding Papadopoulos, he later pleads guilty in October 2017 to making omissions and false statements during his Friday interview with the FBI.

Witness to Treason

On the last day of Week 1, Trump directs his Generals to put together a plan within 30 days for defeating ISIS. He also restructures the National and Homeland Security Councils by downgrading the Chiefs of Staff while appointing Steve Bannon, a Breitbart ultra-right journalist and self-proclaimed political guru as Assistant to the President and Chief Strategist.

The next day is Sunday, the start of Trump's Week 2 in the White House. It is a quiet day with the exception of news from London that the petition launched in October by British citizens to cancel President Trump's state visit to the United Kingdom has passed one million signatures, passing the threshold for requiring a British Parliament debate. The number of signatures dis-inviting Trump to the United Kingdom will eventually exceed more than 1.8 million.

The Muslim Ban

One week after the inauguration, Trump signaled out one ethnic community as being unwelcome in America. He signed an executive order that startled the country and shocked the world. Without any pre-announcement or prior discussion with Congress, he restricted entry into the United States from the citizens of seven Muslim countries he deemed security risks. His order suspended entry for 120 days of all refugees who want to resettle in the United States and barred refugees from Syria indefinitely. The order also prohibited citizens from Iraq, Syria, Iran, Sudan, Libya, Somalia and Yemen from entering into the United States for 90 days. The order was swiftly labeled as a "Muslim Ban" because these targeted refugees were predominately of Muslim faith. He banned citizens from these countries from coming to the US. With such short notice, there was chaos at airports in America and around the world. Legal challenges

were filed immediately and the ban was blocked by federal judges.
Trump defended the part of the order targeting seven Muslim-majority
countries as necessary to fight terrorism even though the large majority
of jihadists committing acts of terror in America have been American
citizens or legal residents. Also, since 9/11, no one in the United States
has been killed in a terrorist attack by someone from the seven
countries. Trump's quick action seemed to be politically motivated to
impress his Midwest, conservative, and southern voting bases. He was
giving notice to Trump America and the world that he could and
would do whatever he wanted to do.

A very noticeable feature about the list was that the targets were the
poorest Muslim countries, the countries where the Trump organization
does not do business or has no plan to do business yet. In January 2018,
during a discussion with Republican Senator Lindsey Graham on a
broader immigration policy, Trump erupted in a racial outburst
demanding fewer arrivals from "shithole countries" in Latin America,
the Caribbean and Africa and displayed his personal aversion to
refugees from poor countries when he complained about people from
"shit-hole countries" being admitted to America and asked legislators
in the same immigration meeting "why we don't have more people
emigrating from good countries like Norway". Trump's callous
comments would threaten to desecrate the tablet in Lady Liberty's
hand with inserting a sad inscription on to it, words not deserving of
our American roots, "Send me your millionaires from Monaco and
your oligarchs from Russia, who can fatten themselves on our common
freedoms." His myopic ban disgraced the millions of immigrants who
were welcomed to America since Plymouth Rock and Jamestown. The
parents and grandparents and ancestors who came here impoverished,
illiterate, and oppressed would've languished in poverty and fear
elsewhere if Trump were President when they came to America. Many

of us would likely be less than who we are today if Trump were
President then. We should be fearful that our children will be less free
to pursue the American dream if Trump, his friends, and his party win
anything again.

The Paris Agreement

During his first weeks as President, Trump's reason d'etre continued to
be his obsession to keep the promises he gave to his voting base during
the campaign regardless of whether a promise was unreasonable,
harmful, pricey, or just loose and dicey. One of his campaign promises
favored by his closest advisor Steve Bannon was to remove the United
States from the "Paris Agreement", an international agreement of
cooperation signed by every nation on earth except Syria and
Nicaragua. This climate agreement is an international accord
previously negotiated by almost 200 countries, aimed at curbing
climate change by reducing greenhouse gas emissions. The Paris
Agreement seeks "to strengthen the global response to the threat of
climate change." One objective is to hold the increase in global average
temperature well below 2 degrees Celsius above pre-industrial levels.
The agreement does not impose penalties on signatories and it does
specify how each country should meet the targets. The underlying
hope behind the agreement is that mutual peer pressure will keep
member nations in line. As major nations emitting enormous amount
of pollutants, the United States, China, and India are strategically
necessary as members in order for the agreement to survive. Trump's
ascendancy to President concerned many environmentalists
worldwide because the United States' departure will weaken the deal,
specifically because the United States' absence will deprive the
agreement's goals of achieving tangible progress without participation
by the world's second biggest carbon emitter.

On June 1, 2017, with the world watching, President Trump stood in the middle of the White House Rose Garden on the soft grass and amid blossoming flowers and announced the United States would pull out of the Paris climate agreement. The agreement was one of the strongest environmental policy legacies of President Barack Obama who called it "a turning point for our planet." In the Rose Garden ceremony, Trump said the United States would exit the Paris agreement, adding "I was elected to represent the citizens of Pittsburgh, not Paris." Later Pittsburgh mayor Bill Pequot tweeted "as the Mayor of Pittsburgh, I can assure you that we will follow the guidelines of the Paris Agreement for our people, our economy & future." A few days earlier Trump had made a decision to shelve another signature environmental effort by Obama, the 2013 Climate Action Plan. This Plan would seek to reduce emissions by 26 percent to 28 percent below 2005 levels by 2025. There were numerous reactions to this Rose Garden announcement. Former President Obama said, "Even in the absence of this administration support I'm confident that our states, cities and businesses will step up and do even more to lead the way, and help protect for future generations the one planet we've got." General Electric CEO Jeffrey Imelda tweeted, "Disappointed with today's decision on the Paris Agreement. Climate change is real. Industry must now lead and not depend on government." *Source: Trump pulling out of Paris climate agreement, By Louis Jacobson, June 1st, 2017 Politifact*

The immediate winner from the United States' departure from the Paris Accord, and the accord's restrictions on air pollutants, will be the coal industry barons. Reducing restrictions on carbon emissions will allow mine owners to re-open the coal mines with less safety and environmental regulations. Work will be available for a limited time, until the mines are bare, or coal is outdated by technology. After, the coal is burned, it will harm the air and land, and lead to irreparable

61

climate changes. The largest certain short-term gain will be the large amounts of cash the coal mine owners and friends of Trump will collect over the next few years before coal use diminishes to zero. The coal miners will work and die, and their land will be left dead and barren, and no one there will remember they voted for it.

Exiting the Paris Accord was not surprising. During the 2016 campaign, Trump was a strong supporter of coal and coal producing areas who were among his most enthusiastic bases of support. Slashing environmental and work safety regulations on the operating mines may not provide enough cost savings to the industry to enable it to turn around in a significant way and exist beyond a few more profitable years. The increasing competitiveness of natural gas secured through hydraulic fracturing, or "fracking", and the technological refinement of renewable energy sources such as solar and wind are now providing an increasing share of the energy used for electricity generation in the United States and overseas.

The Media Is the Enemy

In Feb 2017 Trump called the NY Times and four TV networks "the enemy of the people", echoing similar dictums from at least two of history's notorious dictators: Joseph Stalin and Mao Zedong. Similarly, Trump is at war with the truth. His homegrown muse and mentor, chief strategist Steve Bannon, called the press "the opposition party." President Thomas Jefferson would flip over in his grave on hearing an American in the White House say such a thing. President Jefferson had his differences with members of the press but he was correct when he said, "Our liberty depends on the freedom of the press, and that cannot be limited without being lost."

Trump doesn't read to feed his intelligence. That is obvious. He reads to see his name in the newspapers, magazines, and so forth. So Trump continues to "routinely attack, belittle, humiliate, and delegitimizes the press and its reporters, journalists."

In the first eighteen months of his administration, Reporters without Borders reported the United States has fallen sharply in a global ranking index of press freedom. (Source: Tribune News Service, April 25, 2018.) Citing the Trump administration among other nation governments, the international advocacy group Reporters without Borders said on Wednesday, "The United States has slipped again among countries in an annual ranking of freedom of the press." The study says a "climate of hatred" is growing worldwide toward the news media. Trump's most basic difficulty with the truth is that the truth disrobes him. The truth strips him of the protective cloak of lies that he drapes over himself and over his supporters, family, friends, and relationships he has with anyone and anything, because like King Midas, whatever Trump touches turns into a disaster, more so to others than to himself. *Source: Philly Inquirer editorial, Feb 22, 2017*

Trump's Wiretap Tweet, March 4, 2017

"Just found out that Obama had my "wires tapped" in Trump Tower just before the victory." This was Trump's cry for help and a plea for rage by his voting base and "fried-brained" enablers. It was March 21, 2017, one day after James Comey, FBI Director, testified to the House Committee on Intelligence that the FBI had begun an investigation into reports that some of Trump's close advisers had alleged ties to Russia during the campaign. The announcement of the investigation was damaging to Trump. Trump, as always, lashed out, and he decided to turn the table on his accusers by reporting fabricated information, saying he had proof that Obama wire-tapped his Trump Tower offices before and during the campaign. Devin Nunes, who was upended by Comey's testimony, became a willing pawn in Trump's plan to deflect attention from him and Russia. Nunes, Republican congressman, (CA), an early campaign supporter of everything Trump, and now chairman of the House Permanent Select Committee on Intelligence, gaveled the second day of the House hearing to a close, and arrived for a late-night visit to Pennsylvania Avenue, now referred to as "Nunes' midnight run".

Nunes reportedly went to the National Security Council offices on the fourth floor of the Eisenhower Executive Office Building, right next to the White House, and met with two Trump administration National Security Council staff members. Nunes was shown classified documents that had been gathered for his review and that were related to the purported wiretaps. The next afternoon, without sharing the information with all of the members on his Intelligence Committee, Nunes called a news conference in the Capitol where he announced that "sources" had provided him with evidence that, during the transition, the President or his associates had been swept up in foreign surveillance by American spy agencies. When a reporter asked him if he thought that the American intelligence community was "spying on Trump during the transition," Nunes replied, "I guess it all depends on one's definition of spying." He added: "Clearly it bothers me enough. I'm not comfortable with it." Nunes seemed to be lending credence to Trump's preposterous accusation on Twitter from earlier that month that Obama had his 'wires tapped' in Trump Tower." Nunes then headed back to the White House to brief Trump on his findings - a seemingly unnecessary move considering that the information had been given to him by Trump's own aides.

A few days later, after reporters exposed his visit to the White House, and discovered the ruse that the White House themselves constructed the information it gave to Nunes, he was forced to recuse himself as majority leader of the House's Russia Investigation probe because he misused classified information and did not inform the full committee. Forgotten too quickly was the fact that the Obama-era eavesdropping had been legal, incidental and inconsequential.

Nunes recused himself from the committee's Russia investigation, but he refused to cede the critical subpoena power to his replacement. His retention of the subpoena power and his refusal to use it to force critical witnesses to be called before the panel seriously hampered the House's Russian investigation. It is not surprising that the Republican-controlled House failed to find information it did not wish to find. In December, after the House Ethics Committee concluded that Nunes hadn't illegally revealed classified information, he took back the reins of the Russia investigation. Then, in March, Nunes and the committee Republicans abruptly wrapped up the investigation into Russian meddling, having concluded that there was no collusion between the Trump campaign and the Russian government and that, contrary to the official consensus of the American intelligence community, the Russian government was not even seeking to help elect Trump.

The President soon promoted the findings on Twitter: "THE HOUSE INTELLIGENCE COMMITTEE HAS, AFTER A 14 MONTH LONG IN-DEPTH INVESTIGATION, FOUND NO EVIDENCE OF COLLUSION OR COORDINATION BETWEEN THE TRUMP CAMPAIGN AND RUSSIA TO INFLUENCE THE 2016 PRESIDENTIAL ELECTION."

Note: In July 2018, in Helsinki, Finland, in front of the world, Russian President Vladimir Putin and Donald Trump stood side-by-side at a news conference, and Putin stated, "Yes. I wanted Trump to win the American Presidency."

For House Democrats, particularly Adam Schiff, CA-D, Nunes' "midnight run," represented a fundamental break. Schiff said, "From that point on (March 2017), I think that he considered it his primary mission to protect the White House no matter the cost." Eric Swalwell, a California Democrat and member of the committee, summed up the events concisely. "He is considered to be Trump's Michael Cohen in Congress. He is Trump's fixer."

Foxes in the Hen House

"Drain the Swamp! That's right. Drain the Swamp!" The Republican Presidential Candidate yelled over the crowd in his campaign speeches as the 2016 Presidential election neared.

The guttural populist slogan was handed to him after it had been tested on social media as early as 2015 by professional data collectors hired by Trump Campaign. The candidate immediately embraced the catchy mob chant as his own idea and began using it to incite uncontrolled passion among his crowd of supporters. He was now promising in his campaign speeches to do something he never intended to do if elected. Now he was told by his handlers it was what his frenzied supporters wanted to hear. So he promised to "Drain the swamp!" So what was one more lie? In expected fashion, Trump quickly drained DC of many career professionals and filled the proverbial "hen house" with his own personal den of foxes. Hence, his cabinet of advisers is over-run with diamond-studded tie-tacks, Rolex watches, expensive suits, and private airplanes. Most grievously, all have expensive tastes in travel and luxury items with an affinity for charging all such expenses to the companies they own and now to the government whose taxpayers pay the bills.

There was much interest among the media over his cabinet nominations, as the selections would show America how he intended to govern. President Trump's proposed cabinet was characterized by the media as being very conservative. It was described as a "conservative dream team" by Politico,[53] "the most conservative cabinet in United States history" by *Newsweek,* and "one of the most consistently conservative domestic policy teams in modern history" by the *Los Angeles Times. The Hill* described Mr. Trump's potential cabinet as "an unorthodox team" more popular with conservatives than the establishment Republicans such as John McCain or Mitt Romney who likely would not have chosen them . CNN agreed. They called the proposed cabinet "a conservative dream team of domestic Cabinet appointments." On the other hand, *The Wall Street Journal* stated that "it's nearly impossible to identify a clear ideological bent in the incoming president's" cabinet nominations. In terms of total personal wealth, Mr. Trump's cabinet is the wealthiest in modern American history.[61]

The Wall Street Journal also stated that Mr. Trump's nominations signaled a pro-deregulation administration policy. Several of his cabinet nominees politically opposed the federal departments they were selected to lead. President Trump's cabinet is largely made up of nominees who have business experience but minimal experience in the government when compared to the administrations of the five presidents who immediately preceded him. The Pew Research Center also noted that Mr. Trump's cabinet is one of the most business-heavy in American history. The think tank stated that "A third of the department heads in the Trump administration (33%) will be people whose prior experience has been entirely in the public sector. Only three other presidents are in the same range: William McKinley (three out of eight Cabinet positions, or 37.5%), Ronald Reagan (four out of 13 positions, or 31%), and Dwight Eisenhower (three out of 10 positions, or 30%)."[63]

After the election in November 2016, President-elect Trump announced his first post-election cabinet nominee, Alabama Republican Senator Jeff Sessions for United States Attorney General. Although most positions were simultaneously under consideration by the transition team, the official announcement of offers, and the public acceptance of the offers, usually happens gradually as slots are filled. After three weeks of Trump's presidency, the number of his approved cabinet members stood at 7.

I am a fan of proverbs, wise ones and dumb ones, of fables, of old adages and just plain tidbits of advice wrapped in a thoughtful phrase. I'm sure most of you have heard so many and it is certain you have your own favorites. Me too. In fact, two of my favorites jumped out of my memory bucket as soon as No. 45 began announcing his choices for his Trump cabinet. They fit the situation perfectly. They are: "Birds of a feather flock together" and "You can a tell lot about people by looking at the company they keep." For all of Trump's noisy commotion and verbal blasts to "Drain the swamp", his subsequent actions show a fondness for appointing executives from the industries and financial institutions that surround and occupy large portions of Washington real estate. The alarming difference in his appointments is the people that he chose to be cabinet leaders were recently fierce adversaries of the same departments they will now be responsible for leading. Shocking only if you ever thought Trump cared about anyone but his friends who funded his campaign. Trump's policy is not to lead the departments to improvement nor to provide greater service to America. No, Trump plans to have these cabinet leaders monitor the regression of the agencies into eventual extinction, or ensure they are devoid of any power to accomplish anything except rubber-stamping the wishes of Trump's partnership of corporate businesses, financial interests, and military subservience.

Let's look at Trump's choice to lead the Environmental Protection Agency (EPA), former Oklahoma Attorney General, Scott Pruitt. (Note: Pruitt resigned on July 6, 2018 and was replaced by EPA Assistant and former coal lobbyist, and Senate staffer, Andrew Wheeler.) During Pruitt's eighteen month term as chief of the Environmental Protection Agency, he was under pressure for his abuse of government services and policies. While Attorney General of Oklahoma he allowed a poultry industry leader to dump 300,000 tons of waste from chicken factories into the Illinois River. Pruitt did not even issue a fine. In fact he dismantled an existing Oklahoma state environmental enforcement team and then formed a new team of his choosing and directed them to attack EPA regulations. Under his leadership as State Attorney General, he and dozens of politicians in Oklahoma sued the EPA. It was later reported Pruitt took campaign contributions from the poultry industry. The state GOP and the federal GOP ignored this blatant conflict of interest. Scott Pruitt was rewarded by Trump with the responsibility for safeguarding America's air, lands, rivers, lakes, oceans, and drinking water from his own friends who give him money. Trump put a fox in the hen house.

Trump then looked high and low, and settled on low when he chose Wilbur Ross, an investment banker, as his choice for Secretary of Commerce. Ross, who made a good chunk of his money selling U.S. steel companies to a foreign entity, initiated the Trump's administration's push in 2018 to place high tariffs on steel from foreign countries, steel companies that he competed with earlier. In 2002, Ross and his investing partners bought US steel companies that were either in or near bankruptcy, including LTV Corp., Weirton, and Bethlehem Steel, and consolidated them into the International Steel Group (ISC) and, in 2004, sold that company to the Indian steel magnate Lakshmi Mittal, making some $2 billion in cash on the deal. At the time of the ISG sale, the Washington Post reported that Ross was able to make a stunning 12-fold gain on his initial investment in part by not paying steel workers' pensions and retiree health care costs, and by not putting up millions of dollars to ensure that the environmental messes associated with the plants he bought would be cleaned up before he sold it*.   https://theintercept.com/2018/03/05/steel-tariffs-wilbur-ross-pollution/.

In August 2018, Forbes magazine looked even deeper into Ross' business character and reported that Ross allegedly bilked business associates out of more than $120 million throughout his career as an investment banker. The magazine previously reported that Ross fudged his finances in order to appear on Forbes' elite list of billionaires. Disclosure forms Ross filed after his nomination by Trump showed he had less than $700 million in assets. In July 2018, Ross quietly settled a $4 million lawsuit brought by a former employee, and in 2005, a former vice chairman of Ross's private equity fund, WL Ross & Company, sued him for $20 million in 2005, and yet another lawsuit alleges that Ross and his firm charged at least $48 million in improper fees on investments. SEC fined his firm $2.3 million in 2016, before Trump appointed him the Secretary of U.S. Commerce.

Trump also chose "a cadre of climate-change deniers to lead the agencies that protect the environment" even as the earth is experiencing record-breaking temperature increases which are leading to increasingly vicious flooding, drought, wildfires, and food shortages. Trump's appointee as Interior Secretary, Ryan Zincke, has called climate change a hoax and as a congressman from Montana voted for a bill to give states control over federal lands making them vulnerable to weaker environmental protections and making it easier for the land to be sold to private entities. He staffs his administration with executives from fossil fuel companies including Secretary of Energy Rick Perry (remember him?) who in a moment of embarrassment during a Republican debate forgot the name of the federal department he so forcefully wanted to shut down. Well, he shamefully changed his mind about shutting it down after Trump appointed him to be head of that same department, the Department of Energy. Perry replaced Ernest Moniz, a nuclear physicist. This was a perfect fit for Trump and Perry. After all, Trump only wants to close the department, he doesn't need someone to make it work. It was also either a rare display of magnanimity by Trump, or it was a show of Trump's cruel sense of humor to saddle Perry with the position as Director of a department connected to one of Perry's most embarrassing national moments.

Director of Consumer Financial Protection Bureau Mick Mulvaney, a former congressman from South Carolina, is certainly doing his job for Donald Trump. In the 135 days after Trump appointed Mulvaney to take control of the nation's consumer watchdog agency, it has not recorded a single enforcement action against any banks, credit card companies, debt companies, or any finance companies whatsoever. That's not surprising. Mick Mulvaney once called the agency a "sick, sad dog" of an agency. Now he is simply one of Trump's proud minions doing Trump's bidding of doing harm to the agency or doing nothing at all. As the acting director of this government agency, his mandate is to shrink the bureau's role and take a much softer approach to enforcement (meaning it will no longer protect consumers). Before Mulvaney took over the control of the agency, the agency issued an average of two to four enforcement actions a month. An example of the agency's enforcement successes is when Bank of America was ordered to pay $727 million to consumers for deceptive credit card practices in 2015 and the agency returned $3.97 billion in cash back to American consumers and twice that amount in other types of relief such as lower balances and debt relief, actions to extract billions of dollars in relief for consumers from financial companies who harm the consumers. Because the agency was so effective in protecting consumers from banks' and finance companies' blatant fraud and deception, Mulvaney was given the mission to run it into the ground.

Most disappointing for American parents with children, and for anyone seeking to advance their education, was Trump's choice for Secretary of Education, Betsy DeVos, a longtime Republican donor, and the former chairwoman of the Republican Party in Michigan. DeVos' won Senate confirmation nomination by the slimmest margin possible, a 51-50 margin that needed a tie-breaking vote from Vice President Mike Pence. DeVos is a major advocate for education reform centered on expanding charter schools and private-school vouchers. She headed the American Federation for Children, an advocacy group that pushes for increased school choice for parents. The New York Times reported on her successful effort to kill legislation in Detroit that would have imposed tougher accountability standards on charter schools. Clearly, she wants more charter schools (this action will increase revenue and profitability for charter school owners), but she wants less accountability for the schools performances, (this action lessens the responsibility for charter schools to fully educate their students.)

DeVos is a champion for the privatization of public education. In the 2016 election, billionaires from coast to coast spent record breaking sums to get Trump elected so they could have the opportunity to make billions more from DeVos plan to "reform" education. In elections from Newark, NJ to Los Angeles, CA, many of the same donors contributed to candidates that support their privatization agenda. Once, congress passes a national program to reform the public school system, lobbyists for private investors will flood Washington, DC to persuade DC legislators to approve the plan for more charter schools. In the end, DeVos will award contracts to investors to build and administer the new public school system. In the future, the same rich investors will purchase services from conservative institutions who will provide curriculums laden with layers of libertarian and conservative philosophy. The end result of the "reformed public school system" will be similar to schools in state-controlled countries like Russia and North Korea where free is only applicable to the bland lunch silently and unknowingly purchased at the cost of losing both free expression and the freedom to learn anything that is contrary to the single-party authoritarian government in power. Schools in Eastern Europe and Russia have done this, and it doesn't work, except for those who stand at the top of the pyramid and collect the cash that flows directly to them.

Additionally, there is a record number of "ethics Waivers" for Trump appointees at every level of job in US Government. Waivers are required when appointees cannot meet the requirements of due diligence regarding their association with specific organizations, consulting companies, or designated lobby interests that will conflict with their position with the government agency they will join. *(Source AP, March 9, 2018M. Biesecker, J. Linderman, R. Lardner.) Trump's appointees over-loaded the bucket.*

President Trump's Cabinet and Senior Officials

Trump's cabinet and senior officials have the least amount of government experience than any prior presidential cabinet.
NGE = No gov't experience.

- Vice President, Michael R. Pence
- White House Chief of Staff, Reince Priebus, replaced by Gen. John F. Kelly - **NGE**
- Attorney General, Jeff Sessions
- National Security Advisor, Gen. Michael Flynn, replaced by Gen. HR McMaster, replaced by John Bolton - **all NGE**
- Director of National Intelligence Daniel Coats
- Director of the Central Intelligence Agency, Mike Pompeo, Gina Haspel - **both NGE**
- Director of the Office of Management and Budget, Mick Mulvaney
- Representative of the United States to the United Nations, Nikki R. Haley
- Secretary of Agriculture, Sonny Perdue   - **NGE**
- Secretary of Commerce, Wilbur L. Ross, Jr. - **NGE**
- Secretary of Defense, James Mattis   - **NGE**
- Secretary of Education, Elisabeth (Betsy) Prince DeVos - **NGE**
- Secretary of Energy, James Richard (Rick) Perry
- Health/Human Services, Tom Price, Alex Azar - **NGE**
- Homeland Security, Gen. John Kelly, Kirstjen Nielsen - **NGE**
- Housing/Urban Development, Benjamin S. Carson, Sr. - **NGE**
- Secretary of the Interior, Ryan Zinke
- Secretary of Labor, Alexander Acosta
- Secretary of State, Rex Tillerson, Mike Pompeo. - **NGE**
- Secretary of Transportation Elaine L. Chao

- Secretary of the Treasury Steven T. Mnuchin, - **NGE**
- Secretary of Veterans Affairs, David Shulkin, replaced by Robert Wilkie
- Secretary of Environmental Agency, Scott Pruitt, replaced by Andrew Wheeler
- Small Business Administration, Linda E. McMahon, - **NGE**
- U.S. Trade Representative, Robert Lighthizer

Healthcare

Trump and the GOP held a garden party on the White House lawn on May 4, 2017 to celebrate a big victory that would soon blow up in their faces. A grinning President Trump, House Speaker Paul Ryan, and Senate Majority Leader Mitch McConnell stood together surrounded by brightly beaming GOP members of Congress toasting each other with their first taste of meaningful congressional success in eight years. They had finally struck a death blow (or they thought so) to their personal 'dragon", the Obama Healthcare Affordable Care Act. The House of Representatives had just voted 217-213 to repeal The Affordable Care Act and forwarded it to the GOP-dominant US Senate, and they were as happy with themselves as a room full of fraternity brothers who just all received the answers to the final exams. A great thing had happened for them. The GOP Senators had the necessary votes to pass the repeal bill and would soon send Obamacare to hell, or even further away if that was possible. As the deeply religious Christian fundamentalist likes to say, too often. "Amen. Praise the Lord." Alas!

Here's the deal, a cracker for you, a feast for us. GOP

Their garden party and love-fest was held too soon. Four months later, the President and the GOP-controlled Congress failed to pass Ryan's bill to overturn Obamacare. The Senate failed to pass the GOP Trumpcare bill, 51-49 on September 17 and the shocked, slack-jawed Mitch McConnell was forced to admit defeat and withdraw the GOP attack on Obamacare. The GOP Party of No who throttled America's hope for progress for eight years by refusing to work in common with Democrats, always preferring to haughtily signal "no" to any bill authored by Democrats , could not manage to corral enough "yes" votes to sink it's opposition's proudest accomplishment. Senator McConnell and Congressman Ryan pulled the bill, licked their wounds, and returned to their constituents empty-handed, likely mumbling Scarlett O'Hara's final hopeful words on the barren hill overlooking Tara. "After all, tomorrow is another day."

Trump had earlier provided a clue to the reason the GOP failed to remove Obamacare when he inadvertently admitted his ignorance of both healthcare and governing in a democracy. In a speech at a Governors event on February 27, 2017, he said. "Nobody knew healthcare could be so complicated." Everyone but Trump knew. But years of spiteful comments and hateful rantings of negativism buoyed by tens of millions of dollars from private interests wasn't enough time and money to help them come together with a plan they could all agree to pass. It is easier to say no, than to compromise on a plan. They might have succeeded if they actually considered listening to someone, anyone, outside their own Stepford Politician Club. With Trumpcare seriously lacking sufficient benefits for all Americans, Senator John McCain, seriously ill, rose from his convalesance to enter the voting chamber and cast the final vote to sink 'Trumpscare', and temporarily save Obamacare. McCain's vote was not cast to please his Democratic opponents, it was cast to insist that his party begin working to find solutions, not to continue to wallow in rejection alone. Trump's response was juvenile and mean. Scowling, he vowed to "Let Obamacare die". He vowed he would let it fail. He told America he would do nothing to support it. He took a lower path. Behind-the-scenes, Trump and the GOP began taking actions to sabotage the program, to make the program dysfunctional. Despite the spiteful battles against the Affordable Care Act, it is thriving and the numbers of citizens signed on to the Act keeps growing every year. Presently, it has lasted longer and is more popular in America than Trump is.

In keeping with his march against healthcare progress for women, Trump is backtracking on women's right healthcare, and women's control over making their own decisions on family choices for themselves. Trump and the conservative legislators want to regain the dominance that men had over women in the fifties and throughout the millennium of history. See Epilogue for update through October 2018.u

Here are a few examples of Trump administration efforts against women.

- Weaken Title IX policy that support prosecution of sexual abuse on college campuses
- Create artificial barriers that impede the growing success of Affordable Care for women
- End reproductive services, information, and prenatal care for women in need
- End funding for Planned Parenthood
- Overturn Roe vs Wade
- Then, restrict access to birth control, criminalize abortion

Source: Ricardo Alonzo Zaldivar, David Crary, AP. May 31 delcotimes

Protecting the Rich

Trump signed 24 executive orders in his first 100 days, the most executive orders of any President since World War II. Within hours of entering the Oval Office, Trump began joyfully issuing edicts dismantling government programs and government regulations which his GOP and Democratic predecessors, both Presidents and legislatures, had taken decades to laboriously pass through both houses of Congress. Mirroring himself in the image of dictators and demi-gods, he swore to single-handedly defeat Al Qaeda and his favored enemy, ISIS.

Trump celebrated his election victory by conducting his first weeks as President with an instant rampage of removing regulations established to protect American consumers: removing regulations on banks, investment firms, environmental abusers, industrial safety, and other such regulations. All of these regulations were passed in Congress in response to past flagrant actions taken by business leaders in every business sector. Trump's personal glee and showboating of his Presidential edicts buoyed his megalomania and most alarmingly mimicked the fury that ISIS and tyrants everywhere exhibit upon entering a conquered city's gates and tearing down the physical structures, the social order, and replacing civility with heinous barbaric rule. Trump's actions were tokens of gratitude delivered to the congressional Republicans who rushed to deliver service to the lobbyists and business owners who funded them. Now with control of two branches of government, the White House and the Congress, they could finally remove government regulations from a whole slew of industries from banks to auto manufacturing to mining and drilling companies. Environmental regulations and rules limiting pollution on public lands are among their prime targets. These rules, mostly mandated by Congress, were enacted to safeguard people and our natural resources like air, water and land. But most Republicans argued that regulations have gone too far, and prevent businesses from starting up and thriving. Presidents have generally required that government weigh the cost and benefits of major rules. For example, removing lead from gasoline was costly for some refineries but the health benefits and reduction in medical therapies and treatments — such as reduction of blood lead levels in children—were far greater. Likewise, an Environmental Protection Agency 2011 rule to slash mercury and other toxic air pollution from power plants was estimated to cost the electric power industry $9.6 billion. But the agency calculated that Americans would receive health benefits from the rule valued at three to nine times as much. Trump's executive orders looked only at costs to businesses, not to savings to health and community benefits, and lives.

Here is a partial list of Trump edicts signed in 2017 which de-regulated safety and health provisions for Americans in favor of increased financial gains for large businesses.

- February, 2017 Trump signs a bill that rolls back a needed clean water rule (Waters of the US, WOTUS) to stop toxic runoffs into America's largest rivers and streams.
- Trump announces budget proposal for Fiscal 2018 cuts to EPA by 30% and eliminates 25% employees.
- March, 2017 Trump rolls back DAFE (Corporate Fuel Efficiency standards) for cars and light trucks.
- March, 2017 Trump approved Keystone XL Pipeline to transport crude oil from Canada to refineries on Gulf Coast and announces his support for increasing Canada Tar Sands development which will increase climate changes.
- March 2017 Trump signs exec order for EPA to dismantle Clean Power Plan that would stop reduction of greenhouse emissions. This action will exacerbate climate change.
- June 1, Trump announces exit from Paris Accord.
- Sep 29, Rick Perry, Department of Energy, "Grid Resiliency Pricing Rule." Government pays nuclear and coal power companies to have a 90 day stockpile of fuel. Its real purpose is to prop up coal industry owners (Trump contributors and friends) with tax payer money for 3 months of unneeded power. The Federal Energy Regulators rejected this money-grab proposal, for now.
- Dec 4, 2017 Trump signed proclamations shrinking the size of Federal Parks in Utah, Bears Ears and Grand Staircase. The largest reversal of national monument protection in history. Bears Ears is now open to oil and gas development.

- Dec 22, 2017, Trump signed his tax bill and lifted decades-old ban on drilling in Arctic National Wildlife Preserve in Alaska. This threatens a critical part of the US and the world to oil spillage catastrophes.
- Jan.4, 2018 Trump unveiled a proposal to make 90% of the outer continental shelf of the US available for oil and gas drilling. Threatens America's coastal waters and wildlife and eco systems and tourism. *Source: Delco Times Feb 2, 2018, Rep. Greg Vitalli, Trump vs Environment.*

Longtime regulators predict that Trump's executive orders will create chaos in agencies and stymie the important work agencies do. Margo Oge who headed the Environmental Protection Agency's office of transportation and air quality from 1994 to 2012 under both Republican and Democratic presidents, said her office issued scores of rules that cleaned up the exhausts of cars, trucks, trains, ships and other vehicles, significantly improving Americans' health. She predicts the executive order, which she called "ridiculous," will shut down such work. *Correspondent Elizabeth Shogren writes HCN's DC Dispatches from Washington.* Follow @shogrene

Unleashing the Kraken

Not satisfied with threatening the physical well-being of American citizens, Trump rushed within his first month in office to dismantle restrictions placed on financial institutions by the *Dodd-Frank Wall Street Reform Bill.* The bill was the life boat legislation passed by Congress after GW Bush's Great Recession of 2008/2009. The *Dodd-Frank* bill was not only a life-saving device that kept the American economy afloat but it was fashioned to be a safety measure set in place to prevent a reoccurrence of any "sinking ships" in America's economy in the future. As we saw in 2008/9, the men who put holes in the boat were the first to cry, "Help". They were also the first ones to be heard and rescued. They loaded the life rafts, sent to them by the American taxpayers, with cash and sailed away to their private islands. No harm done to them. The average Americans: homeowners, working men and women, small business owners, college students, and the poor were left to drown in the sea amid the storms of mortgage defaults, closed businesses, and lost jobs, all caused by the greed of bankers and Wall Street financiers.

Trump's orders to de-tooth *Dodd-Frank* will gradually injure the financial health of America. In plain sight, Trump removed the protocols that would prevent the "too big to fail" financial institutions from ushering in a repeat of the Great Recession of 2008/2009. On February 3, after a meeting with his strategic and policy forum, which included Jamie Dimon, a Wall Street financier and current Chairman and CEO at JPMorgan Chase (Note: Dimon sailed away unscathed from the 2008 recession), Trump issued an Executive Order, *Core Principles for Regulating the United States Financial System,* which directed the "Treasury secretary to submit a report on recommended changes to bank regulations in 120 days." Trump announced its purpose was to get "banks to lend money more aggressively" To do so, he wanted to discard or at least, weaken the *Dodd–Frank Wall Street Reform and Consumer Protection Act (2010).* Wall Street wanted to strip the *Dodd-Frank Bill* of any regulatory power and return the banks to the little regulation they enjoyed just prior to the Great Recession. Trump said, "We expect to be cutting a lot out of Dodd-Frank... Frankly, I have so many people, friends of mine, who have nice businesses, that can't borrow money. They just can't get any money because the banks won't let them borrow because of rules and regulations in Dodd-Frank." In an interview on February 3, with The Wall Street Journal, Trump's White House National Economic Council Director, Gary Cohn, (he resigned in Feb 2018) announced the planned rollback of the fiduciary rule, which stated that brokers and advisers who work with tax-advantaged retirement savings "must work in the best interest of their clients" even at the expense of their own profits. One of the first changes to the *Dodd-Frank* bill would be to allow investors to profit even at the expense of their clients, thus resurrecting an old tenant when dealing with untrustworthy businessmen, "caveat emptor", which translates from Latin to "let the buyer beware." The removal of the *Dodd-Frank* restrictions on banking and other financial institutions would allow investment firms, banks, and such institutions to be less responsible for their actions regarding your invested money than used-car salesman are in warranting a car they just sold to you.

Trump and friends insist America will have better choices and better products because we're not going to "burden" the banks and financial institutions with hundreds of billions of regulatory costs. These are the same banks and bank executives whose better choices and better products resulted in losses to hundreds of million American citizens in 2008/2009. The *Dodd-Frank* regulations kept the banks carefully watched and under control for the past decade. Now Trump and his highwaymen are back in business. Presently, the total amount available to be stolen from retired people is approximately $1.3 trillion dollars and this amount will likely rise as investment schemes and risky bank loans wantonly increase until the next Great Recession occurs that will be caused by scaling back the *Dodd-Frank* financial overhaul on bank operations passed in 2010. Source: Killing Dodd–Frank Wall Street Reform and Consumer Protection Act, *Main article: Executive Order 13772, ("Trump Moves to Undo Dodd-Frank Regulations", Wall Street Journal, Feb. 3, 2017).*

Witness to Treason

Neil Gorsuch

Death and retirement like taxes are inevitable. Two of these
occurrences bolted into the political arena during President Trump's
early presidency. Two Supreme Court justices left the court: one died,
and the second retired. This gave Trump and the conservative wing of
the GOP a golden goose, two of them. The chess game between a
forward looking America and a backward looking America had now
favored the regressive party. The GOP would be able to place two
more conservative voices on the country's highest judicial bench. This
was made possible because Mitch McConnell and the GOP refused to
give a sitting president his right to put his nominee on the Supreme
Court. In essence, the GOP appointed two judges to the court because
one was stolen from President Obama and the citizens who voted for
him.

On January 31, 2017, President Donald Trump nominated his first
justice, Neil Gorsuch, to fill a Supreme Court vacancy that had been
vacant for 293 days since Supreme Court Justice Antonin Scalia died on
February 13, 2016. On the same day Justice Scalia died, Republican
Senator Mitch McConnell Senate Majority Leader Mitch McConnell
issued a statement that the Republican legislators would not consider
any nominee put forth by President Obama, and dictated to the
President and the opposition party that this Supreme Court
nomination will be left to the next elected President. The GOP
Republicans controlled both halls of Congress and in a historical back-
step refused to follow centuries-old protocol whereby the sitting
President nominates a candidate for the vacancy and Congress
conducts open hearings to accept or reject the candidate. The GOP
decided to steal this nomination from President Obama and hold it
until a president who they liked was elected. Judge Gorsuch's

84

appointment was announced less than two weeks after Trump's inauguration. It was hurried to cover the stain on American democracy and on the rule of order that occurred when the GOP refused to consider for acceptance any nominee presented by the sitting President of the United States. This refusal was tantamount to any political party refusing to consider voting on any legislation it didn't like until their party had the required number of votes to defeat it. This was a brazen and corrupt act suitable for a tyrant of a captive population on a faraway continent, but not here in America. The seat Trump was going to fill was a position held hostage from the people of America via a distinct disregard for constitutional precedent. Later that day, President Obama responded that he intended to "fulfill my constitutional duty to appoint a judge to our highest court," and that there was no "well established tradition" that a president could not fill a Supreme Court vacancy during a president's last year in office.

On March 16, Obama formally nominated Merrick Garland to the then vacant post of Associate Justice of the Supreme Court of the United States. Judge Garland had more federal judicial experience than any Supreme Court nominee in history and the American Bar Association (ABA) Standing Committee on the Federal Judiciary unanimously rated Garland "well-qualified", the committee's highest rating. Republican Senator McConnell, the Majority Leader of the Senate, refused to consider Garland's nomination, vowing to hold "no hearings, no votes, no action whatsoever" on the nomination. The refusal was highly controversial, with some commentators saying the seat on the Court to which Garland was nominated was "stolen". Over 170,000 people signed a White House petition asking President Obama to independently appoint Garland to the Supreme Court, arguing that the Senate has waived its advice and consent role. On November 17, a U.S. District Judge threw out a lawsuit against Senator McConnell seeking to compel a vote on the nomination, finding that the plaintiff, who had simply alleged he was a voter, had no standing to sue. Garland's nomination expired on January 3, 2017 when the 114th Congress ended.

The senate hearings were set to begin. Judge Gorsuch attended Harvard Law School and was a classmate with Barack Obama. He earned his J.D. in 1991 and he was on the U.S. Court of Appeals for the Tenth Circuit since 2006. A tenuous hearing and a partisan Senate battle on Neil Gorsuch soon commenced with Democrats convening to filibuster the nomination and defeat it, and Republicans responding by invoking the "nuclear option" (an exceptional measure where a bill, an act, or cabinet position can be accepted with at least fifty votes whereas sixty votes are normally required). Setting the table for the showdown, Senate minority leader Chuck Schumer said, "The burden is on Judge Neil Gorsuch to prove himself to be within the legal mainstream and, in this new era, willing to vigorously defend the Constitution from abuses of the executive branch and protect the constitutionally enshrined rights of all Americans." A week after Gorsuch's nomination, Democratic Senator Richard Blumenthal of Connecticut disclosed that Gorsuch had said in a meeting with him that President Trump's negative remarks about the judiciary were "disheartening" and "demoralizing." Blumenthal said Gorsuch made the comments in reference to President Trump's criticism of Judge James Robart, who blocked the administration's controversial travel ban on refugees and citizens from seven predominantly Muslim countries. The president called Robart a "so-called judge" on Twitter and tweeted: "Just cannot believe a judge would put our country in such peril. If something happens blame him and court system. People pouring in. Bad!"

During the Senate hearings, Democrat Dianne Feinstein pressed Gorsuch about a tendency in judicial rulings to favor influential corporations; Senate Minority leader Democrat Schumer said that Gorsuch "was unable to sufficiently convince me that he'd be an independent check" on President Trump. On April 6, when the Senate convened to advance the nomination, the Democratic front mostly held firm to deny the 60 votes necessary to proceed, resulting in the first successful partisan filibuster of a Supreme Court nominee. The Republicans quickly countered with another historic move, invoking the "nuclear option" to lower the threshold for advancing Supreme Court nominations from 60 votes to a simple majority of 50, thereby eliminating the filibuster. With all procedural hurdles fully cleared, Gorsuch was confirmed as the 113th justice of the Supreme Court on April 7 after a vote of 54-45. In the years to come we will all will find out if Senator Schumer's wariness regarding Gorsuch's ability to be independent from Trump's influence, or from any President, when adjudicating on the Supreme Court was justified.

Brett Kavanaugh

On June 27, 2018, Supreme Court Justice Anthony Kennedy announced his retirement. Within days, President Trump received a list of recommendations from the Federalist Society, a conservative legal group dedicated to restoring the good-old buddy rule of law that was dominant since America declared independence from England, a rule of law where white men controlled America without impunity. The list of judges appeared instantly because it had been drawn up even before Trump entered the White House in January 2017. The primary goal of the conservative powers in the U.S. was to control the Supreme Court and roll back all of the decisions made by the court since 1954. Finally, a conservative President and Congress had delivered the pot of gold to their billionaire owners, the final branch of U.S. government, the most influential arbiter of American laws. So now, all those billions of dollars spent over the past two decades have paid off. Roe vs. Wade can be struck down; corporations will remain people for the foreseeable future; the Trump administration can impose any immigration restriction it wants, confident the Supreme Court will have its back; all remaining limits on campaign contributions will end; and, not least, a solid court majority will presumably rule in favor of Mr. Trump on executive power questions.

Immediately, Senate Minority Leader Chuck Schumer, D-N.Y. argued that Kennedy's replacement should not be considered during this mid-term year, citing the same course the Senate Republicans pursued in refusing for 14 months to consider President Obama's nomination of Merrick Garland. "Our Republican colleagues in the Senate should follow the rule they set in 2016 to not consider a Supreme Court nominee in an election year." He added: "Millions of people are just months away from determining the senators who should vote to confirm or reject the president's nominee, and their voices deserve to be heard now, as Leader McConnell thought they deserved to be heard then. Anything but that would be the absolute height of hypocrisy." Reacting to news of Kennedy's retirement, Schumer also said, "This is the most important Supreme Court vacancy for this country in at least a generation. Nothing less than the fate of our health care system, reproductive rights for women, and countless other protections for middle-class Americans are at stake. Senator Richard Blumenthal, D-CT, repeatedly requested for a vote to delay the proceedings and was rebuffed by McConnell. The Democrats protested that Kavanaugh's official letters and documents provided for the G.W. Bush White House had been withheld from them or delivered at the last minute, and some were still withheld as the hearing on his nomination proceeded. Televised hearings and questioning from a range of Democratic senators showed the country a nominee whose responses on topics from abortion rights to executive power were evasive. The hearings concluded on September 7, 2018 and the senators were excused to deliberate on Kavanaugh's suitability for the Supreme Court. A vote on his nomination was expected to take place within the following few weeks, possibly before October 2018.

On September 15, Kavanaugh's nomination to the U.S. Supreme Court was challenged by Diane Feinstein, D-CA, who presented a letter she received from a woman who accused the judge of sexual assault. Democratic members of the Senate Judicial Committee requested that the scheduled quick vote on Kavanaugh's appointment to the Supreme Court be delayed until after the charges were fully investigated. The GOP Party declined and decreed that a hearing would be held on the following Monday, September 24, but later moved to the 27th, where Kavanaugh and his accuser would be questioned by select members of the Senate. The woman, Dr. Christine Blasey Ford, a psychologist, declined to participate in any Senate hearing until after the FBI conducted a full investigation of her charges against the judge. Dr. Ford's lawyers were reluctant to have Dr. Ford participate in the hearing based on the grilling that Anita Hill was forced to endure in a 1991 Senate hearing that was similarly conducted prior to Clarence Thomas' confirmation to the Supreme Court. Nevertheless, the GOP led by Trump and McConnell repeated the same travesty of justice as they did in 1991.

In the week before the bogus hearing, the President defended his nominee at a rally on September 20. Trump, an accused sexual predator, said, "He's a fine, fine man.", and earlier in the same week, "I feel really bad for him.", and on Fox News he told his sidekick, Sean

89

Hannity, "Where was she for 36 years? She should have gone to the FBI then." And again later, "Well, he denies it. Look, he denies it," the president responded. "He totally denies it. He says it didn't happen. And, you know, you have to listen to him also. You're talking about, he said, 40 years ago, this did not happen." Trump's comments are similar to his mindless defense of Alabama judge Roy Moore, Fox News executive Roger Ailes, and Fox personality Bill O' Reilly, when they were accused of multiple sexual indiscretions. Senator Orrin Hatch responded to a news journalist who asked him about the accusation against Kavanaugh. Hatch responded, "He didn't do it. It could've been someone else." Dean Heller, R-NV, assured his constituents, "We have a little hiccup here with the Kavanaugh nomination." Ralph Norman, R-SC, opened his election debate that same evening with his own "joke" about the charges. He said, "Did y'all hear this latest late-breaking news from the Kavanaugh hearings? Ruth Bader Ginsburg came out that she was groped by Abraham Lincoln." The Judiciary Committee Chairman, Chuck Grassley, R-IA, was abruptly dismissive of Professor Ford when he said, "We will proceed with the hearing with or without the woman."

So, they ramrodded the hearing through the GOP-controlled Judicial Committee on Thursday, September 27 in front of a world-wide viewing audience. Neither liberty nor justice were admitted into the crowded hearing room. The next day, the GOP committee scheduled a vote to advance a surly and tainted nominee to the Supreme Court. An ominous trifecta was now possible: America would have a deeply flawed President, Congress, and Supreme Court. Forget Beethoven. Roll over Thomas Jefferson. This was no slap in the face. It was a punch in the gut. See Epilogue for update.

https://www.nytimes.com/2018/09/10/opinion/kavanaugh-democrats-supreme-court.html

Chapter Four
On the Cutting Block

"America was indebted to immigrants for her settlement and prosperity. That part of America which encouraged them most has advanced most rapidly in population, agriculture, and the arts.   James Madison, 4th U.S. President.

Trump's Wall, Mexican Immigration, DACA

In the eighteen months that followed his inauguration, Trump's Wall was the subject of countless discussions in the White House but his pet project hasn't gotten any closer to reality. Mexico may have to watch it rise someday but Mexico will not pay for it. In fact, it is more than likely Trump will have to give something to Mexico, like maybe all of the American Taco Bell franchises along the Mexican border. Trump's deals always boil down to him giving away more than he gets. Stay tuned. As Trump says when he is stumped. "We'll see." He has been repeatedly rebuffed in his obsession to have a wall built. As recently as July 29, 2018, the President's favorite news network reported he wrote on Twitter that border security "includes the Wall! Must get rid of Lottery, Catch & Release etc. and finally go to system of Immigration based on MERIT! We need great people coming into our Country!" Trump added that he would be willing to shut down the federal government if the Democrats do not agree to Republican demands about funding for a wall along the U.S.-Mexico border. During the recent weekly address he said, "One of the critical lessons of 9/11 is that immigration enforcement saves lives. We must enforce the rules against visa fraud, illegal overstay, illegal entry and other immigration violations and crimes, and crimes they are. Believe me, crimes they are." Trump continues his Orwellian misspeaking when according to the conservative-leaning Cato Institute, the Department of Justice and

Witness to Treason

ICE administration data shows that about 40 percent of such cases have nothing to do with terrorism. Instead, they include crimes like petty theft, child pornography and immigration offenses. The institute's own research showed that since the Sept. 11 attacks, only 35 foreigners entered the country and went on to commit terrorism offenses of any kind, including sending money abroad or leaving America to join a group abroad.

Dreamers

The Deferred Action for Childhood Arrivals (DACA) program was designed by the Obama administration for people brought to the United States as children by parents who were undocumented immigrants. The program shielded them from deportation and gave them work permits. These 800,000 people, some now young adults are compassionately referred to as Dreamers. Trump's interest in these lives is only his interest in using the Dreamers as poker chips, pawns, in his "deal" to have his disgraceful Berlin-like wall built. He is foolish enough to sink billions of dollars into building a steel and concrete wall just to fulfill an empty campaign slogan. *Source:, By Tim Dickinson January 17, 2018*

Trump created this mess on September 5, 2017 when he announced an end to the DACA program, which protected the young people from deportation from America, the only home they have ever had. He said then that he wanted these young people to be fully integrated into America but legally. To do that Trump would send them back to a place where they have never lived or belonged. After months of meetings, no agreement on any immigration issue was reached. In December, Trump's tax bill was having difficulty passing and his first federal budget was facing defeat. It was extremely expensive beyond

92

any previous budget. He needed something to bargain with the Democrats as leverage in order to pass both the tax bill and the federal budget, now a whopping 1.3 trillion dollars. On January 9, in desperation but with an outward appearance of compromise, Trump held a bipartisan meeting at the White House. It was uncharacteristically held in front of live television cameras for nearly an hour. At the conclusion of the meeting, he says is willing to compromise on DACA, and adds, "when this group comes back -- hopefully with an agreement -- this group and others from the Senate, from the House, comes back with an agreement, I'm signing it." On January 11, Democrat Dick Durbin and Republican Lindsey Graham visited the White House to propose to Trump a compromise worked out by their group of six bipartisan senators. Trump then invited a set of hardline conservative Republicans to the meeting. After pretending to listen, he rejected the bipartisan proposal.

March 14: With roughly a week to go before the major government spending package known as the omnibus must pass, White House suddenly signals a desire for a DACA-border deal. March 22: Congress passes an omnibus without DACA, it will not be addressed before midterms.

March 23: Trump signs the omnibus, rails on Democrats for, he says, not caring about DACA. CNN's Jeremy Diamond contributed to this report. In an interview with ABC News, Trump said his administration was devising a policy on how to deal with people covered by DACA. "They are here illegally. They shouldn't be very worried. I do have a big heart. We're going to take care of everybody. We're going to have a very strong border," Trump said at the time.

ICE Roundup Patrols

Trump announces plans to add 10,000 immigration agents and 5,000 border agents to his deportation force across America. This is equivalent to placing a new division of military personnel on the border. The images of uniformed agents rounding up men, women, and children across America brings to mind scenes from sci-fi films such as "1984" and "Fahrenheit 451", films that depicted the state's use of uniformed troops to enforce Big Brother's observance and control over all citizens. Trump announced a policy of Immigration Roundups of undocumented immigrants to safeguard America's borders and to prevent more rapists, murderous gangs, and drug lords from entering and living in the US. The Trump administration released a memo that set the policy for the deportation of undocumented migrants accused of any crime. ICE raiding teams multiplied and they were weaponized and spread across the United States armed with the excessive authority of the new administration. Trump's hastiness to remove "illegal"" immigrants from Mexico and Central America, threatens removing many innocent men, women, and children from their homes. "Dreamers", fathers and mothers who abide by US laws and who pay US taxes fairly would be thrown back over the border.

Within the first months of Trump's presidency, General John Kelly, Secretary of Homeland Security, militarized the U.S. Immigration and Customs Enforcement (ICE), and conducted his campaign of deportation with fervor and delight. Newspapers and cable and network television were full of uniformed agents raiding businesses, homes, outdoor functions, and government offices to collect targeted immigrants. Many raids throughout the US were assisted by armed community police. As told in an earlier section of the book, more than half of those arrested were apprehended illegally by the ICE, collateral damage is how Kelly referred to them.

"Zero Tolerance"

ICE increases the number of state and local police officers and sheriffs and immigration officers throughout the US targeting people with dark eyes, dark hair, Spanish surnames, speaking English with accents, and arrests them and hands them over for pickup by "gestapo-like" ICE patrols. ICE backed by the authority of the Department of Justice threatens states with cutting off federal money for city services if they don't cooperate. Now, Trump and the GOP want to dig deeper and increasingly arrest valid American citizens. Critics complain that the ICE roundups are a form of "voter repression". Trump was never able to produce the millions of votes he claims were cast against him by illegal immigrants but now he will remove as many potential democratic voters from the voting rolls in the Border States by terrorizing their Mexican communities. The worse was ahead.

An American first: "Zero tolerance" for compassion

In April 2018, the Trump administration tightened the screws on immigrants to keep his dwindling base loyal to him, and he used the most vulnerable people in his sight: immigrants and the families of immigrants, both legitimate and illegitimate. He decreed that a "zero-tolerance" policy begin immediately calling for the prosecution of all individuals who illegally enter the United States. This "zero tolerance" means that all adults are arrested. Trump knows this policy enforcement will separate parents from their children the moment they enter the country together because when the parents are referred for prosecution, their children are placed in the custody of a sponsor, such

95

as a relative or foster home, or held in a shelter. During a Senate Judiciary hearing on May 23, Richard Hudson, an official with U.S. Customs and Border Protection, said, "658 children were separated from their parents from May 6 to May 19, 658 due to the zero-tolerance policy." He added, "When an adult is referred for prosecution, a child traveling with the adult is turned over to the U.S. Health and Human Services Department. That agency is responsible for placing the child with a sponsor as the child's immigration case is resolved."

Trump argues that processing immigrants for prosecution is not new policy. But prior administrations did not enforce the practice the way Trump has. Before Trump came into office, families were detained together, sent back immediately or paroled into the country, said Peter Margulies, an immigration law and national security law professor at Roger Williams University School of Law. Now, prosecution is happening automatically across the board (zero tolerance) and has become the uniform policy. "The policy has ramped up substantially with the new administration," Margulies said. "Making that a staple of immigration policy is a new feature." Unprecedented, you might say. Now, Trump has symbolically placed white sheets over his ICE patrols and sent them out at all hours to "find" immigrants. The farther they roam from the border, more they will find, and legal and illegal are rounded up. With this ruthless, heartless action, he felt confident that the "immigration haters" section of his voting base would love him even more. He was right. They do love him more. Like flies love crap. But the "zero tolerance" policy showed the world that Trump and his minion Steve Miller must be stopped. By June, the country rejected Trump's public display of meanness, and shivered at the images of children placed in cages.

America's first ladies, current and former, weighed in on the "zero tolerance" policy that led to children being separated from their mothers. Toddlers and infants were pulled forcibly away from crying mothers at the U.S.-Mexico border. This is unprecedented in America. Trump's "zero-tolerance" immigration policy, announced by Attorney General Jeff Sessions on April 8, was accompanied by his own memo advising everyone that anyone entering the country illegally will be met with "the full prosecutorial powers of the Department of Justice." The full force of America's DOJ was in action for all to see. This prompted America's current First Lady and two former first ladies (Laura Bush and Hillary Clinton) to speak out. (Mrs. Barbara Bush was certainly turning over in her eternal sleep.)

- Melania Trump. "Mrs. Trump hates to see children separated from their families and hopes both sides of the aisle can finally come together to achieve successful immigration reform," Melania Trump's communications director, Stephanie Grisham, told CNN Sunday. "She believes we need to be a country that follows all laws, but also a country that governs with heart."
- Laura Bush, wife of former president George Bush, wrote an op-ed in The Washington Post that was published online Sunday night. Bush wrote, "I live in a border state. I appreciate the need to enforce and protect our international boundaries, but this zero-tolerance policy is cruel. It is immoral. And it breaks my heart." Mrs. Bush, whose husband was once governor of Texas where child detention centers are being established, went on to write, "Our government should not be in the business of warehousing children in converted box stores or making plans to place them in tent cities in the desert outside of El Paso. These images are eerily reminiscent of the Japanese American internment camps of World War II, now

97

considered to have been one of the most shameful episodes in U.S. history. We also know that this treatment inflicts trauma: interned Japanese have been two times more likely to suffer cardiovascular disease or die prematurely than those who were not interned."

- <u>Hillary Clinton</u>. Former first lady and President Trump's 2016 presidential opponent, Clinton, began a tweetstorm blasting the administration's immigration policies on June 1. Clinton tweeted, "Like so many others, I am horrified and heartbroken by what is happening to immigrant kids and families because of this administration's disastrous policies. ... As a mother and a grandmother, it's devastating to even imagine." In a further tweet, Clinton wrote, "There is no more important test of our country than the way we treat the most vulnerable among us, especially children. We cannot turn away from what's happening on our watch - we have to act."

The righteous Christian fundamentalists don't have to look any further than St. Mark's gospel, Chapter 9, verses 35-37 to ask what Jesus would do. The answer is clear. *"And he sat down and called the twelve. And he said to them, "If anyone would be first, he must be last of all and servant of all." And he took a child and put him in the midst of them, and taking him in his arms, he said to them, "Whoever receives one such child in my name receives me, and whoever receives me, receives not me but him who sent me."*

A Department of Homeland Security official who declined to be identified said that nearly 2,000 children had been separated from 1,940 adults from April 19 through May 31. The disclosure was the first time the Trump administration has said specifically how many immigrant children have been affected by the zero tolerance policy. On Sunday, Sen. Jeff Merkley, D-Ore., led a congressional delegation to McAllen and Brownsville to inspect the detention centers for children. On the East Coast, Democratic members of Congress from New Jersey and New York met with immigration detainees separated from children at the southwest border who are now being held at a New Jersey immigration facility. The policy remains in place. So does Trump. https://www.krem.com/article/news/nation-now/what-melania-trump-past-first-ladies-have-to-say-on-zero-tolerance-immigration-policy/465-ff0b7a89-3c4b-4db0-8945-4f48a2e73c8a Contributing: John Fritze. Follow Carolyn McAtee Cerbin on Twitter: @carolyncerbin

Selling off National Parks, Drilling Alaska & Grand Canyon.

From the beginning, the Trump administration's interest in the national parks has been aligned with the rich and powerful who have had their predatory eyes fixated on gaining maximum control of the valuable resources that exist inside them. Trump's marching orders from his wealthy GOP contributors includes removing all restrictions on selling federal land - inland or coastal, eastern or western. Trump and the GOP sponsors regard America's natural resources as prizes now won in the national election. With control of all three branches of the federal government, the President, the Congress, and the Supreme Court would join in sharing the spoils of victory. Pristine lands across America can now be sold to corporate prospectors who would repeat what their earlier land barons had done across America in the nineteenth and twentieth centuries. Trump directed his appointees at the U.S. Department of the Interior and related groups to determine out how much coal, oil, and natural gas had been placed off limits in national parks, specifically the Bears Ears' National Monument land area set aside by President Obama. This early activity by Trump confirmed to environmental activists and public lands advocates that he was fulfilling his promise to his friends to reduce the size of national monuments and give mineral extractive industries easier access to drill or mine in protected national park areas. Referencing newly surfaced emails between Trump appointees and Interior Secretary Zinke, League of Conservation Voters Deputy Legislative Director Alex Taurel said in a statement. "We've long known that Trump and Zinke put polluter profits ahead of our clean air, clean water, public health and coastal economies. This is more proof. On Zinke's one year anniversary as secretary, the evidence of just how embedded Trump and Zinke are with the dirty energy of the past could not be clearer." During his review, Zinke looked closely at the potential coal reserves at the Grand Staircase-Escalante National Monument, also located in Utah. Interior Department staff developed a series of estimates on the value of coal that could be mined from a section of Grand Staircase-Escalante. Not coincidently, when the New York Times reported in December that Trump would be reducing Grand Staircase-Escalante to nearly half its original size, the sections with coal reserves were included in the areas that would no longer be protected.

Bears Ears and Grand Staircase Parks

On December 4, 2017 while visiting the Utah State Capitol in Salt Lake City, President Trump, as expected, sharply reduced the size of two national monuments in Utah by some two million acres. It was the largest rollback of federal land protection in the nation's history. The administration shrank Bears Ears National Monument, a sprawling region of red rock canyons, by 85 percent, and cut another monument, Grand Staircase-Escalante, to about half its current size. This move is a brazen reversal of protections put in place by Democratic and Republican predecessors and comes as the administration pushes for fewer restrictions and more development on public lands solely to make the new GOP Republican Party's financial backers richer. Not newly rich, but richer.

The decision to reduce Bears Ears and Grand Staircase is only the first step by Trump and his friends to steal the land's resources and it is expected to set off a legal battle that could alter the course of American land conservation, putting dozens of other monuments at risk and possibly opening millions of preserved public acres to oil and gas extraction, mining, logging and other commercial activities. Speaking for the few land-grabbers who will benefit from this hijacking of federal lands, Trump said. "Some people think that the natural resources of Utah should be controlled by a small handful of very distant bureaucrats located in Washington." And he pompously added while speaking at Utah's State Capitol beneath a painting of Mormon pioneers. "And guess what? They're wrong." "Together," he continued, "we will usher in a bright new future of wonder and wealth." The operative word is "wealth." Trump and his 'friends' want to own America's land for their sole benefit and riches. They do not want it controlled by the federal government for the benefit of all Americans. In America's system of government, the President alone does not have the power to overturn America's conservation laws and traditions. Congress granted presidents the authority to create national monuments, but not to eliminate them, not to reduce their size or sell them out to private interests. If the President attempts a unilateral attack on America's national monuments, the courts and Congress can step in to restore the rule of law. Unfortunately, the GOP has control over all three branches of the federal government, and worse, the three government branches (Congress, President, Supreme Court) are all beholden to, and controlled by, the private parties who have the money and want the land's resources: oil, coal, industrial minerals, forests, real estate.

President Trump's attack on America's national monuments is but one front in his sweeping assault on protected lands and waters. His interior secretary, Ryan Zinke, has overturned a ban on mining on 10 million acres of wildlife habitat in the West and, against the wishes of Republican and Democratic governors there, he is seeking to sell-off the land for mining rights and undermine a regionally developed plan to conserve the sagebrush steppe ecosystem. Mr. Zinke's action will threaten habitat that protects 350 wildlife species and push at least one bird, the greater sage-grouse, closer to the brink of extinction.

Another member of Trump's cabinet leaders is Commerce Secretary Wilbur Ross, a steel industrialist, who is enlisted to rob America of its heritage solely to enrich fellow billionaires. Ross has completed a secret review of national marine sanctuaries and national marine monuments to determine which protected ocean areas should be thrown open for offshore drilling and industrial-scale commercial fishing. On the chopping block are protections for coral reefs and atolls in the Pacific, seamounts and canyons in the Atlantic, and feeding grounds for whales and sharks off California.

Elsewhere in Congress, Republican Senator Lisa Murkowski of Alaska, furtively added an environmental rider to the recent 1.3 trillion dollar Republican tax plan that would require the government to lease part of the Arctic National Wildlife Refuge to private businesses for oil drilling, oil businesses firmly entrenched with Alaskan officials. Senator Murkowski sponsored this same legislation in every term she has served in the Senate. Prior to Trump's presidency, she was rejected every time. The refuge's coastal plain, which has the largest concentration of land-based polar bear dens in the United States and is a calving ground for the Porcupine caribou herd, would be forever lost to an industrial oil field.

The architects of these attacks though disguised as local legislators and as residents of the affected states are working in hand with lobbyists and land speculators who are conspiring to allow private companies to make a quick buck off unspoiled lands and waters. But, more fundamentally, they are seeking to undercut the idea of permanence that is the foundation for the protection of all America's wildlife refuges, national monuments, parks and protected areas.

Trump's actions on national parks are viewed as victories for Republican lawmakers, fossil fuel companies and others. These growing invasions of federal park lands sparked an immediate outcry from Rhea Suh, president of the Natural Resources Defense Council who asked, "What's next, President Trump, the Grand Canyon?"

Drilling and Mining in the Grand Canyon

"There's gold in them hills!" Greedy, seedy, old gold prospectors shouted out that trite old sentence nearly two centuries ago. Much of the gold is gone now but not much else has changed. There are people who still believe there are valuable rocks to be mined into money in some areas of the far western United States. The land surrounding the Grand Canyon National Park has always been coveted as an area of opportunity by land speculators and the investor buzzards have a new partner in Donald Trump and friends. The opportunity to finally begin mining uranium near the Grand Canyon is the latest reason for the Trump administration to open up public lands to the oil, gas, and mining industries. A report issued November 2017 by the new officials at the U.S. Department of Agriculture recommended lifting the 2012 Obama 20-year ban on uranium mining in the Grand Canyon watershed. Right now, the economics of uranium mining in the U.S. aren't strong. The global market is so flooded with abundant uranium that the industry isn't profitable and some existing mines are sitting idle due to record low prices. Regardless, industry has long been pushing for the 2012 ban to be lifted and they know they will never be closer to mining around the Grand Canyon than now.

On March 9, 2018, two of the largest mining interest groups, the National Mining Association (NMA) and the American Exploration and Mining Association (AEMA), filed petitions asking the U.S. Supreme Court to overturn the Obama-era rule banning uranium mining near Grand Canyon National Park. They want the court to reverse the 2012 decision to ban new uranium mining claims on more than 1 million acres of public lands. This comes after the 9th U.S. Circuit Court of Appeals decided last December to uphold the ban on mining in the area after a recent challenge by industry. The ban — implemented by former Department of the Interior Secretary Ken Salazar — restricts mining for 20 years on land that the Havasupai tribe relies on for water. The NMA industry group is now arguing that Salazar did not have the constitutional authority to declare the ban. Their spokesperson told news agencies that uranium mining would not harm the land. Environmental groups disagree. Conservationists say the ban should remain in place until more research is done to understand the risks and impacts of potential water contamination. "Is it worth gambling the future of the Grand Canyon to allow private companies to line their pockets when the risks to groundwater are unknown," Roger Clark, a program director at the Grand Canyon Trust, said in a statement. But scientists may not have the chance to fully study the impacts of uranium mining in the area.

The U.S. Geological Survey (USGS) is currently conducting a 15-year study approved by the Obama administration to determine whether the 1 million acres of public land surrounding the national park would need protection from new uranium mines. But its funding is in jeopardy with the passage of Trump's proposed 2019 budget because all of the funding currently allocated to this research through USGS's Environmental Health Mission — which has been between $800,000 to $1.5 million a year between 2013 and 2017 — will be cut. This means the funding to complete the study will be withdrawn before the USGS can gather enough information to determine whether radioactive elements from mining are harming plants, animals, and the Colorado River — a water source that runs through the Grand Canyon and is relied upon by more than 30 million people across Arizona, Nevada, California, and Mexico. Additionally, Reuters News reported that in May 2017, Vane Minerals in Arizona, a likely investor in uranium mining in the Grand Canyon area, wrote a letter to Secretary of the Interior Zinke stating that its company would appreciate if Zinke could begin the process to "terminate" the uranium mining ban. Conservation groups have said the mining groups' petition to the Supreme Court represents an "attack on the Grand Canyon region". All of this pressure on virgin lands would make a school kid in Alaska wonder aloud, "What's next? Drilling in the Artic?"

Alaska's Arctic National Wildlife Refuge

The US Senate passed the 2018 Tax Bill on December 2, 2017 and buried inside the tax bill is the authority to allow oil drilling in Alaska's Arctic National Wildlife Refuge, fulfilling a priority for a number of Republican legislators. In a vote as part of their sweeping tax overhaul bill early on Saturday morning, Republicans rejected an amendment led by Democratic Senator Maria Cantwell of Washington State to block drilling. The 52-48 vote was an achievement for Republican Senator Lisa Murkowski of Alaska, who is chairwoman of the Senate Energy and Natural Resources Committee. Ms Murkowski

105

has introduced legislation to open a part of the Alaskan refuge to drilling every term since 2002 when she was appointed by her father to serve out his term as Senator after he was elected Governor of Alaska. The Artic area has been closed for drilling since 1975 with most Democrats fiercely opposing the move and she had been blocked each time. "This small package offers a tremendous opportunity for Alaska, for the Gulf Coast, and for all of our nation," Ms Murkowski said before the vote, The Washington Examiner reported. Republican control of Congress and the White House this year emboldened members of the party in the Senate to move to include the provision within their tax reform bill. Democrats in the Senate have criticized the process, saying it is an unfair way to dismantle protections for an area safeguarded since 1960. The 19.6-million acre refuge in northeastern Alaska is one of the most pristine areas in the United States and is home to polar bears, caribou, migratory birds and other wildlife. Billions of barrels of crude oil lie beneath grounds in the refuge known as the "1002 area". "We don't think this has been a fair and open process," Senator Cantwell, who sits on the Energy and Natural Resources Committee, told The Washington Examiner before the vote. "The only way they have been able to get any place on this issue is to throw away the regular process."

Jamie Williams, President of The Wilderness Society, which campaigns for conservation, said "sacrificing the Arctic National Wildlife Refuge has absolutely no place in a tax bill." He said it was "outrageous that some politicians will do anything to sneak this sell-out past the American people". It's outrageous that the oil lobby and their allies in Congress are trying to destroy the crown jewel of America's wildlife refuge system after nearly four decades of bipartisan support for protecting it. Fortunately, this fight isn't over, and we are committed to fighting this legislation every step of the way. The coastal plain is vital habitat for wolves, musk oxen, threatened polar bears, and the Porcupine Caribou Herd. It has value far beyond whatever oil might lie beneath it."

Offshore Drilling

On January 5, 2018, The Trump administration announced a five-year drill plan to award forty-seven leases to drilling companies for oil and gas exploration companies –nineteen in Alaska, twelve in the Gulf of Mexico, nine along the Atlantic Ocean and seven in the Pacific Ocean (including six off California).

The Trump administration was making America's rich and prosperous, richer and more prosperous. Trump's auction of America's natural resources was a huge payoff to his campaign contributors, but the upcoming Republican Tax Bill would be the biggest payoff for all of his largest contributors.

Chapter Five
Comey, Stormy, and Puerto Rico

"I hope you can see your way clear to letting this go, to letting Flynn go."
Donald J. Trump

A Russian Cloud

It will be impossible to adequately explain in decades to come just
what it was like to be alive in the exhausting first year of Donald
Trump's presidency.* Trump is a bratty toddler whose nasty
temperament and raging fits create chaos that never wanes, chaos that
barely abates, resting only to begin its rampages at his next awakening.
His mindless Twitter rants inject frenzy into America's central nervous
system and trigger responses that over-ride traditional political debate
and make days feel like weeks, weeks feel endless, and months feel
infinite. His presidency is an abnormal reign that borders on insanity.
His official pronouncements and his private statements routinely
ravage truth in every corner of national life. In the previous few
chapters you can see the havoc he reeks and the disgrace and
disharmony he unleashes on America. He has not made America great,
he has made America hate.   * *The exhausting first year of Donald Trump's presidency,*
Analysis by Stephen Collinson, CNN, Mon January 15, 2018

Trump and his administrative team entered the White House in
January 2017 under the largest dark cloud of any previous Presidential
administration. It was rumored even before the American people went
to the voting booths on November 8, 2016, that Republican Presidential
candidate Donald Trump, the Trump Organization, and members of
the Trump campaign had been meeting with foreign entities with the
sole intention to illegally influence the 2016 American election? The FBI

had opened an investigation in mid-summer into possible collusion between members of the Trump campaign and Russian operatives. Later the FBI, the Department of Justice (DOJ) and additional American intelligence agencies announced such meetings had taken place before and since the election prior to Trump being sworn in as the 45th President of the United States. How deep was this cooperation? Did Trump's campaign and family members meet with Russian emissaries and Putin fellow-elected officials to seek information and assistance to illegally influence America's most sacred freedom, it's vote? The early rumors morphed into a bi-partisan request to appoint a special counsel to lead a formal investigation into Russian interference with the 2016 election and any related matters that may be uncovered during the investigation. On May 18, former FBI Director, Robert Mueller, was appointed Special Council to lead an investigation. The Mueller investigation continued to gather data, evidence, witnesses and suspects more than a year after its formation by Congress on May, 2017. The amount of incriminating evidence grew and the list of suspects lengthened. Chapter 11 presents more background and details on this major investigation into the possibility of "Russian Collusion" between Trump and Vladimir Putin. Within months, several natural storms, a woman named Stormy, and dark stormy events in two cities in America battered the nation. Trump's performances during each of these news headlines failed to show leadership or sincerity for the American people.

Comey and "the fake Russian probe."

The first strong wind blew across the Trump White House bow on January 26, six days after Trump's inauguration. Acting Attorney General Sally Yates informed the White House that Michael Flynn lied about his contacts with Russian Ambassador Kislyak during the campaign and during the transition period prior to Trump's inauguration. The storms began and the winds became more damaging and never ceased to blow. The dominos began to fall all around the White House.

Brief Summary of Events January 26, 2017- May 17, 2017

Jan 27 Trump invites FBI Director Comey to a private dinner alone at the White House. He asks Comey for a pledge of 'personal loyalty'. Comey says he can 'pledge honesty'.

Feb 13 Lt. General Michael Flynn, accused of lying to the FBI regarding meetings with Russian officials, resigns after three weeks as Trump's National Security Advisor.

Feb 14 in a private meeting in the Oval Office, Trump asks Comey to stop investigating Flynn. Trump says, "I hope you can see your way clear to letting this go, to letting Flynn go."

May 3 Comey testifies before the Senate Judiciary Committee on Russian investigation

May 7 Comey requests more resources from Department of Justice for the investigation

May 9 Trump fires FBI Director James Comey.

May 10 Trump meets in the Oval Office with Russian Foreign Minister Sergey Lavrov and Russian Ambassador Sergey Kislak with only the Russian media in attendance, no US press allowed. TASS, Russian news agency publishes photos. Sensitive info not yet given to

America's Allies is given to Russia. Trump also boasts "I just fired the head of the FBI. He was crazy; a real nut job." He adds, "I faced great pressure because of Russia. That's taken off."

May 11 In a TV interview, NBC's Lester Holt asked Trump about his initial comment that he fired Comey because of a recommendation from by Deputy Attorney General Rod Rosenstein, Trump said, "I was gonna fire him regardless of the recommendation." The President explained how he made up his mind, then called the Russia case a "made-up story" "He [Rosenstein] made a recommendation, he's highly respected, very good guy, very smart guy. But regardless of [the] recommendation, I was going to fire Comey."

May 12 Trump tweets, "Comey better hope there are no tapes of our conversation before he starts leaking to the press." Weeks later Trump says there are no tapes. Five days later, Acting AG Rod Rosenstein appoints Robert Mueller as Special Counsel to the Russian Collusion probe.

𝕆ffice of the 𝔻eputy 𝔸ttorney 𝔾eneral
Washington, 𝔇.𝔆., 20530

ORDER NO. 3915-2017

APPOINTMENT OF SPECIAL COUNSEL
TO INVESTIGATE RUSSIAN INTERFERENCE WITH THE
2016 PRESIDENTIAL ELECTION AND RELATED MATTERS

By virtue of the authority vested in me as Acting Attorney General, including 28 U.S.C. §§ 509, 510, and 515, in order to discharge my responsibility to provide supervision and management of the Department of Justice, and to ensure a full and thorough investigation of the Russian government's efforts to interfere in the 2016 presidential election, I hereby order as follows:

(a)   Robert S. Mueller III is appointed to serve as Special Counsel for the United States Department of Justice.

(b)   The Special Counsel is authorized to conduct the investigation confirmed by then-FBI Director James B. Comey in testimony before the House Permanent Select Committee on Intelligence on March 20, 2017, including:

        (i)   any links and/or coordination between the Russian government and individuals associated with the campaign of President Donald Trump; and

        (ii)   any matters that arose or may arise directly from the investigation; and

        (iii)   any other matters within the scope of 28 C.F.R. § 600.4(a).

(c)   If the Special Counsel believes it is necessary and appropriate, the Special Counsel is authorized to prosecute federal crimes arising from the investigation of these matters.

(d)   Sections 600.4 through 600.10 of Title 28 of the Code of Federal Regulations are applicable to the Special Counsel.

_5/17/17_
Date

Rod J. Rosenstein
Acting Attorney General

Appointment of Special Counsel, Order No. 3915-2017, May 17, 2017

Stormy Daniels

Neither Stephanie Clifford nor her Mom ever imagined she could be someone's "woman of the year" in 2018. In fact, if she is, she will use her professional stage name, Stormy Daniels. Now do you recognize Stephanie? OK. But, who imagines such accomplishments anyway? Well, Donald Trump doesn't count. He imagines everything. He also appears on many of the nation's judicial court calendars. It appears

Trump has often behaved badly towards numerous women, and he's gotten away with it. So far. But this time, his downfall from the highest office in America may happen because he switched tactics and was "nice" to a woman. Well, he didn't assault Stephanie/Stormy. They met in Las Vegas in 2006 reportedly for a vernacular, "one-night stand". Who knew in 2006 that Trump would be the Republican candidate for President of the United States in 2016? Anyone who says they knew or even thought so, can be instantly ranked the second biggest liar in the world, second only to "you know who". Their single-night romance became a life sentence for both when Trump, four weeks before the 2016 Presidential election, paid Stormy Daniel one-hundred and thirty thousand dollars to forget forever, and speak no more, about that now unforgettable night in Las Vegas. It was to remain their secret until The Wall Street Journal reported on January 12, 2018, that Donald Trump's personal lawyer, Michael Cohen, paid Daniels $130,000 in hush money in October 2016 to deny that she had an affair with Trump. Trump's spokesmen curtly denied the affair and accused Daniels of lying. Cohen also initially denied the existence of an affair between Trump and Daniels, but he later stated: "...I used my own personal funds to facilitate a payment of $130,000 to Ms. Stephanie Clifford." The messy lies and tangled responses from the Trump camps heightened interest in another naughty view of Trump's life and character. It became serious on April 9, when FBI agents raided Cohen's home, office, and hotel room and seized emails, sixteen cell phones, tax documents and business records relating to several matters, including payments to Daniels. The FBI issued a statement that raid was carried out by the Southern District of New York's FBI and not under the jurisdiction of the Mueller investigation. Subsequently, Trump admitted he knew Stephanie/Stormy and that he paid her a significant amount of money in October 2017. This admission could open up an investigation to unlawful payments during a personal election campaign with regard to the legal amount paid and the proximity of the payment to the election and if the purpose for such a payment was to solely benefit the candidate. Trump was now in possible violation of the federal campaign finance laws. The efforts to suffocate the payment and the disclosure of the payment as well as the intense pressure placed on Stephanie/Stormy to withdraw her claims also lay open a path to consider obstruction of justice.

Months of denials from both Trump and Cohen his personal lawyer were publicly proven to be lies when Cohen later pleaded guilty to charges of campaign violations and obstruction of justice, both charges were related to the payments to Stormy Daniels. Cohen is cooperating with Mueller's investigators at the time this book went to print in late September 2018.

Puerto Rico

Only the 2017 hurricane season was more disastrous for America than the chaotic first year of Trump's presidency, and his brand of chaos added controversy to the storms fury.

Three large hurricanes hit the United States in 2017. Harvey hit central Texas on August 25, Irma struck the Florida Keys on September 4, and Maria hit Puerto Rico with full force on September 17. All three hurricanes are now listed among the five costliest hurricanes in U.S. history by the National Oceanic and Atmospheric Administration. The storms brought widespread death and destruction to people and properties in its path. Americans stopped to take care of persons who suffered loss of life, property, safety, and threats of disease and starvation. There are no political or social etiquettes to be considered or addressed, just the need to respond to the damaged communities. The recovery work performed in Texas and Florida was responsive and the local services resumed efficiently. The lessons from Hurricane Katrina were incorporated by FEMA. The last storm, Maria, delivered the most problems.

On September 17, Puerto Rico was hit with a massive hurricane after suffering earlier damages from two storms a month or so earlier. This was also the case for the several states hit by these storms. However, critics accused Trump and the FEMA of providing less response for Puerto Rico than was given to the Florida, Texas and Louisiana. President Trump visited San Juan, the island's capitol city, on October 3 in response to this criticism from national news media and from the mayor of San Juan about the less than full federal efforts to aid the island. He also hoped to defuse the appearance that he had less interest in Puerto Rico than he did in Texas and Florida. In a "typically strange and disjointed appearance", Trump applauded his own federal relief efforts and thanked the island's governor. In keeping with his insistence on saying too much, he displayed his crass style of diplomacy and his lack of sensitivity to anyone but himself, when he made remarks that suggested Hurricane Maria was not a "real catastrophe,". He made the comments on the heels of trading public tweets with the mayor of San Juan over her criticism of the recovery efforts by FEMA. It was another case where the President could not take the focus away from himself. He was eager to praise the work of his federal agencies, including FEMA, the Air Force, the Navy, and the Coast Guard, amid a chorus of criticism that Washington's response has been too slow and too small.

"Every death is a horror, but if you look at a real catastrophe like Katrina (August 2005), and you look at the tremendous hundreds and hundreds and hundreds of people that died (1,803), and you look at

116

what happened here and what is your death count? Sixteen people, versus in the thousands," Trump said. "You can be very proud. Sixteen versus literally thousands of people." His statement that Maria was not a "real catastrophe" defied all evidence, and any discussion of the death toll was premature. While the official number on October 3 was at 16, a later number of deaths was confirmed at 51 with many persons still not located. At the time, the Center for Investigative Journalism reported "dozens" of people were dead, with bodies piling up in morgues. Six months later the island government's official death was 64. On May 30, 2018, eight months after the storm, a Harvard study published in the New England Journal Medicine released a report that 4,465 people died due to the storm. The study found that health-care disruption for the elderly and loss of basic utility services for the chronically ill had significant effects across Puerto Rico. Trump's decision to use Katrina as a benchmark belittled the suffering in Puerto Rico as Katrina is both the deadliest hurricane in U.S. history since 1928 and it is a prime example of a mismanaged disaster.

A little later, a photo opportunity in San Juan that was meant to bind the President and the people of Puerto Rico closer together in these hours of turmoil resulted instead into a most disturbing moment captured on video that was and shown across the United States and beyond. In a scene more reminiscent of colonial rule, President Trump presented an image of a "loving despot" tossing out paper towels to his beleaguered subjects in a relief center in a hurricane-ravaged territory in San Juan. (Insert photo). The video shamelessly depicts Trump tossing emergency supplies playfully to men and women who are gathered there to show their concern for their families well-being and who are seeking more than "playtime" and a pack of paper towels. Trump is seen on the video cheering his own generosity and his skillful athletic talent as the needy lunge for the emergency supplies being

117

tossed to them. At the end of his visit, Trump cheerfully remarked how the room is "full of love. Lots of love".

Tossing Paper Towels

He later defended throwing the paper towels. He said in an interview with Christian network Trinity Broadcasting. "They had these beautiful, soft towels. Very good towels," "And I came in and there was a crowd of a lot of people. And they were screaming and they were loving everything. I was having fun, they were having fun," he added. "They said, 'Throw 'em to me! Throw 'em to me Mr. President!'" "And so, I'm doing some of this," Trump added, making a throwing motion, "So, the next day they said, 'Oh, it was so disrespectful to the people.' It was just a made-up thing. And also when I walked in the cheering was incredible." Trump previously said he received nothing but "thank you" after his visit to Puerto Rico on Tuesday.

Source: *Trump Defends Throwing Paper Towels to Hurricane Survivors in Puerto Rico Politics News by Daniella Silva / Oct.08.2017 /*

Trump couldn't resist piling onto his previous criticism of San Juan Mayor Carmen Yulín Cruz, who had been a vocal critic of his administration's response. Trump said Cruz "really did not do a very good job, in fact did a very poor job." The San Juan mayor made an impassioned call for increased federal aid in late September 2017 and criticized Trump's response to the hurricane. She had also taken issue with him throwing the paper towels and other provisions at Puerto Ricans. "The terrible and abominable view of him throwing paper towels and throwing provisions to people, it does not embody the spirit of the American nation," Cruz said in an MSNBC interview with Rachel Maddow the day Trump visited Puerto Rico.

In critiquing the media's overall coverage of him, Trump took credit for coming up with the term "fake." "I think one of the greatest of all terms I've come up with is 'fake,'" he said. "I guess other people have used it, perhaps, over the years, but I've never noticed it," he added. Trump frequently uses the term "fake news" on Twitter when he wishes to dispute media reports. What is not fake is that in September 2018, Trump displayed his trademark pettiness when he told a news reporter that he would never consider statehood for Puerto Rico until its political leaders like Mayor Cruz were removed from office.

Charlottesville, VA

Trump's un-Presidented presidency continued to burrow its way into every nook and cranny of every little town and every big city in America but it took tenacious root in the southern and mid-western states across America. Even after the noisy, raucous Presidential primary, tensions were still rising, inflamed by his caustic attacks on the media and anyone else who criticized him. After his election, he continued to hold campaign rallies in hide-away towns and cities so he could keep his supporters mindlessly faithful to him. He used these campaign "revival meetings' to maintain a steady stream of feeding frenzies for his well-named "base", where he and his supporters gazed adoringly at one another and reveled in repeating chants drawn from his 2016 campaign rallies. It should not have been surprising at all when all of this vituperation rose to an explosive level on an August 2017 weekend in a most-unlikely place.

Charlottesville, VA is a quiet and bucolic small city located in the southeastern part of the US, not very distant from Washington, DC. It was named after Charlotte of Mecklenburg-Strelitz, the queen consort of King George III of the United Kingdom. It has a population estimated at 45,000 and it is in the heart of the Charlottesville metropolitan area which includes four counties and nearly 120,000 people. It was best known as being the home of the University of Virginia as well as home for the third and fourth U.S. Presidents (Thomas Jefferson and James Monroe). The home of the fifth US President, James Madison, is nearby, and Thomas Jefferson's nearby mountain-top home, Monticello, is a major tourist attraction. On Saturday, August 12, Charlottesville suddenly became a landmark centerpiece for what is fundamentally wrong with America: its underlying layer of racial prejudice and a deeply embedded stubborn tribal belief in a master race that spawns an extreme opposition to accepting a diversity of people and cultures. Even before the 2016 election results, hate groups like the KKK and other white supremist groups had been emboldened by Trump's eighteen months-long campaign rhetoric of division and embattlement that he directed at all of his opponents He intentionally inflamed these virulent hate groups' rage and fury against persons of color, race, religion, and he championed their ignorant rejection of diversity. All done to keep their loyalty. The battle over Confederate flags and statues was such an issue.

There had been earlier protests staged in Charlottesville in May and July. All three protests were held to show opposition to a plan announced in June 2017 by local officials to remove a statue of Robert E. Lee, the Confederacy's top general, from Emancipation Park (formerly Robert E. Lee Park) in Charlottesville. Images of Confederate officers who led the South during the Civil War were adopted by white supremist groups as symbols and rallying points to celebrate nostalgia for the Old South, for white dominance, and for blatant intimidation to "other" races, religions, and life-styles. Many communities realized the harm and daily intimidation these century-old statues inflicted on some of its citizens. The Confederate monuments were slowly and quietly being removed or relocated to museums or outlying park areas. This movement to remove divisive symbols from public areas was accelerated across the South in response to a Charleston, SC church shooting in 2015 where twelve African-American church members were killed by a young white man who was sympathetic to racist beliefs.

The May statue protest was led by white nationalist Richard B. Spencer to protest a city council vote to remove the statue from the park. It was followed on July 8 when about fifty Ku Klux Klan members marched in the same area. There were minor incidents reported during both rallies. The August 12 rally was organized by Jason Kessler, a member of the newly energized alt-right movement to unify the white nationalists in the United States. An announcement was placed on social media and other informal communications inviting a wider racist audience to come to Charlottesville. The protesters who came to the city included white supremacists, white nationalists, neo-Confederates, Klansmen, neo-Nazis, and various militias. Over the weekend, some marchers chanted racist, anti-Semitic, and anti-Muslim slogans, and carried swastikas, Confederate battle flags, and semi-automatic rifles. Trump's campaign slogan "Make America Great Again." was heeded as a call to arms by the manic, white, die-hard racists in this self-styled army.   *Source: Follow Maggie Astor on Twitter: @MaggieAstor*

Friday evening through Saturday afternoon

Visitors began to steadily arrive on Thursday and Friday. The main event, billed as a "Unite the Right" March, was to be held on Saturday afternoon. In a prelude to the formal protest, hundreds of white nationalists, some wielding fiery torches, gathered a short distance from the University of Virginia's campus on Friday evening. They conducted a torchlight procession through the center of Charlottesville to the statue of General Robert E. Lee. Their chants included phrases such as "white lives matter," "Jews will not replace us," and the Nazi-associated anthem phrase "blood and soil." Mike Signer, Mayor of Charlottesville, tweeted that evening, "I have seen tonight the images of torches on the grounds of the University of Virginia. When I think of torches, I want to think of the Statue of Liberty. When I think of candlelight, I want to think of prayer vigils. Tonight, in 2017, we are instead seeing a cowardly parade of hatred, bigotry, racism, and intolerance march down the lawns of the architect of our Bill of Rights. Everyone has a right under the First Amendment to express their opinion peaceably, so here's mine: not only as the Mayor of Charlottesville, but as a UVA faculty member and alumnus, I am beyond disgusted by this unsanctioned and despicable display of bigotry, hatred, and intolerance." Before the evening was over, there were physical confrontations and loss of blood near the Robert E. Lee statue.

On Saturday morning at approximately 8:30 AM, groups of alt-right and white supremists began forming in preparation for advancing to the statue. Within several hours, violence erupted between the protest marchers and the counter-protestors who were demonstrating against the marchers. The city police and the State Troopers were reportedly not effective in preventing the brawls and beatings that occurred. Many law-enforcement officers were later accused by witnesses as standing idly by during the violence. Just before noon, Virginia's governor declared a state of emergency in the city and the alt-right marchers and their supporters retreated to another park area to hear their scheduled speakers. Order seemed to be restored but a short time later at 1:45 p.m., a car driven by James Alex Fields Jr.., 20, of Maumee, Ohio, a member of a white-supremist group, plowed a car into a group of counter-protesters and then struck another car a short distance from the rally site. One person was killed and nineteen were injured. Heather D. Heyer, 32, a paralegal from Charlottesville was killed. She was described by her family as "a passionate advocate for the disenfranchised and was often moved to tears by the world's injustices." Two state troopers also died on Saturday afternoon. Lt. H. Jay Cullen and Trooper Berke M. M. Bates were in a helicopter monitoring the demonstrations when the helicopter fell and burst into flames. In total, at least 34 people were wounded in the clashes along the parade route. *Torchlight procession, http://6abc.com/a-timeline-of-events-in-charlottesville-virginia/2305769/*

Trump's response

The reactions across America were swift and sharp, directed at the racism and bigotry displayed by the supporters of the leaders who organized the parade. Trump delivered a tepid response to the incidents shortly after 1 PM, then added a longer comment in the late afternoon. He did not mention any organized groups by name, calling it an "egregious display of hatred, bigotry and violence on many sides." He refused to specifically criticize the white nationalists or the neo-Nazis who had organized Saturday's rally, instead arguing that there was blame to go around on "many sides." After these false starts, Trump later said "We want to get the situation straightened out in Charlottesville and we want to study it." "We want to see what we're doing wrong as a country where things like this can happen." Later that evening, he was criticized broadly for not speaking out specifically against the white supremacists and the Ku Klux Klan.

Witness to Treason

On Sunday morning, a White House spokesperson released a statement saying that the President condemns white nationalists groups. The statement read, "The President said very strongly in his statement yesterday that he condemns all forms of violence, bigotry and hatred, and of course that includes white supremacists, KKK, neo-Nazi and all extremist groups. He called for national unity and bringing all Americans together." On Monday, after receiving more criticism for not singling out white nationalists or neo-Nazis, Trump said, "Racism is evil." He added that "those who cause violence in its name are criminals and thugs, including the K.K.K., neo-Nazis, white supremacists and other hate groups that are repugnant to everything we hold dear as Americans." These comments on Monday came after he mocked the head of Merck pharmaceuticals, who is black, for quitting the American Manufacturing Council in protest of Trump's tepid response to the violence. Within hours, chief executives from Intel and Under Armour also resigned from the same board. A fourth board member, the president of the Alliance for American Manufacturing, stepped down on Tuesday immediately after Trump furiously declared at a Tuesday news conference, "You had a group on one side that was bad. You had a group on the other side that was also very violent. Nobody wants to say that. I'll say it right now." Elsewhere, David Duke, former leader of the KKK, stated that the white supremacists were "going to fulfill the promises of Donald Trump," adding that's why he and other white nationalists voted for Trump.

Indeed, the forces behind this rally run much deeper than the removal of statues. Right-wing extremism, including white nationalism and white supremacy, is on the rise with Trump's candidacy and election. The right extremists feel emboldened by Trump's rhetoric and his warm acceptance of their support. Trump's acceptance of white hatred

124

support and the rise of race-tinted killings in recent months fed the far-right violence that occurred in Charlottesville. This was a deep wound on America's soul and psyche. A wound that a President of the United States would seek to use to turn into a time of community prayer and thoughtfulness. It was a time when America's people were ready for a President to lend his voice and soothing words to calm the waters and direct Americans to find a common shelter through the storm. This did not happen. No one knew then that an even more tragic day was just in front of America. It was to come not so far away, 900 miles south in Parkland, FL.

Parkland, FL

The following paragraph is excerpted from an online article by Andrea Torres posted on Digital reporter on March 23, 2018.

An hour after the Valentine's Day massacre at Marjory Stoneman Douglas High School, President Donald Trump tweeted. "My prayers and condolences to the families of the victims of the terrible Florida shooting," Trump wrote. "No child, teacher or anyone else should ever feel unsafe in an American school." Sarah Chadwick was still trying to figure out who had died and who was injured at her school when she read the tweet and responded in anger. "I don't want your condolences, you [expletive] piece of [expletive], my friends and teachers were shot. Multiple of my fellow classmates are dead," she wrote. "Do something instead of sending prayers. Prayers won't fix this. But gun control will prevent it from happening again." Sarah was the first student from Marjory Stoneman Douglas High School to publicly challenge a politician to take action on gun legislation. Her brazen tweet went viral and is now seen on T-shirts and signs during events organized by activists from the Never Again

Witness to Treason

movement. *Source: Timeline: How the Never Again movement gained momentum after tragedy, Students lead nationwide effort for stricter laws for gun buyers, By Andrea Torres - Digital Reporter/Producer, Posted: 8:52 PM, March 23, 2018 Updated: 4:33 AM, March 24, 2018*

President Trump would continue to get numerous opportunities to lead America away from chaos and division. He predictably missed them all. However, no single opportunity for Trump to act for America's safety and unity would come as timely as on Valentine's Day, February 14, 2018 in Parkland, FL, a small town resting unnoticed in Dade County, FL. But as the saying goes, that was then, this is now. Parkland, FL is now a town whose anonymity is lost forever. On that Friday, seventeen persons were killed, fourteen students and three staff members; and fourteen other persons were wounded in Marjory Stoneman Douglas High School, another high school campus in America. The shooter was a fellow student. The murder weapon was an AR-15 assault rifle. Trump spoke once more to the American people about his concern for the newest school shooting victims. He expressed his identical concern for the victims of previous attacks of gun violence. But he could not keep hidden his lack of commitment to do something to stop the killings. It wasn't expected that he would issue one of his prized Executive Orders and suspend all gun sales, or announce a commission to address the urgent need for gun control and gun culture across America. It was no surprise that he did neither of these things as it was no surprise that he would offer Sarah Chadwick and her community in Parkland "his prayers and condolences." He has no solutions to stop the shootings but he has buckets full of "prayers and condolences". Worse than all of this false piety was his meaningless meeting on television with the Parkland families in the White House to listen to them tell him what they want him to do to stop these tragedies, and then within hours of meeting with the

126

surviving students and their parents, he pledged his allegiance to the National Rifle Association (NRA) as he did in 2016 when he said, "I will never let you down."

Trump did not mention the National Rifle Association (NRA) until students (David Hogg) and parents confront him in the Washington DC town meeting with Parkland student survivors and parents. Trump offered several "original" suggestions that all come from the NRA playlist for taking no action on gun control. Trump proudly declares "that the teachers be armed and trained to defend the students in the schools," and that communities take down existing signs denoting school areas as Gun Free Zones. He mimics the NRA talking points that gun free zones lessen safety and invite people to buy AR-15s and attack schools. He makes a commitment to support a law removing bump stocks from sale, a law already winding its way past the deaf ears of the Republican legislators. The bump stock law received its few days of GOP legislative support just after the shooting in Las Vegas where on the evening of October 1, 2017, a gunman opened fire on a crowd of concertgoers at an outdoor music festival on the Las Vegas Strip in Nevada, leaving 58 people dead and 851 injured, 422 of the injured had gunshot wounds. At the end of the meeting with Parkland parents and children, he repeats his offer of prayers and condolences to FL, and he poses for photos with students and family members. Soon after the Parkland visitors leave the White House, he speaks with the NRA and openly declares his loyalty to them. His most sincere concern that weekend is for the NRA. They can count on him, he tells the NRA. After all, the NRA was his biggest cash contributor in 2016 ($50 million, some of that NRA cash was reportedly from Russia, see Chapter 11. He follows up his sincere concern for Parkland by never mentioning his promises for gun reform again. During the NRA convention in May 4, 2018, he delivers a 45 minute key-note address to his "friends", swearing allegiance to the NRA that is just shy of singing "You've got a friend in me", the best-pal song from the Disney/Pixar animated film, "Toy Story."

The dark forces surrounding Trump's Presidency don't stop churning after the students and adults are mourned and buried in Parkland and missed forever by their loved ones who will remember them as they were in life. Only days later, several GOP legislators and Fox News journalists received their talking points from the NRA and launched attacks against the more vocal students who spoke out against the lack of sensible gun control, and against selling military weapons to the public such as the infamous AR-15, the weapon of choice in mass shootings and a weapon very easy to purchase in any community. Among the gun-related legislation being sought by students of Parkland was to increase the legal age from 18-21 to be able to purchase AR-15 and other military-type weapons to be. The most effective new tool the students introduced to the campaign against gun violence was to unite under a single banner reminding the politicians that these survivors and friends were mindful of the power of the ballot box. They would now join voices and they were "Ready at 18 to Vote" in 2018.

As a consequence, the more immediate positive actions resulting from this tragedy was the student movement for gun control across America which began in Florida's state capital, Tallahassee, and expanded nation-wide with numerous student-led March for Our Lives rallies on March 24, centering in Washington, DC. Unfortunately, the coordinated response from Trump and the Trump White House, the NRA, and the GOP Congress, was to make bogus charges that Parkland student survivors were being fed instructions and directions from leftist and communist entities. This often used tactic of attacking the truth with lies and personal attacks were quickly proven to be lies and such attacks were discontinued. But it was another example of right wing conservative mud-slinging financed by big GOP money sources.

The gun violence did continue across America. On May 18, three months after Parkland's nightmare, Santa Fe High School near Houston, TX was next: 10 people were killed, and 10 were injured. When one high ranking Texas state official was asked how he felt the community would respond to any mention of gun control, he said, "They love their guns". Vigils and processions continued through America's cities and towns, north and south, east and west. Another community shooting occurred only weeks earlier on April 22, 2018 in Antioch, TN, near Nashville. A gunman randomly targeted customers inside a Waffle House chain restaurant, killing four, and injuring several others, before a young man was able to knock him down and wrestle the AR-15 away before more people could be murdered. James Shaw, 29, a father of two, refused to accept himself as being a hero responding that he did what he needed to do to save his life and he was glad to save others at the same time. "It feels selfish," Shaw Jr. "I was just trying to get myself out. I saw the opportunity and pretty much took it." Shaw Jr. rushed the gunman, grabbed the gun's barrel, pulled it away and threw it over the Waffle House counter. He suffered a gunshot wound and burns from grabbing the gun's barrel. Shaw later started a GoFundMe page for victims of the shooting with a goal of $15,000. As of May 12 he raised more than $240,000 in 20 days with donations received from around the world. On May 12, Shaw met Emma Gonzalez and David Hogg and other Parkland students for breakfast at Denny's in FL. Shaw said, "Meeting the young adults of the Parkland incident who have so much fire in their eyes was a great joy." *(Alex Horton, ap article, may 14, 2018) 29-year-old hero from waffle house shooting:*

Witness to Treason

'i saw the opportunity and i took it', jason gonzales, usa today network – tennessee april 22, 2018 | updated april 24, 2018)

The students and community of Parkland are rising as one voice to save lives just as communities in Sandy Hook, Orlando, FL, Antioch, TN, and Las Vegas, NV, Santa Fe, TX and other communities injured by gun violence are working hard to do. It is mind-numbing to continue to see communities who refuse to unite for gun control until after they lose lives in the next school or community shooting. A thunder of voices for gun control must be raised inside the halls of Congress and outside the White House. Sadly, today there are too few voices for legislative action to be found in Washington, DC. Use your vote, at 18 or at 92 to save lives.

The Company He Keeps.

Trump likes the big boys, the tough guys, the men who he says "get things done." He admires crooks, con men, dictators, and tyrants. He makes friends easily with sexual predators, bullies, murderers, racists, misogynists, and he likes to be surrounded and worshipped by small-thinking people. This is not keen insight on my part, nor information gleaned from a White House informant. This is just my plain observation, of watching and listening to 45th's own words and the words and actions of his family and friends. The old adage that applies this time is, "You are known by the company you keep".

Through his first eighteen months as President, Trump aligned himself with the leaders of nations that imprison and oppress their citizens. He congratulated the rulers of Turkey, Philippines, Poland, North Korea, China, and most often, Russia. During his first year in office, his praise for the leaders of these freedom-starved countries is worrisome to the

130

majority of Americans, but it should be worrisome to all Americans. Trump seeks to be identified as an equal among the world's current batch of corrupt "strong men": Philippine President Rodrigo Duterte, Turkey President Erdogan, China's President Xi Jinping, North Korean President Kim Jong Un, and Trump's man-crush, Russian Vladimir Putin. These are the men he publicly admired as great leaders, who he says have "good control" over their individual countries. This should be worrisome to Americans because not one of these "strong men" would be standing at the head of their country if any one of them were required to win a free, democratic election. In 2018, Trump welcomed all of them but Kim Jong Un to the White House. He invited Duterte but Trump postponed the state visit due to resistance from Congress. There is no surprise here. Even before his election, Trump began sniping at America's long-term allies. He intentionally chose to be at uncertain terms with NATO and other members of the free world: the nations who are democratic and who conduct open elections through the processes of free speech, free press, free assembly, and whose citizens are protected from government intimidation. America should be worrisome. Trump has purposely driven clumsy wedges of pettiness between the United States and our NATO allies - the United Kingdom, France, Germany, Canada, Mexico, and other western European nations. It should be of great concern to Americans that Trump prefers the company of tyrants, that he is comfortable amid this band of mega maniacs and psychopaths. If given enough time, Trump will be a leader who mirrors his admired friends; a leader who has "good control" over his citizens who become virtual prisoners under the unopposed rule of one man who would be king.

Here are a few of the "strong men" admired by Trump, their recent claim to fame, and a personal comment from Trump on each one.

- President Rodrigo Duterte, Philippines. He had thousands of citizens murdered under his direction. As mayor of Davao City, he joked about a prison rape of an Australian nun. "I should have been first. What a waste." Trump invited Duterte to the White House, and said "he was very friendly."
- President Abdel Fattah el-Sisi, Egypt. He overthrew the first freely elected President of Egypt, then led a brutal dispersal of opposition leaders, torture and disappearances. Trump said, "He's a fantastic guy."
- President Recep Tayyip Erdogan, Turkey. He is an authoritarian leader who commanded a brutal crackdown on opposition leaders, judges, journalists, educators, and members of parliament. On May 16, 2017, only a few hours after joining Trump in the Oval Office, his bodyguards attacked and seriously injured nine protesters outside the Turkish Embassy in Washington, DC. Erdogan watched the attack from his Mercedes Benz. Afterwards, neither Trump nor Sean Spicer, the White House Press Secretary, would comment on the Embassy assault. In the Oval Office meeting, Trump said, "I give him great credit for turning his country around."
- President Kim Jong Un, North Korea. A brutal tyrant, a self-appointed successor to his father. He murdered his brother, and many citizens, and rules with crushing power. He threatens nuclear war. He and Trump parried with juvenile name-calling in 2017 and 2018, both threatening nuclear war, fire and fury. Trump said, "He's a pretty smart cookie." "I would be honored to meet him."

- President Xi Jinping, China. During the campaign, Trump called China our most dangerous foe, a market cheater, etc. Trump now says, "I think he's a terrific person. We have a good chemistry together.
- President Vladimir Putin, Russia. A fascist in a 'communist' regime, He serves the richest men in Russia. He invaded Crimea and the Ukraine, has ordered assassinations in other countries (8 in 2016), plotted to disrupt US elections, and colluded with the Trump campaign in 2016 election, working directly with WikiLeaks. Trump said, "He is very much a leader. I mean you can say, Oh! Isn't that a terrible thing that the man has so much control over a country?"

Who Betrayed America?
The remaining chapters in this book will show you who paid for Trump's election, who was responsible for getting him elected, and who is responsible for betraying America and for bringing disgrace on her. The book's final chapter will discuss how you can help bring America back onto its destined path to fulfill its commitment to liberty and justice for all Americans, and to be a beacon of light in around the globe.

Chapter Six
GOP, the Party of No
Birds of a feather, flock together.

SNAFU

SNAFU* was a new word when I was growing up in my hometown, Chester, PA, a mid-size city of 70,000 people located just south of Philadelphia. Fathers and older brothers who had returned from the war used the word among themselves when they were in the middle of a mess or trying explain a disaster. I wasn't privy to its hidden meaning, I just knew it meant things were not going well; it meant things were pretty messed up. When I got older and went to work, I discovered what the word meant. Actually, it wasn't a word, I learned that SNAFU is an acronym used to stand for the sarcastic expression *Situation Normal: All Fucked Up*. It is a well-known example of military acronym slang believed to have originated in the United States Marine Corps during World War II. All the GIs used it and later a lot of men who worked for large companies used it too. * A SNAFU describes a tangled mess with no order and no solution in sight, a plan or event that failed miserably, that can't be remedied or solved. It is an earthy and descriptive way to capsulize frustration with any organization that is eternally hopeless in its ability to ever do anything correctly. It is an apt description of the GOP Republican Party in 2018. The new Republican Party in 2018 is an organization worthy of being labeled as a classic SNAFU.   *SNAFU was first recorded in American Notes and Queries in their September 1941 issue.[3] Time magazine used the term in their June 16, 1942 issue.

Witness to Treason

The Party of No Immortalizes SNAFU

It wasn't an easy journey to get to be as confused and as disorganized as the Republican Party was in 2018, but they managed to get there, and they got there all by themselves. Having settled back and prided themselves on capturing the Presidency in 2001 (by judicial decree, Bush vs Gore) and in 2004, the Republicans unleased economic policies that gave free rein to Wall Street banks and investment firms (just as Trump is doing in 2018). Bush loosened financial regulations and favored tax changes for businesses and the wealthy, and turned America's wealth accumulated in 1998 into America's bankruptcy in 2008. On the eve of President Obama's inauguration as the 44th President of the United States, the Republicans were going to escape having to find a way to save the country and themselves, a task they would not have been capable of doing anyway. The nation was on the brink of collapse. The Great Republican Recession was now someone else's work to clean up. Unfortunately, The GOP was going to sabotage that cleanup, even if doing so would possibly destroy America. It is difficult to say it happened, but it was more difficult to watch it happen. The GOP had already proven after eight years of 'rule' that they were not as good at doing something as they were at undoing things. Unfortunately much like Dark Age barbarians, the Taliban and ISIS, the GOP has a penchant for being dysfunctional and destructive.

In the last weeks of December 2008 and in the first weeks of 2009, two years before McConnell had brazenly stated in an interview that, "The single most important thing we (the GOP) want to achieve is for President Obama to be a one-term president", he instructed his Republican colleagues to continue doing what they do best, nothing. His signal was delivered to the Republican senators and representatives even before President Obama was inaugurated. In a

TIME article *"The Party of No,"* published in 2009 and adapted from the book, *The New New Deal: The Hidden Story of Change in the Obama Era,* the article reports "… the Republican plot to obstruct President Obama before he even took office, including secret meetings led by House GOP whip Eric Cantor (in December 2008) and Senate minority leader Mitch McConnell (in early January 2009) in which they laid out their daring (though cynical and political) no-honeymoon strategy of all-out resistance to a popular President-elect during an economic emergency. "If he was for it," former Ohio Senator George Voinovich explained, "we had to be against it." McConnell had demanded unified resistance. Then Vice-President-elect, Senator Joe Biden said, "The way it was characterized to me was, 'For the next two years, we can't let you succeed in anything. That's our ticket to coming back,' "So I promise you - and the President agreed with me - I never thought we were going to get Republican support," Biden said.
http://swampland.time.com/2012/08/23/the-party-of-no-new-details-on-the-gop-plot-to-obstruct-obama/ *TIME published "The Party of No," a 2009 article adapted from the book, The New Deal: The Hidden Story of Change in the Obama Era.*

This irresponsible stance by the GOP in a national emergency was unprecedented and possibly treasonous considering the financial crisis America was facing in 2009. But it was not surprising because the Republican Party had been struggling for thirty years with the increasing influence of the conservative right in the party structure. Now the conservative right, fighting internally, was casting out the moderates and any reasonable members of the party. The unlimited investment of cash from the right wing billionaires was paying off, they meant to buy the entire Republican Party. Meanwhile, there was real governing to be done, and the Obama administration and the Democratic Party succeeded in saving the United Sates from foreclosure.

Witness to Treason

All for Nothing

In 2010, the GOP won control of the House of Representatives and held the majority position to govern the country for the next eight years, but they failed. McConnell and the GOP House Majority Leaders during those eight years, John Boehner and Paul Ryan, were so focused on not allowing Obama to get anything done, they got nothing done themselves. The GOP was so disjointed with this dedicated opposition to all things Obama that they were only effective when they attacked a common foe, or enemy in their eyes. It was an MO (mode of operation) they would continue well past the publication date of this book.

Here is a list of disasters they have achieved from 2010 to 2018. The list explains why they earned their lasting legacy as the celebrated, "Party of No". They were jubilant when opposing the Democratic Party proposals of any kind, but on governing policy, the GOP could never agree with each other. Consequently, their triumphs in Congress came only in battles where the American people lost. A few of the GOP "Party of No" disasters from their list of 'proud' negative accomplishments follows:

- 2013 Republican Party Tea Party's government shutdown
- Republican Party refusal for 14 months to allow hearings before Congress for Judge Merrick Garland nomination to the Supreme Court, stealing the appointment for the Republic Party in 2017. How did they know they would win the 2016 presidency? No Collusion before the 2016 election?
- GOP stonewalled Democratic requests for key witnesses and ended prematurely the House Intelligence Committee investigation into Russian Collusion in US 2016 Presidential Election.

138

In fact, McConnell celebrated the GOP's increased power between 2010 and 2018 by taking tight rein over all Republicans in the House and the Senate and by proceeding to oil his party's SNAFU machine with horse glue partisanship, where glue is substituted for oil to 'gum' up the GOP machine instead of making it work smoother. There was to be no cooperation with Democrats or any other groups who seek to reasonably conduct business in the public interests. McConnell and Ryan were successful at No! They had created a monumental SNAFU at the highest levels of government. Here are a few results of the new GOP's application of horse glue politics funded by dark money:

- As noted above, Republican members of the House or Senate were ordered by McConnell to refuse to cooperate with Democratic members of Congress on anything until President Obama left office. Mike Lofgren, a Republican congressional staff member for 28 years retired from Congress in 2011 and observed the increasingly stubborn obstructionist Republican party-wide behavior when the Tea Party declined to back up the usual increase in America's debt ceiling that led to a government shutdown in 2013. Lofgren is now an author of several books on politics inside the Capitol offices and conference rooms, Following his success with *The Party is Over*, he published another best-seller, *The Deep State: The Fall of the Constitution and the Rise of Shadow Government*, In his introduction to *Deep State*, he warns us, "Our venerable institutions of government have outwardly remained the same, but they have grown more and more resistant to the popular will as they have become hardwired into a corporate and private influence network with almost unlimited cash to enforce its will." In 2018, it is no secret that the Party of No does not get its marching orders from the constituents back home.

- Senator Arlen Specter, PA, a moderate Republican who became a Republican Presidential candidate, left the Party when Republicans refused to support emergency spending at the height of the global financial crisis. Specter announced in April 2009, "As the Republican Party has moved farther and farther to the right, I have found myself increasingly at odds with the Republican philosophy..." His defection gave Democrats and President Obama an important 60th senate vote to overcome a filibuster and it made possible the rescue of the US economy, and US landmark health care reforms.
- Republican moderates are not the only Republicans who no longer have a home in the Republican Party. Now, any Republican member of Congress who works across the aisle with Democrats to try to get something done can face a conservative challenger who is instantly drawn from the Republican conservative fringes' Stepford Wives politician cookie-cutter machine.

Can't get out of their own way.

The Republicans won a majority in Congress in the 2010 election, and continued to gain more seats in the 2012, 2014, and 2016 elections. As noted above, the 112th Congress elected in 2010 was the least productive and most partisan congress in American history even though the Republican members, 242, were the largest number of Republican representatives since the 80th Congress (1947–1949). The Republican- dominated Congress was viewed as one of the most politically polarized Congresses since Reconstruction (1866-1867), and the least productive Congress since the Second World War, with record low approval ratings. Why? Because the new Republican Party and its handlers wanted everything their way, on their terms, with no compromise on their part. Simply stated, without reasonable discussion and compromise from both sides, democracy does not work. Only tyrants and Politburos* can get what they want without compromise. The Republicans continued to refuse to conduct business with Democrats and deadlocked the national government.

In the 2012 elections, (113th Congress, 2013-2015), the seats in the House were apportioned based on the 2010 United States Census, meaning the gerrymandering campaign launched across America by the Koch Organization's political team on behalf of the conservative wing of the Republican Party, enabled Republicans to win district seats rearranged to benefit the GOP. The Democratic Party maintained its Senate majority, while the Republican Party had a House majority. Widespread public dissatisfaction with the 113th Congress increased over its second year, and it was ranked among the worst Congresses in United States congressional history, until 2017. According to a Gallup Poll released in August 2014, the 113th Congress had the highest disapproval rating of any Congress since 1974 when data first started being collected. The results showed that 83% of Americans surveyed said they disapproved of the job Congress was doing, while only 13% said they approved. According to several polls, in October 2013 during the government shutdown championed by the Tea Party, a new branch of the Republican Party, this approval decreased to 10% approval. The Republicans shutdown the federal government.

In the 2014 elections, the Republicans election victories continued, and they now had control of both houses of Congress for the first time since the 109th Congress. With 248 seats in the House of Representatives and 54 seats in the Senate, this Congress began with the largest Republican majority since the 71st Congress of 1929–1931. The Republican majority in Congress increased but its lack of positive activity did not change.

In the 2016 election, the 115th Congress, with seats still apportioned among the states based on the 2010 United States Census, the Senate and the House were both controlled by the Republican Party with Republicans holding 52 senators and 241 representatives, and the Democratic Party holding 48 senators and 194 representatives. Even with overwhelming control, including the executive power of the White House, the Trump administration and the Republican Party failed to repeal and replace Obamacare with a healthcare plan of its own. Senator John McCain, AZ-R, set aside party affiliation to cast a dramatic 'thumbs down' vote* against the Republicans bill to repeal Obamacare. The Republican bill failed to pass, 49-51. On July 27, 2018, only weeks away from undergoing brain surgery for a blastoma tumor, Senator McCain rose from his seat in the Senate to register the final and deciding vote in front of Senator McConnell. Finally, in an urgent effort to have something passed in Trump's first year as President, the GOP scrambled before the New Year holiday and managed to barely pass a tax bill many economists agreed leans heavily towards the very rich and large corporations. The $1.5 trillion Tax Bill was narrowly passed 51-48 just before the end of December 2017.

*http://www.latimes.com/politics/washington/la-na-essential-washington-updates-watch-the-moment-john-mccain-voted-no-1501252122-htmlstory.html

Can the Republican Congress Be A Check on the President?

All of us, even the city kids, are taught at an early age that no farmer would leave the chickens alone with the fox? There is no reason then for anyone to be surprised that the Republican members of the 115th Congress, not a single member, was a check on President Trump through the first nineteen months of his term. It was foolish and negligent for anyone to believe the present Republican legislators in Washington, DC, would display or exert any future control on Donald

Trump. The present GOP has shown neither the principles nor the courage to speak up for all Americans across America, and for America against its rivals who attack our sovereignty and interfere in our basic element of government. It is clear the Republican leaders have chosen party politics, and political deference to financial backers, and their political careers over country. What else explains how they can continue to avoid earnestly seeking the truth about Russian meddling, and reject congressional investigations into growing Presidential malfeasances?

The Republican legislators have been uniformly mute on repeated occasions when the President embraced the Russian ambassador and the Russian Foreign Minister May 2017, and boasted that he got rid of FBI Director James Comey. Trump told them Comey was "a nut job", and how he doesn't have to worry about Russian collusion anymore. He conducted a private meeting with these Russian officials in the White House Oval Office. He allowed Russian news reporters from Russian publications and TV networks to attend the meetings, but refused the same access to American journalists and news outlets. In July 2018, he courted Vladimir Putin, Russia's KGB-President in Helsinki, Finland, choosing to ignore the U.S. Intelligence agencies' proof of Russian meddling inside America. Instead, Trump praised Putin's intelligence and honesty while trashing briefings from his own U.S. Intelligence leaders.

The Republican Party leaders, Mitch McConnell and Paul Ryan, are routinely unavailable for public comment, saving their appearances for the President's biggest SNAFUs. When they do appear, both men say little, defend the President, and exit the stage pleased with themselves. These are not men who will rise and inspire the country with moral leadership.

Witness to Treason

Where Did the New GOP Come From?

The new GOP Republicans in these first two decades of the twenty-first century (2000-2018) are a far cry from the previous generations of staid Republicans when the party's membership was as respectful of the opposition party as it was respectful of honest dissent and reasonable compromise. Today, respect and compromise are as antiquated as a whistle-stop train caravan campaign across America would look in the present mass media world of 24/7 360 electronic cyber communication and Mach-speed air transportation. The GOP in 2018 is dominated by the same hateful and backward mindset of the southern Democrats in 1860. After one-hundred years, and the deployment of a Southern Strategy in the Nixon presidency to welcome segregationists into the dying Republican Party, the Democrats from 1860 are now the force in the GOP Republican party in 2018.

Southern Democrats and New Republicans

Prior to WWII, the Republican Party flourished in the northeast and mid-west, appealing to large and small business owners and citizens in nearby small towns and farming communities. The Democratic Party appealed to new immigrants seeking employment in the large cities growing throughout the nation, and paradoxically, still included the southern states who remained loyal to the Democratic Party even a century after the Civil War, primarily because the Republican Party was viewed as a northern party who thrust Reconstruction and federal control on the southern states; Republicans were not to be trusted in the South. Though institutional slavery no longer separated the two parties and the regions, racial prejudices and overt segregation did. Thus the split in political demographics remain unchanged for a century, until the world caught fire in 1940.

World War II lasted five years and eleven months (September 1, 1939-August 15, 1945). Everything changed. All around the world. All across America. The doors in America- in its small towns, big cities, farms, and company towns- swung wide open and new winds blew through. There was no turning back to a pre-WWII normalcy. How many dynamic changes were ushered in? More than a few. Which changes came first? It's hard to say. The war had awakened America to its racial inequalities and it would never go back to sleep. The war educated a generation of young Americans who led a quiet and gradual upheaval in the two major American political parties.

The inclusion of black citizens into America's war efforts was inevitable and fortunate. America, once described as 'the world's melting pot' is a product of welcoming people from all around the world. People from every continent contributed in great numbers to its rapid rise and its success among nations. No race of people have contributed more to America and benefitted less than black men and women from Africa. Black labor and blood enriched the southern landowners on the eastern side of America for two centuries. Their sacrifice in WWII was offered for America's survival no less than the labor and blood of men and women of Italian, Irish, German, Spanish, Polish, Japanese, Chinese, Native American, and many other people from around the world who came to America and who are all American. In post-war America, a seismic explosion demanding race equality would start raining social changes on America's white European culture and the old world bias of the first immigrants who sailed to the new world, then multiplied and claimed it as home. So it was, in 1948, more than a hundred years after its founding, the GOP would begin to change. No signal of change was as far-reaching as the first national election after the war ended. Men and women of all races, nationalities, rich, poor, educated, and non-educated died on the same field facing a common enemy or worked tirelessly in the same factories in the midst of daily conflict not seen. Equal sacrifice warranted equal rights, and no right was more basically American than the freedom to vote.

Dixiecrats

The change in the Republican Party did not come from within their party, it came from inside the Democratic Party. The defection of the southern Democratic Party was related to the South's original sin: race, the refusal of the southern states to accept black citizens as equal to white citizens, as decreed as the law of the land, and to ensure that equality at all times and places.

The change was hastened with the brutal beating in February 1946 of Sgt. Isaac Woodard, a decorated African-American soldier, in Batesburg, SC. Sgt. Woodard returned from the war and was battered and permanently blinded by Batesburg's police chief. The attack inflamed the nation and shone a strong light on inequality in America. The nation and the leaders in the Democratic Party correctly understood and acknowledged that just as all races and faiths had served in the US Armed Forces during WWII, all of its citizens should share fully in the fruits of America's sacrifices. In preparation for the 1948 Presidential election, Senator Hubert Humphrey of Minnesota wanted the Democratic Party's national platform (its governing plan for America) to reflect the party's demands for equal rights and opportunities such as jobs, equal education for all Americans of all race and all faiths. Immediately, the southern Democrats denounced this civil rights platform and formed a States' Rights Democratic Party vowing to separate from the mainstream Democratic Party. These secessionist Democrats were soon referred to as Dixiecrats and had a brief political life on their own but had little immediate impact on politics. However, they did have a long-term impact. After Harry Truman shocked the country with his unexpected victory over Thomas Dewey in 1948, the southern Democrats began a quiet departure from the national Democratic Party. The Dixiecrats began the weakening of the "Solid South" (the Democratic Party's total control of presidential elections in the South). Race, segregation, states' rights, white supremacy all played a part in the South's differences with the national Democratic Party. The politics embraced by the South in the Civil War had really never changed and its ugliness publicly surfaced again. The southern Democrats began voting against the Democratic Party, and for the Republican Party who enthusiastically welcomed them. The Republican Party won the presidential elections in 1952 and 1956 and became the party of choice for the South. In the ensuing fifty years, the GOP Republicans have become dominated by the most singularly minded citizens in the country.

The control of the Republican Party in the conservative western states by the right-wing business moguls and their partnership with the new southern Republicans created a new force in the American political history, a populist party who can agree on what to dislike but cannot lead because it is divisive in its nature and effective only when it is in agreement with another faction that shares a common enemy. Otherwise, this two-headed creature is not willing to compromise its two distinct single-minded philosophies even within its own party membership. It is akin to having a kindergarten class where all 50 class members manage to capture control of the classroom for themselves but after achieving their goal, all 50 will only agree to play only their favorite game and eat only their own favorite snack. Soon, there are no games, no snacks, and no peace, just a room full, a nation full, of juveniles who will be easily corralled into submission by a kindergarten bully and class dictator who offers to "help" them get along. Can you guess who decides what games are played, what is eaten, and who wins all the games?

The GOP Today

This is who the new Republican Party is today. The southern Democrats from 1860 are at home in the Republican Party. They are a sizable component of the Party and they strengthen it as long as the GOP allows them to hold fast to their white culture and discriminate against anyone who threatens their "old South". The new Republicans are the 1860 Democrats controlled by their prejudices and bibles, and the Republican conservatives and alt-right groups funded by a coalition of conservative billionaires want a free country owned and plundered by them for their wealth-fare. The Republican Party has been routinely embraced by small and large business for its entire existence but now it is controlled by this group of powerful donors seeking to promote their own hard-right agenda. Senator Kristen Gillibrand, NY-D, observed, "Some of the very wealthy patrons of the Republican Party are so demanding, if you deviate from their stated requests, they will fund somebody to run against you in a Republican primary, they will dry up your money." So it is not difficult to understand why Republican leaders fail to stand up to the party's most powerful backers but it is still unacceptable and directly in conflict to their oath of office to defend and protect their constituents.

The new Republican legislators do not embrace the traditional political wisdom of compromise as a solution to end party skirmishes and deadlocks in order to get something done that though not perfectly satisfying to all parties, as is true in most compromises, benefits to some degree all parties. The reality is that these new GOP legislators did not have to raise money to campaign. They do not need to reach inside themselves to skillfully express their heart-felt political views to convince voters to elect them, nor do they have to wrestle with their conscience on challenging issues or listen to the voices of their constituents. The money and the votes they require are provided to them as long as they 'toe the line'. How? The new legislators willingly hire onto a new GOP organization that is funded and controlled by powerful men who provide their candidates with words to say and ideas to express. The announcement that a public official might favor a supporting business or a private benefactor is not a revelation to anyone, anywhere. But the direction the GOP is being driven in now is alarming.

The 2018 GOP, as presently configured and funded, is a threat to the tenets of our founding fathers. Their vision of America is a mockery of the universal application of Declaration of Independence, the carefully stated formula within the US Constitution, and the wisdom of the Bill of Rights. The GOP shamelessly seeks an America that is only for them and for their friends: rich, white, Christian; and littered with cities, states, factories and farms subservient to tyranny. Too many in the Republican Party, rich and poor, no longer recall being born of immigrants who sought refuge in America. In truth, all of them arrived after the wilderness was cleared, the cities were built, and blood was spilled, and after the riches they possess were earned by others and handed to them at birth. They are not pathfinders or roadbuilders.

McConnell and Ryan, King and Prince of No

The GOP gained many seats in the Congress by focusing its strategy and its billions of money campaigning in America's many less populated states. They captured congressional seats and compiled

149

increasing power in Congress. The strategy was applied in all elections in the southern and western states, and now the increasing number of seats from the large states has given them a numerical and strategic edge in Washington: local offices, state offices, federal dominance. The dark money has reaped benefits, the GOP has been successful in the 50 states and they now have the voting power in the House, the Senate, the White House, and the Supreme Court. With such numbers, the GOP instantly secures the senior positions of all congressional committees and special hearing formations, meaning the chairpersons of each committee can direct the committees' work or refusal to work.

The Majority Leader of the House of Representative is Paul Ryan, WI-R, and the Senate Majority Leader Mitch McConnell, KY-R. McConnell and Ryan have instructed the GOP to put politics over country. In the period between 2009 and 2016, the GOP refused to pass bipartisan legislation, deliberate shut down the country's daily operations in 2013, and accomplished nothing during their terms as party leaders. They also failed their major goal, to keep President Obama from being elected to a second term in 2012.

McConnell and Ryan, armed with full control of Congress, the White House, and the Supreme Court, also failed to repeal President Obama's landmark piece of legislation, the Affordable Care Act, aka Obamacare. The GOP attempted to defeat this insurance legislation for eight years, and after having gained control of the House in 2011, the Senate in 2015, the office of President in 2017, and the Supreme Court in 2018, they were still unsuccessful in its repeal and replacement. The Party of No could not get a yes from its own majority. Only months before, the same GOP legislature overwhelmingly voted 'No' to allowing a congressional hearing on President Obama's nominee to the Supreme Court. In all, the majority led by McConnell refused for 293 days to allow the House to hold hearings on Judge Merrick Garland's appointment to the Supreme Court.

McConnell's obstructionist behavior continued into the 2016 Presidential campaign when in September 2016 the directors of the FBI and the Homeland Security learned of Russian interference in the nation's election and requested Congress to draft a bipartisan statement and deliver it jointly to the nation by the leaders of both the Democratic and Republican parties, warning Americans of the Russian plot. McConnell refused, saying he did not believe it was serious enough and he didn't think it was necessary to be shared with his fellow Americans before the presidential election. In hindsight, the better question now is, what did he know? Throughout the debacles of Trump's 2015 – 2016 Republican and Presidential campaigns, both McConnell and Ryan have, at varying times voiced enthusiastic support for, or remained conveniently silent through a steady progression of sex assault charges against Trump, his crude name-calling, the rumors of his treasonous connections with Russia, and his fraudulent practices and lawsuits related to businesses like Trump Foundation, and Trump University.

The blind acceptance of all things Trump is McConnell's and the GOP Republicans cowardly way to survive the quagmire of the Trump administration. Any opposition to the Trump Presidency increases the likelihood of their failure to be re-elected in 2018 and 2020. So, they accept this lasting shame on themselves and their party, and shame America in order to selfishly keep their seats in Congress. Their silence on the events at Charlottesville, Parkland, and Puerto Rico, and their silence on the growing number of indictments from the investigation on Russia collusion is proof of their lack of interest for America's welfare, which they place far beneath their own concerns for money and power.

Through 2017 and 2018, McConnell and the Republican Party obstructed calls for congressional hearings against the President on sexual harassment charges by eighteen women, and turned a dead eye on the continuing list of unethical behavior by the Trump cabinet and miscellaneous White House administrators. In June, 2018, when Trump formally installed tariffs on goods from our closest allies, McConnell finally lifted his voice in opposition to Trump and joined his congressional colleagues in asking Trump to reconsider a fresh round of tariffs levied against US allies in Mexico, Canada and the European Union. McConnell said, "I hope we pull back from the brink here because these tariffs will not be good for the economy, and I worry that it will slow, if not impeded significantly, the progress we were making economically for the country." McConnell added that he hopes it ends soon and he is "not happy about the prospects of a trade war." What occasioned McConnell's unusual though meek retort to Trump's tariff announcement? These newer tariffs created a prompt response of reciprocal actions from effected foreign countries greatly impacting Senator McConnell's home state: a Toyota plant in Kentucky, bourbon distilleries, and small farms throughout Kentucky. In Trump's kingdom, everyone must be prepared to sacrifice for the king, even the little kings in Kentucky. *Mitch McConnell breaks from Donald Trump on tariffs, June 2, 2018, CNN*

Party over Country

The consistent mantra of the new GOP at all levels is no secret, it is 'party over country'. In 2011, the Republican Party finally acquired control of America's three branches of government, the trifecta jackpot of political power formulated by the founders of our great country. How did it come about? It required years of planning and an even bigger expenditure of money: billions of dollars. But the union of three diverse philosophies was achieved when the 1860 southern Democrats completed their sixty years of wandering in disguise as members of the national Democratic Party. These southern states and their voters were now fully out of the closet and they were welcomed as partners with the GOP coalition of conservative and moderate Republican states. These three clusters of voters envisioned a long dynasty of Republican control in Washington, DC. They were ecstatic with their victory and now were anxious to prove they can harness their diverse points of view, lessen their intolerance for compromise, and agree on solutions acceptable to all. In the recent few years of legislative dominance, they proved they could only agree with one another when they agree on opposing a common foe. This trio of factions proved their strength of numbers and combined effectiveness over the past eight years when they defeated every effort of the Obama administration to pass any legislation even when it benefitted American citizens. The mantra of the Party of No had hardened into Party over Country.

As the first two years of the Trump administration was enveloped into one scandal or another, nearly every GOP legislator found themselves taking embarrassing positions or actions to protect their party, and their president. The amount of stonewalling and delay tactics in defense of the president was like most of the past events in the past three years, unprecedented. The almost daily announcement of charges against Trump and his family and his administration forced the GOP Republicans to address the litany of 2016 and 2017 investigations into Trump and friends for suspected wrong-doing, and they answered with loud demands for their own 'investigations of the investigations.' At times, the halls of Congress resembled speed lanes with legislators

Witness to Treason

and witnesses transiting back and forth between the House and the Senate buildings. It was conceivable at one point that Trump's first infrastructure project might not be the Wall but a high speed line transporting the numerous witnesses and committee members between both wings of the Capitol.

The Misogynist

In the present widely-celebrated climate of #MeToo, and #Enough, powerful men in varied professions have been toppled by their bad behavior and by charges of the sexual harassment they imposed upon women. Politicians at every level of government, athletes, movie moguls, sports physicians, are being held responsible for victimizing women and men. It has not ended, and so, on and on the list grows. Abusers are now being held accountable, and when found guilty, they are facing disgrace, prosecution, and removal from their lofty positions. But not all of them. There is one highly visible exception: Donald Trump, the 45th President of the United States. Trump is likely the single individual most responsible for this long-delayed movement to prosecute these sexual predators instead of shaming the victims of their crimes. Some of Trump's accusers had spoken out in the past but were unsuccessful with pursuing justice for themselves. Each of the early accusers were unaware of Trump's other attacks, so the victims were isolated in their efforts to seek justice. Trump's brazen appearance on the national stage as a candidate to be elected President of the United States caused them to bravely speak out again, and they hoped to prevent their attacker from shaming America's highest office. But the Republican Party ignored them.

Despite the presentation of sixteen women who made separate claims of sexual assault against the President, congressional Republicans have

154

been silent on the question of Trump's sexual abuse. During the 2015/2016 campaign when nearly every Republican expected Trump to lose the election, a dozen Republican members of Congress said they wouldn't vote for him in an effort to boost their own political fortunes. But Trump unexpectedly won and Republican members of Congress have been silent ever since his victory. In the midst of #MeToo and transparency, a proper congressional investigation would produce public testimony and determine the truth. The result of the hearings would determine how the country moves forward and whether it is with or without Trump. Either way, there's simply no need for Congress to continue acting as if there's nothing to do about these allegations of sexual harassment against the President. In the past, oversight of the executive branch has been considered a core function of the legislative branch, and such oversight has been vigorously pursued by the Republican congress, spurred on by their conservative cable news channels and talk radio stations. Either it's true that Trump sexually assaulted the eighteen women who accused him or he is innocent of the charges. The GOP's silence and refusal to pursue the truth speaks loudly that there is something for Trump and the GOP to fear if a formal congressional investigation is conducted. Congress should find out which it is and exercise concern for country over party.

So it is less surprising to see that more than 100 days had gone by since the House passed sexual harassment legislation in February 2018 and the Senate had still done nothing to advance the bill. The reason hinted at by Rule Committee members is that some senators don't like the bill's requirement that senators will have to pay out of their own pocket if they are found personally liable for harassing or discriminating against employees. **Rules Committee Chairman** Sen. Roy Blunt (R-Mo.), responded and carefully considered his words. "I think anytime you're dealing with members' personal liability, you ought to be sure that the members understand what they're asked to vote on." It speaks volumes that the Senate is unable to pass a bill to make it easier for victims of sexual harassment or discrimination on Capitol Hill to file a complaint because anonymous senators don't want to have to personally pay for misconduct claims if any one of them is found liable. The real concern should be to focus on removing acceptance of sexual harassment, post haste. The GOP has the ruling edge in both the House and the Senate and in the White House. In this time of active awareness to end sexual harassment the responsibility lies powerfully in their hands. Congress should be holding elected leaders to the highest standards, not the lowest, and taxpayers should never be on the hook to pay for a politician's sexual harassment settlement. Senator Kristen Gillibrand, NY-D, has sponsored a widely supported bipartisan bill to reform this process and bring accountability and transparency to Congress. Senator Blunt as Chairman of the Senate Rules Committee must place the bipartisan bill on the floor of the Senate and support its passage.

The Mueller Investigation

In April 2017, the US Department of Justice appointed a Special Counsel to investigate whether Donald Trump's 2016 presidential campaign colluded with Russian (or other foreign) persons and/or entities to interfere in the 2016 US election, including any possible links or coordination between Trump's campaign and the Russian government, "and any matters that arose or may arise directly from the investigation." The scope of the investigation reportedly also includes potential obstruction of justice by President Trump and others. The Special Counsel took over several related FBI investigations including those involving former campaign chairman Paul Manafort and former National Security Advisor Michael Flynn, both of which started before the 2016 presidential election. The investigation has been led since May 2017 by US Special Counsel, and former FBI Director, Robert Mueller. The bipartisan investigation initially enjoyed bipartisan support, but the special counsel investigation soon came under fierce criticism by President Trump and his surrogates in the conservative media. As the number of indictments and guilty pleas increased, support for the investigation grew. In early September 2018, a Washington Post-ABC News poll showed that a clear majority of Americans supported the special counsel's investigation of Russian interference in the 2016 election and Russia's alleged collusion with President Trump's campaign. Nearly seventy percent of adults said they supported Mueller's focus on possible collusion with Russia.

Unfortunately, the GOP response has been shamefully lacking in seriousness to the charges against the President and to the continuing threat they present to the United States. It is not surprising the GOP hesitates to support investigations into a President they selected to represent their party and who they vigorously continue to support but the GOP's loyalty becomes increasingly misplaced and its judgement is lacking in its regard for the welfare of the country. As the majority leaders in Congress, the Republican legislators in Congress have the power to conduct a thorough investigation, but they have muddied the investigation by refusing to work in communion with its fellow legislators from the opposite side of the House. Devon Nunes, CA-R, the Chairman of the House Committee on Intelligence, and the former manager for the Trump transition team, was forced to remove himself from heading the investigation when he was discovered sharing committee information with the Trump White House. He was making solo visits to the White House to obtain confirmation about unsubstantiated charges that the FBI unmasked Trump associates on intelligence intercepts, and committed FISA court abuse against Carter

Page. All this detailed in Nunes' secret memo. Nunes communicated with the party being investigated, a Republican President, without informing all members of the investigating committee that he was doing so. Where do such legislators come from? Nunes was replaced by another Republican who was appointed chairman but the GOP still remained less than interested in conducting a full and bipartisan inquiry. They refused to subpoena both reluctant witnesses and critical records pertinent to the investigation from Deutsche Bank. The GOP's most glaring fault was their rush to close down the hearings before all the witnesses were questioned to the satisfaction of all committee members. At the conclusion of the House hearings, the GOP-led committee announced that no collusion between Trump and associates and Russia was found. Zero findings was the majority opinion of Nunes' tightly controlled committee. Elsewhere in Washington, DC, the Mueller investigation on the same Russian and Trump collusion matters had so far resulted in seventeen indictments and five guilty pleas. As of this book's printing in October 2018, the independent Mueller investigation, threatened daily by the President, is not yet completed.

To add insult to their slow progress and poor performance on the Russian investigation, the GOP displayed lightning responses when asked by Trump to launch counter investigations on his bogus claims of wiretapping, etc.

- Trump's fabricated charges of unlawful wire-tapping of Trump Tower by President Obama during the campaign,
- Trump's charge that his campaign was infiltrated, spied on by the FBI,
- Trump's charge that the Steele Dossier, a private investigative report detailing Trump's salacious relationship with Russian

contacts in Moscow 2013, was used as the sole evidence to justify the eventual appointment of a Special Council.

- Senate hearings for FBI former investigators, Lisa Page and Peter Strzok, who were accused by Trump of trying to make him lose the election by regularly exchanging anti-Trump messages

All of these allegations of investigators' misconduct were almost immediately debunked, The FBI, the CIA, the NSA all confirmed the dossier was not the reason for the appointment of a Special Counsel. The dossier was taken seriously and added to the information because it corroborated reports the FBI had already received from other sources, including one from inside the Trump camp.

The US Intelligence community had known for months that credible allegations of collusion between the Trump camp and Russia were pouring in from independent sources during the campaign. The New York Times told Congress that they found widespread evidence that Trump and his organization had worked with a wide array of dubious Russians from Manhattan to Sunny Isles Beach, Fla., and from Toronto to Panama, in arrangements that often raised questions about money laundering. None of that information seemed to interest Congress. The New York Times reported the U.S. intelligence agencies were deeply familiar with political operative Paul Manafort's coziness with Moscow and his financial ties to Russian oligarchs close to Vladimir Putin. Nevertheless, GOP leaders in Congress, in their desperation to gain the presidency, elected to keep the American citizens in the dark; even after the election and through this presidency, the GOP has continued to support a cynical campaign to portray America's more noble and loyal institutions as purveyors of rumors and lies when in fact, the lies come from Trump and the GOP.

Witness to Treason

Real investigations, fake investigations, treasonous behavior, dedicated investigators, government officials looking the other way, and truth buried under an avalanche of lies, it all continues. The late Senator Sam Ervin, NY-D remarked in the critical days of Watergate, "it is time to stop chasing rabbits." The public still has much to learn about a man with the most troubling business past of any United States president. Glenn Simpson, the founder of Fusion, GPS, who shared the Steele dossier with the FBI was questioned by Congress. When only pieces of his testimony were released by the GOP committee chairman, only pieces that favored Republican talking points, he responded that "Congress should release all of the transcripts of our firm's testimony so that the American people can learn the truth about our work and most important, what happened to our democracy'.
https://www.nytimes.com/2018/01/02/opinion/republicans-investigation-fusion-gps.html, Obstructing Hearings on Russia Collusion - NY Times, Opinion Page, Glenn R. Simpson, Peter Fritsch, Jan 2, 2018, founders and principles of Fusion, GPS. The Steele Dossier among other reports on Trump.

Trump's Voter Fraud Committee

After the election, Trump was upset by his failure to win the popular vote so he announced he would have won the popular vote "if you deduct the millions of people who voted illegally." He begrudgingly admitted he lost the popular vote to Hillary Clinton. Hillary received 2,864,974 more votes than he did. Americans liked Hillary more than they liked him. The final tally as of December 20, 2016 was 65,844,610 for Clinton, and 62,979,636 votes for Trump. The new President lost the people's vote so he lied and said that voter fraud was committed across the country in the coincidental amount of 3.5 million votes, the same number of votes Trump conveniently needed "to find" in order to surpass Hillary Clinton's votes and support his false claim of winning the popular vote for the presidency. On May 11, 2017, President Trump signed an executive order creating the "Presidential Advisory Commission on Election Integrity". He announced that Vice President Mike Pence would chair the Commission. Kansas Secretary of State Kris Kobach, a leading promoter of the myth of voter fraud and a strong advocate for laws restricting access to voting, was appointed the vice chair and the person primarily responsible for the Commission's duties. The Commission's stated purpose would be to root out widespread voter fraud and uncover the 3.5 million votes stolen from Trump. In fact, the president's invented claim of legions of illegal voters is the most extreme voter fraud claim in recent memory. Many political experts suspected right away that the commission was not a legitimate attempt to study election fraud, but it was another attempt to support conservative Republican long-standing claims of widespread voter fraud that were previously and repeatedly discredited. Critics characterized the Commission's hidden agenda as being focused on imposing voter suppression legislation throughout the nation, similar to the earlier Jim Crow election laws once plentiful in the Deep South.

According to the commission's charter, the General Services Administration would provide the Commission with "administrative services, funds, facilities, staff, equipment, and other support services", all costing about $500,000 over the course of two years. The money would come from U.S. tax payers from around the country. Not only was it doubtful the Commission was necessary but it did not appear to be truly bipartisan? A bipartisan commission would be led by members of both parties, have an equal partisan split among commissioners, and capture a broad range of viewpoints. This Commission, in contrast, was led by two staunch Republicans, has a Republican majority, and counts some of the nation's leading promoters of voting restrictions among its ranks. While five of the 12 members are Democrats, three of the Democrats were recommended by their respective states' Republican chief election officials. To be more transparent on the Commission's political and regional makeup, consider that its charter members included officials from the Heritage Foundation and the Public Interest Legal Foundation, two of the country's most notorious advocates for voter suppression. Both of these right wing conservative political institutions are funded by Charles and David Koch, billionaire businessmen brothers from Kansas who organized and controlled billions of campaign cash donated from conservative billionaires who have invested heavily in the new GOP Republican Party (see Chapter 7). It is not a coincidence that Kris Kobach, the Commission's vice chair, and an announced 2018 candidate for governor of Kansas, has surrounded himself and the Vice-President with mirror political images of themselves. The only certainty is that all of these persons would fit comfortably working closely together on this aptly-named Fraud Committee. The Voter Fraud Commission began activities in May 2017 and faced difficulties communicating with and receiving cooperation from many of the states in the following year. Many states refused to supply general voting records to the Commission, suspecting the data was being collected to provide conservative groups with voters' personal information and provide data to be used to restrict minority voters' access to the polls. On June 5, 2018. Trump disbanded the Voter Fraud Commission. No charges of voter fraud were cited or proven. Hillary still has 2,864,974 more popular votes for President than Trump has.

Gerrymandering

When I was a kid, gerrymander was a buzz word for "the fix is in". I didn't know where the word came from, or really what it meant, or if it was even an English word. I just knew if someone told me that something was "gerrymandered", it meant the result was already decided. Sure, the game needed to be played, and the fight needed to be fought, but the odds were heavily stacked in someone's favor. In 2016 gerrymandering caught my attention again and it still meant the same thing to me as it did when I heard it for the first time on the streets of my hometown, Chester, PA. Today it is the hottest topic in politics. Gerrymandering is being discussed in all the political venues in the United States, as high up as the Supreme Court of the United States. In simplest layman terms, gerrymandering is a process by which electoral districts are drawn with the aim of aiding the party in power. Its origin is traced back to the earliest days of political activity in the thirteen original colonies. Elbridge Gerry was an important and successful American statesman and diplomat during the birth of the American colonies in the late eighteenth century. He supported the colonies' demands for independence from England but he was initially opposed to the idea of political parties, even as he cultivated enduring friendships on both sides of the political divide between Federalists and Democratic-Republicans. He was elected to the Second Continental Congress and signed both the Declaration of Independence and the Articles of Confederation. After the Constitution was ratified, he was elected to the inaugural United States Congress, and as an advocate of individual and state liberties, he was actively involved in drafting and passing the Bill of Rights. He was later elected Governor of Massachusetts in 1810. It was during his second term as governor that the Massachusetts legislature approved creating new state senate districts that favored his party in elections and subsequently led to the coining of the word "gerrymander", a slick combination of his surname and the last part of the word salamander which represented the contorted shape that many of the new voting districts took on the state maps. (See PA 7th District map below). Gerry later served as the James Madison's vice president from March 1813 until his death in November 1814. Unfortunately, his name is more widely remembered for this continuing political strategy of "gerrymandering" than for his contributions to the founding of the United States of America.

GOP Voter Suppression

It may be hard to believe that in America your right to vote is not safe. But it's not. In many states, Republican Party officials are removing voters from registration books, designing ways to prevent your vote from being counted, and not least of all, maintaining and/or creating gerrymandered district voting maps that intentionally favor their party. As Casey Stengel, the baseball Yankees' legendary manager, once said, "You can look it up."

The federal government is responsible to pass laws of national benefit for all citizens across the nation. These laws transcend the individual State laws implemented inside a State's borders. Federal laws pertain to the undeniable freedoms stated in the Declaration of Independence such as voting, speech, religion, etc. The States have the responsibility to make laws that are pertinent to their local citizens for the benefit of its citizens. The State and its citizens must both obey and enforce federal laws. Sometimes, the State wants to break a federal law and do things their way. Usually, it wants to use federal money for the wrong reason, or to deny a basic freedom to all its citizens. This is where your vote falls into danger.

So what are States' Rights? The phrase sounds familiar because it has been the rallying cry for the South since colonial times. It was the first defense against ending slavery. It is now the right-wing conservative and white supremist catchall used to deny freedom to anyone they don't like, or any idea they don't accept. And right-wing conservatives and white supremists don't like people of color, Jews, people who aren't white Christian Protestants, and finally anyone and any idea that didn't evolve from their closed communities. Yes, the good-old boys and their local bully-type sheriffs are still alive in many of the towns in states that worship States Rights.

Unfortunately, not all of the judges on the U.S. Supreme Court believe it, and there are more coming who don't believe it either. In 2013, the Court struck down a key section of the 1965 Voting Rights Act which protected minority voters from state disenfranchisement, an important enforcement clause that was deemed necessary more than fifty years ago. The clause required states to get any changes to state voting policies pre-approved by the federal Justice Department. Can you guess why? Yep. Because some States, mostly southern states, had a history of racial discrimination and aggressively removed registered voters from their rolls for any number of reasons, installed state and local Jim Crow laws that intimidated voters, and physically prevented citizens from voting. Five years ago, the Supreme Court made a mistake. It failed to protect America's most visible freedom and basically enabled the GOP to strip Americans of their right to vote. After reviewing voter purges nationally from 2012 to 2016, the nonpartisan Brennan Center for Justice found that the mostly Southern jurisdictions that had previously been required to get changes to voting policies pre-approved by the Justice Department now had higher rates of purging voter registration lists.

In Georgia, for example, 156 of the state's 159 counties reported an increase in removal rates after the Supreme Court changed the Voting Rights Act clause. It's not only southern states now that are illegally stripping voter lists. The cash-soaked conservative machine is financing more state GOP communities. GOP election officials in Ohio have actively been pursuing voter-removal campaigns in advance of the 2018 and 2010 elections. They control the registration data and they are expeditiously removing valid voters from the books in suspect ways. Jonathan Brater, counsel for the Brennan Center's Democracy Program, said, "There's cause for concern when the (voter) purge rate goes up this much at the same time we're seeing controversial, sometimes illegal voter purge practice, in addition to changes to other voting laws that make it more difficult to participate." The Brennan Center found that election officials were purging voter rolls more aggressively nationwide, too, with some using imprecise or possibly illegal methods to do so. Voter purges - cleaning up and pruning voter rolls down to remove inaccurate information - are a normal part of all election roll maintenance. But when purges are intentionally done too aggressively or with bad information, advocates warn, they can disenfranchise eligible voters, who may not know they've been purged until they go to the polls on Election Day and are unable to vote. Brater added that under the Trump administration, "the Department of Justice has abdicated its responsibility to protect against bad voter purges." "They've actually been encouraging jurisdictions to purge more aggressively," he said.   https://www.nbcnews.com/politics/politics-news/voter-roll-purges-surged-after-changes-voting-rights-act-new-n893056 by Jane C. Timm / Jul.20.2018

The National Census

It is a common practice since colonial times that a local voting district may be reconfigured after a census to reflect the changing demographics in its community, largely due to the mobility of America's population caused by continuing economic and social changes. The party with the majority of elected officials in the subject community is usually responsible for the new voting map. Simply stated, redistricting is meant to be a <u>bipartisan</u> action whereby the changing district will reflect a true demographic and plurality of the voters in a common area. Gerrymandering is the <u>partisan</u> redistricting of unconnected areas into a new district filled with voters overwhelmingly favoring one party. The partisan redistricted salamander-shaped voting communities that are created are an aberration of the democratic process and undermine the Constitution's intent of equality with one person-one vote.

On page 412 of her 2017 national bestseller, "Dark Money", award-winning author Jane Mayer tells the reader, "Gerrymandering was a bipartisan game as old as the Republic." She proceeds to explain that the *Citizens United* ruling by the Supreme Court in 2010 removed restrictions on the amount of campaign contributions and unleashed an avalanche of money from many conservative billionaires that changed the game to favor these big money interests. Worse, the ruling allowed some donors to remain anonymous. The ruling immediately removed any controls that would prevent excessive amounts of money from greatly influencing American elections from the grassroots level to the Presidential election. This disastrous decision by the Supreme Court ensured that "the business of manipulating politics from the ground up was now heavily directed by the unelected rich." The introduction of unlimited money for local politics from "institutions" and "foundations" now more than ever threaten the fundamental democratic principle of equal political power for all citizens: the one man-one vote tenet of American democracy. More alarming, the

Supreme Court's *Citizens United* ruling and the frenzied and heavily-funded 2010 GOP use of extensive partisan gerrymandering on a country-wide scale derailed democracy in several states. States specifically targeted by the GOP since 2010 were North Carolina, Pennsylvania, Texas, Ohio, and Florida. The hundreds of millions of dollars spent by the GOP benefactors such as the Koch Organization on local and state elections throughout the country continued unabated and contributed to the increasing number of partisan gerrymandered districts across the nation. The proof of *Citizens United* damage to equal representation in political debate was shown by the increasing number of gerrymander challenges filed in state and federal courts. Unfortunately, the likelihood in having these wildest-redrawn maps reconfigured rests with some state judiciaries that have already benefitted by the same partisan gerrymandered districts being questioned. The rich get richer.

District	GOP	Dem
1st	83.5 %	18.5 %
2nd	99.6	0.4
3rd	49.5	50.5
4th	99.9	0.1
5th	98.0	2.0
6th	91.6	8.4
7th	91.2	8.9

GOP gerrymandered district

A few examples of gerrymandering cases brought before the courts in 2018 are listed below. Examples of gerrymandered district maps are shown in the following pages

- In January 2018, the Pennsylvania Supreme Court struck down the state's congressional map put into place seven years ago by Republicans as an unconstitutional partisan gerrymander. In February, Pennsylvania Supreme Court drew a new map reflecting a best arrangement for all voters connected by their communities.

- Voting rights cases the Supreme Court were hearing this term include two extreme partisan gerrymandering cases - Gill v. Whitford, a case from Wisconsin, and Benisek v. Lamone, a case from Maryland. Are they constitutional or not? Another challenge to the practice of voter suppression is a ruling on Ohio's system for purging voters from rolls.
- The conservative wing of the court was skeptical of the standard offered by those challenging a Republican gerrymander in Wisconsin.
- Of note is that the Supreme Court has never struck down a voting district that was claimed to be a partisan gerrymander.

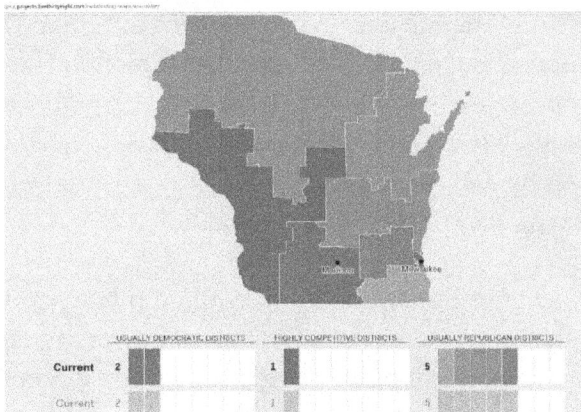

Above map shows 2016 Wisconsin congressional district boundaries, shaded to show how likely each is to be represented by either party over the long term. This is the situational look at the of the 2018 midterm elections.

Witness to Treason

Jane Mayer addresses gerrymandering in Chapter 13 of her best seller "Dark Money". The chapter titled "The States: Gaining Ground", begins with a discussion about conservative Republican operative Ed Gillespie's REDMAP plan (Redistricting Majority Project). Gillespie's Machiavellian plan would redirect millions of dollars from the Koch brothers' political organization and other conservative donors into funding the purchase of state offices across the country. Gillespie and conservative strategist Karl Rove pleaded with the conservative donors to spend their fortunes on gaining the state offices in all fifty states and *then redistricting the congressional districts of the states into a majority of GOP enclaves* described internally as individual "warring partisan camps". The REDMAP plan was successful in North Carolina in 2012, "where Republicans had cemented control of the state legislature and gerrymandered the boundaries of the congressional districts in North Carolina so artfully that despite getting fewer votes than Democrats, the GOP Republicans won more congressional seats." The same pattern was repeated in enough other states that Republicans were able to secure several districts and retain control of the U.S. House of Representatives by a 33-seat margin, all of this despite Democratic candidates having had more of the general vote.

The added effect of unlimited and unidentified money suddenly permitted by the Supreme Court's *Citizens United* ruling created a powerful one-two political punch: combining money spent by GOP donors on these state offices with the GOP campaign of partisan gerrymandering. This proved to be successful for the GOP and it was later repeated in a similar manner when the final results of the 2016 popular vote and electoral vote were tabulated. The redistricting of Wisconsin was so drastic that it became the basis of a case of extreme partisan gerrymandering, Gill v. Whitford. Voters in a district found that elections there were pre-determined due to partisan redistricting.

170

The Supreme Court ruled in June 2018 that the plaintiffs, the Democratic voters, did not have standing against all of Wisconsin. They sent the case back to district court for re-argument. The Court ducked away from its duty. They did not address the core issue that voters in such districts were deliberately legislated out of a meaningful say on a candidate or issue. As Justice Ginsburg opined, "What becomes of the precious right to vote?"

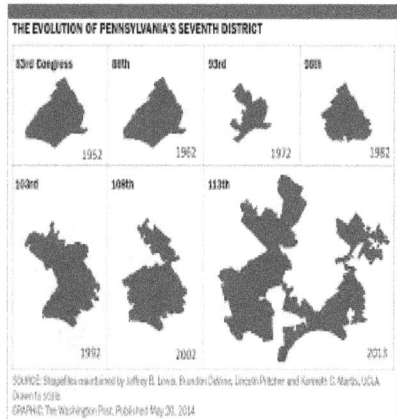

Left, PA 7th Congressional District mutilated by GOP. **Right,** evolution of same district boundaries since 1952 with gerrymandering.

Republican Congressman Mark Meadows of North Carolina, a member of the conservative Freedom Caucus, was a primary beneficiary of gerrymandering in 2012 when the 11th Congressional District was so severely redistricted that there were too few Democrats left in the district to vote against him. The gerrymandering strategy being used by the new GOP Republicans to cement their hold on state and county offices, state legislature seats, and governorships magnified their likelihood to capture subsequent seats in the United States congress. Such ambitions are the goals of any national party. But the goals of the new GOP Republican Party are not to serve the American public but to serve the billionaires who fund the GOP office holders in Washington, DC, and around the country. Extreme partisan gerrymandering has already led to rule by the richest who expand their power. Redistricting, voter suppression, and unlimited money from undisclosed sources dilute the founding father's gift of one person-one vote. Our American experiment in democracy, outlined more than two-hundred and forty years ago, is threatened not from outside but from within.

Stepford Guys, and the Boys from Brazil

Where does the new GOP Republican Party find so many single-minded, fast-talking but saying-nothing, concretely unyielding and identically opinioned political candidates? It cannot be a coincidence that young men and women (mostly men) from fifty different states and five major geographical zones, thousands of cities, towns, and villages, secondary schools, and universities can be so identical in language, expression, thought, and character as the conservative and alt-right wing members of the GOP Republican party. Where do they come from? A dorky prep school in Kansas? Or off a cookie-cutter press somewhere in Kentucky? This question brings to my mind two similarly-themed Hollywood films, "The Boys from Brazil", and "The Stepford Wives", both psychological, sci-fi, thrillers. In the 1977 film "Boys from Brazil", a Nazi hunter discovers a plot hatched by Dr. Josef Mengele, the nefarious Nazi doctor who experimented on men, women, and children at the Auschwitz concentration camp during WWII. The plot involves cloning nearly one-hundred copies of a young Adolph Hitler in hopes that one or more will become the new leader of the underground Nazis who are ready to follow its new Fuhrer in the Fourth Reich. On the opposite end of the gender pool, "The Stepford

172

Wives" involves a group of women, all wives to be exact, who live in a sleepy, but perfect model community in Stepford, Connecticut, and whose personalities and physical features are duplicated and stored into "fembots" programmed with classic loving wife and doting mother traits and unanimously approved and controlled by their husbands, all members of the Stepford Men's Association. Of course, the two films are fictitious, the new GOP Republican legislators are frighteningly real.

They are real because in fact, Pam Vogel, a research fellow at Media Matters provided information for their source in a March 2017 online article. Her researched article lists schools, foundations, scholarship programs, and seminars that recruit candidates for the GOP. The programs include room and board and seek to educate, groom, and regiment in style and thought, the selected multitude into new GOP Republicans. The graduates will advance with religious evangelical fervor the tenets of the conservative, right wing party. The list of such conservative-oriented groups is growing and they are becoming increasingly visible on college campuses throughout the United States. The sponsoring billionaires contribute millions of their excess dollars to establish recruiting teams on college campuses and offer grants and scholarships for curricula advocating their conservative policies. The Ivy League schools were once uninterested in the conservative, right wing arms of the GOP Republican party. Chapter 3 of Dark Money, is titled "Beachheads: John M. Olin and the Bradley Brothers". In the chapter, the Olin family hired Nixon's former Secretary of the Treasury and Energy Czar, William Simon, to lead the development of a student recruitment program. The purpose was to recruit and educate students at college campuses for future "counter-intelligentsia", expecting these students would later advance conservative policies. The program was initially ineffective because it was only targeting little-known colleges

173

where conservative ideas and money were welcome. William Simon and an underling, Michael Joyce, soon realized that 'it needed to infiltrate prestigious schools, especially the Ivy League." An additional program for funding campus recruiting at Ivy League and other politically liberal schools began and it was branded with a typical militarily-minded conservative code name of "beachheads." The beachheads have been successful at nearly all of the Ivy League schools such as Harvard, Princeton, and the University of Pennsylvania, as well as at numerous colleges and universities around the nation. The ticket to get inside the doors of the campuses is money "with no strings attached". In truth, the strings get attached as the increasing donations mount up. The goal is to invade academia by inserting money as necessary to secure a "beachhead". The bait is cast amidst unwitting students, faculty, and administration. Once the relationship is established, and the delivery of money is normalized, the conservative and libertarian dogmas are pitched, expanded, and the trap is sprung. The money is needed and the loyalty to the donor is deepened.

The spending of enormous millions on "counter intelligentsia" combined with gerrymandering, and voter suppression enabled by the _Citizens United_ ruling has resulted in billions of dollars of profit for the wealthy from reduced taxes, removal of controls on banks and investment firms, and elimination on environmental and industrial regulations. All favor only the richest of Americans. The funding of these scholarships and grants to these schools, to all academic institutions, for specific studies in politics, law, and civil and criminal justice bent toward conservative and libertarian ideologies , is purposed to advance conservative policies that though hidden under patriotic buzz words undermine the individual freedoms for all but the richest persons in America. The benefits of controlling a country's government accrue in exponential amounts to those who are in power only for themselves. The recent ruling in *Citizens United* and *Gill vs. Whitford* (gerrymandering) confirms that America is for sale and those with money are investing generously on the new GOP Republican Party's ability to deliver the country to them.   *Source: The Conservative Dark-Money Groups Infiltrating Campus Politics, March 29, 2017, Pam Vogel, Media Matters*

The power of the conservative right wing's access to money is visible when viewing the following list of funding organizations who support the conservative training initiatives and seminars: the Richard and Helen DeVos Foundation, the Donors Trust and Donors Capital Fund, the F.M.Kirby Foundation, the Charles Koch Foundation, the Lynde and Harry Bradley Foundation. The advocacy groups and media outlets who receive the funding include: the American Conservative Union that oversees the CPAC events, the Leadership Institute that trains conservative activists, the College Fix and the Student Free Press Association that receives all its funding from the DeVos Fund and the Donors Trust, the Students for Liberty, Students for Life, Project Veritas, Turning Point USA, Young Americans for Liberty, and Young America's Foundation. Among these conservative foundations are two nationally-identified hate groups: Alliance Defending Freedom, an anti-LGBTQ network of 3,000 allied attorneys with a $46 million budget, and the David Horowitz Freedom Center, an anti-immigrant and anti-black group funded by the Lynde and Harry Bradley Foundation. The fruits of the explosion of funding by the richest families in America has produced a flotilla of foundations across the political landscape. The Cato Institute, Heritage Foundation, Americans for Prosperity, Americans for Freedom, Freedom Partners. The Center to Protect Patients' Rights, State Policy Network, and American Energy Alliance are titles out of a totalitarian wordbook. If any of these organizations appear in your line of sight, be wary of their flags, their hymns, and their support for America. They have usurped the words that Americans and the world use as single-word definitions to describe the essence of American democracy: words such as liberty, freedom, justice, prosperity, heritage, and patriot. These GOP-aligned institutions and foundations use these words that have great meaning for us to disguise their litany of small-minded and prejudiced organizations. All of these right-wing conservative institutions, foundations, centers, etc. are prefaced and labeled with patriotic-sounding names that profess American virtues, but conceal their intent to secure America's freedoms and riches only for themselves, leaving little if anything for those outside their royal caste. Most of the men and women who march under the hijacked conservative banner are ignorant of their own future under its banner. They will become the hapless farm animals on Animal Farm who became subject to the lies and deceptive slogans from selfish pigs who were only interested in "some pigs", and not all pigs.

Whose Side Are They On?

In late July, 2018, just before President Trump scurried off to Helsinki to rendezvous with Russian President Putin, a delegation of conservative Republican congressmen quietly visited Moscow over the previous July 4 weekend, the most important holiday on America's calendar, the one day in history that most dramatically signals to the world the difference between our country and its representative government and the oppressive government in Russia. Why were they there? These conservative Republicans who built their splinter-party on Russian baiting and finding Russian conspiracies behind every tree and door, and in every nook and cranny. Now, in this year when a Russian conspiracy is factual, they rush off to make friends in Moscow and seek to find 'common ground' with their long-loathed enemy. Why?

But it continued. On August 6, Senator Rand Paul, R-KY, travelled to Moscow to meet with Sergey I. Kislyak, the Russian Ambassador to the United States, and other Russian leaders. The meeting was held so that Paul could find his own 'common ground' with the Russians. Senator Paul, a staunch right-wing conservative, had the audacity to meet with the same Russian ambassador who was involved in pre-2016 election secret meetings in Trump Tower with Trump campaign leaders Jared Kushner, Jeff Sessions, and General Michael Flynn. Kislyak was also the same Russian official that Trump invited into the Oval Office in the White House so Trump could gloat that he (Trump) fired America's FBI Director, James Comey. Trump told Kislyak and Russian Foreign Minister Sergey Lavrov, "I just fired the head of the F.B.I. He was crazy, a real nut job," Mr. Trump said. "I faced great pressure because of Russia. That's taken off." Mr. Trump added, "I'm not under investigation." The Russian officials shook hands with Trump and smiled.

These are the Russian officials who are now Senator Paul's new confidants, the men from our nation's strongest adversary with whom he and his 'loyal opposition party' will seek to find 'common ground'. Whose orders are Rand and the GOP following? Whose side are these Republicans on?

Profiles in Courage?

President Trump has been accused of every moral, ethical, or legal offense since he began his campaign in 2015, and up to this day. Tomorrow the list of charges and the number of accusers will likely lengthen. There is no reason to continue to investigate his investigators, or soil his accusers, or deny the obvious. It is time to display courage. It is time for some member or members of the

Witness to Treason

Republican Party to stand up and lead with integrity and courage. Where are the Republican Leaders? Where is their courage?

In 1955, the not-yet President John F. Kennedy wrote a book, *Profiles in Courage*. It remains an unparalleled celebration of that most noble human virtue: courage. The book is a powerful reminder of how strong the human spirit can be even under duress from outside forces, especially when the pressure is placed upon us by family, friends, and close associates. President Kennedy included a popular quote from Dante's Inferno in the book. Dante wrote, "The hottest places in Hell are reserved for those who in times of great moral crisis maintain their neutrality." In the book, eight American statesmen of historical significance, men of different political philosophy and different eras, were singularly faced with a grave decision that required great fortitude and an unselfish regard for themselves. All of them acted with courage and integrity in the face of overwhelming opposition. Granted, the courage displayed in the book occurred predominately in the eighteenth and nineteenth centuries, and the words were written later in the twentieth century, but the lives of such men and their integrity ring even louder now and their example should be remembered throughout our American history.

Today, America is in need of that virtue, courage. It is required from some persons more than others. Where are the men and women of the majority party who have the numbers and power to reign-in tyranny? Where are the Republicans? Their House leaders? Their Senate leaders? Their committee chairpersons? More than half (57%) of Americans across all political leanings are concerned about the current stability of America at home and overseas. Every crisis, or a threat of crisis, requires some measure of action. Inaction rarely creates solutions. John Quincy Adams, Daniel Webster, Sam Houston, and others profiled in the book set aside political conformity and expediency in favor of country and honor. Who, if anyone, among the 288 Republican members of the 115th Congressional (Senators and House legislators) will display personal courage and integrity now, and stand alongside the noble statesmen found inside "Profiles of Courage."? Who among them will chose country before party? Which Republican legislator would you trust enough today to share a "foxhole" with when night comes and tyranny strikes?

Altogether there are a combined total of 288 Republicans in the 115th U.S. Congress (January 2017 to January 2019). This number includes senators and representatives of whom there are 257 men and 31 women, all elected to represent their constituents best interests, but also to represent America's best interest mindful of the laws and essence of the country's fundamental rights of its citizens. The men in Profiles of Courage understood both duty to state and nation, and they valued their responsibility to be true patriots.

There are Republicans who have had an opportunity to elevate themselves into the modern edition of President Kennedy's *Profiles in Courage*; men and women who had multiple opportunities to set party affiliation aside and speak for the country's best interest, but continually failed to do so. There are some who see the tyranny that is silencing debate and fruitful compromise in the Republican Party. They abhor the close-minded allegiance that strangles the freedoms they inherited, and weakens the balance of political institutions in America. But they do nothing. Where is their courage? When will they will rise from their seats to save America from the damage being done to America's core values? Here are a few of the GOP legislators who failed to fulfill their oath to protect America from harm. They may be lost in history, or only remembered for what they did not do, but they are not profiles in courage.

- Paul Ryan, Mitch McConnell? These leaders of the 2015-2019 Republican Party have been largely invisible and nearly inaudible in defending America from the threats and actions of Russian interference in America's domestic affairs. Normally hysterical, vindictive, and righteous whenever opposition party legislators are accused of moral failure to any degree, they have turned away from the sexual assault charges brought against President Trump from eighteen separate women. Their tolerance of Trump's deliberate intrusion of his Executive actions into the functions of the Justice Department and other government agencies is severe negligence. They obstruct justice themselves when they encourage their party's actions in delaying, short-cutting, and restricting full hearings in Congress. With the exception of offering public prayers, they were mute when gun violence continued to kill citizens in our streets, schools, and at public events. McConnell's unwavering support for Trump's actions through 2018 includes Trump's rapport everything Russia. Not broadly known is that in September 2016, before the election, McConnell opposed and blocked the FBI's and Homeland Security's request that the Republican and Democratic leaders in Congress make a joint bipartisan announcement to the nation warning the American public of Russian interference in the U.S. 2016 election. Few knew that McConnell, the majority leader of the U.S. Senate, said he was unconvinced that the reports of Russian interference from U.S. intelligence agencies were sufficient to alarm the public. This was before the election, and McConnell did know the interference was targeted to favor Republican candidates. Why did he refuse to protect Americans voting process? Why did he trust the Russians more than U.S. and allied agents? What did he already know? Congressman Ryan was equally silent as he silently faded away as he retires to some position with a conservative organization. He never displayed leadership or courage. Verdict: Neither are acceptable.

- Devon Nunes, R-CA. This House Republican was a member of Trump's 2016 Transition Team. In 2017, he was appointed as the majority Leader of the House Intelligence Committee. In April 2017, Trump attempted to detract attention from the House Intelligence Committee's investigation into Russia collusion during the 2016 election by accusing the FBI and President Obama with wiretapping his office. During the committee's investigation, Nunes secretly visited the White House to meet with Trump assistants who gave him 'proof' of wiretaps. Nunes announced to the nation he had uncovered information supporting Trump's wiretap claims, but he refused to share all the information and its sources with his full committee, and he denied the information was provided by the White House. Shortly afterwards, the information proved false, and more embarrassing, it was discovered that it came from the White House. After much ballyhoo and delay, he was sanctioned from heading the investigation into Russian Collusion. Verdict: Not acceptable.
- Members of the House Freedom Caucus? Led by Jim Jordan, R-Ohio, and Mark Meadows, R-NC, the Freedom Caucus are House and Senate members are part of the Tea Party faction of the right-wing conservatives in Congress, obsessed with fiscal responsibility and enlarging national defense. Their major success as a political entity is their consistent ability to be

aggressively negative on everything. The few exceptions to their "hell no responses" are when something directly benefits their own constituents, the military, the police, and themselves. In an October 2017 Vanity Fair interview, former GOP House Speaker John Boehner said of the Freedom Caucus: "They can't tell you what they're for. They can tell you everything they're against. They're anarchists. They want total chaos. Tear it all down and start over. That's where their mindset is." None acceptable.

- <u>Senator Ted Cruz?</u> Trump attacked Cruz's wife and father during the GOP campaign. He shared an unflattering photo of Senator Ted Cruz's wife in a tweet that read, "A picture is worth a thousand words." The photo of Cruz's wife, Heidi, was placed next to a glamour photo of Trump's wife, Melania. Trump also tweeted that Cruz should "Look out" as Trump would spill the beans on Cruz's wife. In May 2016, after Cruz's father endorsed his own son as President, Trump alleged that Ted Cruz's father, Rafael Cruz, was with presidential assassin Lee Harvey Oswald shortly before Oswald murdered the president. This claim parroted a National Enquirer story that Rafael Cruz was pictured with Lee Harvey Oswald who was handing out pro-Fidel Castro pamphlets in New Orleans in 1963. During a phone interview with Fox News, Trump said, "His father was with Lee Harvey Oswald prior to Oswald's being — you know, shot. I mean, the whole thing is ridiculous." Trump added, "I mean, what was he doing? What was he doing with Lee Harvey Oswald shortly before the death? Before the shooting?" Trump continued. "It's horrible." Then, after Trump's vicious attacks on him and his family during the campaign, Cruz lowers his self-esteem further by accepting a position of submissiveness as a major supporter for Trump. More recently, in June 2018, after Trump has stated to the world that he can do what he wishes as President including pardoning himself if necessary, Cruz is asked by a journalist, "Do you think President Trump is above the law?" Cruz takes eighteen seconds of 'thoughtful' silence before finally answering the question. His answer is not memorable, but when former NSA Director James Clapper is asked what he thinks of Cruz's reply, he says "Cruz's eighteen second delay is emblematic of the GOP Party silence regarding Trump's words and actions." Not acceptable. *https://www.huffingtonpost.com/entry/ted-cruz-donald-trump-time-100_us_5ad8ba5ce4b029ebe021ed21*

- Senator Marco Rubio? Rubio vacated his Florida Senate seat to run for president and was among the many candidates in the Republican 2016 presidential campaign. He criticized Trump several times: in February 2016, he called Trump a "con artist" and said Trump is "wholly unprepared to be president of the United States"; in June 2016, after Trump became the leading GOP nominee, Rubio said of Trump, we must not hand "the nuclear codes of the United States to an erratic individual." Was this courage and integrity or just campaign muscles? It wasn't courage or integrity. Within a month, after Trump won the Republican Party's nomination, Rubio endorsed him immediately. He had another opportunity to show true grit on October 7 when the Donald Trump *Access Hollywood* controversy grabbed the headlines. Rubio stated that "Donald's comments were vulgar, egregious & impossible to justify. No one should ever talk about any woman in those terms, even in private." But a few days later, party loyalty ruled out and Rubio reaffirmed his support of Trump. On October 25, 2016, it was reported that after Rubio endorsed Trump he was booed off a stage at the annual *Calle Orange* street festival in downtown

Orlando by a crowd of mostly Latino voters. Nevertheless, Rubio was re-elected in November 2016 to the US Senate for Florida. More recently in February 2018 just after a mass shooting occurred at Marjorie Stoneham High School in Parkland, FL, Rubio was given another opportunity to show courage and independency from NRA lobby interests when Cameron Kasky, a Stoneman student, asked Rubio to commit to not taking money from the NRA. Rubio's response was that people buy into his agenda, and he can't help it if people and the NRA support his pro-gun stance.

- Dana Rohrabacher of California? Rohrabacher is a GOP Representative and chairman of the House Foreign Affairs subcommittee on Europe, Eurasia and Emerging Threats. He has persistently taken Russia's side in public debates and backs some of President Donald Trump's controversial comments on Russia. A self-proclaimed "Libertarian conservative," he is a sharp skeptic of the widely held view in Congress, and from US intelligence agencies, that Russia meddled in the US elections -- maintaining that Mueller's probe is a "nonsensical witch-hunt" and the 2016 DNC hack was "an inside job." The inside-job claim has been featured on Russian state-run media to counter the official conclusions by the CIA, FBI and the remaining US intelligence community. He refers to purported Russian mob boss, Alexander Torshin, as the Republican conservatives' favorite Russian." Verdict: Not acceptable. No. Never!

- Others. Rick Perry, Trey Gowdy, Todd Stephens, Chuck Grassley, etc. These are a few of the lesser names in the party who have shown little sign of the character required to stand strong in the face of pressure from the party and influential people. Verdict: None. Never.

- There are several Republican politicians who did rise up and oppose Trump and should be commended for their integrity. The most noticeable is Senator Jeff Flake, R-Arizona, who announced he would not seek re-election in 2018, and has been a sharp critic of Trump and many Republican legislators in the 115th Congress.

There is a lone exception to GOP's current flock of political sheep who lack courage and integrity. Senator John McCain, AZ-R. Senator McCain's dramatic and decisive vote in the Capitol to defeat the GOP's brutal Trump Healthcare Bill was a moment of courage displayed by a man who has served America and his constituents throughout his career as a U.S. Naval officer and a Washington legislator. Senator McCain's deciding vote against Trumpcare on the floor of Congress in 2017 was dramatic, and it recalled a similar act of courage that is recorded in Kennedy's book. On May 16, 1868, Senator James W. Grimes, IA-R, whose was critically ill and near death, displayed personal courage when, after nearing death, he was carried into the voting chamber. There in the face of the mob-like frenzy on the floor of Congress, he cast his vote against the impeachment of President Andrew Johnson who had been pre-convicted on false charges by the Radical Republicans because he would not allow Congress to breach the fine line of power between the three equal branches of government. Senator Edmund Ross, R-Kansas, followed soon thereafter to cast the deciding vote against President Johnson's impeachment.

That period of history was a foreshadowing of the constitutional crisis that we face today, though we have a reverse situation where the Executive branch (Trump) threatens to dominate Congress and the Judiciary branches of government in order to serve his own purpose and pleasure, and thereby corrupt two-hundred and forty-two years of

American democracy. Very few Republicans in Congress (Jeff Flake, Robert Corker, and the late John McCain) spoke out against Trump. But most Republicans, including those mentioned above, deserve only Bronx cheers for their inaction regarding Trump's threat to liberty and justice to all Americans. If this administration worsens, history will record that when the GOP could have made a difference, they were silent.

Abandoning ship. When needed most, away all boats!

A final measure of the new GOP Republican Party impact on its party is to observe the numbers of legislators who are abandoning ship. On average, 22 House members retire each cycle but in 2018, a record number of GOP lawmakers are leaving Capitol Hill. So far, 44 Republicans* have either resigned, retired, been appointed to another position, lost elections or announced gubernatorial bids.

Why?

- They can't win their primary against Trump candidates.
- They don't want to serve under Trump, won't pledge loyalty, and just don't want to be seen with him.
- It is likely that Democrats will win their seat as part of a 2018 Trump backlash
- Made as much money as they could on the job, time to look elsewhere.

Conclusion

In 2018 and forward, the most crucial litmus test for Republicans, incumbent or new office seekers, is to commit personal loyalty to the

President alone and to place his personal policies above their oath of office to protect the Constitution and ensure the welfare of the America people. Republican strategists believe GOP candidates can't win election in 2018 without satisfying both their base and a pro-Trump base, but that same support for Trump will make Republican candidates in many states unacceptable to large swaths of the electorate. There is recent proof in several special elections in 2018 that it is a two-edged sword: when Republicans in different races attempted to avoid either inflaming or embracing Mr. Trump during their campaigns, they were soundly defeated. Pro-Trump candidates even attack Republican rivals for abandoning Trump over his infamous "Access Hollywood" remarks. In the race for Michigan Governor, Michigan's attorney general, Bill Schuette, is assailing his rival for the Republican nomination for governor, Lt. Gov. Brian Calley, because Mr. Calley backed away from Mr. Trump after the "Access Hollywood" tape came out in 2016. The Republican Party is in a quandary, of their own making. I suggest they look back at the example set by one courageous Republican senator who faced a test of character and integrity in 1878, Earning his rightful place in The Profiles of Courage, Senator Lucius Lamar provided this keen observation, "The liberty of this country and its great interests will never be secure if its public men become mere menials to do the bidding of their constituents instead of being representatives in the true sense of the word, looking to the lasting prosperity and future interests of the whole country."

There are as many kinds of courage as there are choices of vocations in life, for parents, soldiers, statesmen, etc. All may face their moment to rise to an occasion. Here in this moment of our nation's great need where are the Republican legislators who will show individual courage?

Chapter Seven
Dark Money

Money often costs too much. --Ralph Waldo Emerson

Quid Pro Quo

A person's viewpoint on money generally depends on how much money they have and how much money they need. You and I have heard the one liners, "Money makes the world go round", "Money is the root of all evil", "Money can't buy love", and "Money doesn't grow on trees". Ayn Rand, the conservative author said, "Money is a tool." Indeed, it is a powerful tool that can be used to enrich lives, destroy lives, enlighten the world, or darken it.

Dark money is an example of money being used badly. It is a tool that corrupts the voting process and is an example because it is used to unduly influence the electoral process in America. Money has always been a major factor in political campaigns as far back as tribal villages and feudal kingdoms. The deluge of money is intended to help it candidate or its cause to win. In many cases, the large amount of dark money is spent on lies and attacks favoring its position. The biggest danger is that dark money is spent and does its work before without anyone but the IRS knowing who donated the money. It could be donated by a saint, a gangster, a 400 pound man in New Jersey, or as possibly happened in 2016, by a foreign government because these nonprofit organizations 501 (c) (4) can receive an unlimited amount of donations and they are not required to disclose their donors.

We all have our own favorite stories or films. Good stories generally have drama, a hero, a villain, conflict, and a denouement that hopefully concludes a welcoming triumph and not a tragic ending. The stories usually contain a carefully sculpted and a carefully positioned scene where money or something else of value is offered by a person with lots of money to the hero or heroine. The storyline can a local business leader to the town sheriff, or a bullying political boss to an honest lawmaker, or an ordinary Everyman (or Everywoman) who faces dilemma and a difficult decision to choose good or bad. This is when a story gets interesting. The gift or a thing of value is presented innocently as a show of support or as a sign of favor from the donor, or maybe simply a display of support for a candidate. Maybe it's an expenditure of time or money or a recommendation of someone to a person in position to choose that person before others. Often the gift is accompanied with a wink or a nod from the donor, a subtle or blatant mannerism which can corrupt both the giving and the receiving of this item of value. You've seen this story; it is too often a common story. Lawyers and people who still use Latin words have a phrase for such a relationship. It is called a "quid pro quo" and it means literally, "something for you, something for me", or figuratively, I pay you, you pay me in like kind, or I do for you, you do for me in due time. More often than not the larger the gift, the greater the debt or homage is possibly owed to, or expected by the donor.

In the film, "The Godfather" Don Corleone has a classic "quid pro quo" response to a vengeful father when the man asks the Godfather how he can ever repay him after the Don promises him 'retaliation' on neighborhood thugs who had earlier brutalized the father's young daughter. "It's OK", Don Corleone replies to the distraught father in his compassionate godfather tone, "Someday I will come to you and ask you to do a favor for me." That moment arrives later in the film just as certain as such moments can arrive in many relationships. The father's indebtedness is repaid to the Godfather with respect and reverence. However, such payback moments are not always as harmless as his repayment was.

This is certainly the long way around for me to say just as campaigns are a necessary part of any election at every level of office, campaign contributions in any form are and have always been a cornerstone of American elections. Money greatly increases the profile in favor of those who can acquire it over those who cannot acquire it. Money can appear in the varied forms other than cash, like whiskey, sex or food, and can increase the likelihood a candidate or a referendum will gain votes. The solicitation for finances and services to support a campaign at any level is necessary and expected in most elections. There is hope that those who agree with you and your cause will support you with something of value that increases your ability to campaign effectively. But hope in the immediate hour of need is not as instantly effective as cash or favors. Hope is like a long-distance runner; it is built for the long run and can move mountains but it might come after the election is over, or when the urgent need has passed. As alluded to earlier, the amount given can largely influence the favor owed when the amount is excessive. What is excessive can be determined by the community or the state in which the election takes place. The United States has addressed this question of reasonable contributions by single individuals and single institutions. Limits were set on annual contributions in campaign laws passed by congressional legislation and are enforced by the Federal Election Commission (FEC). Unfortunately, those limits have been under assault by conservative GOP donors like the Koch brothers and others over the past three decades. Their success in gaining the seats in Congress culminated in the Supreme Court's kingly decree to designate corporations and privately-funded organizations as having the same individual rights as you and I and other single voters. This was realized when the Court issued its 2010 decision on *Citizens United vs. FEC*. The Court ruled in favor of Citizens United, a right-wing conservative organization, in the case, but extended its authority beyond the matter at hand and ruled that corporations and organizations have the same First Amendment rights as a single individual, a reach that benefitted the conservative billionaires who finally received their biggest "quid pro quo."

This ruling on political contributions favored the conservative Republicans who sought the allowance of unlimited contributions from secret sources and threatens democracy's core value where each person's vote is of equal importance to all others, one person-one vote. The resultant ruling in *Citizens United* by the Supreme Court welcomed unlimited money from individuals and private institutions, and money began to flood the political arena. As mentioned earlier, money is an enormously powerful tool, especially when it is used as a weapon against a campaign where donations from individual citizens pale in comparison. The use of this private interest money undercuts America's singular anthem to liberty, one person-one vote. For this reason all political contributions from individuals, businesses, for-profit or nonprofit charities, and all miscellaneous social groups whether for campaign or other reasons must be limited in amount, and all recipients must disclose the source of such funds who contributed to its campaign. This is necessary to prevent third parties from funneling additional money through secondary sources and organizations. This is the 'fault line' that lies beneath the Supreme Court's lame ruling in *Citizens United vs FEC* that is discussed further in Chapter 8.

Apalachin, NY and Indian Wells, California

Fifty years is a long time but somethings don't change. When conspiracies are hatched and secrecy is required, the most remote locations become ideal meeting places. This is a tale of two meetings that were held more than fifty years apart. Both meetings involved large organizations whose goal was to make more money. If their intent was honest, neither group would have met in secret.

The first meeting occurred on November 14, 1957, when local and state law enforcement in upstate NY became suspicious as numerous expensive cars bearing license plates from around the country arrived in "the sleepy hamlet of Apalachin". An occasional expensive top of the line automobile wasn't an unusual appearance in Apalachin. After all, it was no secret to law enforcement personnel that NY mobster Joseph "Joe the Barber" Barbara, a capo regime in the American Mafia, owned a home in Apalachin. However, it was unusual to see so many such cars at one time in this small rural town in mid-November. The license plates signaled that the visitors were from New York, New Jersey, Pennsylvania, Connecticut, Massachusetts, and Illinois and beyond. All of the drivers and their passengers were meeting with Joe the Barber and they parked in his large driveway or wherever they could in between trees on his property. It was a business meeting to discuss various topics including loansharking, narcotics trafficking, and gambling, along with dividing the illegal operations of the late Albert Anastasia, a notorious mob hitman, who did not die of natural causes. He was killed on October 25, 1957, ironically enough in a barber's chair inside a barber shop in the Park Central (Sheraton) Hotel on 56th St. and 7th Avenue in Manhattan, NY.

Witness to Treason

An estimated 100 members of the Mafia from the United States, Italy, and Cuba are estimated to have attended this meeting. Vito Genovese, head of the Genovese family, initially called the meeting as a way to recognize his new power as capo dei capi, translated to mean the boss of all bosses. One of the most direct and significant outcomes of the Apalachin Meeting was that it confirmed the existence of a nationwide criminal conspiracy, a fact that some, including Federal Bureau of Investigation Director J. Edgar Hoover, had long refused to acknowledge. Following the raid more than 60 underworld bosses were detained and indicted for various charges of racketeering.

Criminal minds think alike. In similar fashion during the last weekend in January 2009, fifty-two years later to be exact, a high-level secret meeting occurred in Indian Wells, a desert town on the outskirts of Palm Springs, CA. The meeting was held at an exclusive hotel complex, The Renaissance Esmeralda Resort and Spa. The attendance was controlled by invitation only. It included some of America's richest and most ardent conservative and libertarian political donors, men who were stingy with their billions and who were never satisfied with what they had - and only parted with any of it when they were certain it would deliver more riches to them. Many of these attendees represented the nation's most powerful business and media interests: oil, gas, and coal, retail, communications, banking, and such. There was little if any appearance of law enforcement personnel and highway roadblocks in Indian Wells. If a police presence was requested at all, it would have been in the form of courtesy escorts. The guests of honor at this gathering were billionaires and captains of industry, mostly fortunate sons and daughters of fathers who had made the family fortunes decades before their children had been born. The meeting was hosted by Charles and David Koch, extreme libertarians, long-term political activists, and billionaires. The task at hand was to lay out a plan to stop the newly-elected President Barack Obama and the Democratic Party from advancing an agenda that was enthusiastically voted for just a few months earlier on Election Day, November 2008. These right-wing conservative Republicans had spent hundreds of millions of dollars to win the 2008 presidential election but they were soundly defeated. They needed a new battle plan and this was their dual-kickoff rally for strategy and increased funding. The strategy proposed was multi-prong but most notably different, it was to be united under the Koch's political organization that would be the central command post for all donations made to promote the common cause. The Koch organization would receive donations and distribute the money to foundations and "charities" that support favored GOP causes and the politicians who in turn promised their votes for matters that would benefit the donors. In other words, the strategy was to make America great for them by making laws to benefit the rich, and repealing laws and regulations that hinder them from getting richer. Sometimes it will not involve a legislator's vote, often their legislators or judges will only have to ignore the law or to refuse to enforce it.

Only one of these organizations got caught. The Cosa Nostra didn't have as much money as they needed to protect themselves from law enforcement, and not nearly enough friends in judicial positions to adjudicate for them. Koch and friends had more than enough money and a lot of friends in high places everywhere, or so the rumors went. The Koch gathering in Indian Wells included a top ten list of a billionaires' Who's Who. The meeting included members of America's richest people: Richard Mellon Scaife, John Olin, Harry Bradley, and the Coors, Mercer, and DeVos families. There were a number of large pledges made that weekend and they raised more money than even they could've imagined. So they spent the money all over the United

States as soon as the Supreme Court ruled in favor of Citizens United. Dark money flooded the political landscape after 2010 and in 2017 the rich got richer.

According to the Center for Responsive Politics, "spending by organizations that do not disclose their donors (dark money) has increased from less than $5.2 million in 2006 to well over $300 million in the 2012 presidential cycle and more than $174 million in the 2014 midterms." The *New York Times* editorial board has opined that the 2014 midterm elections were influenced by "the greatest wave of secret, special-interest money ever raised in a congressional election." The amount of dark money spent in the 2016 presidential election cycle is estimated to be more than one billion dollars.

Both parties receive dark money but the GOP Republican Party receives dark money at an 8 to 1 ratio greater than the Democratic Party. Riding the tsunami of money unleashed in the wake of the Citizens United ruling, it is reported that the conservative and libertarian funded Koch Organization unleashed a panzer-like blitzkrieg of campaign attacks on Hillary Clinton and every Democratic candidate that ran for office in 2016. The Koch Organization's objective is to gather America's riches and bounties for themselves; to install a conservative government that spends less on its citizens' health and prosperity; levies the lowest taxes on the wealthy; imposes no restrictions and regulations on their businesses and banks; and secures law and order for their welfare; funding a powerful and loyal subservient military to impose their interests abroad. *Source: https://en.wikipedia.org/wiki/Dark_money#Comparison_to super PACs*

What is Dark Money?

Dark money is a term for a large amount of undisclosed cash (millions) donated by an undisclosed person or organization that is given for the sole purpose of supporting a specific candidate and/or political party (republican, democratic, and such) in a political campaign or political cause. In these classic 'quid pro quo' transactions, the donors wish to remain unknown to the public because their large donations are given in expectation of receiving something of benefit only for themselves.

The term 'dark money' first entered politics with in ruling regarding *Buckley v. Valeo* (1976) when the United States Supreme Court laid out Eight Magic Words that define the difference between electioneering and issue advocacy. The Court limited the reach of campaign finance laws to candidate and party committees, and other committees with a major purpose of electing candidates, or to speech that "expressly advocated" election or defeat of candidates. In footnote 52 of that opinion, the Court listed eight words or phrases as illustrative of speech that qualified as "express advocacy". The eight words and phrases appearing in Buckley were "vote for," "elect," "support", "cast your ballot for", "Smith for Congress", "vote against", "defeat", "reject", or any variations thereof. Under the *Buckley* ruling, speakers that did not invoke any of the eight specific words and phrases of *Buckley*, or similar language expressly calling voters to vote for or against a candidate, were exempt from campaign finance laws. Those eight words were intended to provide examples of the types of things that would lead a reasonable person to conclude the speaker was advocating a particular candidate or ballot measure. The Court felt that limiting campaign finance laws to speech with such express advocacy was necessary to avoid a "chilling effect" on speech about political officeholders and issues that were protected under the First

Amendment to the Constitution. As an example of what would be exempt from campaign laws might be something like the following sentences that do not express a clear request to vote or support the referenced individual. Suppose someone placed an advertisement that went something like this:

Katherine Thornberry is a woman who understands the need for community healthcare. Alice Clark completed her internship at Jefferson University Hospital and has worked in the community for twenty years. Alice also volunteers at the community library on the weekend.

Although the ad might influence potential voters for or against one of the candidates, it does not specifically advocate action to elect a candidate for office. As such, it falls outside of laws that restrict political speech intended to influence elections. This type of ad became known colloquially as "issue ads".

The Internal Revenue Service (IRS) Section 501(c) provides detailed definitions and guidelines regarding the tax exemption status, and the reporting requirements of giving and/or receiving political donations. Thus, the 501 (c) classification is the determinant for tracking where the money comes from, how it is taxed, and how it is used. The various 501 designations assigned by the IRS include 501(c) (3) charitable political, 501(c) (4) (social welfare), 501(c) (5) (unions,) and 501(c) (6), (trade association) groups.

Today, most political fund raising and expenditures are handled by political action committees (PACs). PACs are organized for the purpose of raising and spending money to elect and defeat candidates. Most PACs represent business, labor or ideological interests and they can give $5,000 to a candidate committee per election (primary, general or special). Super PACs, officially known as "independent-expenditure only committees", may not make contributions to candidate campaigns or parties, but may engage in unlimited political spending independently of the campaigns. These larger Super PAC organizations are designated by the IRS as 501(c) (3) organizations and can receive unlimited contributions from individuals, corporations, and unions. They can be registered as a nonprofit organization if its primary activities are charitable, religious, educational, scientific, literary, and so on. However, money contributed to Super PACs registered as nonprofit, charitable, or social organizations (501(c) (3) must disclose their donors. But a new class of organizations 501(c) (4) that perform benefits for the social welfare are prohibited from political activity, but they are not required to disclose their donors publicly regardless of how much money they receive. This lack of disclosure has led many political-purposed organizations to lie and register as 501(c) (4) organizations. They lie and are actively involved in political lobbying and campaigns. That is why the 501(c) (4) designation has become controversial. The spending from these organizations on political TV ads has exceeded spending from Super PAC. The increase of dark money, primarily donated from 501(c) (4), and used in political spending in political campaigns, has increased from less than $5.2 million in 2006 to well over $300 million in the 2012 election. It is directly caused by the 501(c) (4) organizations that do not have to publicly disclose their donors. An example would be money from Russian given to the NRA and donated to the Trump campaign does not have to be disclosed to anyone, except it does have to be shown on their tax return filing. This is the primary reason it is referred to as dark money. These 501(c) (4) dark money groups are distinct from (501(c) (3) Super PACs. While both types of entity can raise and spend unlimited sums of money, Super PACs "must disclose their donors" whereas 501(c) (4) groups "must not have politics as their primary purpose but don't have to disclose who gives them money."

However, a single individual or group can create both types of funds and combine their funds, making it difficult to trace the original source of funds. ProPublica explains: "Say some like-minded people from both a (501(c) (3) Super-PAC and a nonprofit 501(c) (4) want to pool their money. Corporations and individuals could then donate as much as they want to the nonprofit 501(c) (4) (a dark money fund), which isn't required to publicly disclose funders. The nonprofit could then turn-around and donate as much as it wanted to its own Super-PAC, which lists the nonprofit's donation but not the original contributor name." During the 2016 election cycle, "dark money" contributions via shell LLCs became increasingly common. The Associated Press, Center for Public Integrity, and Sunlight Foundation all "flagged dozens of donations of anywhere from $50,000 to $1 million routed through non-disclosing LLCs to super PACs" backing various presidential candidates." According to the Sunlight Foundation, "untraceable dark money" is a preferred tactic of right-wing conservatives, while Democrats tend to use traceable super PACs." "Charitable" is broadly defined as being established for purposes that are religious, educational, charitable, scientific, literary, testing for public safety, fostering of national or international amateur sports, or prevention of cruelty to animals and children.

What Makes Dark Money "Dark"?

As noted above, a nonprofit 501(c) 4 can donate as much as it wants and does not have to donate its source of funds because it has formally registered as "a social group who confirmed that politics is not their primary purpose." In at least one high-profile case, a donor to a super

PAC kept his name hidden by using an LLC formed for the purpose of hiding their personal name. One super PAC, that originally listed a $250,000 donation from an LLC that no one could find, led to a subsequent filing where the previously "secret donors" were revealed.

In the 2012 presidential election cycle, more than $308 million in dark money was spent, according to the Center for Responsive Politics.[11] An estimated 86 percent was spent by conservative groups, 11 percent by liberal groups and 3 percent by other groups. The three dark money groups which spent the largest sums in 2012 were Karl Rove's American Crossroads/Crossroads GPS ($71 million), the Koch brothers' Americans for Prosperity ($36 million) and the U.S. Chamber of Commerce ($35 million), all conservative groups. The three liberal groups with the largest dark-money expenditures were the League of Conservation Voters ($11 million), Patriot Majority USA, a group focusing on public schools and infrastructure ($7 million), and Planned Parenthood (almost $7 million).

The 2014 election cycle saw the largest amount of dark money ever spent in a congressional election; the New York Times editorial board described 2014 "the greatest wave of secret, special-interest money ever."[5] On the eve of the election, Republican-leaning dark money groups dominated, with $94.6 million in expenditures, exceeding dark money expenditures by Democratic-leaning dark money groups by $66 million, and received expenditures of $1.9 million that could not be classified.[13] Karl Rove's dark money group *Crossroads GPS* alone spent over $47 million in the 2014 election cycle. In the Senate elections, dark money spending was highly concentrated in a handful of targeted competitive states, especially in Alaska, Arkansas, Colorado, Kentucky, and North Carolina. In the eleven most competitive Senate races, $342 million was spent by non-party outside groups, significantly more than the $89 million spent by the political parties. In Kentucky, the "Kentucky Opportunity Coalition," supported Republican Senator Mitch McConnell, whom the New York Times editorial board has described as "the most prominent advocate for unlimited secret campaign spending in Washington." The Kentucky Opportunity Coalition, a 501(c) (4) "social welfare" group, raised more than $21 million and was linked to Karl Rove's Crossroads groups. Described as "mysterious," the group was listed only by a Post Office box. A citizen watchdog organization Citizens for Responsibility and Ethics in Washington said that the Kentucky Opportunity Coalition was "nothing more than a sham."

Altogether, in ten competitive 2014 Senate seats, the winners had $127 million in dark-money support, according to an analysis by the Brennan Center for Justice at New York University School of Law:

Winning Candidate	Dark Money in Support	Dark Money as % of Outside Spending
Thom Tillis (R-NC)	$22,888,975	81%
Cory Gardner (R-CO)	$22,529,291	89%
Joni Ernst (R-IA)	$17,552,085	74%
Mitch McConnell (R-KY)	$13,920,163	63%
Tom Cotton (R-AR)	$12,502,284	65%
David Perdue (R-GA)	$11,098,585	86%
Dan Sullivan (R-AK)	$10,823,196	85%
Pat Roberts (R-KS)	$8,454,938	78%
Gary Peters (D-MI)	$4,226,674	28%
Jeanne Shaheen (D-NH)	$3,478,039	35%
Total Dark Money	$127,475,231	71% Outside $

In North Carolina, the pro-Tillis group "Carolina Rising" received nearly all (98.7%) of its funds from Crossroads GPS; a 501(c) (4) group that "evades limits on political activity through grants" to other 501(c) (4) groups. In the 2014 cycle, Crossroads GPS also gave $5.25 million to the U.S. Chamber of Commerce, $2 million to the American Future Fund, and $390,000 to the Kentucky Opportunity Coalition. In total, Crossroads GPS spent more than $13.6 million on grants to other groups, which it described as being for the purposes of "social welfare." The large amounts of money were moved in interconnected circles reminding me of the old sidewalk "shell game" where you were challenged to find the small object stuffed under a half shell that was swiftly shuffled back and forth across the table. This was the same game. You always lose.

During the 2016 election cycle, "dark money" contributions via shell (there's that word again) LLCs became increasingly common. The Associated Press, Center for Public Integrity, and Sunlight Foundation all "flagged dozens of donations of anywhere from $50,000 to $1 million routed through non-disclosing LLCs to super PACs" backing various presidential candidates, including Marco Rubio, Hillary Clinton, Ted Cruz, John Kasich, Jeb Bush, and Carly Fiorina. According to the Sunlight Foundation, "untraceable dark money is a preferred tactic of conservatives, while Democrats tend to use traceable super PACs."

The sources behind most of the money raised by politicians and political groups are publicly disclosed. Candidates, parties and political action committees — including the super PACs that are allowed to accept unlimited amounts of money — all report the names of their donors to the Federal Election Commission on a regular basis. Or, to be technical, they regularly disclose the names of all their donors who each give more than $200. But when the source of political money isn't known, that's *dark money*. The two most common vehicles for dark money in politics are politically active nonprofits and corporate entities such as limited liability companies. Certain politically active nonprofits — notably those formed under sections 501(c) (4) and 501(c) (6) of the tax code — are generally not required to publicly disclose their donors. So, when limited liability companies are formed in certain states, such as Delaware and Wyoming, they are essentially black boxes: the company's name is basically the only thing known about them. These LLCs can be used to make political expenditures themselves or to donate to super PACs. During the 2012 election cycle — the last time the presidency was at stake — dark money groups pumped about $300 million into political messages that called for the election or defeat of federal candidates, according to the nonpartisan Center for Responsive Politics. Additionally, dark money groups spent hundreds of millions of dollars on political advertisements that focused more on issues than candidates. The most notable example is Americans for Prosperity, the flagship nonprofit of the conservative billionaire brothers Charles and David Koch. Also worth noting: dark money doesn't affect every election. It frequently targets the most high-profile political state and federal races, the election that if won, will benefit the very rich.

Do Democrats use dark money? Yes. Neither party wants to be left behind in the political money arms race. The result: dark money groups are multiplying — and thriving — on both ends of the political spectrum. However, according to the Center for Responsive Politics, conservative dark money groups that reported expenditures to the FEC during the 2012 election cycle outspent liberal ones by about 8-to-1. In 2016, Democrats had their dark money allies as well, but they spent far less than their Republican counterparts, accounting for just 17 percent of reported spending by these groups.

Dark Money vs PACs and Super PACs,

Political action committees are groups that collectively seek common goals by supporting political party candidates for public office. In the United States, we have a two-party system, with the right and left catching almost every piece of the ideological spectrum. Donations to and spending by political parties is highly regulated by the Federal Election Commission (FEC).

How is a PAC different from a super PAC? A PAC is a political action committee that basically collects campaign contributions to donate to campaigns for or against a particular candidate or issue. An organization becomes a PAC when it receives/spends more than $2,600 on influencing a federal election. Federal PACs can donate specified amounts to candidates, political parties and other PACs, and can donate unlimited amounts independent of a candidate or political party. PACs can be single issue or oriented towards an ideology or group of voters (e.g. minorities, women).

Super PACs are committees that can raise funds from individuals, corporations, unions, and other groups without any legal limit on donation size, but they cannot donate directly to candidates or political parties. They can, however, spend an unlimited amount independent of those two entities. There is also no limit on how much money an individual or group can donate to a Super PAC, unlike a regular PAC. Super PACs were made possible by two judicial decisions: the aforementioned Citizens United v. Federal Election Commission in October 2010 and, two months later, Speechnow.org v. FEC when the Supreme Court shutdown limits on campaign contributions from corporations.   *source: https://en.wikipedia.org/wiki/Dark_money*

The DISCLOSE Act and the US Congress

Democrats in the United States Congress have repeatedly introduced the DISCLOSE Act. This is legislation to require disclosure of election spending by "corporations, labor unions, super-PACs, and, most importantly, politically active nonprofits."[44] The DISCLOSE Act would require covered groups, including 501(c) (4), to reveal the source of election-spending donations of $10,000 or more. The bill also targets the use of pass-through and shell corporations to evade disclosure by requiring that such groups disclose the origin of contributions. Senate Republicans, led by Mitch McConnell, "have blocked earlier iterations of the DISCLOSE Act since 2010." According to Columbia Law School's Richard Briffault, disclosure of campaign expenditures, contributions, and donors is intended to deter corruption.   *Source;* *https://en.wikipedia.org/wiki/DISCLOSE_Act*

The Federal Elections Commission, which regulates federal elections, has been unable to control dark money. According to the Center for Public Integrity, FEC commissioners are voting on many fewer enforcement matters than in the past because of "an overtaxed staff and commissioner disagreement." This is likely a result of Trump's appointment of GOP persons to leadership positions in the Commission. The IRS (rather than the FEC) is responsible for oversight of 501(c) (4) groups. The IRS "found itself ill-prepared for the groundswell" of such groups taking and spending unlimited amounts of money for political purposes in the wake of the U.S. Supreme Court's decision in *Citizens United v. Federal Election Commission* in 2010. The agency particularly "struggled to identify which organizations appeared to be spending more than the recommended 50 percent of their annual budgets on political activities—and even to define what 'political spending' was." When the IRS began looking at nonprofit spending, GOP donors accused the IRS of improper targeting.

In August 2011, immediately after the Supreme Court ruling for *Citizens United*, nine academics from universities across the U.S. petitioned the Securities and Exchange Commission (SEC) "to develop rules to require public companies to disclose to shareholders the use of corporate resources for political activities." The petition received over a million comments in the following month, "a record amount for the SEC, with the overwhelming majority of voters asking for better disclosure." According to a Harvard professor of law, economics, and finance who helped draft the petition, the request had drawn the support of "nearly a dozen senators and more than 40 members of the House." Under current SEC regulations, public corporations must file a Form 8-K report to publicly announce major events of interest to shareholders. The Sunlight Foundation has proposed that the 8-K rule should be updated to require that aggregate spending of $10,000 on political activities (such as monetary contributions, in-kind contributions, and membership dues or other payments to organizations that engage in political activities) should be disclosed and made publicly available via the 8-K system.[46]

In 2015, Republicans in Congress successfully added a rider in a 2015 omnibus spending bill that bars the IRS from clarifying the social-welfare tax exemption to combat dark money from advocacy groups that claim to be social welfare organizations but that are actually political committees. Other provisions in the 2015 bill bar the SEC from requiring corporations to disclose campaign spending to shareholders, and a ban application of the gift tax to nonprofit donors. All these efforts by the GOP ensures that the dark-money provision allows "the door to secret foreign dollars in U.S. elections to remain wide open through secret contributions to these ostensibly 'nonpolitical' groups that run campaign ads without disclosing their donors."

Wisconsin, Pennsylvania, Ohio. Michigan, and North Carolina

Do any of the states listed above sound and look familiar? They should. They were the death knell for Hillary Clinton and the Democratic Party around midnight Eastern Standard Time on November 8, 2018. They were the final state electoral votes announced for Donald Trump that sent him over the targeted number to win the Presidency. It was a cold blast of impossibility hitting us in the face. These four northern states and one border state sped America at Mach speed into a position as a third-world political state. How did it happen? No, Spike Lee, it wasn't the shoes! It was money that sunk America, *dark money* discussed in this chapter; money donated in the shadows from within and from outside America; money unleashed and spent in states across the nation, especially in Wisconsin, Pennsylvania, Ohio, Michigan, and North Carolina.

The following table on page 178, "2016 Outside Spending, by Group" is taken from Open Secrets website. The column labeled Outside Money indicates money donated via 501c accounts by some unspecified person or group located outside the state, a person or business that does not reside in that state. This is how lots of money buys elections and undermines our colonial founding fathers' one-person, one-vote concept of democracy. Some Congressional races are seeing more dark money being spent by super PACs and outside groups than by the candidate themselves.

2016 Senate Election, Top Ten States with Largest Outsider Spending

Rank	Race	Total	Candidate	Outside
1.	Pennsylvania Senate	$179,531,628	$47,163,884	$132,367,744
2.	New Hampshire Senate	$141,392,457	$38,049,238	$103,343,219
3.	Nevada Senate	$126,994,871	$30,350,691	$96,644,180
4.	North Carolina Senate	$97,299,067	$24,113,463	$73,185,604
5.	Florida Senate	$90,780,270	$41,112,578	$49,667,692
6.	Ohio Senate	$90,356,396	$37,073,656	$53,282,740
7.	Missouri Senate	$79,909,903	$28,982,689	$50,927,214
8.	Wisconsin Senate	$76,310,148	$44,946,682	$31,363,466
9.	Indiana Senate	$76,191,263	$25,020,652	$51,170,611
10.	Illinois Senate	$34,631,376	$28,688,676	$5,942,700

*https://www.opensecrets.org/outsidespending/summ.php?cycle=2016&chrt=V&disp=O &type=U , Based on data released by the FEC on 05/18/17, **2016 Outside Spending, by Organized Groups,***

Conservative groups registered as 501(c) nonprofits account for $144 million. Liberal groups registered as 501c nonprofits account for $17 million. The groups use funds from undisclosed donors on independent expenditures and electioneering communications.

Here below are the top twenty major nonprofit contributors who funneled $161 million 'dark money' in 2016.

⭕ = No disclosure of donors,	C = Conservative, L = Liberal,	X = type

Group	Total	View	Super	527s,	501c
National Rifle Assn⭕	$35,157,585	C			X
US Chamber of Commerce⭕	$29,106,034	C			X
45 Cmte⭕	$22,010,337	C			X
Americans for Prosperity⭕	$13,309,199	C			X
American Future Fund⭕	$12,735,724	C			X
Majority Forward⭕	$10,116,977	C			X
Environmental Defense ⭕	$4,285,793	L			X
League Conservation Voter⭕	$4,162,118	L			X
Club for Growth⭕	$4,061,719	C			X
One Nation⭕	$3,405,810	C			X
Ending Spending⭕	$2,636,359	C			X
Fair Share Action⭕	$2,541,465	L	xSuper		_
Planned Parenthood⭕	$2,237,207	L			X
American Chemistry Council⭕	$1,806,663	C			X
Citizens for Respon Energy ⭕	$1,443,122	C		X	
National Assn of Realtors⭕	$1,373,941	X			X
NARAL Pro-Choice America⭕	$1,325,556	L			X
Libre Initiative⭕	$1,227,098	C			X
VoteVets.org⭕	$1,195,208	L			X

Koch Organization

Among the top twenty donors listed as 501c organizations in 2016 was Americans for Prosperity who is on record as having donated

$13,309,199 to the Republican Party in the 2016 general election. Americans for Prosperity is a nonprofit right-wing conservative institution that is fully-funded by Charles and David Koch, Kansas City businessmen who inherited a major energy and manufacturing company from their father Fred Koch. Among the largest private companies in America, the Kochs have since spent hundreds of millions of dollars to flood legislative chambers across America's mid-west and southwest with Pavlov-trained legislators who espouse a Koch brand of arch-conservative dribble that champions states' rights, lower taxes on the wealthy, little to no government regulation over industry and banking, and increasing expenditures for military institutions.

The brothers maintain a "permanent campaign", the Koch Organization that manages control over countless municipalities, cities, and states by finding, funding, and controlling a myriad army of legislators in the Midwest but now throughout the U.S. In their wisdom, all of these programs which benefit them and their fellow billionaires, they will invest their money into gaining control of America's judges and legislators for now, but be reimbursed quickly once they have the power in Washington to reduce the legacy services for the average American citizen (Social Security, pensions, Medicare, income tax deductions), reduce their own personal taxes while increasing the individual taxes, and increase the cost of goods and services bought by those same citizens. In January 2018, they recouped almost all of the $900 million dollars they spent for the election.

The Koch Organization is carefully and minutely exposed in Jane Mayer's national bestseller *Dark Money. The Hidden History of the Billionaires behind the Rise of the Radical Right*, published in 2016. The deeply researched book broadcasts to the general public the silent, secret war of espionage that has been carried on by rich right-wing men and women (much fewer women are included in the leadership, as would be expected in view of the radical right's position on women as that of subjugation of women and domination by men. Chapter Five opened with these leaders meeting near Palm Springs in 2009 to join forces with corporate icons to strategize and bankroll the new GOP Republican party. In 2016, the Washington Post reported in January 2015 that the Koch-backed network (400 or so wealthy sponsors, aka "Kochtopus") was prepared to spend nearly a billion dollars on the general elections. In fact, the Kochs have mastered a prolonged influence-buying approach over the past 40 years. In preparation for the 2016 presidential election, the Koch's private network of political groups had a bigger payroll than the Republican National Republican Committee. *Dark Money, xvii*

Koch's beginnings

The Koch brothers' father, Fred Chase Koch, developed business interests with Adolph Hitler and Joseph Stalin in the 1930s. In 1927, Koch and co-workers invented an improved process for extracting gasoline from crude oil (p.33) but after trying to market the new technology himself, he was sued circa 1929 for patent infringement by several American oil companies. Koch went to Europe with his refining methods and contracted with foreign governments to build refineries in England and Russia, helping to establish fifteen oil refineries in Russia during the general global depression. When Hitler became the German Chancellor in 1933, Koch assisted Germany with completing a massive refinery in 1935, knowing as everyone did that the new oil was needed for Hitler's military machine and his plan for conquest, specifically as a source for high-octane gasoline for Nazi fighter planes. *Dark Money, pg. 36.* Fred Koch said in a letter to a friend in 1938, "although nobody agrees with me, I think I am of the opinion that the only sound countries are Germany, Italy, and Japan, simply because they are all working and working hard."(Does this sound familiar, ref. Trump on Putin, Korea, China?) The Second World War interrupted Koch's prosperous arrangement with Hitler and Stalin. Strangely, in the post WWII era, Fred Koch would slide to the authoritarian right when he was one of the original founders in 1958 of the arch-conservative right wing group, the John Birch Society that was known for its wild conspiracy theories about communist plots to take over America. During this time Fred Koch expressed enthusiasm for a strong state and federal position for racial segregation and an abolition of income taxes.

Charles Koch, Like Father, Like Son

Charles Koch interests were not exactly like his father but there are more similarities than dissimilarities. The largest similarity is Charles' interests in politics and the use of his money to purchase political influence to benefit the family fortune. In this regard, Charles funded his first nonprofit group, the Freedom School, founded in 1957 by Robert Lefevre. *Dark Money pg 53*. By 1966, Charles Koch became the Freedom School's major financial supporter, and an executive and trustee. The school taught a revisionist version of American history wherein the early nineteenth century American industrialists were not robber barons but heroes; taxes were considered a form of government theft; and the Progressive Movement, the New Deal, Lyndon Johnson's War on Poverty were ruinous turns to socialism. Those Americans who were weak and poor were to be aided by charity, not by the government. Those who attended the school believed that the South should have been allowed to secede; that the Civil War should never have been fought, an idea most certainly offered in hindsight since the

South did not end up winning the war that the slave owners and the segregationists all crowed for in 1860. This initial entry into funding political activist education became a life-long obsession for Charles and his brother, David, was dragged along.

Charles continues his life-long, single-minded, tax-deductible sponsorship for libertarianism into this present-day battle between a faulty libertarianism and Jefferson and Madison's American democracy. Koch's Freedom School was followed by many more patriotic-sounding institutions founded as nonprofit centers for social order, social justice, social fiscal responsibility, even social law enforcement, and social criminal sentencing. Shamefully, all of the following institutions were created with American sounding titles but are groups hidden under misleading titles in order to deceive their real purposes which is to sabotage exciting sensible reforms and replace them with conservative and libertarian ideologies: the Cato Institute, Heritage Foundation, Alliance for Justice, Americans for Prosperity, Americans for Tax Reform, American Enterprise Institute, Center for Strategic and International Studies, Center for Public Integrity, Center to Protect Patients' Rights, Common Cause, Federalist Society, Freedom Partners, National Association of Criminal Defense Lawyers, North Carolina History Project.

Koch's Political Protégés

The Koch brothers' money has made many political friends for themselves. Truly, the money hasn't made them political friends as it has created them. Most of the legislators in their fold have been recruited from local colleges and businesses, men and women who were measured for their likelihood of being easily trained and persuaded to adopt the Koch Organization's conservative/libertarian

214

philosophy and create a small government beholden only to the wealthy who will decide who gets an opportunity to earn money and prosper. Among the Koch brothers' hand-picked protégés were former PA Senator Rick Santorum, House Speaker Paul Ryan, Vice President Mike Pence, and former Kansas congressman, and current Secretary of State Mike Pompeo who was the recipient of the largest donations from Koch so often that he was referred to as the congressman from Koch. Although Donald Trump was never on Koch's list, Koch's influence filled Trump's 2017 pre-inauguration transition team with several Koch political favorites and members of the Koch billionaires club: Wisconsin building supply billionaire, Diane Hendricks and Las Vegas Sands casino owner Sheldon Adelson.

Koch Inroads into Universities, Feigning Support on Minority Issues

The Koch Organization took thirty years to realize that all the money in the world can't buy you victory at anything when you consistently develop poor strategy, have slower runners, smaller athletes, restrict an exchange of ideas, and rely solely on graduates who never exceed B-average grades through graduation. In 1980, William Simon, who was a millionaire many times over and a former energy czar and Treasury Secretary under Presidents Nixon and Ford, was recruited to head a new conservative think tank, the John Olin Foundation. The impetus for the formation of the Olin Foundation was the several years of lawsuits and fines from President Nixon's newly organized Environmental Protection Agency (EPA) that led to the Olin Company being indicted in several states for polluting the land and rivers on which their chemical plants were built. In one tiny community in Appalachia, Saltville, VA, the company had been spilling one hundred pounds of mercury per day between 1951 and 1970. Prior to 1970, there had been no local, state, or federal restriction on such contamination. Only common senses was expected to be the safeguard. After a legal battle between the EPA and Olin, the cost of cleaning up Saltville was estimated to be $35 million, and the plant was shut down, and the cleanup was never done.

John Olin's reaction was typically brazen and revengeful, not repentant. He used his abundance of polluted money to establish his Foundation to educate students to become advocates for his conservative obsession with an unlimited free market, devoid of regulations. His goal was to develop members of an elite "conservative counter-intelligence" operation that would insert persons favorable to business into positions of political leadership in local, state, and federal offices. After William Simon's direction, the funding was increased to recruit the needed "counter intelligentsia". Soon, Simon and his team concluded that they needed to penetrate America's best universities and capture inside the classroom and campus students who had the highest quality minds and incentives. The strategy to infiltrate these universities was code-named "beachhead theory", and would establish conservative cells, or "beachheads." It was agreed that the elements for success in Ivy League schools and other highly regarded universities would "include subtlety, indirection, and perhaps even some misdirection." The program became successful and it is active. Many Ivy League schools now have received multi-million dollar grants to finance specific conservative curricula. The grants sometimes fund chairs in these universities to be held for conservative professors dedicated to advocating far right conservative policies and initiatives that promote elitism and threaten American democracy. An example of this type of deceit that ropes in Ivy League schools is shown below when the University of Pennsylvania in Philadelphia warmly accepted a grant in excess of $2 million dollar for the study of criminal justice system. The study sounds reasonable but Koch's interest is to interject

216

only their conservative viewpoint and support for strict sentencing and specific sentencing benefitting a conservative cause; not to teach, learn, or share an open discussion and a free exchange of thoughts and ideas.
Source: Jane Mayer's Dark Money Pg125- 26, 145, 461

Likewise, Koch has opted for a public-relations opportunity by enlisting former Dallas Cowboy pro football player, Deion Sanders to join Kochs in a sizable aid venture to help fight poverty in Texas. The partnership will raise $21 million over 3 years and fund anti-poverty in Dallas*. Sanders says, "Charles Koch trying to make the world a better place." It would be prudent for the community and its leaders in Dallas and elsewhere to remember the conservative pledge to infiltrate and lull others to sleep with "subtlety, indirection, and perhaps even some misdirection." The Koch Foundation and the conservatives will donate money to win favor and votes for its own interests but once elected, they will not support programs that benefit the most vulnerable: Medicare, Medicaid, Social Security, etc. Political offices won by conservatives will use their votes to pass only programs that benefit conservatives, any other program will be removed. *AP article from Colorado Springs.*

Dark Money and Campus Politics

Conservative dark money is now a big man on American college and university campuses. Increasing amounts of private money is arriving more steadily to fund conservative clubs for recruiting and underwriting the introduction of far-right conservative ideas and policy into the school's curriculums. In a March 2017 online article by Pam Vogel, Media Matters, the author provided detailed information on the conservative right-wing dark money groups who are targeting college campuses who have long served as unique places for the free exchange of ideas. But the Conservative group's purpose is not to promote an exchange of ideas; it is to establish "beachheads"* on campuses, or landing sites, where they can create pleasant intellectual playgrounds that espouse right-wing conservative and liberationist diatribe. An abundance of funding is provided by ideologically driven, right-wing billionaires through their conservative strategists. Media Matters has mapped out some of the biggest actors behind the conservative campus activism, creating an echo chamber of seemingly grass-roots right-wing student media and campus groups that are actually propped up by a handful of the same conservative funders and, sometimes, even prominent hate groups. An example of inroads to establish "beachheads" on campuses nationwide is a Philadelphia Inquirer article regarding the Koch Foundation's grant given to the University of Penn in March, 2017. The grant is to fund the study of individual rights of those involved in the criminal justice system. Sounds noble? The actual purpose of funding this study is at least two-fold, get on campus and get credibility and access to intelligentsia, and to influence the study results. The Koch Organization is not interested in improving criminal institutions except for streamlining sentences, restricting appeal processes, and most importantly, privatizing prisons and reform institutions to allow their friends who are waiting in the wings to profit from private control of prisons and to be subsidized whenever they have begun to lose profit. There is an old adage suitable for offering here to Penn and to other credible universities, "Beware of Greeks bearing gifts".

https://www.mediamatters.org/research/2017/03/29/conservative-dark-money-groups-infiltrating-campus-politics/215822 ,

Charles Koch Foundation gives $2.2m to Penn Law School
source: *http://www.philly.com/philly/business/law/koch-foundation-gift-to-penn-law.html*

The foundation of libertarian Charles Koch has given a grant of up to $2.2 million to the University of Pennsylvania law school for research on ways to improve fairness in the criminal justice system. The funding, from the Charles Koch Foundation, will go to the Quattrone Center for the Fair Administration of Justice at the law school. The center focuses on whether the rights of disadvantaged populations are adequately protected when they interact with the criminal justice system. One study last year of hundreds of thousands of criminal cases in Philadelphia and the Houston area found criminal defendants who couldn't make cash bail were more likely to plead guilty and become trapped in a cycle of criminal conduct. The billionaire brothers Charles and David Koch made a fortune in petrochemicals and manufacturing with their Wichita, Kan.-based Koch Industries. Democrats have criticized their extensive political giving, claiming it distorts the legislative process. The gift to Penn law school is but one of several that the foundation has announced in recent months, including a $3.25 million grant to Villanova University Charles Widger School of Law last October. Source: march 8, 2017 by chris mondics, staff writer email@cmondics ,*

Penn said the Koch foundation gift would further its work in finding ways to improve fairness in the criminal justice system. "With the generous support of the Charles Koch Foundation, the Quattrone Center will expand on its groundbreaking, cross disciplinary work advancing the study of criminal justice," said Penn Law dean Ted Ruger. "These efforts will help victims of injustice caught within the criminal justice system." Koch wants to have a voice in reform but to see that justice is done. It is more like insider espionage.

Witness to Treason

This book's author sent the following letter to the President of the University of Penn, to the university's student newspaper, The Daily Pennsylvanian, and to the Philadelphia Inquirer in response to the above news release printed in the Philadelphia Inquirer newspaper on March 8, 2017.

Note: Author's letter to the Editor in response to above news article

Dear Editor

The University of Pennsylvania's acceptance of any donation from Charles Koch is alarmingly bad news. Koch's wealth funds foundations, politicians, and pseudo-intellectuals who encourage extremist libertarian actions to undermine the American system of justice. They seek to cripple and remove justice from America's courtrooms. Jane Mayer's book 'Dark Money' details Koch's expenditures many millions to congressmen, local officials, and judges across America who obediently support his personal agenda of no business taxes, no industry and bank regulations, no social programs; seeking an unfettered path to increasing his personal wealth. He knows the only institution in America to thwart him is the judiciary and the Supreme Court. This is why he funds a "beachhead" program (pg 126) with Ivy League schools. I have asked Penn's President Amy Gutman to give this 'dark money' back to Koch. This money is like biting the poisoned apple. It will make Penn a contributor to the death of our American justice and democracy.

All money is not evil

Before I leave this chapter on dark money, it is important to reflect on the good that is done with money when it is used selflessly by anyone, by the richest, and by many of us not so rich. The Koch bothers, Robert Mercer, the Mellons, Sciafies, DeVos, Bradleys, and Coors (all exposed in Jane Mayer's bombshell book, Dark Money) are enamored with an abhorrent libertarianism view of government, one where the government exists only to safeguard individual property, where police and armies serve to protect the possessions of the elite. What they seek is a kingdom where kings and royalty rule; where they get richer. These men and women want to turn America away from its march forward to a place in the future where equality of opportunity and freedom is given to all its citizens. These families are remnants of the parents and grandparents who left them rich. They don't understand the promise that lies in the heart of the pledge of allegiance first written in 1892, "I pledge allegiance to the Flag of the United States of America and to the Republic for which it stands, one nation, indivisible, with liberty and justice for all." It is so clear, "with liberty and justice for all." Men and women who think as they do are a real threat to America. Their money makes them super-threats.

Fortunately, the past, present, and future blessings that buoy us in times of struggle are the many people who donate, sacrifice, and provide largess to assist others, and who do so without expecting or demanding something in return. One such person who represents that largess is a man who is much-maligned by right-wing conservatives – George Soros. What the right-wing elements in America say about Soros is representative of how they mudsling everyone who actually makes the world a better place for mankind, all mankind. It could also possibly be so because Soros is Jewish.

Witness to Treason

George Soros has given away more than $32 billion of his personal fortune to fund the Open Society Foundations' work around the world. He is also the founder and primary funder of the Central European University in Budapest, a leading regional center for the study of the social sciences. The Open Society Foundations have supported individuals and organizations across the globe fighting for freedom of expression, accountable government, and societies that promote justice and equality. The foundations have also provided school and university fees for thousands of promising students who would have been excluded from opportunities because of their identity or where they live.

Soros experienced intolerance firsthand. Born in Hungary in 1930, he lived through the Nazi occupation of 1944–1945, which resulted in the murder of over 500,000 Hungarian Jews. His own Jewish family survived by securing false identity papers, concealing their backgrounds, and helping others do the same. After working in London as a part-time railway porter and as a night-club waiter, he completed his studies at the London School of Economics, emigrated to America where he launched his own hedge fund, Soros Fund Management, and went on to become one of the most successful investors in the history of the United States.

Soros used his fortune to create the Open Society Foundations to educate the world that no philosophy or ideology is the final arbiter of truth, and that societies can only flourish when they allow for democratic governance, freedom of expression, and respect for individual rights. In 2017, the Open Society Foundations announced that Soros had transferred $18 billion of his fortune into an endowment that would fund the future work of the foundations, bringing his total giving to the foundations since 1984 to over $30 billion. Others who

222

share their wealth without strings attached are Bill & Melinda Gates ($50B), Gerry and Marquerite Lenfest ($1B), Warren Buffet, Mark Zuckerberg, Larry Page, Jeff Bezos. They shame the Koch family, the Mercers, and the Koch Organization secret club members who dole out pieces of their billions only as an investment to get more leverage on tax breaks, or get industry safety regulations, environmental regulations eliminated that enables them to pollute the air, water, stream, and oceans we value. Their donations are selected to fool the doubters and to control the political discourse in America so that laws passed and judgements levied favor them and generate billions more to the fortunes left to them by the family members who actually created their wealth.

https://www.opensocietyfoundations.org/people/george-soros

Chapter Eight
Citizens United vs FEC

"Until we abolish soft money, Americans will never have a government that will work as hard for them as it does for special interests." Sen. John McCain,

A Brief Background

To safeguard the power of individual voters in our democracy, campaign contribution laws were have been enacted to limit the amount of money, goods, and services that can be contributed by a single entity in a single campaign. Understanding the influence that money can exert on candidates and political parties, Congress carefully monitors such activity and makes periodic adjustments to address any potential abuses to these laws. In 2002, amendment § 203 of the Bipartisan Campaign Reform Act of 2002 (BCRA) was passed and it states that federal law prohibits corporations and unions from spending their general treasury funds on "electioneering communications" or for speech that expressly advocates the election or defeat of a candidate. An "electioneering communication" is any broadcast, cable, or satellite communication that (1) refers to a clearly identified candidate for federal office, (2) is made within 30 days of a primary election or 60 days of a general election, (2 U.S.C. § 441b), and (3) is publicly distributed (11 CFR § 100.29(a)(2)).

Political contributions were commonly limited by law and every person who made a disbursement for the direct costs of producing and airing electioneering communications in an aggregate amount in excess of $10,000 during any calendar year" had to disclose "the names and addresses of all contributors who contributed an aggregate amount of $1,000 or more to the person making the disbursement". This § 203

amendment was challenged in 2008 by Citizens United, a conservative advocacy group which receives individual donations and corporate funding to promote its demand for increased rights for corporations.
Source: The Story of Citizens United v FEC, <u>Annie Leonard</u> and <u>Allison Cook</u>, Yes Magazine, Feb 21, 2011 Wikipedia.

Who/What is Citizens United?

It is two different but related things: (1) a Political Action Committee (PAC) in Washington, D.C., and (2) a Supreme Court case about election spending in which the aforementioned PAC was the plaintiff. Both lie at the center of a debate over the role corporations play in society.

- Citizens United, the PAC, is a conservative political advocacy group that produces television commercials, web advertisements, and documentary films in support of right-wing conservative causes. David Bossie had been its president since 2000 but in 2016 he took a leave of absence to be deputy campaign manager of Donald Trump's campaign for President of the United States.
- The Citizens United ruling is a decision handed down by the Supreme Court in 2010 that removed restrictions on the amount of money that a single donor or corporation can contribute to political campaigns.

Citizens United, a Political Action Committee

Citizens United is a Political Action Committee (PAC) that gained fame in 2009 when it sued the Federal Election Commission, leading to a controversial Supreme Court case (now known as *Citizens United*) which eliminated restrictions on how much money corporations can

226

spend money in elections, and how they can avoid public disclosure of these donations. Citizens United was founded in 1988 by Floyd Brown, a longtime Washington political consultant, with major funding from the Koch brothers (industrialists who own "the second largest privately owned company in the United States"). The Citizens United (CU) group promotes corporate interests, socially conservative causes and candidates who advance their goals, which are "…limited government, freedom of enterprise, strong families, and national sovereignty and security." CU is one of the many institutions and groups that are given patriotic names to disguise their real purpose which is to undermine the freedoms of unsuspecting American citizens. Their mission to increase rights for corporations is a legal gambit to place recognized corporations on an equal standing in citizenship as you and I. The fact that corporations have access to power and money far beyond a single citizen shifts the likelihood that corporations will exert greater influence on policy and law. One citizen's vote will compete poorly for attention against one multi-billion dollar corporation's vote.

In 2008, Citizens United produced and released a negatively opinioned 90 minute documentary film entitled *Hillary: The Movie* about then-Senator Hillary Clinton, who was a candidate in the Democratic Party's 2008 presidential primary elections. The movie expressed opinions about whether then-senator Hillary Clinton was fit for the presidency. Citizens United distributed the movie in theaters and on DVD, but also wanted to pay cable companies to make the film available for free through video-on-demand. Citizens United planned to make the film available within 30 days of the 2008 primary elections and planned to pay for the video-on-demand distribution and the advertisements from its own general treasury funds but doing so would violate the 2002 Bipartisan Campaign Reform Act (known also as the McCain–Feingold

Act), which barred corporations and unions from paying for media that mentioned any candidate in time periods immediately preceding elections. Citizens United was subsequently blocked by the Federal Election Commission (FEC) which sets campaign finance laws and election rules, from releasing the film immediately preceding the 2008 primaries. Citizens United challenged the law, suing the Federal Election Commission. After the case made its way through lower courts, the District Court denied Citizens United a preliminary injunction and granted the FEC's motion for summary judgment. The Supreme Court showed immediate interest in the proceedings and noted probable jurisdiction in the case, and the case was forwarded to the Nation's highest court.

Citizens United vs FEC

Citizens United's appeal was granted by the U.S. Supreme Court. The Supreme Court heard oral arguments on March 24, 2009 and then asked for further briefs on June 29; the re-argument was heard on September 9, 2009. In a brazen act of judicial activism, the Supreme Court decided to consider the much broader issue of corporate spending to influence elections which wasn't even presented in the original case down in the lower courts. Citizens United's single appeal was only on the ruling that the content was solely an "expressed advocacy" for a definitive political purpose, and that it would be communicated within the restricted period of time, only days immediately prior to the targeted election campaign. The case was now being expanded to a discussion of whether corporations should be considered individual citizens.

Supreme Court Ruling

In a 5-4 decision on January 21, 2010, the U.S. Supreme Court issued a ruling in Citizens United v. Federal Election Commission that corporations and unions have the same political speech rights as individuals under the First Amendment. The conservative members of the Court spear-headed the majority decision and overturned a century-old precedent allowing the government to regulate such spending. The Court declared unconstitutional the government restriction on "independent" political spending by corporations and unions, and determined the negative political broadcast should have been allowed. The ruling stunned democracy advocates and trampled a number of campaign finance laws. The majority ruled that corporations—including for-profit corporations—do indeed have a right to spend as much money as they want to elect or defeat candidates in American elections. They ruled that the free speech clause of the First Amendment to the Constitution prohibits the government from restricting independent expenditures for communications by nonprofit corporations, for-profit corporations, labor unions, and other associations. The decision was highly controversial when announced and initiated a continuing deluge of pervasive discussions. It struck down a federal law banning corporations and unions from using their general treasury funds to make election-related independent expenditures and also overruled two of its prior decisions, Austin v. Michigan State Chamber of Commerce (Austin) that allowed prohibitions on independent expenditures by corporations, and also overruled the part of McConnell v. Federal Election Commission that held that corporations could be banned from making electioneering communications. The Court's decision called into question laws in 24 states which prohibit corporations from making independent expenditures from their

Witness to Treason

general treasury. The case did not affect the federal ban on direct contributions from corporations or unions to candidate campaigns or political parties. Soon after the ruling, an explosion of easy money cascaded across America's conservative right-wing political landscape. This was not unexpected. Wealthy corporations and wealthy families in the GOP Republican Party already had their checkbooks opened, knowing the money invested now will reap them ten-fold profit once their favored candidates benefit from the contributions and ruled the White House and Congress. *Citizens United* showered billions of dollars on the conservative right wing candidates and swept the subsequent elections since the Supreme Court's ruling in 2010.

Included below is the briefest version of the Supreme Court official *Citizens United* ruling

SC: XX 603. The provisions of the Bipartisan Campaign Reform Act restricting unions, corporations, and profitable organizations from independent political spending and prohibiting the broadcasting of political media funded by them within 60 days of a general election or 30 days of a primary election violate the First Amendment's protections of freedom of speech. United States District Court for the District of Columbia reversed.

Attending Justices: Chief Justice John Roberts, Associate Justices John P. Stevens · Antonin Scalia, Anthony Kennedy · Clarence Thomas, Ruth Bader Ginsburg ·Stephen Breyer, Samuel Alito · Sonia Sotomayor

The Court majority (Justices Kennedy, Roberts, Alito, Scalia, and Thomas) favoring CU argued:

1. Barring independent political spending would squelch free speech protected by the First Amendment.
2. The First Amendment protects not just a person's right to speak, but the act of speech itself, regardless of the speaker. Therefore, the First Amendment protects the speech of corporations and unions, whether we consider them people or not.
3. Although government has the authority to prevent corruption or "the appearance of corruption," it has no place in determining whether large political expenditures are either of those things, so it may not impose spending limits on that basis.
4. The public has the right to hear all available information, and spending limits prevent information from reaching the public.

The Court minority (Justices Stevens, Ginsburg, Breyer, and Sotomayor) against CU argued:

1. The First Amendment protects only individual speech.
2. A government may prevent corruption, and campaign spending can be corrupt when it buys influence over legislators. Therefore, government may impose spending limits on corporations and unions.
3. A government may prevent the appearance of corruption which undermines public confidence in democracy. Limits on corporate and union political spending are an expression of that authority.
4. The public has the right to hear all available information, and when corporations spend money individuals can't match, messages from corporations drown out messages from others, and that information fails to reach the public. *Source: http://reclaimdemocracy.org/cu_fec_coverage/*

Witness to Treason

The decision was controversial. The conservative wing of the GOP celebrated the decision. They claimed it advanced free speech and allowed any company to compete on equal footing with media organizations. Some neutral observers thought the decision would only boost the volume of political ads, but wouldn't affect public discourse for better or worse. The Democrats were critical, saying the decision "gives the special interests and their lobbyists even more power in Washington, reducing the influence of average Americans who make small contributions to support their preferred candidates."

(Slip Opinion)   OCTOBER TERM, 2009   1

Syllabus

SUPREME COURT OF THE UNITED STATES

Syllabus

CITIZENS UNITED *v.* FEDERAL ELECTION COMMISSION

APPEAL FROM THE UNITED STATES DISTRICT COURT FOR THE DISTRICT OF COLUMBIA

No. 08–205.   Argued March 24, 2009—Reargued September 9, 2009—Decided January 21, 2010

As amended by §203 of the Bipartisan Campaign Reform Act of 2002 (BCRA), federal law prohibits corporations and unions from using their general treasury funds to make independent expenditures for speech that is an "electioneering communication" or for speech that expressly advocates the election or defeat of a candidate. 2 U. S. C. §441b. An electioneering communication is "any broadcast, cable, or satellite communication" that "refers to a clearly identified candidate for Federal office" and is made within 30 days of a primary election, §434(f)(3)(A), and that is "publicly distributed," 11 CFR §100.29(a)(2), which in "the case of a candidate for nomination for President . . . means" that the communication "[c]an be received by 50,000 or more persons in a State where a primary election . . . is being held within 30 days," §100.29(b)(3)(ii). Corporations and unions may establish a political action committee (PAC) for express advocacy or electioneering communications purposes. 2 U. S. C. §441b(b)(2). In *McConnell* v. *Federal Election Comm'n*, 540 U. S. 93, 203–209, this Court upheld limits on electioneering communications in a facial challenge, relying on the holding in *Austin* v. *Michigan Chamber of Commerce*, 494 U. S. 652, that political speech may be banned based on the speaker's corporate identity.

In January 2008, appellant Citizens United, a nonprofit corporation, released a documentary (hereinafter *Hillary*) critical of then-Senator Hillary Clinton, a candidate for her party's Presidential nomination. Anticipating that it would make *Hillary* available on cable television through video-on-demand within 30 days of primary elections, Citizens United produced television ads to run on broadcast

The Effects of Citizens United

As expected, an explosion in independent political spending ensued in the decision's aftermath, as the chart shown below illustrates. Spending was on the rise even before *Citizens United*, but the post-decision increase was dramatic. The 2012 presidential election was the first following *Citizens United*, with more than twice the political spending as any previous election. Independent political spending of the kind *Citizens United* allows accounted for all of that increase. (See below). Is this new spending determining the winners of elections?

What are the objections to unlimited spending and the private protection given to large campaign contributors? Well, it might happen that a foreign entity (like Russia) or a mob king (from Russia) delivers the money with strings attached or with no strings attached. Wouldn't it be prudent for the general public to know who donated it? How much? And why? Doesn't it seem sensible and responsible to visibly track the present and future actions taken by the persons benefitting from receiving the contribution?

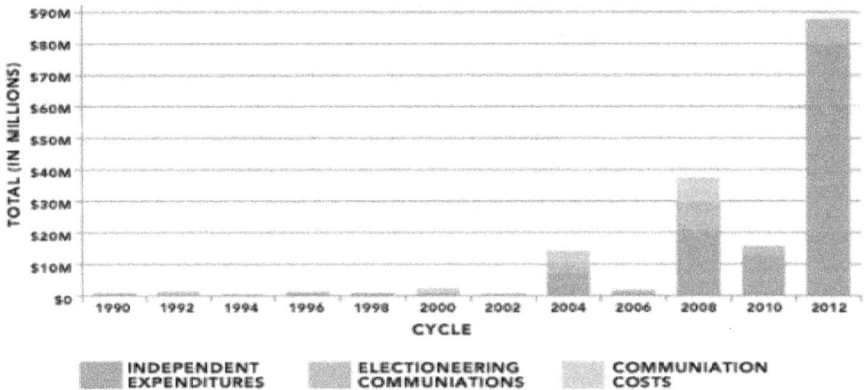

Source: the Center for Responsive Politics:

The founding members of America were enlightened individuals who understood the eternal and all-pervasive threat that money and power have on individuals and institutions throughout all of history and that such threats are as ever present as the air we breathe. Thus, they wisely imposed strong restrictions on the use of influence by private individuals and business entities to seek political favor for their own personal gain; they clearly didn't intend the richest individuals and eventually the largest corporations to enjoy constitutional protections. They understood the government has the authority and the responsibility to prevent corruption or the appearance of it. Now, the *Citizens United* majority opinion says the government has no right to decide whether independent political spending drives those things. In fact, the history of America and of any nation inhabited by mankind suggests this isn't just a theoretical problem because evidence of government-corporate relations has shown sometimes to appear to be corrupt to the electorate, and too often those relations are in fact corrupt.

The majority's claim that spending limits prevent full information from reaching the public ignores reality. We're bombarded by information. We register only a fraction of it, and money spent on advertising and promotions strongly determines what information we are likely to see. When wealthy groups can spend whatever they want, they can make sure their messaging drowns out other voices.

The Court had to overturn one of its own decisions to decide Citizens United as it did. The Court normally honors a custom called *Stare Decisis*, which means it tries not to overturn its own decisions if it can avoid doing so, by deciding a case on narrower grounds. In this case, the path was clear: the Court could have ruled the McCain-Feingold law doesn't apply to video-on-demand, a decision which would have aligned better with previous decisions. The Justices went far beyond what Citizens United's own lawyers asked for.

Why Is Citizens United ruling dangerous?

Who does it harm?

1. Candidates at every level of government will need public exposure to win office
2. The candidates must find money for Campaign Ads, staff
3. Donations create allegiance to the source of the money
4. Allegiance means favors for donors
5. More money, bigger favors
6. This quid pro quo process (see Chapter 7) creates 'personal politicians'
7. Ergo, personal politicians: "in for a penny, in for a dollar."

Unlimited political spending by corporations and unions causes problems. Unlimited political spending allows ideas to dominate not by merit, but by their supporters' ability to finance their creation and broadcast them, and it has incalculable influence far beyond the ads it buys. The more money a politician needs to compete for office, the more he/she must court the wealthy, leaving less time to govern and less contact with average citizens. Legislators' become too familiar with wealthy supporters in ways that have led to decisions favoring the wealthy and powerful. Unlimited political spending such as used in *Citizens United* allows a crude, counterproductive form of political dialogue, framed by acute partisanship and purposely presenting misleading images and sound bites. Lastly, it gives large corporations and nonprofit groups anti-competitive advantages over small businesses and community groups. The founding fathers knew the importance of limiting the influence of money on candidates and elections, and safeguarding a fair democracy emphasizing the constitution's model for one-person, one vote. The government formed at our country's birth, and improved upon cautiously in subsequent centuries, has to ensure that an innumerable number of single citizen votes are not swamped by a single entity flashing an uncontrollable, and unaccounted for, amount of money. Indeed, the Supreme Court has shepherded America through challenges to the Constitution and to the evolving concepts of humanity and equality. It must look again and correct its damaging decision regarding Citizens United.

The Big Picture

Citizens United is a symptom of a bigger, longstanding threat. In recent decades the largest corporations and its sponsors have been regaining their power over America's political process - power that comes at the expense of citizens. One of the main instruments of this influence is the legal concept of "corporate personhood," wherein corporations receive the same Constitutional protections as individuals. Corporations use these protections to claim the "right" to lie to the public, for example, or to influence elections in various ways. Corporations have lobbied for and received these protections for decades, despite our country's founders intending no such thing. The *Citizens United* decision is just the latest in a long line of decisions granting Constitutional rights to corporations but the Court majority didn't say corporations have free speech rights because they're people, instead, they stated non-persons have free speech rights, leading a person who follows their train of thought that they believe if your toaster could talk, it would have those rights too.

The case did clarify, however, that a Constitutional Amendment is the only way to strip corporations of "constitutional rights." Many kinds of electoral reform, such as public campaign financing that truly levels the playing field, are legal impossibilities without first amending the Constitution. There is a growing grassroots movement afoot to amend the Constitution in this regard. Move to Amend is a broad national coalition with chapters nationwide and Reclaim Democracy is a co-founder. More than 400 cities and towns have passed resolutions or ordinances calling to end corporate personhood or have serious efforts underway. The measures typically pass by huge margins. Even more impressive, 10 states now have passed measures in opposition to *Citizens United*. Most recently, Colorado and Montana voters did so in early November 2012. Montana's measure opposed not just *Citizens United* but also the Supreme Court's creations of corporate personhood and "money-speech" (*Buckley v Valeo*), and it passed by an overwhelming 75%-25% margin. It is time to get involved in the effort to revoke *Citizens United* and the illegitimate corporate power it granted. Chapter 12, Call to Action, will provide more information on this Movement as well as discussions on many actions you can take to save America from the greed and tyranny threatening it now, and return our founding fathers' America to all its citizens.
http://reclaimdemocracy.org/who-are-citizens-united/, By Nick Bentley Reclaim Democracy

"Dangerous to Our Democracy"

Supreme Court Justice John Paul Stevens published a dissenting opinion to the majority ruling on Citizens United vs FEC in a ten page written address. He said in part, "This decision effectively gifted corporations the same First Amendment Free Speech protections granted to real live people. The fact is that corporations are not people. There are some big and significant differences between people and

238

companies. For starters, people need a healthy environment and a stable climate to thrive. Corporations are legal entities, created for business and for profits, having a distinct code of business law, and have no inherent reason to safeguard the environment." Justice Stevens continued, "Corporations have no consciences, no beliefs, no feelings, no thoughts and no desires." Instead, corporations—by both law and the demands of the market—are under enormous pressure to focus on one thing: maximizing profit. "The corporations' single minded focus on profits and their enormous scale makes them potentially dangerous to our democracy." He reminds us a corporation can disproportionately influence election outcomes, they can easily overwhelm the contributions from real people, skewing election results to favor corporate interests, which aren't always the same as the interests of workers, families, and the environment. They might sell guns, opioids, cigarettes, emit deadly carbons, and consider the lives of others later.

Organizations working for solutions to issues as diverse as climate change, toxics in consumer products, and the wastefulness of bottled water know the biggest obstacles to progress in these areas is corporate influence in the political process. (Koch, etc). The *Citizens United* decision makes the age-old problem of less control over corporations and their political relationships even more difficult. Reversing this Supreme Court decision is a critical step to reclaiming our democracy and if it requires a new Constitutional Amendment and a national campaign to get corporations' dirty money completely out of our democracy, then it must begin now.

Federal law prohibited any corporation (or labor union) from making an "electioneering communication" (defined as a broadcast ad reaching over 50,000 people in the electorate within 30 days of a primary or 60 days of an election), or making any expenditure advocating the election or defeat of a candidate at any time. The court found that these provisions of the law conflicted with the U.S. Constitution.

Excerpts from Judge Stevens' 2010 dissenting opinion on Citizens United vs FEC.

It is an interesting question "who" is even speaking when a business corporation places an advertisement that endorses or attacks a particular candidate. Presumably it is not the customers or employees, who typically have no say in such matters.

I have taken the view that a legislature may place reasonable restrictions on individuals' electioneering expenditures ...in recognition of the fact that such restrictions are not direct restraints on speech but rather on its financing.

A century ago Theodore Roosevelt delivered speeches to Congress that, in time, led to the limited prohibition on corporate campaign expenditures that is overruled today.

The distinctive threat to democratic integrity posed by corporate domination of politics was recognized at "the inception of the republic" and "has been a persistent theme in American political life" ever since. It is only certain Members of this Court...who have agitated for more corporate electioneering.

A Government captured by corporate interests...will be neither responsive to their needs nor willing to give their views a fair hearing. The predictable result is cynicism and disenchantment: an increased perception that large spenders "'call the tune'" and a reduced "'willingness of voters to take part in democratic governance.'".

Politicians who fear that a certain corporation can make or break their reelection chances may be cowed into silence about that corporation.

The Court's blinkered and aphoristic approach to the First Amendment may well promote corporate power at the cost of the individual and collective self-expression the Amendment was meant to serve. It will undoubtedly cripple the ability of ordinary citizens, Congress, and the States to adopt even limited measures to protect against corporate domination of the electoral process.

Justice Supreme Court continued, "While American democracy is imperfect, few outside the majority of this Court would have thought its flaws included a dearth of corporate money in politics. I would affirm the judgment of the District Court."

DISCLOSE Act, 2010

The DISCLOSE Act, formally known as the Democracy Is Strengthened by Casting Light On Spending in Elections Act, H.R. 5175 (S.3628-Senate), was a bill introduced in the U.S. House of Representatives by Chris Van Hollen (D-Maryland) on April 29, 2010 and in the U.S. Senate by Charles Schumer (D-New York). On July 2010 only seven months after the SC ruling, the US Senate was scheduled to vote on The Disclosure Act a piece of emergency legislation to undo some of the damage from the Citizens United Supreme Court decision. President Obama addressed the American people from the White House Rose Garden on the evening before the vote was to be taken. He said the reforms in the pending Disclosure Act were necessary to prevent corporate and special interest takeovers of our elections. "The ruling is damaging to our democracy." He urged the members of the Senate to imagine the power special interests will have over America's politicians at every level of government if the Citizens United ruling is not mitigated by having the Disclosure Act passed to restrict Citizens United's danger to democracy in America. The Republican Party, the Party of No, predictably voted No. The Citizens United decision essentially opened the floodgates for the greater influence of huge corporations, including foreign-owned corporations and countries on our elections (see Chapter 7, Dark Money, and Chapter 11, Russian Collusion). In the local, state, and federal elections held since 2010, new limitless flows of undisclosed money allowed special interests, powerful men, to buy millions of dollars of television ads -- and they don't even have to reveal who's actually paying for the ads (presently, the FBI is investigating whether Russia funneled money to the Trump 2016 campaign through the National Rifle Association). Instead, a group can hide behind a name like "Citizens for a Better Future," even if a more accurate name would be "Companies for Weaker Oversight." President Obama knew these shadow groups were already forming and building war chests of hundreds of millions of dollars to influence the fall elections throughout America. "Now, imagine the power this will give special interests over politicians. Corporate lobbyists will be able to tell members of Congress if they don't vote the right way, they will face an onslaught of negative ads in their next campaign. And all too often, no one will actually know who's really behind those ads. Once again, with a solution at hand, Republican leadership in the Senate stands in the way, hoping to deny an up-or-down vote." The House has already passed a bipartisan bill that would change all this before the next election. The DISCLOSE Act would simply require corporate political advertisers to reveal who's funding their activities. So when special

242

interests take to the airwaves, whoever is running and funding the ad would have to appear in the advertisement and claim responsibility for it — like a company's CEO or the organization's biggest contributor. Foreign-controlled corporations and entities would be restricted from spending money to influence American elections -- just as they were in the past.

This degree of simple transparency is about as commonsense as you can get. You would expect that reducing corporate and even foreign influence over our elections would not be a partisan issue; you'd expect a rush of bi-partisan support to protect America's most treasured possession, its election process, its single-most sacred expression of freedom, the right to vote without interference from anyone, anywhere. Still, the Republican leadership in the Senate once again used every tactic and every maneuver to prevent the DISCLOSE Act from even coming up for an up or down vote. President Obama added, "As they did on issue after issue, as we are trying to move America forward, they keep on trying to take us back. Americans voices shouldn't be drowned out by millions of dollars in secret, special interest advertising. The American people's voices should be heard."

Since 2010, the GOP Republican Party and its right-wing Conservatives, and the Libertarian Party have received and spent hundreds of millions, approaching billions. It is unfathomable to realize that the GOP's first dark money effort in 1972, Nixon's Plumbers, had a "slush fund" of a few thousands of dollars to do dirty tricks like burglarizing the Democratic Party's National headquarters in the Watergate Hotel, and that amount of money is like the Our Gang clubhouse's treasury compared to the millions of dollars in the "slush funds" that are available for use today by the GOP's army of the Potomac.

Citizens United's journey to the Supreme Court was not a happenstance. It was a strategy inside a plan, and funded generously by an enemy, not an opposing political party, but an enemy whose purpose is to make America in their image, and under their thumbs.

Chapter Nine
The NRA: Instruments of Death

"Your Second Amendment rights are under siege. But they will never, ever be under siege as long as I'm your president, we've got to get Republicans elected."　　　　　*President Trump, NRA convention, May 4, 2018*

Blood Money

The National Rifle Association (NRA) is exempt from income tax as a section 501(c) (4) social welfare organization. Any group or institution that identifies themselves under the guise of performing services for the social welfare of its community can lobby without limit and, of particular importance, can engage in campaign intervention – supporting or opposing candidates for public office – so long as such activity is not their primary activity.

The NRA's national website advertises training programs and other community services for its members and affiliated organizations and therefore it qualifies for tax exemption protection under the tax code designation listed above. It seems reasonable to grant a harmless nonprofit organization group with an always appreciated tax break. In 1871, the NRA began with well-meaning intentions as detailed further on in this chapter. In those early days of the Union, familiarity with a rifle, acquiring improved weapons skills, and receiving safety training with weapons benefitted America's mostly rural population and farming communities. After all, weapons, then small caliber pistols and rifles, were confined to usage by their owners for hunting and guarding against wildlife. Or, on the rare occasion when unwelcome intruders may unwisely stray too close on someone else's property, they provided some protection. The NRA's motivation was clear then.

Times change and it appears the NRA's motivation has changed also. Today, their motivation is money.

Today the NRA is too closely aligned with enterprises who make guns, and accessories for guns. Gun manufacturers make money making and selling guns, all kinds of guns – rifles, handguns, shotguns, high-powered rifles, and high capacity automatic rifles. The National Rifle Association (NRA) makes money promoting gun sales and gun use to everyone, everywhere. The NRA lobbying arm, the Institute for Legislative Action, has trumpeted pledges by some gun makers, such as Sturm, Ruger and Co.'s August 2016 commitment of $2 from each gun sale, with a goal to raise $4 million. Many politicians in the Republican Party secure contributions and important NRA-ratings by aligning their political influence with the NRA and gun manufacturers business. In turn, the NRA can ensure its business associates that all state and federal gun legislation favor the gun manufacturers' unrestricted right to continue to sell bigger and improved guns. This cycle of greed is maintained amidst increasing gun violence across America's communities, where too often prayers are offered somewhere in the United States for yet newer victims of a mass shooting, domestic shooting, crimes, and suicides. The NRA, the GOP, and Trump all celebrate their power over our government to impede citizens in their own cities, towns, and communities from being better protected with common sense regulations and restrictions on some guns and some gun owners.

Trump and NRA

In 2015 and 2016, candidate Donald Trump made fears about gun violence a central part of his campaign, but as president he has done little to curb that violence. Instead in 2018, he praised the NRA leaders

and members, and he has taken steps to relax the few
gun control policies that are in place.

- His administration's Justice Department tightened the
  definition of who qualifies as a "fugitive from justice" when it
  comes to gun ownership, making it easier for some people with
  arrest warrants to possess firearms.
- He signed a bill in February 2017 just after moving into the
  White House prohibiting the Social Security Administration
  from reporting recipients with mental impairments to a
  national background-check database. The
  NRA applauded these actions.

During the first half of 2017, the NRA spent $3.2 million to successfully
lobby for a resolution overturning an Obama-era Interior Department
rule that restricted sport hunting on national wildlife refuges in Alaska,
including banning hunting from planes and killing predators like bears
and wolves while near their dens or their cubs. President Trump
approved it in April. His administration's Interior Department
removed a ban on hunting with lead ammunition on federal lands,
ensuring continued sales and profits for gun ammunition
manufacturers.

In 2016, the NRA, a nonprofit, spent nearly $140 million on legislative
programs and public affairs, an increase of about $75 million overall
from 2015. These categories are not itemized further in the financial
report, but they likely encompass the lobbying efforts and campaign
contributions that have become a cornerstone of the NRA's political
power. This $140 million figure includes a $30 million investment in
Donald Trump's presidential campaign as well as at least $20 million
more to help GOP Senate candidates, though recent reports suggest

spending on congressional races may have been significantly higher. As the Center for Responsive Politics notes, much of that funding came in the form of "dark money" disbursed by the NRA's Institute for Legislative Action (NRA-ILA), a 501(c) (4) social welfare organization that is not required to disclose its donors.

The love affair between Trump and the NRA is not surprising. The NRA spent $30 million* in 2016 to back his 2016 candidacy for president: $10 million to directly promote his election and another $19.7 million to attack Democratic nominee Hillary Clinton. (The 2010 Supreme Court ruling, *Citizen United*, allows such record amounts of donations from sources that are not required to be identified to the public.) Trump has spoken at NRA events before and after his election and enthusiastically pledged his loyalty to the group at the NRA's annual meeting in April 2017 when he said, "You came through for me, and I am going to come through for you." On May 4, 2018, less than two months after meeting at the White House and commiserating with surviving students and grieving parents of teenage children who were murdered in February at Marjory Stoneman Douglas High School in Parkland, FL, the President set aside his insincere promise to them to protect schools and all citizens from gun violence when he travelled to the NRA national convention and spoke glowingly in support of the NRA, vowing that gun owners' rights, "will never, ever, be under siege as long as he is President."

Trump was the biggest beneficiary of NRA cash in the 2016 election. Here's the top 10 biggest beneficiaries of donations from the NRA.

Donald Trump — $31,194,646
Sen. Richard Burr (R-N.C.) — $6,297,551
Sen. Marco Rubio (R-Fla.) — $3,298,405

Sen. Roy Blunt (R-Mo.) — $3,105,294
Sen. Todd Young (R-Ind.) — $2,888,132
Former Rep. Joe Heck (R-Nev.) — $2,529,305
Sen. Rob Portman (R-Ohio)— $2,319,755
Sen. Ron Johnson (R-Wis.)—$650,745
Rep. Lloyd Smucker (R-Pa.)—$215,786
Sen. Richard Shelby (R-Ala.)—$167,411

These numbers above, compiled by CRP and calculated by The Hill,
include only the NRA's outside spending. It encompasses the money
spent to help get the candidates elected and defeat their opponents.

*http://thehill.com/business-a-lobbying/business-a-lobbying/354317-the-nras-power-by-the-numbers ; published in the Hill, **The** nra's power: by the numbers, by megan r. wilson - 10/08/17*

2018   "a gun in every pocket"

Who is the NRA? The National Rifle Association of America's (NRA)
website is all-American clean and brightened with patriotic images
trimmed in America's proud colors: red, white, and blue. It is
identified as an American nonprofit organization (501c) that advocates
for US citizens' gun rights.

 According to the NRA, it had 6 million members as of May 2018, and
it is recognized as one of the top three most influential lobbying groups
in Washington, DC. The NRA is nearly one-hundred and fifty years
old and was formed by former two Civil War officers who were
alarmed at the poor weapon skills of the Union soldiers during the war
and wished to improve private gun owners' weapon skills and general
marksmanship. The initial focus for the first century of its existence
was to target hunters and sportsmen. In 1934, the organization began

249

to inform its members about gun safety and firearm-related legislation. In 1975, the organization began directly lobbying Congress for and against firearms legislation and formed a strong relationship in Washington politics, primarily within the Republican Party.

A lot changed at the NRA over the last forty years. The NRA is now politically aggressive in its pursuit of "gun rights' under the Second Amendment. The organization is extremely successful and influential at all levels of our state and federal government. It has helped Republicans gain control of Congress by contributing more money to GOP election campaigns than any other conservative group aside from three Super PACs formed to back GOP presidential candidates. The NRA poured tens of millions into the 2016 election, breaking its own record of $31.7 million from just two years before, according to data compiled by the Center for Responsive Politics. They devoted huge sums of money to winning back the White House and maintaining Republican control of Congress by electing their candidates up and down the ballot. Those investments paid off. All but a few of the candidates who received NRA backing won their respective elections. The NRA's spending on elections has soared since 2010, after the Supreme Court's controversial *Citizens United* ruling.

https://www.thetrace.org/2016/10/nra-breaks-campaign-spending-record/, *The NRA Has Broken Its Record for Election Spending.by Dan Friedman, ·October 12, 2016 published in Trace, online.*

1871, in the beginning.

A few months after the Civil War started in 1861, several Americans living in England sent a letter to President Lincoln proposing that a national rifle organization similar to the British National Rifle Association be formed in America. They suggested building a shooting range on Staten Island in New York. Due to the onset of the Civil War in April 1861, no action was taken on the proposal. In 1871, six years after the war ended and some order and normalcy was beginning to return to a scarred nation, Union veterans Col. William C. Church and Gen. George Wingate formed the National Rifle Association. According to a magazine editorial written by Church, they were disappointed by the lack of marksmanship shown by their troops during the recent war and hoped to improve the dismal shooting abilities of the average Union soldier. According to an official study, Union troops fired 1,000 rounds for every bullet that struck a Confederate soldier. The primary goal of the new association was to "promote and encourage rifle shooting on a scientific basis." After being granted a charter by the state of New York on November 17, 1871, the NRA was founded and Civil War Gen. Ambrose Burnside became the fledgling NRA's first president. In 1872, a shooting practice site was opened on Long Island and its first annual matches were held there in 1873. Later, political opposition to the promotion of marksmanship in New York forced the NRA to find a new home for its range, and it was moved to Sea Girt, New Jersey.

The association's original mission focused on hunting, conservation, and marksmanship; there was no mention of protecting the Second Amendment right to bear arms. Indeed, for nearly a hundred years, the organization actively lobbied for gun control, co-authoring gun restrictions with the government right up until the 1970s. "Historically," says UCLA law professor Adam Winkler, "the leadership of the NRA was more open-minded about gun control than someone familiar with the modern NRA might imagine." It is supposed that marksmanship and gun safety were equally important to its leadership and its membership. In fact, the NRA backed the nation's first federal gun laws after the Prohibition Era, when tommy gun–wielding gangsters warred in the streets of Chicago. The National

Firearms Acts of 1934 and 1938 placed heavy taxes and regulations on machine guns, sawed-off shotguns, and silencers; prohibited felons from owning weapons; and required gun owners to register with the federal government. NRA leader Karl T. Frederick not only endorsed the legislation, he went so far as to state, "I have never believed in the general practice of carrying weapons. I think it should be sharply restricted and only under licenses." In 1934, the National Rifle Association created a Legislative Affairs Division and testified in front of Congress in support of the first substantial federal gun control legislation in the US, the National Firearms Act.

Legislation, 1934-1968

The NRA remained a neutral political organization over the following forty years. The NRA President in 1934 testified during congressional NFA hearings, "I have never believed in the general practice of carrying weapons. I seldom carry one. ... I do not believe in the general promiscuous toting of guns. I think it should be sharply restricted and only under licenses." Four years later, the NRA backed the Federal Firearms Act of 1938. The NRA supported the NFA along with the Gun Control Act of 1968 (GCA), which together created a system to federally license gun dealers and established restrictions on particular categories and classes of firearms. The organization did oppose a national firearms registry, an initiative favored by then President Lyndon Johnson.

National Rifle Association Position on Federal US Legislation

Bill/Law	Year	Supported	Opposed
National Firearms Act	1934	✗	
Federal Firearms Act	1938	✗	
Gun Control Act	1968	✗	✗
Federal Assault Weapons Ban	1994		✗
Protection of Lawful Commerce in Arms Act	2005	✗	
Disaster Recovery Personal Protection Act	2006	✗	
Assault Weapons Ban	2013		✗

The NRA opposed parts of the Gun Control Act of 1968, which broadly regulated the firearms industry and firearms owners, prohibiting interstate firearms transfers by anyone other than licensed manufacturers, dealers and importers. The law was supported by America's oldest manufacturers (Colt, S&W, etc.) in an effort to forestall even greater restrictions which were feared in response to recent domestic violence. The NRA supported elements of the law such as forbidding the sale of firearms to convicted criminals and the mentally ill.

Legislation 1975, the NRA and the Second Amendment

Until the middle 1970s, the NRA mainly focused on sportsmen, hunters and target shooters, and downplayed gun control issues, leaving gun control in the hands of local, state, and federal governments. However, according to political scientists John M. Bruce and Clyde Wilcox, the NRA shifted its focus in the late 1970s to incorporate political advocacy, and began seeing its members as

253

political resources rather than just as recipients of goods and services. The Institute for Legislative Action (NRA-ILA), the lobbying branch of the NRA, was established in 1975. The politicization of the NRA has been consistent ever since The NRA Political Victory Fund (PVF) PAC was established in 1976 to challenge gun-control candidates and to support gun-rights candidates.[62]. After 1977, the organization expanded its membership by focusing heavily on political issues and forming coalitions with conservative politicians, most of whom were Republicans.[41].

- In 1986, the NRA successfully lobbied Congress to pass the Firearm Owners Protection Act (FOPA) of 1986 and worked to reduce the powers of the federal Bureau of Alcohol, Tobacco, Firearms and Explosives (ATF).
- In 1994, the NRA unsuccessfully opposed the Federal Assault Weapons Ban (AWB), but successfully lobbied for the ban's 2004 expiration. The organization has not lost a major battle over gun control legislation since the 1994 Federal Assault Weapons Ban.
- At the federal level, the NRA successfully lobbied Congress to effectively halt government-sponsored research into the public health effects of firearms.
- In 2005, the NRA lobbied Congress to ensure the passage of legislation protecting gun manufacturers and dealers from lawsuits.
- In the shadow of the many gun deaths in towns and cities across America, the NRA continues its lavishly-funded campaigns to influence state governments to eliminate local governments ability to regulate guns, and restrict carrying guns in public places (such as bars and campuses).
  https://en.wikipedia.org/wiki/National_Rifle_Association

In 1993, with Democrats in the majority of both the U.S. Senate and House of Representatives, "The Brady Bill", was signed. Named after James Brady, Ronald Reagan's press secretary who was shot and paralyzed during the 1981 assassination attempt on President Reagan, the bill created a mechanism for background checks in order to enforce the Gun Control Act of 1968 and prevent criminals and minors from purchasing guns. In addition, the Violent Crime Control and Law Enforcement Act of 1994 included a 10 year ban on the sale of assault weapons. According to a CBS poll in 1994, the ban was favored by 78% of Americans. However, during the 1994 midterm elections, Yale Professor Reva Siegel reported, "The NRA spent more than $3.2 million on GOP campaigns and helped win nineteen of twenty-four races the organization targeted, leading to a House with a majority of members who were 'A-rated' by the NRA". The NRA seeking to expand interpretation of the Second Amendment to include an individual right to a gun, joined together with the 'New Right', a political movement that wanted less gun control, and advocated for school prayer and for banning abortion.

The NRA in the U.S. Congress

The NRA ranks as "one of the biggest spenders in congressional elections" as of 1998. In 1999, Congressional lawmakers and their staffers considered the NRA the most powerful lobbying organization three years in a row. The NRA influenced the writing of the Firearm Owners Protection Act and worked for its passage. In 2004, the NRA opposed renewal of the Federal Assault Weapons Ban of 1994. The ban expired on September 13, 2004. In 2005 President George W. Bush signed into law the NRA-backed Protection of Lawful Commerce in Arms Act which prevents firearms manufacturers and dealers from being held liable for negligence when crimes have been committed with their products.[104] The NRA's contributions to cash-hungry politicians campaigning for office continued to rise, and the NRA's influence on gun-related legislation increased.

In 2012, 88% of Republicans and 11% of Democrats in Congress had received an NRA PAC contribution at some point in their career. Of the members of the Congress that convened in 2013, 51% received funding from the NRA PAC within their political careers, and 47% received NRA money in their most recent race. In large part, these percentages were increasingly delivered to GOP Republican legislators in both Houses of Congress. The NRA donated to Congressional races for both Republicans (223) and Democrats (9).

The NRA leadership assured its members that Republicans would be defenders of Second Amendment rights and repeal recently passed gun control legislation.[69]

- The NRA spent $40 million on US elections in 2008, including $10 million in opposition to the election of Senator Barack Obama in the 2008 presidential campaign.
- Colorado state senators John Morse and Angela Giron helped to pass expanded background checks and ammunition magazine capacity limits after the 2012 Aurora, Colorado, and Sandy Hook, Connecticut, shootings. Then the NRA spent over $360,000 in a Colorado recall election of 2013, which resulted in their ouster from the state senate.
- On May 20, 2016, the NRA endorsed Donald Trump in the 2016 US presidential election. The timing of the endorsement, before Trump became the official Republican nominee, was unusual, as the NRA typically endorses Republican nominees towards the end of the general election.

NRA and the ATF

It would be expected that the oldest and largest gun club in America would maintain a good relationship with its government's primary institution responsible for the manufacture, sale, and safe use of firearms. In America, you would be wrong. Very wrong.

For four decades, the NRA fought to limit the ability of the federal Department of Alcohol, Tobacco, and Firearms (ATF) to regulate firearms. The NRA blocked nominees to the department who did not support the NRA's interests, and lobbied against reforms that would ease the ability of the ATF to track gun crimes. On numerous occasions, the NRA, has successfully forestalled the ATF's efforts to implement an electronic record of gun ownership that would replace the current system of using paper records.[85] How can a private social organization that is both tax exempt and free to accept and spend charitable donations be able to reach inside a government agency and determine public policy? How did the NRA do that?

In 2006, the NRA lobbied US Representative F. James Sensenbrenner to add a provision to the Patriot Act reauthorization that requires Senate confirmation of ATF director nominees, thus assuring that every senator influenced by the NRA would not vote for a nominee opposed by the NRA. Did it work? For the next seven years, the NRA lobbied against and "effectively blocked" every presidential nominee to that director position. First was President George W. Bush's choice, Michael Sullivan, whose confirmation was held up in 2008 by three Republican Senators who said the ATF was hostile to gun dealers. One of the Senators was Larry Craig, who was an NRA board member during his years in the Senate.[89] The NRA has been criticized by gun control and gun rights advocacy groups, political commentators, and politicians. They have been the focus of intense criticism in the aftermath of high profile shootings, from Columbine High School (1999) and Sandy Hook Elementary School (2012) to Marjorie Stoneman Douglas High School (2018), and Sante Fe High School (2018).

The NRA and the Gun Industry

Does the NRA really care about the Second Amendment rights of Americans? The evidence shows that the NRA is more interested in the revenue it receives from the gun manufacturers and gun accessory makers who make up the billion dollar gun industry in America. The NRA receives tens of millions from its corporate allies. Donors include firearm companies like Midway USA, Springfield Armory Inc, Pierce Bullet Seal Target Systems, and Beretta USA Corporation, Cabala's, Sturm Rugar & Co, and Smith & Wesson. The NRA also draws in tens of millions of dollars from selling advertising to industry companies who market products in its many publications, according to the IRS filings by the NRA. All this money is in addition to gun industry companies donating portions of their sales directly to the NRA for each gun it sells. One gun maker forwarded $1 to the NRA for every gun it sells. That company sells millions of guns.

"The NRA is a virtual subsidiary of the gun industry," said Josh Sugarmann, executive director of the Violence Policy Center. "While the NRA portrays itself as protecting the 'freedom' of individual gun owners, it's actually working to protect the freedom of the gun industry to manufacture and sell virtually any weapon or accessory." There are two reasons for the gun industry support for the NRA. The first is that the NRA develops and maintains a market for the gun industry products. The second, less direct function, is that the NRA absorbs criticism in the event of a public relations crises when gun attacks occur. It's possible that without the NRA, Americans would be protesting outside of gun industry plants and offices used in the gun massacres, forcing their CEOs in front of cameras and Congress. The NRA doesn't mind the heat and criticism from the public. After all, it gets paid well for doing so, and it can always rely on the President and the GOP to support them. So, despite prayers and condolences from the President, and his loyal local, state, and federal GOP legislators, history will repeat itself and NRA CEO Wayne La Pierre and NRA poster woman, Dana Loesch, along with other NRA mouthpieces will be front and center after the next gun massacre threatening foes and arming themselves with the same dumb arguments they've used in every gun control debate. Meanwhile, gun manufacturer executives will remain safely out of the spotlight.

Russian Money for the NRA

In 2017, the NRA reported 2016 revenue of $444 million and expenses of more than $480 million. In more detail, the NRA spent $55M on 2016 elections, $30M alone for Trump's election. It was the most spent by any one organization, and by an arm of the NRA "not required to disclose its donors." That is a lot of new money, far exceeding its revenues and expenses in prior years. The excessive increase from its previous annual amounts is so great that, as of January 2018, the NRA is under federal investigation for accepting money from Russia to aid and abet the Trump Campaign in the 2016 presidential election. The questions are simple and few.

- How much money did the NRA collect?
- Where did it come from?
- What did they spend it on? Why?
- Who are the NRA friends and board members?
- What are the NRA's financial relationships to gun manufacturers, military contractors, political legislators, Russia, and foreign donors?

In January 2018, the FBI began investigating whether a senior Russian banker with Kremlin ties channeled funds through the NRA to support President Trump's 2016 presidential campaign. In February, Sen. Ron Wyden (D-Ore.) wrote to the U.S. Treasury Department seeking financial records related to alleged links between Russian banker Alexander Torshin and the NRA after he read published reports suggesting Torshin's interest in the NRA and the organization's hefty campaign spending in support of then-candidate Donald Trump were related. *NRA discloses two dozen additional contributions from Russian donors, by pete madden, matthew mosk, Apr 11, 2018,*

Initially, John C. Frazer, the NRA's Secretary and General Counsel, reported that only one Russian donated to the controversial gun-rights group in 2016. That single donation was less than $1,000. Soon, the NRA revised its total of Russian donations in an April 10 letter to Sen. Wyden wherein the NRA's Frazier corrected his response to Wyden, "Given your focus on potential Russian influence between 2015 and the present, we reviewed our financial records for that period. During that time, the NRA received a total of approximately $2,512.85 from people associated with Russian addresses (which may include U.S. citizens living in Russia), or known Russian nationals living in the United States." The number of Russian donors during that period from 2015 quickly climbed to more than two dozen. An aide to Sen. Wyden told

ABC News that as ranking member of the Finance Committee, the senator is considering making a push for "additional oversight actions" in light of recent inquiries. "Sen. Wyden will be referring his correspondence with the NRA to the Federal Elections Commission to contribute to their inquiry," the aide said. "After three letters, the NRA continually, and specifically avoided detailing what measures it takes to vet donations, including from shell companies, a known means for Russians to funnel money into the United States.

Alexander Torshin and Maria Butina

In January 2018, reports began circulating that the FBI was investigating whether a top Russian banker with ties to the Kremlin illegally funneled money to the National Rifle Association to help Donald Trump win the presidency. The Russian was identified as Alexander Torshin. Most interestingly, the single individual Russian donor first identified by the NRA was Alexander Torshin, a former senior member of the Russian Senate and former deputy governor of Russia's central bank. He was identified in news articles as "a vociferous Putin ally," and close friend of the Russian president. He has also been implicated in money laundering by Spanish* authorities who have characterized him as a "godfather" in Taganskaya, a major Russian criminal organization. Torshin coincidentally holds a lifetime membership in the NRA, and in May 2016, he sat at a dinner table with Donald Trump Jr. at the 2016 National Rifle Association convention in Kentucky. (Note: It is reported in this same article that Donald, Jr. was sent to Kentucky to meet Torshin as a "first contact" in creating a link with Russians interested in aiding the Trump campaign). Since then, he has been the subject of scrutiny from lawmakers and Special Counsel Robert Mueller regarding possible attempts by Russia to influence the 2016 presidential campaign. Additionally, his friendship with accused

Witness to Treason

Russian spy Maria Butina who previously worked as a special assistant
to Torshin when he was the deputy governor of Russia's central bank,
and Butina's close relationships with NRA officials and her attendance
at NRA and Trump administration functions, reveals more
uncomfortable links between the NRA and Russian officials at the
highest levels.

*The Spanish prosecutors, who have cooperated with the FBI for years,
say Torshin has a dark side. They have accused him of laundering
money for the Russian mob, an allegation Torshin has denied. During a
visit to Washington, chief Spanish prosecutor Jose Grinda spent several
hours meeting with FBI officials, according to two people familiar with
his itinerary. Both sources spoke on condition of anonymity due to the
sensitivity of the matter. Grinda also met with journalists at the
Hudson Institute, where he revealed that a few months ago he
provided the FBI with 33 audio recordings of Torshin, including one in
which a since-convicted Russian money launderer called him
"godfather," according to Yahoo News.

The NRA has denied these links as being anything more than Russian
individuals having an interest in the NRA. The NRA continues to deny
receiving money "from foreign persons or entities in connection with
United States elections," but questions continue to swirl around the
organization's seemingly close relationship to Torshin. When Torshin
was added to the list of Russian nationals sanctioned by the U.S.
Treasury Department in response to the Kremlin-ordered invasion of
Eastern Ukraine and Moscow's meddling in the 2016 elections,
questions were raised about his long-standing relationship to the NRA.
There were already red flags regarding Kremlin links to NRA," Rep.
Ted Lieu, a California Democrat, told ABC News following Torshin's

meetings with NRA designees. "This (money from Russia) just supercharges it."

Torshin Hosts the NRA in Moscow

In 2015, the Torshin lavishly wined and dined a NRA delegation that included high-dollar NRA fundraiser, Joe Gregory, and Pete Brownell, the head of a major U.S. firearms firm who later became the NRA's president. A Politico article published in January 2108 stated, "Torshin hosted two dinners during the NRA's week-long visit to Moscow that included meetings with influential Russian government and business figures. The two dinners went very well." In the same article, it was reported that Arnold Goldschlager, a major fundraiser for the NRA, said, "They were killing us with vodka and the best Russian food. The trip exceeded my expectations by logarithmic levels." But not everyone was pleased with the Russian/NRA détente. "U.S. Kremlin analysts sharply criticized a meeting between the NRA delegation and Deputy Prime Minister Rogozin, who oversaw Russia's defense and firearms industries because Rogozin had been placed under U.S. sanctions..," Steve Hall, an ex-CIA Russian specialist who worked earlier as the CIA's Moscow station chief, believes that Torshin's involvement with the NRA was no accident, and neither were meetings between NRA representatives and Deputy Prime Minister Dmitry Rogozin and Sergei Rudov, manager of a far-right Russian religious foundation. Hall said, it looks like the Kremlin was pulling the strings at every turn, in a country where that happens "to a degree that cannot even be dreamed of here," Hall added, "Everybody knows the consequences of not doing what the Kremlin wants you to do." In light of all of the revelations about Torshin, the NRA reevaluated its relationship with him. NRA spokesman Arulanandam says Torshin's NRA membership was now "frozen".

Witness to Treason

In a subsequent letter, NRA General Counsel Frazer stated that the organization is "reviewing [its] responsibilities" with respect to Torshin. The NRA did not respond to questions about what that review might entail or what actions might be taken. If this accusation that the Kremlin secretly funded Russian efforts to boost Trump's election proves to be the case, the donations would violate US campaign laws that prohibit the use of foreign money to support a candidate in US elections. The NRA did not reveal the extent to which the group traces the true origins of its $350 million in annual funding. Most interestingly, Torshin is also being investigated whether this Russian banker with ties to the Kremlin illegally funneled money to the National Rifle Association to help Donald Trump win the presidency.

https://washingtonmonthly.com/2018/01/18/did-a-russian-crime-boss-fund-trump-through-the-nra/   Did a Russian Crime Boss Fund Trump Through the NRA? , Political Animal, by Martin Longman, January 18, 2018,

https://www.mcclatchydc.com/news/politics-government/article214075459.html   Russia investigators likely got access to NRA's tax filings, secret donors, by greg gordon and peter stone, ggordon@mcclatchydc.com, july 02, 2018

However, Rep. Dana Rohrabacher of California refers to Torshin as "conservatives' favorite Russian." And it's true. Conservatives seem to love the guy. This past February, Republican bigwig donor George O'Neill Jr. hosted "a fancy four-hour dinner" for Torshin at a Capitol Hill restaurant that attracted Rohrabacher and a host of other conservatives. Torshin was even slated to have a meeting with President Trump until his mob connections came up and the meeting was cancelled. Torshin is the founder of the Russian gun rights group Right to Bear Arms. He has been trying to find common cause with the National Rifle Association. Torshin's ties with the NRA have flourished in recent years. In late 2015, he hosted two dinners for a high-level NRA delegation during its week-long visit to Moscow that included meetings with influential Russian government and business figures.

According to the Times, shortly before the NRA's May 2016 convention, a NRA fundraiser named Paul Erickson, (later reported to be having a personal relationship with Russian spy Maria Butina) emailed Trump campaign aide Rick Dearborn about the possibility of setting up a meeting between Putin and Trump during the campaign. Erickson's email to Dearborn bore the subject line "Kremlin Connection." In it, Erickson solicited advice from Dearborn and Dearborn's boss, Sen. Jeff Sessions of Alabama, then a top foreign policy adviser to Trump's campaign, about the best way to connect Putin and Trump. The email was sent to top Trump campaign officials including former campaign chairman Paul Manafort, campaign official Rick Gates and eventually Jared Kushner. Kushner's attorney says his client said to "pass on this" and warned campaign officials to "decline such meetings." In other words, Erickson pitched the campaign on a meeting with Torshin and a possible Trump/Putin meeting and this pitch made the rounds before Kushner allegedly spiked the idea. Yet, it's not clear if the idea was truly spiked or if it was modified. What actually wound up happening is that Donald Trump Jr. made a trip to Louisville for the NRA conference at the Kentucky Exposition Center. The conference ran from May 19 to May 22. And while Donald Jr. was at the NRA convention he had a meeting with Torshin. The length and nature of this meeting is in dispute, with the Trump camp characterizing it as more of a brief conversation about firearms than a formal sit down. But the truth here is going to matter because the FBI now suspects Torshin of illegally financing the Trump campaign using the NRA as a cutout. Most notable was that within two weeks after Don, Jr. met with Torshin in Kentucky, Don, Jr. hosted the meeting with more Russians in the Trump Tower on June 9.

https://www.nytimes.com/2017/12/03/us/politics/trump-putin-russia-nra-campaign.html

John Aquilino, a former NRA spokesman, is also baffled by the NRA's outreach to Torshin and Moscow. "The NRA has fallen into a public relations trap, and the Russians knew damn well what they were doing," Aquilino said in a phone interview. He added, "The NRA and the gun control issue is a perfect example of an issue that would fire up the populace and sow discord," He pointed to the fact that a Russian troll farm bought dozens of Facebook ads on gun rights as part of a 2016 social media blitz aimed at dividing Americans and helping Trump. Michael Carpenter, a senior Pentagon and National Security Council official specializing in Russia issues during the Obama administration, said a relationship between Russia and the NRA would be "mutually beneficial." Carpenter tweeted that "NRA lawyers know how to use Google and were no doubt familiar with their contacts' links to the Kremlin and to organized crime."

Ex-CIA Russia specialist Hall said he cannot fathom what the NRA officials hoped to obtain from Russia. Putin opposes arming his citizenry with anything more than hunting rifles. Russia, though, may have had an agenda for its gun makers. The NRA visit included a tour of the Russian firearms manufacturer Orsis, perhaps to highlight Moscow's hopes that victory by the right candidate could bring the 2014 sanctions to an end and the Russians could sell guns in America. Moscow had also sought to lift earlier limits on Russian gun imports to the US, including the iconic Kalashnikov. "So Russia turned to the NRA and other gun enthusiasts to try to promote the issue," he said. The Torshin-led mating dance between Moscow and the NRA culminated at the NRA's convention in Louisville in late May 2016, when Trump received an early endorsement from the pro-gun goliath.

Torshin tried unsuccessfully that week to arrange a personal meeting with Trump, but he did cadge a short chat with Donald Trump Jr.., an avid hunter.

After the election, Torshin came to Washington in February 2017 to attend the annual National Prayer Breakfast, an event where he'd been a regular for more than a half dozen years, Erickson said. Torshin also was feted at a four-hour Capitol Hill dinner organized by George O'Neill Jr. a Rockefeller heir. Attendees included Erickson and Republican Rep. Dana Rohrabacher of California, considered by some analysts to be Putin's best friend in Washington. Rohrabacher, in a phone interview last year, said that conservative American gun rights groups no longer look at Russia with Cold War angst, but rather "in friendly terms." He remembered meeting Torshin in Moscow a few years earlier, calling him a "mover and shaker." Presently, US Russian sanctions include barring Torshin from entering the United States.

Money laundered from Russia to the NRA.

In November 2017, the Chairman of the Senate Judiciary Committee, Sen. Chuck Grassley of Iowa, had to send a sternly worded letter to Jared Kushner's lawyer, Abbe Lowell, complaining that Kushner's production of requested documents and records was incomplete. There were several items on Grassley's list, including emails pertaining to WikiLeaks, communications with Sergei Millian, a variety of phone records, and a copy of Kushner's SF 86 security clearance form. Maybe the most explosive omission pertained to a Russian mob boss, Alexander Torshin, a former senior member of the Russian Senate, who has been described as "a vociferous Putin ally," as well as a "mafia godfather." Jared Kushner didn't initially disclose that he had emails pertaining to Mr. Torshin, but the Judiciary Committee had received copies from Paul Manafort and Rick Gates who had been copied on the email chain. The Spanish authorities have 33 audio recordings of phone conversations where Torshin is referred to as "boss" or "godfather." These recordings also implicate Torshin in a vast money laundering scheme.

The extent to which the FBI has evidence of money flowing from Torshin to the NRA, or of the NRA's participation in the transfer of funds, is under investigation. However, the NRA reported spending a record $55 million on the 2016 elections, including $30 million to support Trump – triple what the group devoted to backing Republican Mitt Romney in the 2012 presidential race. Most of that was money was spent by an arm of the NRA that is not required to disclose its donors. (*Citizens United* SC ruling 2010). Two people with close connections to the powerful gun lobby said its total election spending actually approached or exceeded $70 million. The reporting gap could be explained by the fact that independent groups are not required to reveal how much they spend on Internet ads or field operations, including get-out-the-vote efforts.

https://www.bing.com/search?q=peter+stone+is+a+mcclatchy+special+correspondent%2C+mich ael+woodel+contributed+to+this+report.+greg+gordon%3A+202-383- 152%3B+%40greggordon2%2C&form=EDGEAR&qs=PF&cvid=c655fcb7ccb744f98b2b23b57b 0d72c8&cc=US&setlang=en-US Peter Stone is a McClatchy special correspondent, Michael Woodel contributed.

Maria Butina and Republican 'leaders' back channel to the Kremlin

In mid-July 2018 the FBI and presented an affidavit for the arrest of an accused Russian spy and influential NRA member, Maria Butina. One of the many explosive charges included in the affidavit is this alarming nugget shown below.

31. On October 4, 2016, U.S. Person 1 sent an email to an acquaintance. The email covered a number of topics. Within the email, U.S. Person 1 stated, "Unrelated to specific presidential campaigns, I've been involved in securing a VERY private line of communication between the Kremlin and key POLITICAL PARTY 1 leaders through, of all conduits, the [GUN RIGHTS ORGANIZATION]." Based on my training, expertise, and familiarity with this investigation, I believe that this email describes U.S. Person 1's involvement in BUTINA's efforts to establish a "back channel" communication for representatives of the Government of Russia.

It is reported that POLITICAL PARTY 1 is the Republican Party as is said to be clear from reading the rest of the document. It is not clear which "key leaders" of the Republican Party had secured a "VERY" private line of communication to the Kremlin, in October of 2016.

Person 1 specifically says it is "unrelated" to a presidential campaign; that doesn't leave too many other options. While figures like Dana Rohrbacher, R-California or Scott Walker, R- Wisconsin, may hug the NRA tightly, neither can be considered a "key party leader." Only House leaders, Senate leaders, or top GOP party officials would fit that bill.

According to this affidavit, an unknown number of those leaders had a secure line of communications to the Kremlin in October of 2016, immediately before the elections. For what possible purpose? Are we going to find out who? And do government investigators already know? *Monday, Jul 16, 2018 · Hunter*

NRA Protects Our Right to Kill Ourselves with Guns

The NRA spends millions of dollars in law suits and influences politicians and judges all over America to protect their freedom to sell Americans larger and more deadly assault rifles, automatic pistols, unlimited ammunition, and numerous gun accessories. Then they want to tell us they do all that to protect our freedom under the second amendment, the freedom to kill ourselves, and/or others. This is not what our founding fathers had in mind when they wanted to ensure that Americans had the right to bear arms.

The NRA filed an amicus brief with the Supreme Court in the 2008 landmark gun rights case of District of Columbia v Heller. In a 5 to 4 vote, the Supreme Court ruled that the District of Columbia's gun laws were unconstitutional, and for the first time held that an individual's right to a gun was unconnected to service in a militia. Some legal scholars believe that the NRA was influential in altering the public's interpretation of the Second Amendment, providing the foundation for the majority's opinion in Heller.

- In 2009 the NRA again filed suit (Guy Montag Doe v. San Francisco Housing Authority) in the city of San Francisco challenging the city's ban of guns in public housing. On January 14, 2009, the San Francisco Housing Authority reached a settlement with the NRA, which allows residents to possess legal firearms within a SFHA apartment building.
- In 2010, the NRA sued the city of Chicago, Illinois (McDonald v. Chicago) and the Supreme Court ruled that like other substantive rights, the right to bear arms is incorporated via the Fourteenth Amendment to the Bill of Rights, and therefore applies to the states.

- In March 2013, the NRA joined a federal lawsuit with other gun rights groups challenging New York's gun control law (the NY SAFE Act), arguing that Governor Andrew Cuomo "usurped the legislative and democratic process" in passing the law, which included restrictions on magazine capacity and expanding the state's assault weapons ban.
- In November 2013, voters in Sunnyvale, California, passed an ordinance banning certain ammunition magazines along with three other firearm-related restrictions. The ordinance was passed with 66% in favor. The ordinance required city residents to "dispose, donate, or sell" any magazine capable of holding more than ten rounds within a prescribed period of time once the measure takes effect. The following month the NRA joined local residents in suing the city on second amendment grounds. A federal judge dismissed the suit three months later, upholding Sunnyvale's ordinance.
  https://en.wikipedia.org/wiki/National_Rifle_Association - cite_note-Chokshi-116
- San Francisco passed similar ordinances a short time later. The San Francisco Veteran Police Officers Association (SFVPOA), represented by NRA attorneys, filed a lawsuit challenging San Francisco's ban on the possession of high-capacity magazines, seeking an injunction. A federal judge denied the injunction in February 2014.
- In 2014 the NRA lobbied for a bill in Pennsylvania which grants it and other advocacy groups legal standing to sue municipalities to overturn local firearm regulations passed in violation of a state law preempting such regulations, and which also allows the court to force cities to pay the NRA's legal fees. As soon as it became law, the NRA sued three cities: Philadelphia, Pittsburgh, and Lancaster. In Philadelphia, the NRA sued to overturn seven regulations including a ban on

271

gun possession by those found to be a risk for harming themselves or others, and overturn a requirement to report stolen guns to the police within twenty-four hours after discovery of the loss or theft.

- In Lancaster, a city of fewer than 60,000, Mayor Rick Gray, who has chaired the pro-gun control group <u>Mayors Against Illegal Guns</u>, was also named in the suit. In that city, the NRA challenged an ordinance requiring gun owners to tell police when a firearm is lost or stolen within 72 hours or face jail time. The basis for the lawsuits is "a 1974 state law that bars municipalities against passing restrictions that are pre-empted by state gun laws". At least 20 Pennsylvania municipalities have rescinded regulations in response to threatened litigation from the NRA.

NRA releases 2016 financial statement showing revenue and expenses 5/05/17 I by Daniel Terrill published online on Guns.com

During the 2016 election year, the National Rifle Association saw a 10 percent rise in revenue from 2015, but also spent $42 million more than it earned, according to a financial statement given to members at last week's annual conference. The statement consolidates revenue and expenses from six NRA-affiliated organizations, including its political action committee, according to the statement. It lists $433.9 million for total revenue and other support along with $475.9 million in expenses. The biggest increase in spending for 2016 went toward program services (generally paid with non-disclosed dark money) to the tune of $288 million, a 52 percent jump from the year before. The statement does not go into great detail about it,

Finances, NRA and its subsidiaries, pre-2016 election

Name	Year	Income in Millions	Expenses in Millions
National Rifle Association (NRA)	2011[174] 218.9		231.0
NRA Institute for Legislative Action	n/a	n/a	n/a
NRA Civil Defense Fund	2012[175] 1.6		1.0
NRA Civil Defense Fund	2013[176] 1.3		0.9
NRA Foundation	2012[177] 43.0		29.1
NRA Foundation	2013[178] 41.3		31.4
NRA Freedom Action Foundation	2012[179] 2.1		2.3
NRA Freedom Action Foundation	2013[180] 0.5		0.1
NRA Political Victory Fund	2012[172] 14.4		16.1
NRA Political Victory Fund	2014[173] 21.9		20.7

Expenses the NRA accrued in 2016 included:

- Leading up to the 2016 election, the NRA also spent more than $30 million in support of Republican presidential candidate Donald Trump, who has maintained a close relationship with the organization since becoming president.
- According to the statement, the NRA generated the majority of its revenue from membership dues, $163.5 million, down about $2 million, and contributions, $171 million, up 24 percent, in 2016. Program fees accounted for the third largest amount with

$69 million, up $4 million. And investments, royalties and assets accounted for approximately $30 million. *Filed Under: Gun Laws, Politics & 2nd Amendment, Product & Industry News*

Ka-ching! The Gun Industry $$

Critics have charged that the NRA represents the interests of gun manufacturers rather than gun owners. For example, in 2011, Violence Policy Center executive director Josh Sugarmann, said: "Today's NRA is a virtual subsidiary of the gun industry. While the NRA portrays itself as protecting the 'freedom' of individual gun owners, it's actually working to protect the freedom of the gun industry to manufacture and sell virtually any weapon or accessory".

In 2010, the NRA reported revenue of $227.8 million and expenses of $243.5 million, with revenue including roughly $115 million generated from fundraising, sales, advertising and royalties, and most of the rest from membership dues. Less than half of the NRA's income is from membership dues and program fees; the majority is from contributions, grants, royalties, and advertising. Corporate donors include a variety of companies such as outdoors supply, sporting goods companies, and firearm manufacturers. From 2005 through 2011, the NRA received at least $14.8 million from more than 50 firearms-related firms.[184] An April 2011 Violence Policy Center presentation said that the NRA had received between $14.7 million and $38.9 million from the firearms industry since 2005. In 2008, Beretta exceeded $2 million in donations to the NRA, and in 2012, Smith & Wesson gave more than $1 million. Sturm, Ruger & Company raised $1.25 million through a program in which it donated $1 to the NRA-ILA for each gun it sold from May 2011 to May 2012

Gun Control

In February 2013, USA Today editors criticized the NRA for flip-flopping on expansion of universal background checks to private and gun show sales, which NRA now opposes., and in March 2014, The Washington Post criticized the NRA's interference in government research on gun violence. However, a survey of NRA members found that the majority of members support certain gun control policies, such as a universal background check. For instance, 84% of gun owners and 74% of NRA members (vs. 90% of non-gun owners) supported requiring a universal background-check system for all gun sales; 76% of gun owners and 62% of NRA members (vs. 83% of non-gun owners) supported prohibiting gun ownership for 10 years after a person has been convicted of violating a domestic-violence restraining order; and 71% of gun owners and 70% of NRA members (vs. 78% of non-gun owners) supported requiring a mandatory minimum sentence of 2 years in prison for a person convicted of selling a gun to someone who cannot legally have a gun.

It appears that the NRA leadership speaks for only a minority percentage of NRA members when it fervently opposes any reasonable gun control. Who is the NRA representing when it vehemently opposes any gun control legislation? Gun manufacturers? Right wing conservatives? Renegade militias? It is clear the NRA is not responding to gun violence and repeated tragedies across American cities and communities.

The Pennsylvania House was busy on firearms and gun safety legislation in 2018. Did any pass? PA Rep. Leanne Krueger-Braneky says, "Twenty-six bills have been introduced on common-sense gun safety reform so far in these sessions (2018). Some of these bills were introduced last session and the session before that. But the only common theme is that as of today, none of these bills have yet had a vote." Not even a vote! *"The Subject was Guns", Sunday, April 22, 2018.*

List of deadliest US mass shootings 1999-2018. Only incidents with ten or more fatalities are included. Shootings are listed by number of lives lost.

Incident	Year	Deaths	Injuries	Type of firearm(s) used
Las Vegas shooting	2017	59	851	Modified semi-automatic rifles and pistols
Orlando nightclub shooting	2016	50	53	Semi-automatic rifle and pistol
Virginia Tech shooting	2007	33	23	Semi-automatic pistols
Sandy Hook Elementary School shooting	2012	28	2	Semi-automatic rifle and pistol
Sutherland Springs church shooting	2017	27	20	Semi-automatic rifle
Stoneman Douglas High School shooting	2018	17	17	Semi-automatic rifle
San Bernardino attack	2015	16	24	Semi-automatic rifles
Columbine High School massacre	1999	15	24	Shotguns, semi-automatic rifle, bombs, semi-automatic pistol
Binghamton shootings	2009	14	4	Semi-automatic pistols
Fort Hood shooting	2009	14	33	Semi-automatic pistol and revolver

Incident	Year	Deaths	Injuries	Type of firearm(s) used
Washington Navy Yard shooting	2013	13	8	Semi-automatic pistol and shotgun
Aurora shooting	2012	12	70	Semi-automatic rifle, pistol, shotgun
Geneva County massacre	2009	11	6	Semi-automatic rifles, revolver, and shotgun
Atlanta shootings	1999	10	13	Semi-automatic pistols and revolver
Red Lake shootings	2005	10	5	Semi-automatic pistols and shotgun
Umpqua Community College shooting	2015	10	8	Semi-automatic pistols, Rifle (Not used) and revolver
Santa Fe High School shooting	2018	10	14	Shotgun, bombs, and a revolver.

https://en.wikipedia.org/wiki/Mass_shootings_in_the_United_States

NRA responses to mass shootings, 2012-2018

Sell guns to teachers, school security guards, and street crossing guards, they urge communities to "harden" security. Shortly after the FL school shooting, The NRA filed an immediate complaint against a Florida law banning gun sales to anyone under 21.

Trump responses to mass shootings, 2012-2018

Provide guns for teachers (extra pay), then train teachers (only the smart ones.); remove all Gun Free Zone signs outside schools. He pledges undying support for NRA weeks after FL shooting.

GOP responses to mass shootings, 2012-2018

The GOP responses to more shootings across America are more and bigger prayers and condolences, more empty promises, more delays on gun safety because it is not a good time to talk about guns, and more promises that they will do something next time. Instead, after every mass shooting, the GOP allows the NRA to speak for the Republican Party. Following the high-profile December 2012 shooting at the Sandy Hook Elementary School, the NRA announced a press conference. The NRA backed an effort to assess the feasibility of placing armed security officers in the nation's 135,000 public and private schools under a National School Shield Program. The announcement came in the same week after President Obama had stated his support for a ban on military-style assault weapons and high-capacity magazines. In January 2013, after the Sandy Hook shooting, the NRA released an online video which attacked Obama's stand against assault weapons and mentioned guns with reference to Obama's daughters*. A senior NRA lobbyist later characterized the video as "ill-advised". -"
https://www.youtube.com/watch?v=RB4lDYSv_KY

2017 Las Vegas shooting

After the October 2017 shooting at a concert in Las Vegas, which left 58 people dead and 851 injured, the NRA issued a statement opposing additional gun control laws, which they said would not stop further attacks, and calling for a federal law allowing people who have a concealed carry permit in one state to carry concealed weapons in all other states. The organization also suggested additional regulations on so-called bump fire stocks that the Las Vegas shooter had used, which allows a semi-automatic weapon to function like a machine gun.

2018 Marjorie Stoneman Douglas High School, Parkland, FL

In February 2018 this school shooting at a high school in Parkland, Florida left 17 dead, and student survivors organized a movement called Never Again MSD to demand passage of certain gun control measures. Many of the students blamed the NRA, and the politicians who accept money from the organization, for preventing enactment of any gun control proposals after previous high profile shootings. An NRA spokesman responded by blaming the shooting on the FBI and the media. The NRA also issued a statement that the incident was proof that more guns were immediately required in schools in the hands of a bolstered force of armed security personnel in order to "harden" them against any further similar assaults. A Florida law passed in the wake of the shooting, which includes a provision to ban the sale of firearms to people under 21, was immediately challenged in federal court by the NRA on the grounds that it is "violating the constitutional rights of 18- to 21-year-olds."

In May 2018, Cameron Kasky's father and other Parkland parents formed a super PAC, Families vs Assault Rifles PAC (FAMSVARPAC), with a stated goal of going "up against NRA candidates in every meaningful race in the country". The organization seeks federal legislation to ban "the most dangerous firearms", while not affecting the second amendment.

Witness to Treason

Santé Fe High School, Santé Fe, TX

After the May 18, 2018, shooting deaths of 8 students and 2 teachers in this small school, Texas Gov. Greg Abbott suggested that Texas should look for ways to keep guns away from people who pose an immediate danger to others. One such idea had already been enacted in six states since the shooting deaths in February at Parkland, FL. Known as "red flag" laws, the state law allows law enforcement to deny guns or take guns away from an individual who has mental health problems, or who has demonstrated incidents of violence. In August, the Governor and his Lt. Gov. Dan Patrick have back-peddled, and will not consider a red law, or any gun control action. Since the shooting the Texas Rifle Association, and arm of the NRA, and a gun-carrying organization, Open Carry Texas, have "visited" the two men and all of the legislators to lobby for guns.

Gun deaths in urban communities in addition to mass shootings: Homicides during 2017 in the 50 largest cities

City	Homicides	Change	Per 100,000
Baltimore	343	25	55.8
Boston	57	10	8.5
Chicago	650	-112	24
Dallas	166	-5	12.6
Denver	56	-1	8.1
Detroit	267	-36	39.7
Houston	269	-32	11.7
Indianapolis	154	6	23.3
Jacksonville	141	21	16
Kansas City	149	18	31
Las Vegas	141	-17	22.3
Los Angeles	286	-7	7.2
Memphis	200	-28	30.6
New Orleans	158	-16	40.4
New York City	290	-45	3.4
Philadelphia	317	40	20.2
Phoenix	152	6	9.4
Washington, D.C.	116	-19	17

SOURCE: USA TODAY analysis of police department crime data

Parkland 2018 NRA boycott

The NRA offers corporate discounts to its members at various businesses through its corporate affiliate programs. For several years, and increasingly in the aftermath of the Stoneman Douglas High School shooting, companies affiliated with the NRA have been targeted in social media as part of a boycott effort to terminate their business relationships with the NRA. As a result of this boycott movement, several major corporations such as Delta Air Lines, United Airlines, Hertz, Symantec, and MetLife have separated themselves from the NRA, while others, such as FedEx continue their business relationships.

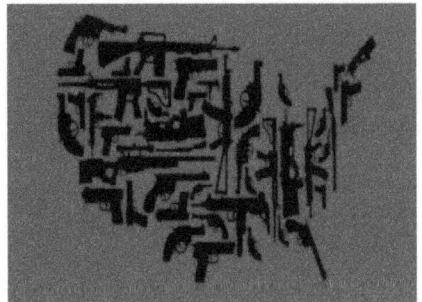

Companies end NRA affiliation in 2018.   How the NRA sees America

Plastic Guns and 3-D Printers

Also in Texas, Cody Wilson is hawking the next hot weapon, a "ghost gun". The NRA has begun pressuring legislators to make it legal and abundant. It is destined to appear soon at the conservative Republican latest favorite place, the U.S. Supreme Court. Cody is the owner of Defense Distributed CAD Company located in Houston, TX, and he prides himself as a cowboy version of Julian Assange of WikiLeaks fame. He created 3-D blueprints for DIY printable guns, making blueprints initially for an AR-15 killer-rifle, but he is marketing a plastic gun that shoots real, deadly bullets, one at a time. States are banning access to the site and denying any downloading of CAD files. Not Texas.

Pointing Fingers

It is immoral that any Republican legislator who enables constituents to casually purchase guns, will not pass common sense gun control legislation to ensure gun owners and non-owners are uniformly safe, or who receives generous health care at the expense of US taxpayers will not support reasonable medical care for it citizens who are at risk to random gun violence. The NRA is more likely to lobby for government subsidies for all US citizens to purchase guns to protect themselves, to hunt, to become skilled marksmen, to exercise their Second Amendment rights, to even kill other citizens, in order to sell guns to fill the pockets and bank accounts of the NRA and the 'business interests" they serve who benefit from the sales that put a gun in every pocket, and an automatic rifle under every long coat.

Chapter Ten
E Deplorabus Unum

"If the shoe fits, wear it." Anonymous.

A Test of Character

Here is a simple self-assessment examination that I created to allow anyone to quickly determine if they have what it takes to be included in Donald Trump's basket of deplorables. The first question is simple. Did you ever, or do you still, support Donald Trump. OK. That's settled. Let's proceed. First, I apologize in advance to anyone who might be offended by the similarities of the stated examples and Trump's actual behavior. The questions may seem to mirror Trump's actions, but that is more coincidence than intention. Believe me. The requested responses are simple, a simple yes or no will do. Once completed, count the number of yes answers. The bad news is that just one yes answer qualifies you to be in Donald Trump's 'basket of deplorables', and suggests you are strong-willed, stubborn, watch Fox News a lot, and are prone to follow the crowd that surrounds you. The good news is that it is not too late to stop supporting Donald Trump and the Republican legislators who enable him.

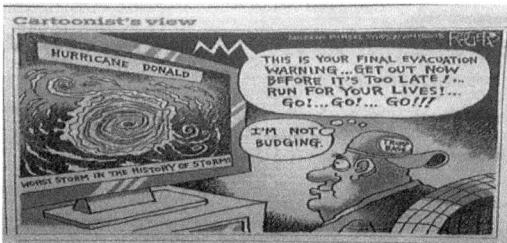

Syndicated in Delaware County Daily Times, Chester, PA September 20, 2018

Witness to Treason

Am I a Deplorable?   Test yourself. No cheating allowed.
1 or more correct = a deplorable;   13 correct = a perfect deplorable

Scenario: You wake up in the morning and the richest and most powerful man in your community admits that he has done all of the 10 things listed below.
Here's the question: Do you still admire or like this rich neighbor? Answer yes or no after reading each numbered sentence listed.

1. He cheated his business partners, bankrupted his businesses, borrowed money from the mob, and refused to pay contractors for work performed on his construction projects.
2. He committed fraud, and cheated college students and parents of tens of thousands of dollars they paid for phony college courses.
3. He established a charity foundation and used other people's donations for his own purposes
4. He sexually assaulted eighteen women.
5. He paid hush money to two women a few months before his election to public office.
6. He used Russian money and its government officials against American interests.
7. He announced on TV, there were good people on both sides at a Nazi, white power, brawl.
8. He bragged that he could shoot 'you' on Fifth Avenue in NYC, and get away with it.
9. He said he could grab your sister, wife and daughter in a sexual manner, they let him do it because he is rich and famous.
10. He hates all your friends and neighbors, and his best friend is the town bully who hates you.
11. **Bonus question**: Will you let him marry your daughter?

A basket of deplorables

What happened in New York City on Sept. 9, 2016? Democratic
Presidential candidate Hillary Clinton spoke at a fundraiser and
identified half of Donald Trump's supporters as belonging in a "basket
of deplorables, people who she said were "racist, sexist, homophobic,
xenophobic, Islamaphobic." She went on to say that the other half of
Trump supporters were people who were frustrated by government
and felt they were forgotten by representatives already in Washington.
This last part of her message was lost in the uproar that accompanied
the 'basket of deplorables" phrase she uttered. While Trump didn't
directly deny her assertion regarding his 'basket of deplorables', he
blasted her attack as being against all of his supporters.

The next day, after facing criticism from the Trump campaign and
others, Clinton issued the following statement: "Last night I was
'grossly generalistic,' and that's never a good idea. I regret saying 'half'
-- that was wrong. But let's be clear, what's really 'deplorable' is that
Donald Trump hired a major advocate for the so-called 'alt-right'
movement to run his campaign and that David Duke and other white
supremacists see him as a champion of their values. It's deplorable that
Trump has built his campaign largely on prejudice and paranoia and
given a national platform to hateful views and voices, including by
retweeting fringe bigots with a few dozen followers and spreading
their message to 11 million people. It's deplorable that he's attacked a
federal judge for his 'Mexican heritage,' bullied a Gold Star family
because of their Muslim faith, and promoted the lie that our first black
president is not a true American. So I won't stop calling out bigotry
and racist rhetoric in this campaign. I also meant what I said last night
about empathy, and the very real challenges we face as a country
where so many people have been left out and left behind. As I said,

many of Trump's supporters are hard-working Americans who just don't feel like the economy or our political system are working for them. I'm determined to bring our country together and make our economy work for everyone, not just those at the top. Because we really are 'stronger together." *Politifact, September 9, 2016*

Here are Hillary Clinton's original comments made on September 9, 2016 in NYC. Clinton began the night with a standard welcome before criticizing Trump and the types of judges he might appoint to the U.S. Supreme Court if he were elected. She then noted that she had "a special commitment" to LGBT community and spoke in support of gay rights. She continued:

"In too many places still, LGBT Americans are singled out for harassment and violence. You can get married on Saturday, post your pictures on Sunday and get fired on Monday. That's why we've got to continue the forward march of progress." "And we cannot do it alone. I cannot do it alone. I'm not like Donald Trump, who says, 'I alone can fix it.' I've never quite figured out what it is he alone can fix. But that's not what you'll hear from me. I think we have to do this together. So, together we're gonna pass the Equality Act to guarantee full equality. We're going to put comprehensive quality affordable healthcare within reach for more people, including for mental health and addiction. We're going to take on youth homelessness, and as my wonderful, extraordinary, great daughter said, we are going to end the cruel and dangerous practice of conversion therapy. We're going to keep working toward an AIDS-free generation, a goal that I set as secretary of state, and with your help we're going to pass comprehensive gun laws. ..."

288

"I know there are only 60 days left to make our case -- and don't get complacent, don't see the latest outrageous, offensive, inappropriate comment and think, well, he's done this time. We are living in a volatile political environment. You know, to just be grossly generalistic, you could put half of Trump's supporters into what I call the basket of deplorables. Right? The racist, sexist, homophobic, xenophobic, Islamaphobic -- you name it. And unfortunately there are people like that. And he has lifted them up. He has given voice to their websites that used to only have 11,000 people -- now 11 million. He tweets and retweets their offensive hateful mean-spirited rhetoric. Now, some of those folks -- they are irredeemable, but thankfully they are not America."

"But that other half of Trump supporters are people who feel that the government has let them down, the economy has let them down, nobody cares about them, nobody worries about what happens to their lives and their futures, and they're just desperate for change."

Unfortunately, Clinton's clarification of her "deplorables" comment was too late to prevent Trump from slamming a backhand volley onto Hillary's side of the court, forcing her campaign to back-pedal when it was gaining in the election polls. Trump, a master at twisting the truth around other people's windpipes, trumpeted those four words into a rallying cry for his mob and invigorated his fading chances for victory. Clinton later wrote in her book *What Happened* that the deplorables comment was one of the factors for her loss. She said after the 2016 election that her decision to label many Trump supporters "deplorables" was a "political gift" to President Trump.

Source: *The Fix* Analysis the Washington Post by Aaron Blake March 13 2018

Witness to Treason

After the election, Diane Hessan, who had been hired by the Clinton campaign to track undecided voters, wrote in *The Boston Globe* that "all hell broke loose" after the "basket of deplorables" comment, which prompted what she saw as the largest shift of undecided voters towards Trump.[36] In an interview with CNN on December 4, 2016, Hillary Clinton's campaign manager Robby Mook said that the statement "definitely could have alienated" her voters.[37] Meanwhile, Courtney Weaver of *Financial Times* believed that Clinton's comment had no effect on the election, stating "To argue that one word cost Mrs. Clinton the election is foolish." However, Weaver acknowledged that the statement "did not hurt her opponent". *From Wikipedia, the free encyclopedia.* Hillary Clinton had previously expressed her concerns about Donald Trump and his supporters. *The New York Times* and *CNN* cited Clinton's earlier articulation of similar ideas to the phrase in her August 25, 2016 campaign speech at a rally in Reno, Nevada. In that speech, Clinton had criticized Trump's campaign for using "racist lies" and allowing the alt-right to gain prominence, claiming that Trump was "taking hate groups mainstream and helping a radical fringe take over the Republican Party". Clinton also criticized Trump for choosing Steve Bannon as his chief executive officer, especially given Bannon's role as the executive chair of the far-right news website, *Breitbart News*. On the same day, Clinton posted a video on Twitter depicting white supremacists supporting Donald Trump. Within the video is a CNN interview wherein Trump initially declined to disavow white nationalist David Duke.   https://en.wikipedia.org/wiki/Basket_of_deplorables_-cite_note-Background-4

Hillary Clinton was right when she made the (bizarrely phrased) assertion that half of Donald Trump's supporters could be put in a "basket of deplorables." While the immediate post-basket days were spent arguing if Clinton's assessment was accurate (yep, it was), most

290

people agreed that the statement was a 'gaffe'. But Clinton's comments were still perceptive. She correctly labeled a significant portion of Trump's base as being "racist, sexist, homophobic, xenophobic, Islamaphobic." And she limited her critique—it was broad, but not overreaching. Trump's campaign was forced into a tight spot: Mike Pence, for instance, had to argue that no Trump supporters deserved to be called deplorable—not even Ku Klux Klan leader, David Duke— because what else was Pence supposed to do? If Pence denounced some on the list, for instance acknowledging truthfully that Duke was a deplorable because he hated blacks and people of color and Jews, Pence would be agreeing that Clinton was right, or partly right. So he and the Republican Party embraced all of the persons who Clinton included in the basket. However, it didn't hurt the Republican Party at all. Trump's base - deplorables and others - became more passionate in their commitment to vote for Trump. The new GOP Republican Party couldn't be happier. They sent out a loud dog whistle. And waited for November.

Who are the deplorables?   Some of the people, all of the time

Many Trump supporters absolutely don't care about his adultery, his misogyny, his lies, his crookedness, his racism, or the possibility that he committed treason against his nation in order to sit at the most powerful desk in the White House. Trump's deplorables as pointed out by Hillary Clinton in September 2016 are not invisible boogie-men and women who only come out at night. The hard-core supporters, the deplorables, are men and women who peddle their hate brazenly in the light of day, at their jobs, and in their kitchens, as well as in the firelight of torches and bonfires that excite their hate. They are not bothered by doctors being murdered in their Kansas churches; and they accept that "children of color are placed in detention camps for fear that a terrified 8-year-old child might be a hardened gang leader. They have open contempt for anyone not in their own small tribe, and are obsessed with helping Trump harm every other tribe not like them because it makes them feel better about their own lot in life." Who are the deplorables? Anyone who still supports Trump after watching and listening to Trump steer our ship into and onto the rocks must surely qualify.

The Times finally gets to the bottom of Trump supporters: It turns out they're garbage human beings , Hunter , Daily Kos Staff Wednesday July 04, 2018 · 4:00 PM USEDT

Left: Donald Trump, Jr. wearing his button of honor at a campaign rally.
Right: Poster at Trump rally after Clinton unmasks Trump supporters.

KKK and White Supremists

An article in the Washington Post in July 2018, provides some insight into the support Trump receives, and welcomes, from racist hate groups like the Ku Klux Klan. One such place is Ulysses, PA, a tiny, suitably quaint, town in rural Potter County in far north-central Pennsylvania. Ulysses is staunchly Republican and voted Democratic once since 1888. Trump received 80 percent of the vote in 2016, tying Herbert Hoover for the highest percentage of votes ever won. On the north side of town, there is a home dedicated to Adolf Hitler, where star-spangled banners and Nazi flags flutter side by side and wooden swastikas stand on poles. White supremacy has had a continuous presence in Ulysses since the Ku Klux Klan arrived a century ago. It hosted the World Aryan Congress, a gathering of neo-Nazis, skinheads and Klan members, in the mid-2000s, when August Kreis III, 63, a neo-Nazi from New Jersey moved to town in the 1990s and made Ulysses the national headquarters. (In 2015, Kreis was sentenced to 50 years in prison on a child-molestation conviction.) Neo-Nazis and their opponents here say that white extremists have grown more confident - and confrontational - since the rise of Donald Trump. Two months before the 2016 presidential election, the KKK established a "24 hour Klan Line" and sent goody bags containing lollipops and fliers to hundreds of homes. "You can sleep tonight knowing the Klan is awake," the message read. A regional newspaper ran Klan advertisements saying, "God bless the KKK." In 2018, federal prosecutors charged six members of a local Aryan Strike Force cell with weapons and drug offenses, contending that they had plotted a suicide attack at an anti-racism protest. The group met and conducted weapons training in Ulysses.

A member of another group, the National Socialist Movement (NSM), a far-right group that was founded in Detroit in the mid-1970s, noted the increase in activity, "I can tell you with certainty that since November 2016, activity has doubled, whether it's feet on the street or money orders or people helping out," The NSM has a presence in many states, according to the Southern Poverty Law Center, and the NSM was among the groups that took part in the violent August 2017 rally in defense of Confederate statues in Charlottesville. They see Trump as a politician who has amplified long-standing white-nationalist views at the right time. Pennsylvania has 36 racial hate groups, more than Alabama, Arkansas or Kansas, according to the

Southern Poverty Law Center. Some residents think the racist presence has worsened since Trump's election, that Ulysses has been more divided since Trump's victory: "I think Trump has opened the gate. It was not a license, but a subtle, 'It's okay.' I think we are seeing that now." "It bothers me," the resident said, "because we have good people in this town, then added, "I think a lot are racially insensitive," she said, "and Trump has allowed that to grow."

https://www.washingtonpost.com/politics/how-white-supremacists-split-a-quiet-rust-belt-town/2018/07/28/15a7e414-85df-11e8-8f6c-6cb43e3f306_story.html?utm_term=.d11e274ec8de

White Nationalist is the Republican candidate for Senator in VA

Corey Stewart lives in Woodbridge, VA and he is a strong supporter of Donald Trump and admires what Trump is doing to make America great, and whiter, again. Stewart was born in Minnesota but styles himself as a champion of the Confederacy and its statues, and, as he puts it, "taking back our heritage." He makes it clear he means "the South", and not Minnesota. His adoption of the uglier side of the southern culture has made him a popular figure with white nationalists, and as one of the new fringe politicians in the new Republican Party, he is eager to embrace the racist members of his party in order to advance his Trumpian appeal. He praised President Trump's statement that there were "very fine people on both sides" at the Unite the Right white nationalist protests in Charlottesville in August 2018. "I don't think he said anything bad there," Mr. Stewart, 50, said.

There are many people who believe and say what Stewart is saying, but Stewart is most notable because he is the 2018 Republican candidate for Senator in Virginia. His campaign volunteers include white supremists, and several of his aides and advisers have used racist or anti-Muslim language, or maintained links to outspoken racists like Jason Kessler, the organizer of the hate rallies in Charlottesville, VA in 2017 and in Washington, DC in 2018. Trump admires Stewart and has enthusiastically endorsed him, tweeting in June 2018, "Don't underestimate Corey, a major chance of winning!" Stewart has contended that the term 'white supremacist' is a concoction of the left. The former state Republican Party executive director lamented that "the alt-right has taken over the Virginia Republican Party." After Mr. Stewart secured the nomination in June, the Republican Party chairman resigned in a rare display of personal character from anyone in the national GOP party. But many Republican leaders haven't publicly disavowed Mr. Stewart, mindful that Trump is supporting him, and that the president has strong influence with the party base — many of whom supported Mr. Stewart in the primary.

Stewart was aware of, but brushed aside, Robert E. Lee's prophetic warning that Confederate monuments could "keep open the sores of war." Kevin Chandler, president of the state's N.A.A.C.P., called Mr. Stewart "treasonous" for his embrace of the Confederate flag. "It symbolizes hate. It symbolizes white supremacy." Rev. Chandler added, "And something such as that should not be displayed openly in the public." In addition to his racist stand, Stewart assailed David Hogg, a teenage survivor of the 2018 high school shooting in the Parkland, FL, and now a gun control activist, as "that punk" who has "been brainwashed." Stewart became an ardent defender of Alabama's Roy Moore amid allegations of Moore's sexual misconduct with underage girls. During the summer of 2018, several neighbors blamed him after Klan fliers landed on local lawns around Woodbridge. "This isn't a coincidence that this happened in my neighborhood," said a local teacher. "Our chairman (Stewart) can't stop talking about the

Confederate flag." Stewart later issued a statement condemning the Klan.

Such associations have dogged Stewart. He called a Wisconsin Congressional candidate, Paul Nehlen, "one of my personal heroes," long after Mr. Nehlen suggested American Muslims should be deported. Nehlen's anti-Semitic rants finally prompted Mr. Stewart to disavow him. Previously, Stewart said of Nehlen, "...many people said very kind things about him, even President Trump and Ann Coulter and Sarah Palin and Laura Ingraham." According to court documents Brian Landrum, a county staff member employed by Stewart, has close ties with Jason Kessler with whom he recently took part in a Facebook chat with about 20 people, including violent racists, who were planning a second Unite the Right rally in Charlottesville. In a July 2018 deposition in a dispute with the city over the proposed rally in Charlottesville, Mr. Kessler described Mr. Landrum as a friend. The company they keep: Jason Kessler, Donald Trump, and Corey Stewart proves the old adage that, "...birds of a feather, flock together."

Hillary haters

In trying to understand the seemingly eternal phenomenon of hatred for Secretary Of State Hillary Clinton, Michelle Goldberg published a lengthy article about the "Hillary haters" in July 2016, four months before hell froze over. She began her article, "I've spoken to people all around America who revile her. Recently, Morning Consult polled people who don't like Clinton and asked them about the reasons for their distaste. Eighty-four percent agreed with the statement "She changes her positions when it's politically convenient." Eighty-two percent consider her "corrupt." Motives for loathing Clinton have evolved. But the loathing itself has remained constant." Among the myriad reasons given by men and women for hating Hillary, not just disliking her, the range was unlimited. Consider the following:

An accountant who lives in Chicago said, "I thought she was someone who came off as a bit entitled and kind of full of herself." He adds, "She strikes me as so programmed and almost robotic." A woman whose father emigrated from Palestine is horrified by what she sees as Clinton's "hawkishness and allegiance to Israel. Most "Hillary haters" abhor Clinton for petty, personal reasons, egged on by radio and TV personalities; there seems to be few people who don't like Clinton because they don't like her record and her proposals.

For many, resistance to Clinton goes beyond policy. "It's not that I just don't like Hillary's positions," many will say. "I don't like her." Their antipathy doesn't follow a precise ideological trajectory. This same woman says, "I don't like her support for the Iraq war." She was also disappointed that Clinton did not support universal healthcare. But in her next breath, she admits she would happily vote for Joe Biden, who also voted for the Iraq war, and as a presidential candidate, he didn't support universal healthcare. She says, "He has a certain kind of humanity that touches me," she says. Several of the people I spoke to see Clinton as lacking in humanity. It's not just that they don't like her—they also feel, on some level, that she doesn't like them. OK. Let me get this straight. All these Hillary haters don't like Hillary because she is 'high and mighty', didn't oppose the Irag War, is the embodiment of avarice and deception, and they think Hillary doesn't like them. Yet, they all chose Trump who is truly the embodiment of all the faults mentioned in the preceding sentence, and who is an accused sexual predator who only months after his inauguration was forced to refund $25 million dollars to students and parents of his short-lived Trump University. OK? Some who loathe Clinton see her as the living embodiment of avarice and deception. Both of these personal shortcomings are the opposite of who Hillary Clinton is. How can all this hatred be understood when it sounds and seems confusing and disorganized.

It appears that millions of Hillary haters take at face value every charge the conservative and moderate Republicans have ever hurled at her, as well as the dark accusations and looney conspiracy theories the right wing parties feed Fox News and the far-out internet sites. As former New York Times editor-in-chief Jill Abramson wrote, "I would be 'dead rich,' to adapt an infamous Clinton phrase, if I could bill for all the hours I've spent covering just about every 'scandal' that has enveloped the Clintons." After all that investigation, Abramson concluded that Clinton "is fundamentally honest and trustworthy." But the appearance of perpetual scandal surrounding Clinton can make it seem as if she must be hiding something monstrous, especially to those who are predisposed against her.

Many Hillary haters express a loathing that transcends political ideology. One young man admits he always disliked Hillary, and his distaste intensified when, as first lady, she was put in charge of health care reform. "I felt like it was not her job to be involved with legislation," he says. I would like to think otherwise but I am certain that Eleanor Roosevelt, another champion for the neediest people in our nation, wouldn't be surprised to hear that statement, even more than a half-century later. (The visceral resistance to Hillary's campaign for US President showed that this particular glass ceiling may be reinforced with steel and its removal will require a laser-beam intensity.)

Yet like most Hillary haters, a middle-aged man rejected the idea that gender has anything to do with his antipathy. "Not at all," he says. "Absolutely not. Nope." He just doesn't like the fact that Hillary feels entitled to his vote. He places his words in her mouth. "Vote for me because I'm a woman," he says. "Ignore the fact that I have accomplished practically nothing significant in my whole career in the public eye, but I'm a woman, so vote for me."

So people hated Hillary Clinton for being one sort of person, and in response to that she became another sort of person who people then hated for different reasons. But this doesn't explain why the emotional tenor of the hatred seems so consistent, even as the rationale for it has turned inside out. Is it because she is a woman, the first woman who was qualified to lead the country, to lead men and women? No doubt, gender still matters. Americans tend not to like ambitious women with loud voices. Women who are successful in areas that are culturally coded as male are typically seen as "abrasive, conniving, not trustworthy, and selfish." There are millions of people, men and women, who will say about a woman: "She's really good at her job, I just don't like her. They think they're making an objective evaluation, but when we look at the broader analysis, there is a pattern to the bias." Among hardcore Trump supporters, the misogyny often isn't subtle; it can be brutal. The Republican National Convention seethed with a highly personalized, and highly sexualized contempt toward Hillary Clinton. Men wore T-shirts that said, "Hillary Sucks but Not like Monica" on one side and "Trump That Bitch" on the backs. Buttons and bumper stickers read, "Life's a Bitch: Don't Vote for One." One man wore a Hillary mask and sat behind a giant yellow sign saying "Trump vs. Tramp." The Make America Great Again voting masses were denigrating Hillary, and America.

Witness to Treason

In the months approaching the 2016 election, in my own limited way, I
made a sincere effort to find out why some of my friends and family
would vote for Donald Trump. The biggest number of answers were
that they "did not like" Hillary Clinton. So I asked them why they
didn't like her. The answers I received were of course varied but they
could be sorted into 4 or 5 boxes which I present below. What is
interesting is that after receiving a one or two word answer: Benghazi,
Bill Clinton, abortion, and so forth, I did not receive any supporting
details from them on the reason given, only a repeated response that
re-emphasized their doubts about Hillary's personal character and
performance. They were reluctant or unable to offer facts deeper than
"I don't like her," or "I don't trust her." It bothered me then; it bothers
me now. It bothers me because the automatic response they delivered
with such unsupported certainty resembled traces of brainwashing. Is
it possible that years of repetitious hateful accusations and charges
piled on endlessly from paid-commentators and radio hosts have
convinced tens of millions of people, and too many people I know and
admire, that Hillary Clinton is the monster and dragon lady these
mercenary TV hosts say she is simply because they said it for so long
and so loudly that it has found a home in a dark corner deep inside
them. I worry because maybe someday that can happen to me. That I
will hate somebody I hardly know only because someone else I hardly
know told me I should.

The hatred for Hillary is so pervasive that it seems like something was
put in America's water. It was. The viciousness and intensity of
people's rejection of Hillary Clinton is founded and centered on the
effects of mob-hysteria generated by the proliferation of conservative,
right wing, alt-right, talk radio programs, and racist internet blogs, and
Fox News where 'fake news' is programmed as entertainment, and
factual news is ignored and "shit-canned." I offer one example of a

leading trumpeter of all the Hillary haters, one of the most vitriolic poison mixers: Alex Jones is a Texan radio host and Trump supporter who is described by the Southern Poverty Law Center as "the most prolific conspiracy theorist in contemporary America". He boasts that all of the 9/11 attacks and the Boston Marathon bombings were plots staged by the government. In a loud, uproarious performance on the BBC's Sunday Politics in 2013, Jones inspired BBC host Andrew Neil to twirl a finger around his temple, saying, "We have an idiot on the show today." Alex Jones is one of the echoes that Hillary haters hear over and over again.

Four Top Reasons given by Hillary Haters, and the true facts.

Benghazi attack: As Secretary of State at the time, Clinton takes responsibility for the attack on the US mission that killed four Americans in 2012 even though several congressional hearings have failed to prove wrongdoing on her part. The hearings, chaired by congressman Trey Gowdy, R-SC, were dominated by the Republican majority in power who spent two years and $ 7.8 million, and found no evidence of wrong-doing by either Secretary of State Clinton or any US government agency or representative. In comparison to the Benghazi panel, the Department of Justice's Special Counsel's investigation into Trump and Russian collusion during the 2016 election is only in its 16th month and has secured five guilty pleas and 14 indictments of individuals. It also gave a referral to the U.S. attorney's office for the Southern District of New York that resulted in a raid on the office, home and hotel room of presidential lawyer and fixer Michael Cohen. Note: In August 2018, Cohen pleaded guilty to committing bank fraud and tax fraud and breaking campaign-finance laws to cover-up Donald Trump's sexual affairs.

Witness to Treason

Use of a private email server: An FBI investigation requested by the GOP members of the House was conducted into the use of a special email server used by then Secretary of State Clinton in 2014, a period adjacent to the Benghazi investigation. The FBI concluded that no "reasonable prosecutor" would bring a criminal case against Clinton, but that she and her aides were "extremely careless" in their handling of classified information.

Clinton Foundation: Questions over potentially inappropriate relations with wealthy foreign officials and businesses were levelled by Trump, but Clinton's campaign pointed out that Trump, too, was a Clinton Foundation donor. Clinton stressed the lifesaving work of the Foundation and denied allegations of corruption. In comparison, the New York state Attorney General began investigating the Trump Foundation charity in January 2018.

Sex scandals: Donald Trump brought women who accused Bill Clinton of sexual assault to the forefront of his 2016 campaign rallies. The Clintons responded previously that the allegations are baseless, though the former president has acknowledged consensual affairs. Trump did not invite the eighteen women who have accused him of sexual assault, and no hearings into the charges have been ordered by the Republican dominated Congress.

The dark depths of hatred for Hillary Clinton,
https://www.bbc.com/news/magazine-36992955, By Jasmine Taylor-Coleman
BBC News, Washington DC 12 October 2016.

Christian Fundamentalists

Politics and religion were two subjects that were always taboo at family dinners and friendly gatherings, unless everyone in the room was in full agreement with both subjects; even then, sports and stories about family were preferred. If you wanted to enjoy your meal, digest your food, and gather peaceably again, you saved diverse opinions for your school's Civics class or for the local borough hall's monthly meeting. Politics and religion don't mix well, we were cautioned. It is a history lesson that our founding fathers learned from the nations that existed around them and the many others that came before them. They were so fearful of religious domination and/or religious persecution in a secular world that they protected their new 'experiment in democracy' by addressing that major concern in the first amendment to the US Constitution. The first of the ten amendments (the Bill of Rights) to the US Constitution includes the words, "Congress shall make no law respecting an establishment of religion, or prohibiting the free exercise thereof." The two parts of that declaration, the "establishment clause" and the "free exercise clause" form the basis for the separation of church and state. The two can co-exist in the community but the government cannot make laws that favor one religion over another. It is also meant to ensure that belonging to any religious affiliation, or to none, does not advantage or hinder a citizen's standing in the community. That single-issue Christian voters will determine their choice of candidates on one specific issue such as abortion, gay marriage, homosexuality, or sin in general, is understandable, and as American as the concept of "one person, one vote" can be. But, single-issue voting can invite the loss of so many additional important freedoms. It is important to be prudent in judgement, to have foresight, and to Stop, Look, and Listen to the candidates' entire message and measure their full character before you make a decision that can cause you to throw the baby out with the bath water.

The Christian Bible, the Separation of Church and State

In Matthew 22:21 Jesus said "Render to Caesar the things that are Caesar's; and to God the things that are God's." This is an oft-quoted passage from the Christian bible that is referenced whenever a church and state discussion is presented. At the time of Jesus' mission, there were two major groups in the Jewish community, a semi-secular one who supported Herod and an orthodox religious one, the Pharisees. They were at opposite ends of the political spectrum but their common hatred of Jesus was enough for them to join forces to try to destroy him. Here is the back-story of Jesus' command to "render to Caesar the things that are Caesar's".

Jesus had just returned to Jerusalem for the final time and finished sharing several parables with the crowd. His enemies saw an opportunity to put him on the spot in front of his followers. They asked Jesus, "Tell us, then, what you think. Is it lawful to pay taxes to Caesar, or not?" It was a trick question. If Jesus answered, "No," Herod's followers would charge him with treason against Rome. If he said, "Yes," the Pharisees would accuse him of being disloyal to the Jewish nation, and he would lose the support of the crowds. Jesus' response was brilliant, "Show me the coin for the tax." And they brought him a coin used as the tax money at the time. It was made of silver and featured an image of the emperor with an inscription calling him "divine." The Jews considered such images idolatry, forbidden by the second commandment. If Jesus answered, "Yes," He would be in trouble. His acceptance of the tax as "lawful" could have been seen as a rejection of the second commandment, thus casting doubt that Jesus' could be the Son of God. With the coin displayed in front of them, Jesus said, "Whose likeness and inscription is this?" The men who asked the questions said, "Caesar's." Then Jesus replied, "Therefore render to Caesar the things that are Caesar's, and to God the things that are God's." Upon hearing this, his enemies went away.

Jesus' answer echoes across two millennium. He outlined a sharp distinction between the two kingdoms. The kingdom of this world which Caesar held power over, and God's world to come which God holds power over. Christians, people who choose to believe in their God, are part of both kingdoms, at least temporarily. Under Caesar, Jesus tells his followers they have certain obligations that involve material things, social rules, regulations, and government laws. While in the flesh, we must accept the laws where we live (and in America, practice our faith in peace), but we must not legislate our faith into other people's secular lives.

The US Constitution, the separation of church and state

America was founded and committed to an individual "pursuit of happiness" and to a clear separation of church and state. Mindful that the terrible history of war and persecution were often initiated as religious wars by kings or ruling factions who demanded allegiance to a specific faith and beliefs, the Framers of the US Constitution acted to prevent America from falling down that hole. They accepted that religious groups have a right to set their own rules of behavior for those who share their faith, but they make it clear that they cannot enlist the authority of the state to compel others to conform their behavior to the commands and demands of a religion they do not accept. The first amendment to the Constitution makes it crystal clear to all. We can practice our own religion as we wish, but we cannot force others to practice our faith and follow its rules. It is imperative that America adhere to the Framers' commitment that religious dogma shall not dictate the meaning of secular law and shall not serve as an excuse for denying fundamental freedoms to all Americans. Laws enacted by the state for the common good of the country shall rise above the religious beliefs of its citizens.

When Religion Looks the Other Way

It is religious hypocrisy when any religion reserves love and charity only for their neighbors who look like them, talk like them, think like them, and believe in the same God as them. In a democratic society, a just rule of law is prominent and foremost for the equal benefit of the community. A mind-set that believes that their God loves them and what is theirs but hates all others who don't accept him, has a common affinity with all religious fanatical movements in history: the Protestant Reformation, the Spanish Inquisition, Al-Qaeda, ISIS, and the Taliban.

History records occasions where religions have accepted the worst evils that prevail in exchange for being able to survive, or sometimes, to be accepted as the state religion; in essence, they have been able to negotiate a "devil's deal" where the religious leaders will not be inconvenienced, imprisoned, persecuted, or murdered as long as they are complicit with government laws and actions and do not speak or act against the government for any reason. They see no evil, hear no evil, and do nothing to stop evil. As mentioned above, single issue voters must guard against voting for a preferred candidate to gain that single issue, to the point where they willfully trade issues important to the common good, then realize later they welcomed the devil himself into the parlor.

White Christian Fundamentalists voters are willing to vote against their own interests if they can be convinced their vote will make sure the minorities are hurt more than them. Afterwards, they will still be white and superior to minorities, and still be favored by their white God, as their parents, themselves, and their children were all taught the same for so many repeating generations. Racist views are more a product of in-trenched ignorance than animosity. They were taught they are superior because they are white, made in God's white image. The CF communities pray continually to God for the same things that all Americans want, deliverance from job loss, an end to declining property values, more opportunities for their children, and an equal voice in determining a better future in a safer and more peaceful world. In the last decades, many towns with a robust economy and well-kept homes morphed into failed businesses, dilapidated homes. Who has stayed, who has left? What can be done to change this collapse of community?

Complaining that the government won't help them but electing the same GOP party candidates to office hasn't worked. How could it? As long as voters keep electing the same people who bring them nothing good, the community will keep getting nothing good. A 'chicken in every pot' won't put gas in the car, or keep the bank from demanding that the mortgage or rent be paid, on time. The voters must check the food cabinets, refrigerators, and driveways of the politicians they vote into office every year. The signs of 'plenty' are there.

The CF won't support the main issues on a Democratic Party platform that will improve their lives such as healthcare, minimum wage increase, union representation, infrastructure spending, alternative energy growth, and climate change policies to prevent regional damages. All of these will be able to help rural America, where most Christian fundamentalists live.

Cynthia Dagnal-Myron, Award-winning former features reporter for the Chicago Sun Times and Arizona Daily Star, HuffPo contributor and author. Jun 28, 2017, https://medium.com/@bioko/a-must-read-an-insider-explains-why-rural-christian-white-america-will-never-change-ac0baf4df02e

What do CFs fear most? Why?

Education. Learning is valued only up to a certain point: reading, writing, arithmetic. Rural America may not accept the real causes of their own situations and fears; they will infer that they have no interest in finding out, especially if their leaders steer them away from finding out the facts. Religion is their education. They will cite Adam and Eve to teach the lesson 'that a little knowledge is a dangerous thing', thus laying a communal prohibition against seeking new ideas and change, instead of encouraging the better view that 'a little knowledge goes a long way.'

Isolation. Fundamentalists are victimized by right-wing conservative propagandists on radio and cable television because they are isolated with little connections beyond their community. They have a "closed-off belief system" that doesn't encourage new information coming into their sphere of influence. Radio and TV persons like Hannity, Limbaugh, formerly O'Reilly, and others tell them the news; these wealthy men convince them that they are "one of them" and spit endless venom against intellectuals, science, and race equality. The listeners are being told what they want to hear by the familiar radio personalities they trust; in turn, the radio station owners collect dollars from advertisers who sell their products to listeners, a cycle that works the same as many 'radio ministers' who bring God's voice to them, collect dollars from faithful listeners. When it is necessary, Republican politicians and business owners provide CFs with scapegoats to blame for every failure in our country. In 2009, they were likely told banks failed because minorities got mortgage loans when most defaults were caused by deficient loans for large homes, apartment buildings, hotels, and corporate real estate. They believe Obama was responsible for 2008/2009 Great Recession, when the truth is Republican president GW Bush, and Republican politicians John Boehner and Mitch McConnell, de-regulated banks and investment firms circa 2002, removing safeguards against risky investments not supported by the borrower's sufficient equity. Their religion often trumps common sense and compassion. They believe there is no Climate Change threat because they believe only God can change the weather? They believe women must be servient to men.

What Can Change a Christian Fundamentalist?

The CFs might say to themselves, only God knows. I would dare to suppose that a personal experience might force them to change: maybe a loved one is gay, a black person becomes a friend, athletics, work, at school, on an athletic team, a book they read from the library, serving in the army, hell, maybe even at church services. The two most striking commonalities are to get away from home, and to meet people, as many good people who want the same things as they do. Religion is limited. Education is unlimited. The heart is unlimited.

The Christian Fundamentalists are taught in their bible schools and churches to "Do unto others as you would have others do unto you." It's not complicated. Pray for that. Vote for that. That is how you find truthful leaders.

These CF Truths Are Not Self-Evident

The CF communities have lived without positive change for too long. The myths they have accepted have been causes for their misfortune. Here is the truth about some myths the CF voters believe can harm them.

- Supply-side economic policies, aka trickle-down economics, favor the rich, not the un-employed
- Immigrants haven't taken jobs away from Americans. In fact, America needs workers
- Republican businessmen, not liberals, move companies overseas
- No one is coming for their guns, just trying to make schools and communities safer
- Gay people getting married won't threaten them, their children, or their community
- A woman who uses birth control has the right to decide if she wants children or not
- People of all races want to work and have a job that enables them to feed their families
- Eliminating government support for black and white neighbors leaves people destitute
- White people in need receive the largest share of food stamps, health care, SS, etc.
- Apple phones, guns, ammo, hunting gear, trucks, all are part of a global market
- Using illicit drugs for their health crisis is the same as "others living elsewhere" using drugs, a person's race or hometown does not determine moral inferiority.

- Jobs to feed families may require some people to relocate for work
- Taxes from the larger states on the coasts pay for their farm subsidies, highways, etc
- Refusing to welcome new residents and commerce in their communities will stop growth and leave the communities without businesses, jobs, and new neighbors

Fox News

Trump's deplorables have to get their news from somewhere, so it makes sense that they get it from Fox News, a place that thinks an awful lot like them, and shows a lot of television programs. These Trump supporters watch a lot of television; they don't read much of anything in print, and don't use the internet. So, with all their TV hosts, Fox News has a larger audience of TDs (Trump deplorables) than Briebart News (billionaire Robert Mercer's alt-right, jaundiced internet blog). Briebart's army of racist and anarchist correspondents led by Trump throwaway Steve Bannon does attract most of the younger deplorables who use the internet. It is a mixed bunch. However, there is one thing Russia's TASS, Briebart, and Fox News have in common. None of them will let truth get in the way of their mission to broadcast lies, falsehoods, and conspiracy theories to keep their viewers entertained. Fox News is an entertainment network, not a news station with factual news – the stories are fussed with, not vetted, and most are slanted and infected with purposeful errors and outright lies. In August 2018, as the scent of treason begins to thicken the air around Washington, Trump wants to make everyone accept it as though it was a good thing, so the Fox News celebrities echoed Trump's short-lived tagline #Treason Might Be Good Now to die-hard Trump supporters who will repeat and retweet it willing and eagerly. They are good medicine for whatever gets under Trump's skin, riding to his rescue with new lies and old charges against his 'tweeter target' of the day. For both Fox News and Trump, facts are dull. They both use innuendos to sensationalize stories and vilify their enemies, and never retract their many proven misprints and lies.

Additionally, in the name of defending the new Republican conservative philosophy, Fox News provides a platform for guests to defend alt-right and white nationalists personalities such as Milo Yiannopoulos, Richard Spencer, and Jason Kessler, men who disgrace America. Christian fundamentalists know that one of the Ten Commandments is "do not lie." Yet, the No. 1 source for their news is Fox News. How do the CFs reconcile the two?

The Fox News celebrities

Who besides Donald Trump feeds the fires for the majority of Trump's passionate voters? Certainly, conservative talk radio hosts and Briebart internet bloggers do, but most famously, it is a stable of Fox News TV journalists listed below.

Sean Hannity is reportedly the most popular member in the Fox News corral. His popularity is connected with his promotions of falsehoods and conspiracy theories, among them being his repeated doubts of President Obama's citizenship and his refusal to accept that Obama was born in America. Yes, Sean, Hawaii is part of America. Hannity reported false stories and false evidence about Hillary's 'poor health' during the 2016 election campaign, even falsely claiming that Clinton was drunk at a rally. All not true. Since Trump's election, he often acted as a conduit for Trump's messages, criticizing the media and attacking the Special Counsel inquiry on Trump and Russian collusion in the 2016 election as a "witch-hunt".

In May 2017, Hannity was still at it. He became a prominent promoter of the conspiracy theory that Hillary Clinton and the Democratic Party were involved in Seth Rich's murder. Rich, a DNC staffer, was killed on July 10, 2016. He was shot to death about a block from where he lived in Washington, DC. Hannity was among a host of right-wing conservatives who insisted that Rich, who was the director of DNC voter expansion data, was the real source of the WikiLeaks emails. This false story was a convenient distraction to draw attention away from the Russia and Trump investigation. Hannity and others reported that Rich was a supporter of Sen. Bernie Sanders and leaked the emails to help Sanders just before the Democratic National Convention was to begin. Hannity faced a tremendous backlash for the false charges, and lost several advertisers, including Crowne Plaza Hotels, Cars.com, Leesa Mattress, USAA, Peloton and Casper Sleep. In March 2018, Seth Rich's parents filed a lawsuit against Fox News for pushing conspiracy theories about their son's death. The suit alleges that the network "intentionally exploited" the tragedy for political purposes.

Hannity had some legal controversy in his earlier career. In 2010, The Federal Trade Commission filed a complaint after three organizations and the IRS alleged that the country music-themed "Freedom Concerts" that Hannity sponsored to raise money forwarded only a small percentage of the money raised by the concerts to the charity, and Hannity was "falsely promoting that all concert proceeds would be donated to a scholarship fund for the children of those killed or wounded in war." The complaint filed with the IRS claims the organizing group, Freedom Alliance, had violated its 501(c)3 charity status. The concerts stopped around the same year that the complaint was filed. *https://en.wikipedia.org/wiki/Sean_Hannity*

Ann Coulter is a conservative author and frequent radio and television commentator and guest on many Fox News conservative republican programs. She has written politically conservative books and opposes immigration so it is not surprising that she would support the most disturbing scenes of Trump's immigration policy: the current separation of families at the US Mexican-American borders. It is alarming to hear her describe to the world that the defenseless, scared, children being separated forcibly by ICE agents on the direct orders from the President of the United States, the US Attorney General, and the Director of Homeland Security are not suffering children at all, but that the "crying immigrant children are actors".

The May 2018 "zero tolerance" immigration enforcement policy rolled out by the Trump administration became a lightning-rod, political issue; an emotional wedge that cut across partisan lines in the national debate about immigration. More than 2,000 children were separated from their parents in the first month of the hardline policy: pictures and audios were leaked. A photograph by Getty Images' John Moore depicting a 2-year-old crying as her mother was patted down by a border agent before the two were separated ricocheted around the world becoming a stand-in for what some see as the abject cruelty taking place in America, land of the free and home of the brave. It did not stop Coulter. She continued. "These kids are being coached," she said. "They're given scripts to read by liberals. . . . Don't fall for the actor children." she directed her remarks to President Trump. "These child actors weeping and crying on all the other networks 24/7 right now; do not fall for it, Mr. President," she said, staring directly into the camera. "I get very nervous about the President getting his news from

TV." Duh! Trump doesn't read or watch actual news; he gets his 'news' as entertainment from Fox News and people like Coulter. Sadly, her remarks went unquestioned by Fox News host Steve Hilton, or by two other guests present at the time, former congressman Republican Jason E. Chaffetz, and Fox News Kimberly Guilfoyle.

This is interesting because Coulter is a descendant of immigrants. In October 2015 while on a book tour, she was defending her opposition to immigration on the TV talk-show, <u>The View</u> when she told the audience that she was not an immigrant, she was a settler. The View's guest host Ana Navarro responded, saying, "Let me point out that you're sitting at this table next to two immigrants ... What is your family's immigration story?" Coulter's reply was curious: "Yes, I am. I'm a settler. I'm descended from settlers. Not from immigrants ... I'm not living in the Cherokee Nation. I'm living in America, which was created by settlers, not immigrants." Coulter's ancestors arrived in America in the mid-nineteenth century from Ireland, likely to escape famine and religious prosecution. But she refuses to accept that she is descended from family members who immigrated to America just as others did who came here from somewhere else. Why is she so embarrassed to be an immigrant? Would she recognize her own ancestors if they stepped off the boat and stood next to her today? Would she even let them enter America today, or would she go on Fox News and tell them to go back to Ireland and starve? I feel that someone she owes so much to is crying in heaven in shame.

https://www.washingtonpost.com/news/arts-and-entertainment/wp/2018/06/18/migrant-kids-are-child-actors-ann-coulter-says-on-fox-news-telling-trump-not-to-be-fooled/?utm_term=.a05c504c7e2b

Laura Ingraham. Sometimes you just need to get away from the office to clear your mind. Fox News host Laura Ingraham did that when she took a much-needed, and reportedly forced, vacation from her regular spot on Fox News. She took an Easter break vacation with her children and fill-in hosts appeared in her normal cable TV slot. Ingraham's show is often the fourth most-watched program in all of cable news with about 2.6 million viewers nightly. A Fox News representative said her absence was planned and was not at all related to advertiser reaction to Ingraham's social media taunting of Parkland high school shooting survivor David Hogg. That didn't ring true to everyone. Liberty Mutual, Office Depot and Entertainment Studios, maker of the film "Chappaquiddick," were Fox News sponsors who no longer run commercials in the conservative commentator's nightly prime-time program. Other cancellations include Nestle, Johnson & Johnson, TripAdvisor, Nutrish, Expedia, Jos. A. Bank and Hulu, the streaming video service that is one-third owned by Fox News parent 21st Century Fox.

Ingraham was under criticism for her tweet about Hogg, the Marjory Stoneman Douglas High School senior, who has become a highly visible gun control activist following the deadly shooting at his Parkland, FL school in February. He mentioned in an interview elsewhere that he was not accepted by four University of California schools. Ingraham took this information as an opportunity to malign the recent high school senior, possibly, because he offends Ingraham's sensibilities that favor the NRA and gun rights because he is leading the youth movement to push guns off the streets of America. Ingraham tweeted, "David Hogg Rejected By Four Colleges To Which He Applied and whines about it," Ingraham issued an apology Thursday after David urged his followers to pressure sponsors to pull out of her show. Ingraham's apology came quickly, considering that Fox News commentators typically resist backing down when under attack for their controversial statements. But the support and sympathy for David and other Parkland students prompted advertisers to continue to bail from her program. Hogg did not accept Ingraham's apology, calling it "an effort just to save your advertisers."

"I will only accept your apology if you denounce the way your network has treated my friends and I in this fight," he tweeted Thursday. "It's time to love thy neighbor, not mudsling at children." The thinned herd of advertisers was apparent during the Friday edition of "The Ingraham Angle." The commercial breaks were filled with Fox News promotional spots and commercials from direct response advertisers — usually a sign of ad cancellations.
Information excerpted from article written by stephen.battaglio@latimes.com, Twitter: @SteveBattaglio

Only months later, in August, Ingraham struck again. She must have been confident the storm had passed and the Fox advertisers were once again enamored with her sizable audience. She pronounced her narrow views on who she judges is an American and who can become American, stirring her proverbial 'pot of sh*t' again, producing another political turmoil. She explained in her righteous manner how alarmed she was that "changing demographics" are destroying America. Her side-kick host, Tucker Carlson, shared the Fox News pulpit that evening but the show's highlights belonged to Ingraham. Shortly after her rant on "demographics", former Ku Klux Klan leader and a White Nationalist ally, David Duke tweeted a link to what Ingraham said, calling her comments "one of the most important (truthful) monologues in the history of MSM." He later deleted the tweet.

Usually, it's Tucker Carlson who pops up on Fox News spouting unabashed white nationalism on-air, railing against the problems with immigration, that is, that more non-white people are immigrating here. But Ingraham gave Carlson a run for his money on this night unleashing a white nationalist rant that suggested "the America we know and love" has been destroyed by "massive demographic changes" due to both illegal and legal immigration. She said outright that allowing non-white people to come here may threaten the majority power enjoyed by White America, that non-white immigration is tantamount to destroying America. In her formulation, whiteness defines the United States, with white people at the center of American life. Which they are, for now. The center of American life 700 years ago was Native Indian. To Ingraham, America is not a daring experiment in self-government based on the principles of liberty, equality before the law, and self-determination, which anyone can be a part of if they work hard and buy into these values. To Ingraham, America is white people's turf. Native Americans may have gotten here first, but it is white now. The problem folks like Carlson, Ingraham, and Trump have is that 'certain people' are coming here, too many 'certain people'. They want more people to come, but people from countries like Norway, or they don't want anyone coming at all. "None of us ever voted for this", Ingraham said. This discussion used to center on how we can better enforce our immigration laws. Now it's about whether anyone should be allowed in at all. Fox News knows that emphasizing people's fears gets their attention, rallies them to unite, to become loyal to the broadcaster and the network, to Fox News. Reminding white people they are losing majority status—and power—due to changing demographics in America makes them hostile to social safety net programs that benefit poor minorities, even though those same programs benefit all races. Fox News has sold white resentment as a primary product. It serves a double purpose: it gives frightened viewers what they want, and tricks them into supporting policies favored by the luxury class in America, the 1% of Americans who own the Republican Party and who pay tens of millions annually for the programming on Fox News, yet pay a smaller percentage of their

income in taxes than you and I, the remaining 99% of Americans pay.
https://www.esquire.com/news-politics/a22685107/laura-ingraham-white-nationalism-fox-news-tucker-carlson/

Fox News Is Trusted Less Than CNN, MSNBC.

With all of the noise about who is broadcasting "fake news", Fox News inadvertently posted a graphic on a Sunday program showing it trailed other cable news networks in trustworthiness, giving a stinging certitude to the observation that sometimes the truth hurts. Fox News host Howard Kurtz was discussing with a Republican pollster Frank Luntz a Monmouth University poll which asked respondents if the media regularly or occasionally reports fake news. Unfortunately for Fox News, the graphic that came up on screen showed results from another question in the poll, Question 38, which asked what cable news outlets did poll respondents trust more. The Monmouth poll chart, shown below, listed Fox News last at 30%, behind CNN and MSNBC, both regular targets of attacks by President Donald Trump. Overall, CNN @ 48% was chosen as the most trusted followed by MSNBC @ 45%, and trailed lastly by Fox News at 30%. Fox News was last in credibility. The chart was quickly removed from the broadcast and most likely so was the employee who inserted the chart with the true data onto the shocked Fox News TV host's screen. Kurtz, the author of an admiring book about the Trump White House, realized the mistake too late. "That is not the graphic we are looking for," he said. "Hold off. Take that down, please."

The truth in this incident is that Trump, who was also included in Question 38 (shown below), finished first as being the most untrustworthy. That was most fitting for the man who started claiming 'fake news' every time anyone said or printed anything negative about

319

him: things not untrue, just negative. Trump brandished his life-long disregard for the truth and initiated an avalanche of doubt on the truth in America. He has given lying a position of prominence all across America. This is the personal legacy that he emblazoned on America's soul in less than two years.

Monmouth University Polling Institute, 04/02/18. https://www.monmouth.edu/polling-institute/documents/monmouthpoll_us_040218.pdf/

The Fake News Epidemic. Who Do You Trust?

The Trump administration has accomplished a lot of negative 'firsts' in its short, but seemingly 'been-around-forever' stint as the face of America seen by the world and the American citizens. In less than two years, the operative and most descriptive word to describe Trump's presidency is "out of control". No. 45 has turned America upside down and inside out. If Peter Sellers and his grand army from the Duchy of Grand Fenwick landed on America's shores today, he might want to turn around immediately, fearful that whatever illness is infecting America is something that he and all of the citizens of Grand Fenwick should want to avoid at all costs. Monmouth University Polling Institute located in West Long Branch, NJ published a poll on April 2, 2018 announcing some interesting observations that should worry all Americans.

The Monmouth report indicated large majorities of the American public believe now that traditional media outlets engage in reporting fake news. The March poll indicates that more than 3-in-4 Americans believe that traditional major TV and newspaper media outlets report "fake news," including 31% who believe this happens regularly and 46% who say it happens occasionally. The 77% who believe fake news reporting happens at least occasionally has increased significantly from 63% of the public who felt that way in 2017. Just 25% say the term "fake news" applies only to stories where the facts are wrong. Most Americans (65%), on the other hand, say that "fake news" also applies to how news outlets make editorial decisions about what they choose to report. "These findings are troubling, no matter how you define 'fake news.' Confidence in an independent fourth estate is a cornerstone of a healthy democracy. Ours appears to be headed for the intensive care unit," said Patrick Murray, director of the independent Monmouth University Polling Institute. The belief that major media outlets disseminate fake news at least occasionally has increased among every partisan group over the past year, including Republicans (89% up from 79% in 2017), independents (82% up from 66%), and Democrats (61% up from 43%). When it comes to the meaning of "fake news," a majority believe that it involves editorial decisions as well as inaccurate reporting. The public feels that social media platforms are partly to blame for the spread of fake news and are not doing enough to stop it.

Trump versus Cable News. The poll chart for Question 38 (shown below) finds that President Trump continues to be less trusted than three major cable news outlets as an information source. Nearly half the American public (48%) trusts CNN more than Trump, compared with one-third (35%) who trust Trump more than CNN, 13% trust both equally as a source of information. The results are similar when Trump is pitted against the left-leaning MSNBC where 45% trust MSNBC more than Trump, 32% trust Trump more, and 16% trust both equally. The right-leaning Fox News also bests the President as a trusted information source – 30% trust Fox more, and 20% trust Trump more, 37% trust both equally.

Witness to Treason

The Monmouth University Poll was conducted by telephone from March 2 to 5, 2018 by the Monmouth University Polling Institute in West Long Branch, NJ, 803 adults were contacted in the United States. The results in this release have a margin of error of +/- 3.5 percent. Question 38 is shown below.

Question 38. I'm going to read you some names of information sources. For each pair of names I read, please tell me which one you trust more as a source of information, or whether you trust both sources about equally.

Donald Trump and CNN   March 2018: Trust Trump more 35%, Trust CNN more 48%, Trust both equally 13%, (VOL), don't know 5%. (n) (803)

Donald Trump and Fox News TREND: March 2018: Trust Trump more 20%, Trust Fox News more 30%, Trust both equally 37%, (VOL), don't know 13%. (n) (803) (801)

Donald Trump and MSNBC TREND: March 2018; Trust Trump more 32%, Trust MSNBC more 45%, Trust both equally 16%. (VOL) Don't know 6%. (n) (803) (801)

https://www.monmouth.edu/polling-institute/documents/monmouthpoll_us_040218.pdf/

WHO DO YOU TRUST MORE?

	NETWORK	TRUMP
CNN	48%	35%
MSNBC	45%	32%
FOX NEWS	30%	20%

MONMOUTH UNIVERSITY
MARCH 2-5
803 ADULTS +/- 3.5%

FOX NEWS

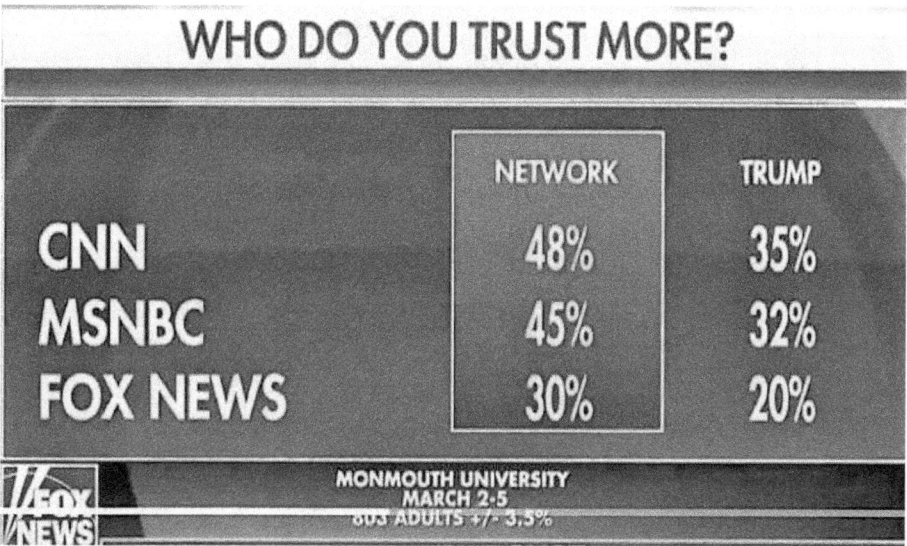

Monmouth University Poll shown on Fox News on April 2, 2018

Where Have All the Foxes Gone?

The Fox News organization is a part of billionaire Rupert Murdoch's Entertainment Empire. Sex, gossip, scandal, conspiracy theories, murder, espionage and treason are money-making events (truth or lies) for Murdoch's empire, but only if his empire is not part of the scandals. Since 2017, Fox News and its business guru, Roger Ailes, have become part of the scandals. In 2017, Fox News became a large part of their own cable news entertainment when the network's on-air and off-air leaders were involved in a wide range of exposes. The continuing scandals alienated sponsors, thus effecting revenues (money). Murdoch and his underlings rushed to quietly manage the accusations of sexual harassment, racist behavior, and bigoted comments levelled at the network's executives, top hosts, senior managers and staff. Roger

Ailes, his number two person, Bill Shine (hired in August 2018 as Trump's deputy manager of public relations), top Fox host Bill O'Reilly, and on-air hosts Anne Coulter and Laura Ingraham, and Judy Slater, Fox company comptroller, and others have been dismissed, retired or reprimanded. Bill O'Reilly, once Fox News top TV host, was fired in April 2017 after the disclosure of a series of sexual harassment allegations against him. Now that the #Enough and #MeToo movements have blasted open the previously-closed door on sexual harassment behavior charges, is it possible that even Fox News will consider conducting real news investigations into the sexual accusations against Trump? (See paragraph below). Meanwhile, the Foxhole is getting crowded. Who will jump out of the Foxhole first? The GOP, Fox, Russia, or Trump? It appears that Fox News qualifies as a different definition of the word deplorable.

In one instance, Fox News did finally stand-up when it defended its own host, Megyn Kelly, after Trump attacked Kelly in 2015 calling her "sick" and "overrated" because of her hard-hitting questioning at a GOP campaign debate in August 2015. The question from Kelly that triggered Trump's temper was about Trump's prior statements in which the real estate developer called various women "fat pigs," "slobs" and "disgusting animals." Kelly's aggressive stand against Trump's language toward women infuriated Trump who cannot accept anything less than submission from women. Fox News attacked Trump saying his words are "beneath the dignity of a presidential candidate." Following that debate, Trump tweeted that Kelly was a "loser" and a "bimbo." He also told another cable news network that Kelly had "blood coming out of her eyes—blood coming out of her whatever." In retrospect Trump's misogynist treatment of women makes him a candidate for employment at Fox News after he leaves the White House.

Soon, it was Trump's turn in the barrel. During the stretch run prior to the November 2016 election, eighteen women came forward and accused Trump of sexual assault. Many of the charges were not new but none of the cases were ever fully adjudicated in a court of law. All the women said they decided to speak out after Trump stated in several of his election press conferences that he had never sexually harassed a women. Fox News fell back into its true form as a leading voice for the conservative wing of the Republican Party. They did not convene any panel discussions in support of any of the women accusers, and presented no commentary or requests for committee investigations into the President's serial behavior. Fox News and the Republican congress would have others believe that all of these eighteen women lied, and that only Donald Trump told the truth. Can anyone give a better definition for the word deplorable? Maybe George Orwell's Oceana wasn't a fictional place, Fox News seems to have much more in common with Big Brother's newspeak than it would like to admit.

The GOP Is Still Loyal to a Fault. Why?

Trump's approval among Republicans has remained strong since he entered office and various polls indicate there is very little the President can do wrong in the eyes of the new Republicans, even while he denies Russia's interference in the 2016 election, and Russian officers, businessmen, and spies are beginning to fill-in the calendar on Washington DC courthouse dockets. The GOP, who prior to Trump's candidacy, voraciously demanded that every person running for a political office must share their personal income tax returns with the general public, feverishly supported Trump's refusal to do so, and still support refusal, despite all of the alleged skullduggery that has arisen during the past two years: Russian loans, hush payments, hundreds of millions in debt, and so forth.

Throughout his 18 months in office, Trump has never received less than 78% percent approval from Republicans in Gallup's poll. According to Gallup Polls in late summer 2018, Trump registered a 90% approval rating from Republicans, while only 8% of Democrats and 38% of independents offered approval. The recent findings suggest a strong shift within a Republican Party that was staunchly anti-Russia for decades. Starting with notorious Wisconsin Senator Joseph McCarthy and his firebrand style known as "McCarthyism," the GOP has long been firmly anti-Communism and viewed Russia as the nation's greatest enemy. Now the GOP and Russia are friends? After Trump's visit to Helsinki in July 2018, 79% of Republicans approved of Trump's performance alongside Putin, while 91% of Democrats and 62% of independents disapproved. Overall, Trump received 58% disapproval and only 40% approval. Those results backed up a Reuters/Ipsos poll released in mid-July which showed 55% overall disapproved of Trump's work on Russian relations, but, the poll also reflected approval from 71% of Republicans, reflecting the Republican Party leadership and voters choice of Party over country.

His Republican base was loyal and supportive even after the debacle at the Helsinki meeting on July 24, 2018 where Trump was out-shone and overwhelmed by Putin, to the embarrassment of America. The leaders of the two most powerful countries in the world, traditional rivals, met on the world stage amidst the ongoing problems of a tragic war in Syria, continuing ISIS terrorism, and Russian military interference in Ukraine. They shared a two-hour private conversation with one another, then came out of the meeting smiling and pleased with one another. But neither shared the contents of their discussions nor provided any meeting notes. Their secret session was followed by a public press conference where Trump accepted Putin's denial of meddling in the U.S. 2016 election, with Trump still insisting that it could've been anybody (but certainly not the Russians). In the same press conference, Trump was asked by an American reporter who he trusted most, Russia or the accuracy of his own US intelligence agencies' previous confirmation that Russia did meddle in 2016, and that it was now meddling in the 2018 US election. His reply did not reflect his full confidence in his own intelligence agencies, leaving most of the world to witness Trump accepting Putin's word above all others. Incredible! This happened only days after his own administration's Department of Justice issued indictments on twelve Russian military officers and other Russian citizens for interfering in the US 2016 election (indictment cover page shown below). Trump may have with-held judgement against Russia but the indictments make it clear these Russians were operating with the full cooperation of Putin's government.

Defining Trump's appeal to his deplorables: one disgrace after another.

- Russian Collusion. Trump covertly sought and accepted Russian support to win the 2016 Presidential election.
- Helsinki capitulation. He sided with Putin and Russia while expressing less faith in America's FBI, CIA, and additional intelligence agencies.
- Charlottesville. He finally addressed the white supremist riot in Virginia, after being pressured by news media, saying 'there were good people on both sides.'

- Sexual Assault Charges. He denied all 18 women's charges of aggressive sexual assault, he is avoiding facing any one of the women in a court of law.
- Immigration roundup squads. He questioned aloud why we accept immigrants from "shit-hole' countries who are predominantly people of color and little educated.
- The free press is the enemy. He attacks the mainstream press as "enemies of the American people", calling reputable and accurate news reporting "fake news" and his personal fake news as the only 'real' truth.
- Mass shootings, Parkland, Las Vegas, others. Insincere homage to victims followed by heart-felt pledges of loyalty to the NRA. No action from Trump. "Not a good time to discuss guns."
- Hush payments. Sexual assault sex wasn't Trump's problem this time. He paid thousands in hush money to two women (Stormy $130K, and Karen $150K) just before the 2016 Presidential election took place, violating Federal campaign laws.
- Tried to Repeal and Replace Obamacare. Trump's biggest campaign promise was to remove Obamacare, though he failed, he set roadblocks to sabotage Obamacare through 2018.
- Muslim Ban. He arbitrarily restricted people from Muslim countries from entering America.
- Tossed paper towels to hurricane Maria survivors in Puerto Rico, disgracing the citizens of Puerto Rico and America when he visited the island and had 'a great time.'
- He placed America (Guam and Hawaii first) on the brink of nuclear war twice - when he exchanged insults with North Korea's President, and did the same in with Iran.

- Damaged relations with western Allies, picked arguments with the members of the North American Treaty Organization: all this benefitting Russia.
- Attempted to bully women leaders of Germany and United Kingdom, banned from visiting London in 2017 by popular vote, insulted Prime Ministers of France, Canada and Australia while embracing and praising Turkey, Russia, and China tyrants.

Trump supports and admires bullies and dictators.

Vladimir Putin, Russia   Erdogan, Turkey   Kim Jong-un, North Korea
Xi Jingping, China   David Duke (KKK) Sheriff Arapio, Arizona
Roy Moore, Alabama   Richard Spencer (WS)   NRA gun peddlers

Informal Deplorables Clubs arose in Trump country shortly after Hillary Clinton's remark in NYC was applauded and celebrated by Trump and Donald, Jr. The young Trump was so proud of his automatic membership into the club that he displayed the deplorables button on his suit coat lapel. All of the men listed above have likely been admitted as charter members in the Deplorables club. I am hopeful they won't get the opportunity to be 'pinned' by Trump on the White House lawn. That, by itself, would be further definition of deplorable.

Pardons for Sale at 1600 Pennsylvania Ave

Trump has watched close associates and members of his 2016 campaign organization being indicted (some already convicted) on a variety of different charges uncovered during the Special Counsel's investigation into possible collusion between the Trump campaign and

Russia during the 2016 election. Trump publicly voiced his intention to pardon his associates after they are convicted. He added that he can pardon himself if he needed to, though he didn't do anything wrong. He was 'just saying.'

In order to send a signal to his already-indicted associates, General Michael Flynn and 2016 election campaign manager Paul Manafort, he began showing them his pardoning power by pardoning friends of his friends. In a six month period, March to July 2018, he pardoned six persons. Trump's plan is to display his intention to be loyal to his convicted associates and hopefully convince them from 'spilling the beans'. The message is clear: if they go to jail protecting him, he will pardon them before the sentencing ink will dry. Quid pro quo. Here is a list of Trump pardons through July 2018. Are there more to come?

PARDONS GRANTED BY PRESIDENT DONALD TRUMP 2017-2018

AUGUST 25, 2017   Download PDF Clemency Warrant

Joseph M. Arpaio,

Offense: Contempt of court (District of Arizona)

Sentence: N/A

MARCH 9, 2018   Download PDF Clemency Warrant

Kristian Mark Saucier

Offense: Unauthorized retention of defense information (District of Connecticut)

Sentence: 12 months' imprisonment and three years' supervised release, conditioned upon six months' home confinement performance of 100 hours' community service (August 19, 2016)

APRIL 13, 2018 Download PDF Clemency Warrant

I. Lewis Libby, aka Scooter Libby, aka Irve Lewis "Scooter" Libby

Offense: Obstruction of justice; false statements; perjury (two counts) (District of Columbia)

Sentence: 30 months' imprisonment, two years' supervised release, $250,000 fine (June 14, 2007)

MAY 24, 2018 Download PDF Clemency Warrant

John Arthur Johnson, aka Jack Johnson

Offense: Violation of the White Slave Traffic Act (Northern District of Illinois)

Sentence: One year and one day's imprisonment; $1,000 fine (September 14, 1920)

MAY 31, 2018   Download PDF Clemency Warrant

Dinesh D'Souza

Offense: Campaign contribution fraud (Southern District of New York)

Sentence: Five years' probation, conditioned upon eight months' community confinement and the performance of one f week of community service; $30,000 fine (September 23, 2014)

JULY 10, 2018   Download PDF Clemency Warrant

Dwight Lincoln Hammond, Offense: Use of fire to damage and destroy property of the United States

Sentence: 3 months' imprisonment; 3 years' supervised release; amended to 60 months' imprisonment on Oct 7, 2015.

JULY 10, 2018   Download PDF Clemency Warrant

Steven Dwight Hammond, Offense: Use of fire to damage and destroy property of the United States (two counts)

Sentence: 12 months' and one day's imprisonment; 3 years' supervised release; amended to 60 months' imprisonment o

Russian Collusion

Russian Collusion

Chapter Eleven
Russian Collusion

"No prior president has ever abased himself more abjectly before a tyrant."
John McCain, July 2018

On Treason

Cicero, a Roman statesman in 42 BC, addressed the Roman Senate two thousand years ago on the dangers imposed on a nation from an enemy from within its nation when he said, "A nation can survive its fools, and even the ambitious. But it cannot survive treason from within. An enemy at the gates is less formidable, for he is known and carries his banner openly. But the traitor moves amongst those within the gate freely, his sly whispers rustling through all the alleys, heard in the very halls of government itself. For the traitor appears not a traitor; he speaks in accents familiar to his victims, and he wears their face and their arguments, he appeals to the baseness that lies deep in the hearts of all men. He rots the soul of a nation, he works secretly and unknown in the night to undermine the pillars of the city, he infects the body politic so that it can no longer resist. A murderer is less to fear."

From Russia with love

A question of treason has been raised. Along with treason, espionage, blackmail, spies, sex, greed, murder, and betrayal are all actors in this day to day story that suffocates us all. This chapter in America's history surpasses the imagination of even the greatest story-tellers, because the truth in this case is stranger than fiction. James Bond and Ian Fleming, spy and author, are both dead. The rumor among librarians is that they both died on the same day. But if they were alive today, neither would believe the events that have encircled the world in the last several years. "Poppycock" is probably how they might react to it all. After all, it would be too hard for them to believe that the President of the United States and his family and friends are accused of conspiring, colluding is the word choice in the official indictments, with a foreign agent (Russia) to seriously influence America's 2016 presidential election. That's a big enough statement, but there's more to this very complicated spy story of an America on the ropes. Fleming, a British naval intelligence officer during WWII, must be turning over in his grave, trying to get back up here to read the craziest, damn spy novel even he couldn't have dreamed up. I don't blame him for trying either. Anyway, here are the facts, the rumors, the denials, the testimony, the witnesses, the betrayals, the deception, the murders, the shame, and the danger that have been visited like a plague upon America. Most of all, it reminds us that we must be diligent about democracy, about the truth, all the time, beginning at the local ballot box in our own communities. Here in 2018, less than a few months before the 2018 mid-term elections, I want to paraphrase New York Yankees baseball Hall of Famer Yogi Berra's famous quote, "It ain't over, yet!"

Something Is Going On

The first warnings given to U.S. officials that America was under attack from Russian came from several countries friendly to America. In July 2016, these countries provided information to US intelligence agencies that Russia was waging a full attack on America's sovereignty. The Russian government appeared to be orchestrating an effort to disrupt the American political process and interfere in America's 2016 presidential election. Russia decided they could seriously influence who would be the 45th president of the United States. Russia's sole purpose for this brazen attack was to prevent Hillary Clinton from becoming President, and in doing so, ensure that its favored candidate, Donald J. Trump, would be elected. The plan had a more fictional plot than the 1960 Hollywood film, *The Manchurian Candidate*, but it was it all true.

John Brennan, And the GOP Failure to Act

On August 4, John Brennan, CIA chief, took the first direct action against Russia. He called Alexander Bortnikov, Russia's director of the FSB, the successor to the KGB, and warned him in blunt language that America would respond heavily if such interference was conducted by Russia or its agents. Brennan then proceeded to contact both GOP and Democratic congressional leaders to arrange an emergency meeting to inform them of Russia's activities, and to recommend immediate action to counteract the Russian aggression. The response from the GOP was slow, and then even slower as the reason for the meeting became clear to the GOP leaders. While the GOP leaders refused to find time to participate in a meeting to address Russian attacks, Jeb Johnson, the homeland-security secretary, began contacting all 50 of the nation's secretaries of states to seek agreement from them to designate their state voting mechanisms as "critical infrastructure", thereby entitling their state to receive priority assistance from federal cyber-security if anyone interfered with their voting system. Later, in congressional testimony, Johnson said this suggestion of assistance was met with "a wall of resistance" from dozens of secretaries of states in GOP controlled states. The homeland-security secretary reported that the reaction from GOP political officials "ranged from neutral to negative". Why the resistance? Brian Kemp, the Republican secretary of state for Georgia accused Johnson of "an assault on state's rights." Why such slow response form GOP leaders in Washington, and from GOP politicians around the country?

Finally, a meeting with all members of the "Gang of Eight" (the majority and minority leaders of both houses of Congress, and the GOP chairmen and the highest ranking Democrats in the Senate and House intelligence committees) took place after Labor Day. The meeting addressed by FBI and Homeland Security senior officials began with the legislators being told that they had evidence that the Kremlin might be trying to actively involve themselves in helping Donald Trump be elected as President of the U.S. These officials who were appointed to protect and defend the United States of America fully expected bipartisan acceptance of the information and a like expectation of a joint resolution for action from America's most powerful legislators, but to their dismay, the meeting ended in a partisan squabble. The Democrats took the information seriously and were ready to act and to tell the American people of the Russian interference; the GOP, the Party of No, did nothing. The GOP leaders of the House and the Senate, the GOP House Intelligence and the Senate Intelligence Committee chairmen - all four GOP leaders - closed party ranks and decided there was insufficient information to take any action, neither to confront Russia, nor to tell the American public about Russian activities. GOP Senate Leader, Mitch McConnell, and GOP House Leader Rep. Paul Ryan, led their party down the path of inactivity again. The Party of No remained consistent in its ability to do nothing when confronted with America's common good. Why did the GOP leadership do nothing?

The Plot to Hack America

I read Malcolm Nance's e-book *"The Plot to Hack America."* in mid-October 2016, just before the election that I will never forget. The book was published in an eBook format likely because there was not enough time to prepare it for release in a printed format because the author and the publisher wanted the book in the public eye while the election was in the news. They were hopeful it would serve as a warning cry to America's voters, all of them. The eBook became a 21st century version of Paul Revere's ride to save America, with Nance substituting Revere's famous words with his own warning that "the Russians are coming." I heard it, others heard it, but not everyone heard it. And some leaders who heard it, ignored it.

Here are excerpts from a book review by Michael Lipkin. (*online link provided below*).

Malcolm Nance served the nation as a career naval intelligence officer with expertise in counterterrorism and national security, and he has deep knowledge of similar matters in his book. As a Russian language interpreter, he studied the Soviet Union intensely, especially its espionage arm, the KGB. *"The Plot to Hack America"* is an essential primer for anyone who wants to be fully informed about the unprecedented events surrounding the 2016 U.S. presidential election. Published shortly before the election, the book still provides the basic framework for understanding all that came after the election, much of which corroborates Nance's claims and speculation. Remember, many people disputed or downplayed Russian involvement at the time. Subsequent developments show that Nance was way ahead of the curve. The book begins in summer 2016 when Guccifer 2.0 and WikiLeaks released embarrassing emails hacked from the Democratic

National Committee showing, for example, that DNC leaders had a
clear preference for Hillary Clinton as their candidate. This information
immediately caused discord between Clinton supporters and the
Sanders people. The harmful hacks had begun in March, as the
intruders stole emails, voicemails, and donor data, timing the release at
the worst moments for the Democrats. Cyber investigators noticed
important things about the hacks, Nance explains. First, the complex
patterns and tools pointed not to amateurs, but to state-sponsored
actors, based on past history and other electronic "fingerprints."
Second, from this evidence, the prime suspects immediately became
two Russian-sponsored hacking groups, FANCY BEAR and COZY
BEAR (collectively called CYBER BEARS). And third, while most hacks
collect and hoard stolen information, these hacks made the data public.

Based on the evidence, the investigators thus developed a theory:
Russia was trying to influence the election against Hillary Clinton in
favor of Donald Trump, who supported policies in line with Russia's
geopolitical agenda. After the DNC hacks and information dumps,
massive investigations were begun by civilian, U.S., and NATO
nations. Some politicians were still telling American voters that this
was no big deal and that you can never know where a hack comes
from—maybe from a hostile power, maybe from a 400-pound guy in a
bed in New Jersey. But as Nance explains in great detail, you *can* trace
the origin of a hack. There are many methods of tracking down the
source. In the case of the DNC hack, all indicators showed patterns that
were recognizable to just about every intelligence officer, and it all
continued to point to the Russian-sponsored CYBER BEARS.

Why Only the Democratic Party?

The question remained. Why did only Democratic information get released and why at especially crucial and damaging times? Was it a coincidence that all the information that was hacked and revealed damaged the Democratic Party and Hillary Clinton and was helpful to Donald Trump? To explain that "coincidence," Nance digs deeply into the histories and personalities of Putin and Trump, and adds one real fact, Putin's mind-set is "Once KGB, always KGB." One great skill Putin learned in his KGB tenure was how to turn people against their own country and into spies, wittingly or unwittingly, for the Soviets. Putin could also blackmail his targets with a technique the Russians call Kompromat (compromising material), using embarrassing or compromising information to turn individuals into Russian sympathizers. As his political power and his wealth grew, Nance explains, Putin's political agenda developed—a desire to increase Russia's power and wealth against an economically crippled and isolationist United States under pro-Russian leadership. This, according to Nance, is where Donald Trump enters the picture.

"If there were ever a candidate for recruitment by a hostile intelligence agency, then Trump would be moved to the head of the class," suggests Nance. Trump had been visiting Russia since 1987 seeking business deals and favor among the nation's wealthy elite he so admired. He proudly stated after one meeting that "almost all of the oligarchs were in the room." After Trump's many well-documented bankruptcies, he turned to Russian sources—including criminal ones—for financing of his projects. Meanwhile he developed a great affinity for Putin and the nation of Russia. This was tailor-made for Moscow, "...Putin saw Trump as an asset to be developed," The powerful pro-Russian ties of many of Trump's closest associates, including Paul

343

Witness to Treason

Manafort, Howard Lorber, Carter Page, Richard Burt, Dimitri Simes, Michael Caputo, and perhaps most importantly, General Michael Flynn who went from forced resignation as director of the Defense Intelligence Agency to being a contributor for the Kremlin-controlled television propaganda outlet Russia Today, fit perfectly. Nance puts forth a powerful and informed opinion: "The revelations of the Kremlin Crew's (Trump's advisers) proximity to Moscow are stunning. They reveal how easily some Americans will accept money to work against their national interests. . . . Such riches would surely be issued with invisible strings, allowing the Russia's FSB, the former KGB, to gain access to the highest-level players in a new American administration." Nance wrote in 2016 that Putin: "sees the election of Donald Trump as the fastest way to destabilize the United States and damage its economy as well as fracture both the European Union and NATO [in order to end NATO's obstruction of Russian aggression in Eastern Europe]. These events . . . would allow Russia to become the strongest of the world's three superpowers and reorder the globe with a dominant Russia at the helm."

Conveniently, Russia was able to use WikiLeaks and the Russian intelligence's own fake source, Guccifer 2.0, to "launder" the public disclosures of the DNC rift and negatively impact Hillary Clinton's campaign. Nance insists that the Russians "have achieved this goal." He believes that these individuals have been won over "to further their own financial interests at the behest of a hostile government." In a particularly dramatic statement, Nance states that, by their choices, actions, and statements, "Trump and Pence chose Russia's values over America's." *https://www.nyjournalofbooks.com/book-review/plot-hack-america* book review by: Michael Lipkin

Cambridge Analytica

Cambridge Analytica (CA) is a UK data collection company created by
Robert Mercer, an American billionaire patron of right-wing factions
who was also the primary investor of the alt-right, on-line, junk-news
outlet, Breitbart News. The company (CA) was contacted by the Trump
campaign after Jared Kushner, who was overseeing Trump's digital
operations, hired a Texas-based digital expert named Brad Parscale,
whose company collected $90 million for its services. The decision to
hire Parscale was reinforced by Steve Bannon, Trump's campaign
manager at that time. Bannon, a political guru to Robert Mercer, had
been vice-president at CA, then president of Mercer's Briebart News
prior to joining the Trump campaign. Throughout its business life-
cycle, CA worked in the U.S. only for clients with Republican Party
ties. Cambridge Analytica became an added partner to this expansive
endeavor to adversely influence Clinton's campaign. (Note: CA filed
for insolvency in May 2018).

The principal role CA played for the Trump campaign was that it
reportedly gathered data from 87 million Facebook accounts in the
United States and created profiles on US voters that were later used to
target them with false and misleading ads during the 2016 election
with the sole intention to help Trump get elected. *The Wall Street
Journal* reported that Cambridge Analytica turned over internal
documents to the Mueller team as part of its investigation into possible
collusion between the Trump campaign and Russia during the 2016
election. So, another foreign player enters the investigation, and the
question gets louder; did Trump's campaign team, with the help of this
data company, share the data and its strategic significance with
Russia, and facilitate Russia's meddling in the US presidential election?

How It Worked

Cambridge academic Alexander Kogan's company Global Science Research (GSR) developed an app used by CA to pull in data from people who used the app as well as pulling in data from their Facebook friends. Once the information package from CA become operational in August, pro-Trump programmers "carefully adjusted the timing of content production during the debates, strategically colonized pro-Clinton hashtags, and then disabled activities after Election Day." These online ads were spread primarily through bots (computer auto-commands) on social media platforms. The ads that got liked, shared, and retweeted the most were reproduced and redistributed based on where they were popular and who they appealed to. The benefit of this kind of data is that it allows companies like Cambridge Analytica to develop more sophisticated psychological profiles of internet users (more data points means more predictive power). Cambridge Analytica was able to use this real-time information to determine which messages were resonating where, communicate this information to interested parties who could then shape Trump's travel schedule around it. So, if there was a spike in clicks on an article about immigration in a county in Pennsylvania or Wisconsin, Trump would go there and give an immigration-focused speech. When you consider how a few thousands votes in a handful of swing states determined the election, this is no small thing. Clinton Watts, a senior fellow at the Center for Cyber and Homeland Security at George Washington University, told Senate investigators that many social accounts created during the election to nefariously push fake news looked just like real voters in states like Wisconsin and Michigan. The Russian operatives, he noted, would "inhale all of the accounts of the people in Wisconsin" and "identify the most common terms in it" to "recreate accounts that look exactly like people from Wisconsin..." Even the smallest impact from this disinformation campaign could change the election result. So how damaging would such collusion be to America's election process? How much impact might it have had on the election? Particularly in three key states where "Clinton lost the decisive states of Michigan (5,353), Wisconsin (11,375), and Pennsylvania (22,147) after 13.9 million votes were cast".

Research and timing are common strategies in electioneering, but sharing skill sets, and coordinating intelligence, and schedules to target specific states, even precincts, with Russian trolls trained and paid by Russia, are crimes under federal law, and such acts are tantamount to treason. To what degree were Russians involved is the focus of a *Wall Street Journal* article by Shane Harris who interviewed a man named Peter Smith, a pro-Trump GOP operative, who sought to acquire the 30,000 deleted emails from Hillary Clinton's private server? Of the several hacker groups Smith reached out to, he said at least two had connections to Russia. Smith told Harris that he was in regular contact with Gen. Michael Flynn, who at the time was one of Trump's closest confidants - and of course later, Flynn became Trump's National Security Adviser. Later, in an amended public financial filing, Flynn was forced to disclose "a brief advisory role with a firm related to a controversial data analysis company that aided the Trump campaign." The "data analysis company" is none other than Cambridge Analytica. The precise amount of money Cambridge paid to Flynn is unknown, as are the details of Flynn's role. But we know that congressional and DOJ investigators believe that Trump's campaign might have aided Russia's voter targeting scheme in knowing when and where to flood vulnerable states, cities, and precincts with specific fake news, scare ads, etc with the intent to influence voters' decisions. Flynn, who worked for Trump's campaign and with Cambridge Analytica, is suspected of having extensive ties with Russian operatives.

347

Witness to Treason

https://www.vox.com/policy-and-politics/2017/10/16/15657512/cambridge-analytica-facebook-alexander-nix-christopher-wylie Cambridge Analytica, the shady data firm that might be a key Trump-Russia link, explained

After the fact

The plot to hack America succeeded. Hillary Clinton was removed as a threat to Russia, and Donald Trump was elected President of the United States. A January 2017 assessment by the United States Office of the Director of National Intelligence (ODNI) delivered to the highest officials in Washington reported that Russian president Vladimir Putin favored presidential candidate Donald Trump over Hillary Clinton and personally ordered an "influence campaign" to harm former Senator and Secretary of State Clinton's electoral chances and "undermine public faith in the US democratic process."[27]:7 It is now clear that the Russian government interfered in the 2016 U.S. presidential election and that they are suspected of funneling tens of millions, possibly hundreds of millions of dollars, in dirty money to the Trump campaign to get Trump elected.

Due to his participation in activities related to the investigation, Jeff Sessions, Trump's Attorney General and former campaign aide, was pressured to recuse himself from any contact with the investigation into Russian interference and Trump collusion in the 2016 election. Therefore in May 2017, Deputy Attorney General, Rod Rosenstein, serving in the capacity of Attorney General, appointed former FBI director Robert Mueller, to be the Special Counsel for the United States Department of Justice (DOJ). The instruction for the investigation was to examine Russian interference in the 2016 United States elections, including exploring any links or coordination between Trump's 2016 presidential campaign and the Russian government, "and any matters

348

that arose or may arise directly from the investigation",[30] and any other matters within the scope of 28 CFR 600.4 – Jurisdiction.

On the following page is the letter from Rosenstein appointing Robert Mueller as the Special Counsel for the investigation into Russian interference into the United States 2016 election, aka the Russia/Trump collusion probe. As stated above, Sessions' repeated pre-election contacts with Russian officials make him a likely witness in the investigation, and as such he would have a potential conflict of interest in the probe's investigative proceedings.

Witness to Treason

Office of the Deputy Attorney General
Washington, D.C. 20530

ORDER NO. 3915-2017

APPOINTMENT OF SPECIAL COUNSEL
TO INVESTIGATE RUSSIAN INTERFERENCE WITH THE
2016 PRESIDENTIAL ELECTION AND RELATED MATTERS

By virtue of the authority vested in me as Acting Attorney General, including 28 U.S.C.
§§ 509, 510, and 515, in order to discharge my responsibility to provide supervision and
management of the Department of Justice, and to ensure a full and thorough investigation of the
Russian government's efforts to interfere in the 2016 presidential election, I hereby order as
follows:

(a)   Robert S. Mueller III is appointed to serve as Special Counsel for the United States
Department of Justice.

(b)   The Special Counsel is authorized to conduct the investigation confirmed by then-FBI
Director James B. Comey in testimony before the House Permanent Select Committee on
Intelligence on March 20, 2017, including:

   (i)   any links and/or coordination between the Russian government and individuals
          associated with the campaign of President Donald Trump; and

   (ii)   any matters that arose or may arise directly from the investigation; and

   (iii) any other matters within the scope of 28 C.F.R. § 600.4(a).

(c)   If the Special Counsel believes it is necessary and appropriate, the Special Counsel is
authorized to prosecute federal crimes arising from the investigation of these matters.

(d)   Sections 600.4 through 600.10 of Title 28 of the Code of Federal Regulations are
applicable to the Special Counsel.

5/11/17
Date

Rod J. Rosenstein
Acting Attorney General

Contrary to the Trump administration's insistence that the Russia
investigation was prompted solely by the infamous Steele Dossier

350

(which included alleged details of Trump's scandalous sexual antics in a Moscow 5-star hotel), the probe originated at the direction of the House Intelligence Committee after the FBI learned that a Trump campaign aide, George Papadopoulos, was approached by a Russian agent, and before the dossier surfaced. Papadopoulos then mentioned to an Australian diplomat that the Russians had "dirt" on Clinton. The Australians contacted the U.S. government, and the FBI began to take a look. The investigation into Russian/Trump collusion during the 2016 campaign had already indicted several persons, before the appointment of a Special Counsel by the Department of Justice. The appointment of the Special Counsel followed a series of events that included President Trump's firing of FBI director James Comey, and Comey's allegation that Trump asked him to drop an FBI investigation into former National Security Advisor General Michael T. Flynn. On August 3, 2017, Mueller empaneled a grand jury in Washington, D.C., as part of his investigation. The grand jury has the power to subpoena documents; require witnesses to testify under oath; and issue indictments for targets of criminal charges if probable cause is found. The grand jury has since issued a number of subpoenas to those involved in a pre-election Trump campaign–Russian meeting held on June 9, 2016, at Trump Tower in New York City.

That same day, the Mueller investigation subpoenaed Randy Credico, whom Roger Stone, a Trump associate, described as his "backchannel" to WikiLeaks founder, Julian Assange who published the DNC email leaks. At the beginning of 2017, Fox News' Sean Hannity travelled to the Ecuadorean Embassy in London to meet that embassy's longest-tenured visitor, Julian Assange. Hannity was a big fan of Assange and went to get Assange to confirm what only Hannity and President Trump believed, that Assange did not get the emails from Russia. Hannity asked Assange with a straight-face where he got the emails that were stolen from America's Democratic National Committee (DNC) and from Democratic presidential candidate Hillary Clinton's campaign chairman. (The sudden publication of the emails created havoc just a few months before the election. The leak of these emails just weeks earlier impacted the November 2016 election.) Assange who is a fugitive from the law in two countries was asked by Hannity if he could tell the American public and the world that he did not get these documents "…from Russia or anybody associated with Russia." Assange said, "Our source is not the Russian government and it is not a state party." Seven months later, the US Department of Justice indicted 12 Russians military officers with stealing and disseminating the emails to WikiLeaks. Interestingly, on July 27, 2016, Trump encouraged a foreign adversary to illegally hack into messages by a former U.S. secretary of state that might contain sensitive information, then asked them to release them publicly. This was only a few days after WikiLeaks began publishing some DNC emails. Trump on world-wide TV, pleads with Russia for their help in finding the 20,000 additional missing emails, "Russia, if you're listening, I hope you're able to find the 30,000 emails that are missing. I think you will probably be rewarded mightily by our press." In an indictment issued against Russian hackers on July 13, 2018, it is reported that Russian hackers tried to hack Clinton's emails on the same day as Trump's plea. *Charges undermine Assange denials on hacked emails. AP, July 15, 2018*

The Steele Dossier

Russian prostitutes, "golden showers", espionage, secret deals, British spies, Russian spies, Christopher Steele, Fusion GPS, oligarchs are words, names, phrases that first gained our national attention in late 2016 after the presidential election. Now as the US mid-term elections are approaching in November 2018, the public's fascination with them has waned but the legal implications of the source of these words has gotten the singular attention of Robert Mueller's special investigation team.

'Why did Mr. Trump repeatedly seek to do deals in a notoriously corrupt police state that most serious investors shun?' was the question that private investigative firm Fusion GPS was contracted to seek answers to in October 2015 by the conservative political website *The Washington Free Beacon* that hoped to obtain political opposition research for use against Trump. When Trump became the presumptive Republican Party presidential nominee, they ceased interest in the information. In April 2016, Fusion GPS was hired to investigate Trump on behalf of Hillary Clinton's campaign. In June 2016, Fusion GPS subcontracted Steele's firm to compile the dossier. His instructions were much the same, seek answers to why Trump would "repeatedly seek to do deals in a notoriously corrupt police state". Steele completed research and was reportedly paid directly by Fusion GPS co-founder Glenn R. Simpson. The completed dossier was later handed to British and American intelligence services.

The Steele Dossier is a private investigator's intelligence report that should be viewed not as evidence in a trial, but as a road map for investigators. In January 2017, BuzzFeed News published this intelligence dossier developed by a former British MI6 intelligence officer who was deemed credible by U.S. intelligence officials. The Dossier raises profoundly disturbing questions about whether there was improper contact between the Trump campaign and the Russian government and about the existence of compromising personal and financial information about Donald Trump. At the time BuzzFeed published the Dossier, BuzzFeed acknowledged that the allegations it contained were "unverified" and that the document contained "some clear errors." As the Russia Trump collusion investigation continues through its second year in 2018, the dossier's high level of accuracy is rapidly becoming clear. There are some significant facts to be noted about the Dossier and its author.

Christopher Steele is a former UK MI-6 officer who also worked on behalf of the FBI in the successful FIFA (international soccer) investigation. Steele wrote the Dossier in real time (before Trump's candidacy) and it largely contains intelligence related to internal Russian efforts to interfere in the election, not intelligence about the Trump campaign. The Dossier was credible enough for former FBI Director James Comey and Director of National Intelligence James Clapper to brief President Obama and then-President elect Trump on the contents of the dossier, and credible enough that Steele was concerned about his and his family's safety after the Dossier was released and he and his family went into hiding.

While much attention has gone to the salacious tape described in the Dossier, more should be paid to the allegation that for at least 5 years Trump was passing information to Russian intelligence operatives on Russians expats living at his properties. All of the sources indicate that he had a vast surveillance system on his properties, a system that kept a close tab on Russian oligarchs. The information could be useful to Putin and his FSB spy agency who were assigned to spy on Russian expats and Russian oligarchs living and visiting in America, surveillance that could benefit Putin sometime in the future. So, Putin's friendship with Trump was valuable.

There was also ample and separate intelligence that UK, Dutch, French, German, Estonian, and Australian intelligence agencies picked up on meetings between Trump associates and Russian intelligence going back to 2015.

Steele cites many sources for the data in his dossier, one of the sources was a former Russian intelligence figure who was found dead in his car on December 26, 2016, only days after the dossier was published. The spy network across eastern and western borders hint strongly at murder, but after a thorough Russian investigation conducted by local authorities, no reason has been given for the death, but foul play has been definitely ruled out. Case closed.

An excerpt from the Dossier is provided on the next page. It shows the reporting style and structure of the Steele Dossier follows.

Company intelligence report 2016/080
US Presidential election: Republican candidate Donald Trump's activities in Russia and compromising relationship with the Kremlin.

Summary remarks

- "Russian regime has been cultivating, supporting and assisting TRUMP for at least 5 years. Aim, endorsed by PUTIN, has been to encourage splits and divisions in western alliance, and
- "he (Trump) and his inner circle have accepted a regular flow of intelligence from the Kremlin, including on his Democratic and other political rivals,"
- -Former top Russian intelligence officer claims FSB has compromised TRUMP through his activities in Moscow sufficiently to be able to blackmail him. According to several knowledgeable sources, his conduct in Moscow has included [REDACTED BY THE MOSCOW PROJECT] arranged/ monitored by the FSB

Witness to Treason

The most attention to the Dossier was its description of Trumps reported 'salacious' behavior in a Moscow Hotel room in February 2013 while he was attending his Miss Universe contest. The 'sexcapade' included Russian prostitutes, Trump, and the presidential suite previously occupied by President and Mrs. Obama. This alleged incident along with alleged Russian 'deals' formed the basis for the observations in the report that Trump was in a position to be compromised by Putin. The more damaging revelation was that Russia's understood that Trump and associates were in agreement that a quid pro quo arrangement would be in play, such that any Trump decisions that may arise in his administration related to the Ukraine and Crimea, and Russian sanctions, would favor Putin, the oligarchs, and Russia.

The Steele Dossier has been attacked by every Republican leader in Congress as being unsubstantiated, as though a Russian citizen who provided the information would stand up in Moscow and claim to be the source. Hell, the Republicans in congress don't have the courage to say the President lies, about anything: when the easy truth to tell is that he lies about everything. The Dossier is being more fully corroborated as each new witness testifies before the Special Counsel. The fact that its author and his family had to flee for their safety when it was published, confirms the truthfulness of the Dossier. The credibility of the report is further testified to after the mysterious deaths of at least two sources likely exposed when they were referenced in the dossier: one was found dead died in his car in Moscow the day after Christmas 2016, a second was forcibly removed from a meeting in Moscow in the same month and is still missing.
https://themoscowproject.org/dossier/

Trump and Russia

"I am not involved in Russia." This 2016 election campaign statement, uttered by Trump in his "Believe me." voice will echo in the museum of lies until the end of time. Trump visited Russia for the first time in 1986, then returned in 1987. He like what he saw and decided there were real estate opportunities for him in and around Moscow. However, the Berlin Wall came down in 1989 and Russia's economy fell with it. Soon, the Soviet empire faded as each Soviet state was permitted to go its own way simply because the government in Moscow could neither support the economies for all of its fifteen separate republics, nor did it have the finances to enforce control over them. Trump's fortunes also took a gigantic tumble during this period as it was reported in the latter part of the decade that he was more than $3 billion dollars in debt and that even the banks who knew him well wouldn't lend him money. Trump's access to money and his fascination with any Russian investment waned. But something happened in the latter part of the decade. Throughout the first half of the decade, economic chaos reigned in Russia as the Union of Soviet Socialist Republics transitioned into the Russian Federation, and democracy and capitalism struggled to replace communism. Then, like vultures to a carcass, a new block of Russian power brokers began to swiftly take pieces of businesses they coveted, and sought to enrich themselves and fashion their own favored type of national government, "an economic oligarchy, composed of politicians, banks, businesspeople, security forces, and city agencies,." Wikipedia: economic history of Russian federation. These oligarchs partnered with a former political hold-over from the communist party, Vladimir Putin, and a new Russia was born, but it was resurrected in the image of an old tsarist regime.

Witness to Treason

In 1996, Moscow was again interesting to Trump, and he made a third visit to Russia. The Kremlin made a decision to place all of Moscow's economic infrastructure development under the control of the city's mayor, Yuriy Luzhkov. At the same time, organized crime maintained an almost equal and important role in the city's growth, accounting for Moscow's "rate of protection rackets, contract murders, kickbacks, and bribes all of which were intimately connected with the economic infrastructure." Now that "Luzhkov's city government was responsible for all banking, hotels, and construction", this "allowed Luzhkov's planners to manipulate resources efficiently, and with little or no competition." After his visit, Trump soon applied for his first trademark in Russia, and announced his intention to invest there. In 1998, Deutsche Bank setup a credit line for Trump business ventures worth $98 million. After one visit to Moscow, Trump, who was considered a bad risk to most US banks, was back in the real estate business. Shortly, thereafter, Trump began construction of Trump World Tower, and it is completed in 2001, and sold to Russians in 2002. Additionally, during this period, Trump sells numerous Trump NYC condominiums to Russians, and in 2005, Trump Organization and the Bayrock Group agree on a site for a Trump Tower in Moscow. Not so bad for someone who told NBC in 2007 that he has no property or investments in Russia. "I am not involved in Russia," he said, and also sent a letter to Sen. Lindsey Graham, R-SC stating, "I have no business connections with Russia."

http://www2.needham.k12.ma.us/nhs/cur/Baker_00/03-04/baker%20poland%20p1/ussr.htm, Russian Economy in the Aftermath of the Collapse of the Soviet Union, By Marshall Poland

"I am not involved in Russia," Donald J. Trump, Sr.

A chronological list of Trump's business activities with Russians.

1984   *Russian* mobster purchases five condos in Trump Tower for $6 million to launder money from illegal criminal activity.

1996   Trump goes to *Russia*, applies for first trademarks in *Russia*, to invest in *Russia*

1997   Trump begins to sell condos to *Russian* buyers.

1998   Deustche Bank provides $98M line of credit to Trump, begins construction on Trump World Towers, completed in 2001, and then sold to *Russians* in 2002

1998   August, *Russian* money flows into NYC, in October Trump buys vacant lot for new Tower World Tower near the United Nations, by 2004 *Russians* purchased 8 floors.

2000   *Russian*-linked Bayrock Group, a suspected money-laundering conduit for *Russian* mob and oligarchs, partners with Trump. More Trump condos sold to more *Russians.*

2002   Trump World Towers sold to *Russians*

2005   Trump and Bayrock find site for a Trump Tower in Moscow, *Russia's* capital city

2006   Trump partners sell their condos to *Russians*

Witness to Treason

2002   *Russian* oligarchs begin buying Trump condos in Sunny Isles, FL, $109M, all cash

2008   July, US recession and market crash, Trump sells FL home to a *Russian* billionaire for $98M, Trump paid $41M three years earlier.

2013   April, *Russian* spies target Trump aide Carter Page as an agent for *Russia*

2013   June, *Russia* paid $20M to host Trump's Miss Universe contest in Moscow, the site of Trump's alleged 'sexcapade' incident detailed in the Christopher Steele Dossier

2014   June, Eric Trump tells golfing companion, James Dobson, "Well, we don't rely on American banks. We have all the funding we need out of *Russia*."   *https://themoscowproject.org/collusion-chapter/chapter-1/; https://themoscowproject.org/collusion/russian-criminal-purchases-trump-condos/*

No Contacts with Russian Officials by Trump Campaign

Throughout the past two years, Trump's and his campaign team's steady denials of having any contacts between Russian officials and government operatives before the 2016 election, and before Trump's inauguration as President of the United States, threatened to become more numerous than the number of grains of sand on a Miami beach. Quotes from his surrogates Jeff Sessions, Michael Flynn, Jared Kushner, Don, Jr.., and others abounded and ranged from ridiculing the journalist and television new broadcasters for asking such a frivolous question to launching a verbal accusation against anyone who would doubt the veracity of their denials.

Therefore, I won't deposit any of their now embarrassing denials and outright lies about Russian contacts. As we say these days, "google it." But what follows are a few tidbits that might let you determine for yourself how truthful and innocent of Russian collusion Trump and his team are.

Kushner's 'back channel' to Moscow

The Washington Post reported in May 2017 that Jared Kushner, Trump's son-in-law and senior adviser, was willing to go to extraordinary lengths to establish a secret line of communication between the Trump team and Russian government officials during the presidential transition period before Trump was sworn in as President. On December 1, 2016, Kushner met in the Trump Tower with Michael Flynn and Russian Ambassador, Sergei Kislyak, and floated the possibility of setting up a secure channel. Kushner wanted those talks to take place in Russian diplomatic facilities inside the U.S. which would prevent disclosure of such communications to the American government. Kushner did not disclose this Kislyak meeting to U.S. officials during his background check—the White House only acknowledged it after news outlets reported on it. It was part of a pattern of many off-the-book interactions that took place between the Trump campaign officials and Russian officials. In response to additional questioning, Kushner declared that no further discussions were held on the subject of a 'back channel.' But, someone investigated further. He was wrong, or he forgot, or he has the same memory-defect that his other campaign associates have. He did have another meeting on the subject, and more than one more meeting. The bigger question is why, why did Kushner and the Trump campaign need a 'back channel' setup to communicate directly with Russia even before Trump was inaugurated as President? A second question soon became important. Where is Seychelles? And why does Robert Mueller care about it? The answers to these two questions have been pursued at length by the FBI since January 2018 when George Nadar, a well-connected Washington businessman, was first interviewed by members of the Mueller investigation team.

The Seychelles Meeting

Once, Kushner put the 'back channel' ball in motion, Russian Ambassador Kislyak carried it to Russia. Soon, George Nadar was tapped to help organize, and to attend, a meeting in Seychelles on January 11, 2017, just a few days before Trump's inauguration. (Seychelles is in the Indian Ocean, equidistant from nothing). The meeting brought together Trump representatives and more Russians. Erik Prince, brother of Secretary of Education Betsy DeVos, and founder of the private security company Blackwater, and Kirill Dmitriev, a Russian sovereign wealth fund manager, believed to be connected to Vladimir Putin.

Anonymous sources claim to reporters that the purpose of the Seychelles meeting was for Trump's team to covertly communicate with Putin's team. The meeting was in response to Jared Kushner telling the Russians that he wanted to set up a 'back channel'. What actually happened there — and why those involved wanted so badly to keep it secret, is of major interest to the FBI. Here are some reasons floated publicly that the US government might be suspecting.

1. One, "whether Russia could be persuaded to curtail its relationship with Iran, including in Syria," a topic that was very much of interest to the United Arab Emirates (UAE).

2. Two, was money involved? The Russian who went to the meeting, Kirill Dmitriev, is a moneyman, and his fund was once part of the Russian government-owned bank, VEB.
3. Three, Mueller "appears to be examining the influence of foreign money on Mr. Trump's political activities," and who might've "funneled money from the Emirates to the president's political efforts."
4. Four, there's the possibility that this meeting allowed Trump's team and Putin's to secretly communicate about Russian interference in the 2016 campaign.

Shhh! Other Russian Contacts That Never Happened.

One of Trump's top surrogates during the campaign, Senator Jeff Sessions, R-AL, met with Kislyak several times, but told his colleagues during his confirmation hearings for attorney general that he had no contact with Russians during the campaign. Two other campaign aides, Carter Page and J.D. Gordon, spoke to Kislyak following a panel at the Republican National Convention. And Trump's first national-security adviser, Michael Flynn, was forced to resign after mischaracterizing his several conversations with the former ambassador before the election and again before Trump's inauguration.

Hot to Trot

Just days after Trump took office, the Trump administration looked into lifting the sanctions that former President Barack Obama had imposed on Russia over its meddling in the 2016 election. Before stepping down in January 2017, Tom Malinowski, Obama's assistant secretary of state for human rights, scrambled to lobby Congress to halt the development of a sanctions-lifting package being pushed by the Trump White House. Other government officials began ringing "alarm bells about possible concessions being made" to Russia. From the legislative side, a bi-partisan pair of senators, Democratic Senator Ben Cardin and Republican Senator Lindsey Graham, quickly introduced the Russia Sanctions Review Act on February 8, 2017. The legislation called for new penalties on Russia and included a provision that gave Congress veto power over any sanctions-lifting package proposed by the Trump White House that would benefit Russia. It passed that summer with a veto-proof majority, and forced Trump to sign the bill. Trump let two deadlines pass before he finally imposed the new sanctions as required by law, but Trump implemented them in slow waves in March, allowing the Russians to take salvaging actions (move their money, etc) before the sanctions took place.

List of a few of the Trump associates' illegal contacts with Russians prior to inauguration

April 2016, Jared Kushner, senior Trump adviser and responsible for coordinating the campaign's digital projects, meets Russian Ambassador Kislyak at Mayflower Hotel.

June 3-8   Don, Jr. receives and responds to e-mails from Russians, agrees to meet Russians

June 9, 2016, Trump Tower meeting, Russians, Don, Jr.., Manafort, Kushner

Nov 10, 2016, Obama meets presidential-elect Trump at White House. Obama warns Trump that Flynn has met illegally with Russian contacts and received money from foreign governments.

July 27, 2016   "Russia, if you're listening, I hope you're able to find the 30,000 emails that are missing." Trump's televised plea to Putin.

From Russia, to Trump

Known connections between the Russian government and the Trump campaign.

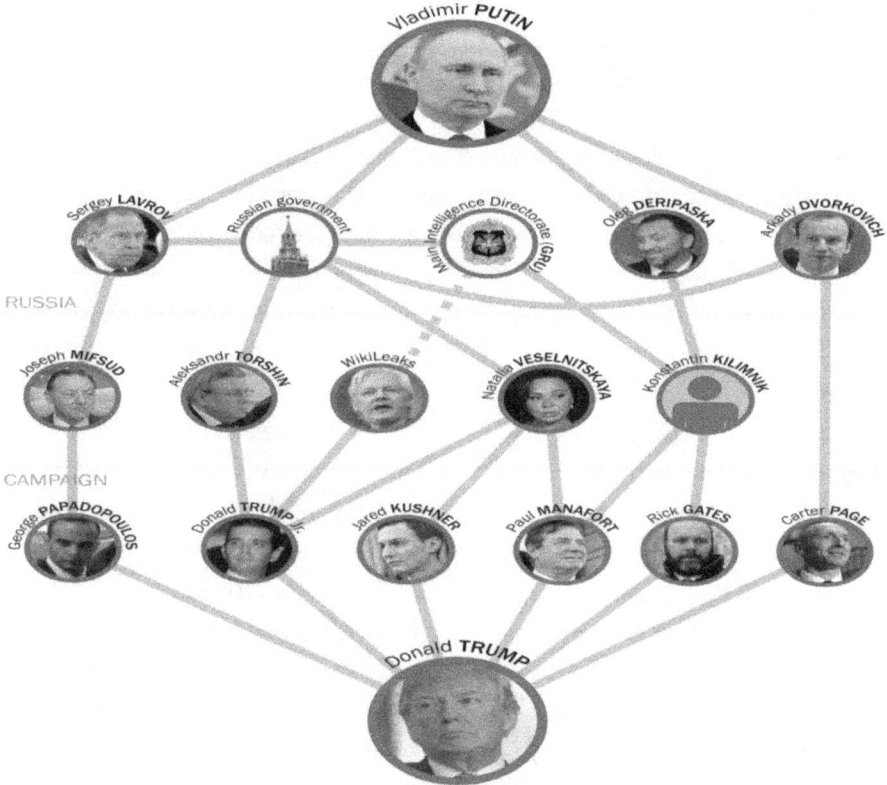

The web of connections between Trump and Putin, chart as of March 28, 2018

https://www.washingtonpost.com/news/politics/wp/2018/03/28/the-web-of-connections-between-trump-and-putin-visualized/?utm_term=.f55db9daef9f

Manafort, from Russia with love?

Paul Manafort, a Washington lobbyist, turned political consultant, and third-world nations kingmaker, brought his dirty-tricks activity kit to Donald Trump's presidential campaign team in March 2016, and he was soon elevated to campaign chairman from June to August 2016. Now, he is a convicted felon.

On August 21, 2018, Paul Manafort, Trump's 2016 campaign manager, was convicted of five counts of tax fraud, two counts of bank fraud, and one count of failure to report foreign bank accounts. He was charged on ten other counts of similar crimes but the jury was unable to render a verdict on them, leading to a mistrial for those ten counts charges. He will be re-tried on the remaining ten charges. He is also scheduled for another separate trial in September 2018 for more federal offenses. This second of a possible three trials is related to obstruction of justice charges brought by the Special Counsel Investigation team. The Federal Bureau of Investigation (FBI) has had an active criminal investigation on Paul Manafort since 2014 regarding his business dealings while he was lobbying for the Ukraine's former President Viktor Yanukovych. He became a person of interest in the FBI counterintelligence probe looking into the Russian government's interference in the 2016 United States presidential election. Where did Manafort come from so late in the 2016 presidential campaign? How did he rise so quickly inside Trump's campaign? One thing the FBI knows now, he did get paid well.

Before his work for Ukraine and the Trump campaign, Manafort spent decades and earned millions serving as a political consultant for third-world countries led by a slew of international dictators such as Ferdinand Marcos of the Philippines, Zaire's Mobutu Sese Seko,

Angolan's guerrilla leader Jonas Savimbi, and advised crooked regimes in Kenya, Pakistan, and Nigeria. His lobbying firm was ranked among the top five firms who received the most money from regimes who had the world's highest number of human-rights abuses reported against them. That distinction earned his firm a listing among the lobby industry's specialty niche referred to as The Torture Lobby. As recently as 2004 through 2014, Manafort worked in the Ukraine and in other Russian-hinged republics to further Putin's regime in Moscow. Viktor Yankukovich, Ukraine's president was a Russian puppet controlled by Putin, and sympathetic to Russia's conspiracy in annexing the Ukraine. Does any of that sound familiar? Once inside the Ukraine government, Manafort 'pitched' a plan to Putin in 2005 that benefited Putin and the Russian oligarchs, and led to Putin's camouflaged Russian soldiers invading the Ukraine and the annexation of a key southern region of the Ukraine by Russia.

In the August 2018 trial proceedings in Virginia, the prosecutor showed that Manafort was paid $60 million through 2010 to 2014 for his work in aiding Putin's annexation of Ukrainian territory. In March 2016, Manafort joined the Trump campaign expecting to possibly do the same things for Trump in America: help Trump to become President of the United States, whatever it cost Trump, or Putin. So, Manafort might suppose the attempted assassination of a Soviet spy and his daughter in England is a blatant warning to Manafort that he is not safe from Putin's reprisal if he turns on Trump. Putin's plan for restoration of Russia and recovery of riches to the oligarchs needs Trump to remain President for at least 4 years, hopefully 8 years. Manafort has a lot on his mind besides the tens of millions in cash he received from Russia.

Witness to Treason

Manafort has these ugly scenarios to consider:
- Plead the fifth, and go to jail for the rest of his life
- Get pardoned by Trump soon after sentencing, maybe as long as a year.
- Turn on Trump, and fear assassination by a Russian tourist, in jail or out of jail
- Turn on Trump, be safe in jail but have his family and associates vulnerable to Putin,

There are some dots that can be reasonably connected between Manafort, Russia, and Trump. Ten years earlier in the spring 2005, Manafort worked for Ukraine and had contacts with Russia and Putin, then come forward to April 2016 when Trump's ratings were low and his campaign was in retreat and disarray. Trump was in trouble and he needed cash, lot of cash, for his campaign. (Note: Trump never uses his own money when he can use someone else's money.) At this time, Felix Sater, a known Russian associate and a former business principal of Bayrock Group and Trump associate, announces that he wants to help to "engineer" the Trump campaign. However, Manafort suddenly appears in April, is brought in as a campaign team member, and two months later is personally appointed Trump's campaign manager. He resurrects the Trump election campaign, Russian trolls begin hacking the Democratic National Committee (DNC), and Trump associates begin communicating with Russian agents. Coincidence? Is it possible that Manafort and the influx of money was a final investment by Putin to ensure that his initial investment would survive at least into the November election? All this leaves a final question to consider. Who paid Manafort?

Note: Paul Manafort pleaded guilty on September 14 to charges related to defrauding the U.S. and to obstruction of justice. The deal is dismissal of additional charges, major leniency in sentencing in turn for providing information on everything about the 2016 campaign that he knows. See **Epilogue** in rear of this book.

The NRA and Russia, 2013-2016

One of Trump's major campaign contributors and a loyal booster for his run for the presidency was the National Rifle Association. The NRA spent more money to get Donald Trump elected President, and to maintain Republican control of Congress, than it did on any other election in history. The NRA had poured $55 million into the 2016 election and most of the spending was on the presidential race. The NRA spent $32 million to support Trump's campaign, using a little less than half of the total amount to attack Democratic nominee Hillary Clinton, and the balance for literature, rallies, ads, and campaign salaries to directly support Trump. That far exceeds the $13.6 million the group spent on the entire 2012 presidential race. Where did all that money come from? *Dan Friedman, ·October 12, 2016, Trace, online.*

In 2017, the NRA reported revenue of $444 million in 2016, and expenses of more than $480 million. In more detail, the NRA spent $55M on 2016 elections. It was the most spent on the 2016 election by one organization, and by an arm of the NRA "not required to disclose its donors." That is a lot of new money, far exceeding its revenues and expenses in prior years. The excessive increase from its previous annual amounts was so great that it prompted a closer look. Consequently, the NRA has been under federal investigation since January 2018 for accepting money from Russia to aid and abet the Trump Campaign in the 2016 presidential election. *Dark Money source.*

Witness to Treason

In Chapter 9, <u>The NRA, Instruments of Death,</u> information is provided showing the numerous contacts and relationships that developed between NRA leadership and Russian agents during the years leading up to the 2016 election. The FBI has indicted several of these Russian citizens, but as of September 1, 2018, no NRA officials have been charged. The Special Counsel investigation is ongoing, and its agents continue to look for instances where money was accepted for any reason from foreign individuals, agents, or governments. For more details on Russian contacts within the NRA, please go to Chapter 9.

Why do so many of Putin's enemies 'end up dead'?

In Helsinki, Finland, Fox News host Chris Wallace on Monday pushed Russian President Vladimir Putin after the leader brushed off the death of his political enemies. Wallace asked how come "so many people who were political enemies of Vladimir Putin are attacked?" He was referring to the recent nerve agent attack on former Russian spy Sergei Skripal in the United Kingdom and the fatal 2015 shooting of Putin's political opponent Boris Nemtsov. "Well, first of all, all of us have plenty of political rivals. I'm pretty sure President Trump has plenty of political rivals," Putin told the Fox News host. "But they don't end up dead," Wallace responded. Putin pointed out that U.S. presidents and Dr. Martin Luther King Jr. have been assassinated on American soil. "All of us have our own set of domestic problems," Putin said.

Source: Chris Wallace asks Putin why so many of his political enemies 'end up dead' Morgan Gstalter July 17, 2018, The Hill

The bold assassination attempt mentioned above was carried out in daylight. The UK investigation confirmed that Russian agents were pictured on video, so the question shifts from who to why. Why were a

Russian spy and his daughter attacked publicly in England with a Russian-developed poison easily traced to Russia? The British investigators determined that they were poisoned earlier this month using Novichok - a Soviet-era nerve agent that the British government says is linked to Russia's spy agencies. Prime Minister Theresa May's government has accused Russia's government of being involved in both poisoning incidents. But why be so bold to announce yourself as the killer? It is possible that Putin wanted all Trump associates, especially Manafort to see how easy it is to kill them or their family members, even across oceans and time. Even if the killer is caught and a nation is responsible, the target is still dead. The message is clear. Don't cooperate. Putin does not fear America or its reprisals. He has a friend in the White House.

Who Should Worry?

Dead Russians pockmarked Trump's campaign and post-election. US law enforcement and intelligence officials believe that some of the Russian diplomats expelled from the U.S. in March 2018 were suspected spies who were tracking Russian defectors and their families who had resettled in America. In at least one instance, the officials said Russian spies were watching a Russian citizen who was part of a CIA program that provided new identities to protect resettled Russians. That episode and other US intelligence information heightened concerns that the Kremlin was formalizing a program to spy on Russian émigrés in the US who the Kremlin labeled as traitors or enemies. Russian oligarchs who live and travel to the US are also targeted for the Kremlin's 'special attention'. Are these resettled Russian men, women, and children safe from Russian violence, even on American soil?

Witness to Treason

There is more concern now following the poisoning in the UK of a former Russian spy, Sergei Skripal, and his daughter, who are Russian citizens. British and U.S. officials have blamed Russian intelligence for the use of a nerve agent in the attempted poisoning. Officials in both the US and UK have warned that the Russian government appears emboldened to carry out assassinations in western Democracies. Democrats on the Senate Foreign Relations Committee produced a report earlier this year raised the issue of the suspicious deaths of more than two dozen critics of Russian President Vladimir Putin during his time in power. The Russian security services are suspected in many of the deaths, the report said, noting a Russian law passed "in July 2006 that permits the assassination of 'enemies of the Russian regime' who live abroad." "The trail of mysterious deaths, all of which happened to people who possessed information that the Kremlin did not want made public, should not be ignored by Western countries on the assumption that they are safe from these extreme measures," said the Senate Democrats in their report.

Source: Expelled spies included Russians suspected of tracking compatriots who resettled in US CNN online, By Evan Perez and Shimon Prokupecz, CNN, April 26, 2018.

Russian has a long history of political assassination since 1917. Now, dead Russians litter Trump's campaign and post-election. Here below is a litany of assassinations, beginning with two notorious assassinations prior to Trump.

Nov 1, 2006, a former KGB officer and whistleblower Alexander Litvinenko was poisoned with radioactive polonium-210 that was placed in his tea by two Russian friends.

2012, whistleblower Alexander Perepilichny died from a toxin while jogging in England, per a New York Times report at the time.

Nov 2015 a senior adviser to Putin, Mikhail Lesin, who was also the founder of the media company RT, was found dead in a Washington hotel room according to the New York Times (NYT). The Russian media said it was a "heart attack," but the medical examiner said it was "blunt force injuries."

Dec 2016, Russia's Ambassador to Turkey, Andrei Karlov was assassinated by a police officer at a photo exhibit in Ankara on December 19, 2016.

Nov 8, 2016, on the morning of the 2016 election, Russian diplomat Sergei Krivov was found unconscious at the Russian Consulate in New York on November 8 and died on the scene. Initial reports said Krivov fell from the roof and had blunt force injuries, but Russian officials said he died from a heart attack. BuzzFeed reports Krivov may have been a Consular Duty Commander, which would have put him in charge of preventing sabotage or espionage.

Dec 2016, Ex-KGB chief Oleg Erovinkin, who was suspected of helping draft the Trump dossier, was found dead in the back of his car December 26 2016, according to The Telegraph. Erovinkin also was an aide to former deputy prime minister Igor Sechin, who now heads up state-owned Rosneft.

Dec 2016, on the same day, another diplomat, Peter Polshikov, was shot dead in his Moscow apartment. The gun was found under the bathroom sink but the circumstances of the death were under investigation. Polshikov served as a senior figure in the Latin American department of the Foreign Ministry.

Aug 2017, Russia's ambassador to Sudan, Mirgayas Shirinsky, was found dead in his swimming pool in Khartoum.

That's the seventh Russian diplomat to have died since November, 2016 in addition to an aide to a former deputy prime minister, a lawyer for a Putin-foe, a former Russian MP. All but two of the seven died on foreign soil. Some were shot, while other causes of death are unknown. Note that a few deaths have been labeled "heart attacks" or "brief illnesses." Here's what you need to know:

2017, Russia's Ambassador to the United Nations, Vitaly Churkin, died in New York. Churkin was rushed to the hospital from his office at Russia's UN mission. Initial reports said he suffered a heart attack, and the medical examiner is investigating the death, according to CBS.

Jan 2017, Russia's Ambassador to India, Alexander Kadakin, died after a "brief illness" January 27, which The Hindu said he had been suffering from the illness for a few weeks.

Jan 2017, Russian Consul in Athens, Greece, Andrei Malanin, was found dead in his apartment January 9. A Greek police official said there was "no evidence of a break-in." But Malanin lived on a heavily guarded street. The cause of death needed further investigation, per an AFP report. Malanin served during a time of easing relations between Greece and Russia when Greece was increasingly critiqued by the EU and NATO.

Mar 2017, a lawyer for a Putin-foe, Nikolai Gorokhov, was reportedly thrown from a window March 21, 2017 in Moscow. However, Russian press and Russian security forces reported Gorkohov fell while trying to move a bathtub into his apartment. Gorokhov was set to testify as a U.S. government witness in a money laundering case in New York.

Mar 2017, former Russian MP, Denis Voronenkov, was shot dead in Kiev March 23, according to the BBC. Voronenkov was to testify against deposed Ukrainian President Viktor Yanukovych and had ruffled feathers in Russia for calling the Crimean annexation illegal. Kiev police said it was likely a contract killing but the Kremlin rejected the remarks as "absurd."

Aug 2017, Russia's ambassador to Sudan, Mirgayas Shirinsky was found dead at his Khartoum home August 23. He was found dead in the residence's swimming pool, but Sudanese police said he had died of natural causes. Russia's foreign ministry spokeswoman Maria Zakharova said an ambulance was called but he "could not be saved."

Mar 2018, Sergei Skripal and his daughter, Yulia, were found unconscious on a public bench in the English city of Salisbury. Skripal, was a former colonel in Russian military intelligence who betrayed Russian agents to Britain's MI6 foreign spy service. Britain blamed Russia for the poisonings and identified the poison as Novichok, a deadly group of nerve agents developed by the Soviet military in the 1970s and 1980s. Russia has repeatedly denied any involvement in the attack. The motive for attacking Skripal, who was exchanged in a spy swap in 2010 involving the infamous Russian spy Anna Chapman, is still unclear, as is the motive for using a nerve agent which is clearly linked to Russia. Two Russian agents posing as tourists were later identified visiting Skripal's town outside London at the time of the poisoning.

Apr 2018, in at least one instance, Russian spies were believed to be casing someone who was part of a CIA program that provided new identities to protect resettled Russians. U.S. law enforcement and intelligence officials said that episode and other similar reports raised concerns that the Russians were targeting Russian émigrés in the US. These persons are labeled by the Kremlin as traitors or enemies, The CIA declined to comment. The White House declined to comment.
Source: Russian diplomats keep dying unexpectedly, by Ivan Sekretarev / APShannon Vavra Aug 24, 2017, Axios, BuzzFeed News, start with Part 1: "Poison in the System,"

Trump and Putin, Puppet and Puppeteer

The mystery surrounding the high-regard, and the "do anything to please him" behavior that Trump flagrantly displays for Russia's murderous leader, Vladimir Putin, deflects attention away from the actions that Trump as America's president was putting in place to make America, if not subservient to Putin and Russia, at least ineffective as an obstacle to Russia's aggressiveness in every aspect of its resurgence as an international bully.

America is more powerful than Russia, but by nurturing a 'new friendship of cooperation' between Russia and America, via duplicity, blackmail, or Putin's charm, Russia can walk assuredly along its chosen path to reposition itself as the biggest threat to all western democracies. In closer inspection, Trump's actions aid and abet Russia on that journey. In addition to being misogynistic and narcisstic, Trump and Putin share a loathing for democratic rule. They see democracies as troublesome, weak, and complicated. They like power in a single ruler's hands; preferably in their hands. So, how can Trump and his corporate friends aid Russia, and at the same time benefit themselves? That depends on what Putin wants. Unlike the Republican Party of No who abhor compromise, and subsequently win nothing, Putin understands compromise. He understands that compromise means there are situations when you bend a little, but never a lot, in order to move towards getting everything you want. He is willing to settle for 80%, and give you 20%; his 80% comes easy, and your 20% comes hard. To keep yours, you must keep your hands and your eyes on your 20%, at least until he is out of the room. Then, don't let him back in the room. Big dogs don't share, they eat other dogs. For now, both men promise allegiance to one another, and to the billionaires and the oligarchs in their respective countries. Let's look at what is happening right now.

Russia's economy is energy based. That's the source of its major income. Russia sells military equipment and has raw material resources for export, but oil and gas reserves drive its economic engine. They are a Euro-Asian version of an oil-rich, middle-eastern country, but with nuclear weapons. It was no surprise that Rex Tillerson, Exxon Oil's CEO, was one of the first appointees to Trump's cabinet. Tillerson was one of Trump's first gifts to Putin. Weakening the 2016 Republican Party's national platform on Ukraine and Crimea was first, and lifting the sanctions on Russia's banks and billionaires was supposed to be second, but more on that subject later. (*Note, Rex Tillerson was fired by Trump in March 2018 the day after he said the chemical used to attack a former Russian spy on UK soil "clearly' came from Russia."*)

But Tillerson's short term as secretary of state further entrenched Putin comfortably in place at the highest level of US government. Putin was glad that he would never have to sit across the table, any table, from his nemesis, Hillary Clinton, again. Putin and Tillerson had been friends since 1999 as a result of closing business deals between Exxon and Russia. Tillerson was elevated in 2006 to chief executive officer of ExxonMobil, holding that position until he accepted the job as Trump's Secretary of State. Prior to that appointment, Putin awarded Tillerson with Russia's Order of Friendship medal in 2013, after Exxon and Russia's state-controlled oil company had completed a deal enriching both Exxon and Putin. "One of the enormous deals that Vladimir Putin and Rex Tillerson worked on was a $500 billion oil exploration partnership between Exxon and the Russian government's oil company, Rosneft. The Obama administration blocked the deal when it imposed sanctions against Russia for its intervention in the Ukraine in 2013 and its annexation of the Crimea in February 2014." Tillerson opposed the US sanctions. Joe Romm, founding editor of Climate Progress, wrote in December 2016, "This deal could explain why Putin appears to have interfered in U.S. elections in favor of a Trump victory." Romm goes on to say, "if the sanctions are lifted—something a new Secretary of State could help make happen—it would pay off big time for Exxon. ... Imagine ... if the oil giant is freed to produce and sell oil on the staggering 63.7 million acres of Russian land it leases," It's always money.

https://www.democracynow.org/2016/12/12/could_massive_russian_oil_deal_with Could Massive Russian Oil Deal with Exxon Explain Why Putin Appears to Have Meddled in US Election? Story December 12, 2016

Ukraine

Ukraine's flirtation with European Union in 2013 emboldened Putin to risk war with NATO when Russia invaded both the Crimea area and southeastern Ukraine. Putin's vision for Russia included Ukraine despite Ukraine's independence from Russia since August 1991. Ukraine is Russia's border neighbor and though it has no oil or gas, its land and its ports on the Black Sea serve as conduits for delivering Russia's black gold to markets in the west. The last thing Putin wanted on the border of his new Russian empire was a western-leaning, future member of NATO.

Russia quickly began inserting Ukrainian Russian nationalist into southeastern Ukraine arming them for 'revolt' against Ukraine's government in Kiev, the capital city in the northwest. The Russian-installed Ukrainian nationalists "rose up", 'claiming' that they were always Russian, spoke Russian, and wanted their part of the Ukraine to be part of their motherland, Russia. This ruse of protecting Russian citizens was used by Putin to invade the Ukraine and protect the 'best interests' of the Ukrainian nationalists. (Note, Hitler annexed Austria under the same guise.) Unwillingly, to withdraw its poorly-concealed presence in the Ukraine, the US and its western allies imposed economic sanctions on Russia's banks and its billionaire oligarchs. The economic sanctions hurt Russia where all powerful people can be hurt the most, in the wallet. These sanctions motivated Russia's intensive and expensive interference into America's 2016 presidential election. (Note, it is possible the oligarchs funded the entire cost of the election interference, after all 63.7 million acres of proven oil leases is a lot of money.) Despite many denials by Russia that they were arming the unmarked, uniformed pro-Russian rebels with full-scale offensive military weapons, the truth came forth in the few minutes it took for a non-existent missile to be fired by a non-existent Russian soldier at a commercial airliner flying from Amsterdam to Kuala Lumpur. Malaysia Airlines Flight 17 was shot down on 17 July 2014 over eastern Ukraine, killing all 283 passengers and 15 crew on board. A Dutch-led investigation team issued a formal report afterwards that a Russian BUK SAM missile launcher fired a missile at the plane from a separatist-controlled territory in southeast Ukraine by "'pro-Russian rebels".

The intelligence report that followed confirmed that the rocket launcher originated from the 53rd Anti-Aircraft Rocket Brigade of the Russian Federation, and returned across the border to Russia immediately after its missile struck its target. In May 2018, Russia continued to deny it was responsible, stating that it never deployed missile weapons to Ukraine.

The Russians weren't the only persons trying to have the sanctions removed. California Representative Dana Rohrbacher, reported in some news sources to be Russia's favorite US politician, proposed removing sanctions imposed as part of the Magnitsky Act, a bipartisan bill passed by the U.S. Congress and signed by President Obama in December 2012. The Magnitsky Act was passed in November 2013 to punish Russian officials responsible for the death of Russian tax accountant Sergei Magnitsky who died in a Moscow prison in 2009 after being imprisoned on bogus charges because he filed legal action against Putin and Russian oligarchs. (Note: It is alleged that the primary purpose for the Trump Tower meeting in June 2016 was to discuss what Russia could offer Trump and associates in trade for Trump's removal of the economic sanctions imposed by the Magnitsky Act.) These sanctions were particularly problematic for Russian billionaires who were millions of dollars, and patience with Putin. The Magnitsky Act is linked to the adoption of Russian orphans because Putin's first action after the US sanctions were implemented was to immediately end an American/Russian adoption program, thereby punishing Americans hoping to adopt children, and Russian children hoping to be adopted. The subject of child adoptions were never discussed at the June 9 meeting.

NATO

The North Atlantic Treaty Organization, NATO, is unique in American history because it was the first peacetime military alliance that America joined. Today, the alliance consists of 29 North American and European countries and its reason for existence is unchanged in nearly 70 years: prevent the Soviet Union (then a federation of countries subjugated to Russia after 1945) from expanding any further into Western Europe.

During WWII, the alliance of western democratic nations and Joseph Stalin's communist Russia was one of convenience, more correctly, it was an alliance for survival. With the alliance, Germany would have to defend itself on two battle fronts, this two-prong attack would pinch Germany. The combination of American and allied forces advancing from the west towards Germany and the Russian forces advancing from the east into Germany hastened, after 7 long years, the Germany's defeat. The alliance succeeded but its future was short-lived. The ideological differences between communism and democracy were incompatible, especially regarding the imposition of political slavery on individuals. In the East, the countries 'liberated' by Russian troops were in fact, 'captured' and taken into the growing Soviet empire. Russia was full of its power and envisioned expansion westward across Europe, basically it sought to replace Hitler's Germany as master of the continent. The Soviet Union, since dissolved after 1991, was strong in numbers in 1949, and it was a large threatening force to any single country on the European continent.

In 1949, observing soviet Russia's expansion westward across Europe, the United States and 11 other Western nations met to form the North Atlantic Treaty Organization (NATO) and stand against the Soviet

Union. Its charter announces to all that the members agree that if any country outside of NATO was to attack any country inside the NATO pact, all of the countries signature to the NATO agreement would act in defense of its fellow-member country, even to the extreme measure of going to war to end the threat. The organization's system of collective defense remains prepared today to respond to an attack by Russia. In response to the NATO pact, the Soviet Union and its affiliated communist nations in Eastern Europe founded a rival alliance, the Warsaw Pact, in 1955. This created an alignment of nearly every European nation into one of the two opposing camps and formalized the political division of the European continent that had taken place since World War II (1939-45). This alignment provided the framework for the military standoff that continued throughout the Cold War (1945-91), until the Berlin Wall came down, and the Soviet Union was dis-membered by decree by Russia.

The Soviet Union is since dissolved, and the many former member-nations are independent of Russia, which is now referred to formally as the Russian Federation. The decline of the Soviet Union 27 years ago was swift and there was some reason to believe that the giant threat from Russia was ended. That belief in the 21st century has faded as a new Russia under Vladimir Putin has risen that warrants distrust and caution from its European neighbors and from America. Presently, the late 20th century cold war between America and Russia has returned. War is not imminent but acts of aggression, inattention, and careless mistakes can hasten war.

Therefore, what was necessary in 1949, is still necessary in 2018 and beyond: stop Russian aggression and prevent any war in Europe that would likely ignite WWIII. America and Europe's, best interests are to keep the member countries cooperative and strong, economically and militarily. The 2014 invasions of Crimea and the southern Ukraine by Russia are examples of more aggression planned by Putin's Russia. Russian military force is not powerful enough to conquer a cooperative NATO alliance, but Russia's newest weapons are invisible and are used to create division among member nations and sow chaos inside their enemies' camps. This is the war that Russia wages now on America and on all nations across Europe. It is the same war that Trump wages within America. The fifty different states compromising the United States of America are in a similar position as NATO's 29 countries: both are subject to the daily attacks against the truth, and the endless flow of deceit, lies, and hate-mongering from these two men who would be kings. Together, our 50 states must stem the venom that Trump injects into America to divide us, just as the 29 countries must be of one mind to repel Russia's false news that seeks to weaken the alliance. The wisdom of forming an alliance of democratic countries with common borders and shared interests was sound in 1949, and after so many decades, it is still sound and necessary. Though sometimes agitated, the reason for the common pact of friendship has not lessened, it has become more important under the increasing shadow of Putin's Russia.

How Does Trump's Position inside NATO Assist Putin and Russia?

- Trump gives Putin a fox inside the hen house. Putin doesn't need a spy, or a code. Trump is the worm inside the apple; the virus let loose in a crowd. Putin's voice will come out of Trump's mouth.
- Trump can create rifts that can weakens the alliances, thereby strengthening Russia and assisting Putin's restoration of Russia.
- Trump's Svengali hold over the spineless Republican Party brethren will enable favors to be handed to Putin, possibly

giving Putin full access to Ukraine and other countries on its borders. Trump's secret conversations with Putin in Helsinki alludes to that likelihood.

- Trump's sanctions on Iran in January 2017 are more examples of Trump's crude gamesmanship, and his positions are consistent with Putin's position on Iran.
- Trump's insistence on bringing Russia back into G-8 is a divisive plan to have two votes in Russia's bag, Putin's and Trump's. *Trudy Rubin, July 12, 2018, Philadelphia Inquirer*

In summary, Trump is America's gift to Russia. He is doing Putin's dirty work from inside NATO. He undermines support for NATO in America to a degree that only 40% of GOP voters think America should stay in NATO, and incredibly, 56% of GOP voters consider Trump's friendship with Putin good for America. There has been a 166% rise in GOP favorable approval of Putin since February 2017, one month after Trump inauguration, and this is due to Trump's constant love-pining for Putin's attention. "Trump's open contempt for representative democracy and his vocal admiration for autocrats and dictators is the biggest 'fault line' in the alliance today, and the greatest chasm in NATO's history". *Bookings Institute Fellow Constanze Stelzenmuller.*

Mueller Indictments

In the midst of watching the Trump administration cuddle closer and closer to Russia and identify warmly with despots and tyrants in Turkey, Philippines, and other undemocratic countries, the Special Counsel that was formed to investigate Russia's election interference, has been working quietly and steadily for seventeen months. It has nearly 30 indictments and 7 convictions through August 2018, and there's no sign it's winding down. President Trump thinks the investigation has dragged on too long. But it is still six years away from the longest special-counsel probe—Iran-Contra under former President Ronald Reagan—that lasted nearly seven years, the Whitewater and Monica Lewinsky inquiry involving former President Bill Clinton lasted four years, and the investigation of the Valerie Plame affair under former President George W. Bush lasted three-and-a-half years. In comparison to the aforementioned investigations, Mueller's pace has been at breakneck speed, especially considering it is a complicated counterintelligence investigation that involves foreign nationals and the Kremlin, an adversarial foreign government already linked to the crime. Hindering progress of the investigation are the numerous misdirection congressional charges and their subsequent self-serving investigative panels created to block the truth about "Russia's interference" and who in America, if anyone, may have assisted them from being uncovered, and when uncovered from being heard by the American people. If "block" is too strong a description of the majority party's intent, a kinder sounding fitting adjective like "obstruct" might be applicable.

As the Russia/Trump collusion probe marches on, the fundamental legitimacy of Trump's presidency hangs in the balance. Did his campaign conspire with Russia to undermine Hillary Clinton, and work undercover with Russian agents to damage Clinton's candidacy, and bolster Trump's candidacy, thus aiding Trump to win the 2016 presidential election?

https://www.theatlantic.com/politics/archive/2018/05/the-lingering-mysteries-of-a-trump-russia-conspiracy/560465 *The Lingering Mysteries of a Trump-Russia Conspiracy, by Natasha Bertrand may 16, 2018*

According to a poll in late summer 2018, many Americans don't think the Department of Justice (DOJ) Special Counsel investigation on Russian and Trump campaign collusion has uncovered any crimes. But

Witness to Treason

Robert Mueller's number of indictments and convictions, as listed
below, speaks for itself and it is advancing additional indictments as
this book is being sent to publication. The biggest convictions through
August 2018 were against Trump's personal lawyer and self-
proclaimed 'fixer', Michael Cohen, and Trump's former 2016 campaign
manager and frequent Russian traveler, Paul Manafort. Persons and
companies indicted to date include four former Trump advisers (Gen.
Michael Flynn, George Papadopoulos, Paul Manafort and Rick Gates),
13 Russian nationals, 12 Russian military personnel, 3 Russian
companies, one California man, and one London-based lawyer. Seven
(including four former Trump aides) have either pleaded guilty, or
been found guilty. Granted, none of the charges have so far included
directly conspiring with Russians to interfere with the campaign, but
several pleaded guilty to making false statements about their contacts
with Russians to investigators. No formal charges of collusion with
Russia on the 2016 election, nor any charges of obstruction of justice by
Trump and his family, nor anyone on the Trump campaign team, have
been announced through September 1, 2018. The investigation
continues and each week brings forth more testimony, more immunity,
and more incredulous head-shaking in America.

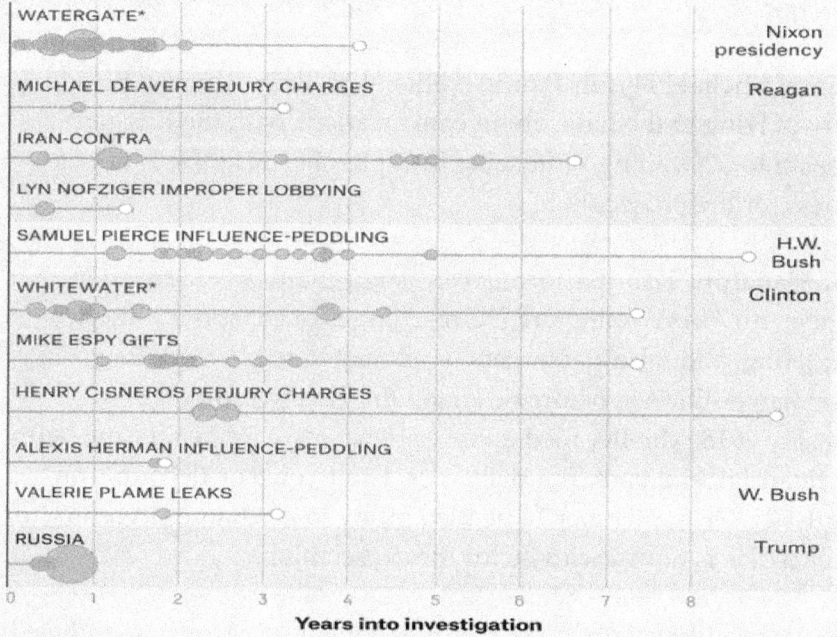

The Mueller investigation: one year in

Special investigations since 1973 that resulted in charges, by number of indictments and guilty pleas per week, as of May 17, 2018

INDICTMENTS AND PLEAS

WATERGATE* — Nixon presidency

MICHAEL DEAVER PERJURY CHARGES — Reagan

IRAN-CONTRA

LYN NOFZIGER IMPROPER LOBBYING

SAMUEL PIERCE INFLUENCE-PEDDLING — H.W. Bush

WHITEWATER* — Clinton

MIKE ESPY GIFTS

HENRY CISNEROS PERJURY CHARGES

ALEXIS HERMAN INFLUENCE-PEDDLING

VALERIE PLAME LEAKS — W. Bush

RUSSIA — Trump

Years into investigation

* Indictments occurring before the official investigation started are not shown.

Some defendants were indicted and later pleaded guilty, and some defendants were initially charged with one set of crimes and then indicted again on other charges. In both cases, only the first indictments or charges are included. Indictments of businesses are excluded.

FiveThirtyEight   SOURCES: CONGRESSIONAL RESEARCH SERVICE, NEWS REPORTS

https://fivethirtyeight.com/features/how-muellers-first-year-compares-to-watergate-iran-contra-and-whitewater/

Below is a list of the up-to-date indictments, plea deals, and convictions that have resulted from the Mueller special counsel investigation from its formation in May 2017 to September 21, 2018.

Witness to Treason

George Papadopoulos, former Trump campaign foreign policy adviser, pleaded guilty in October 2017 to making false statements to the FBI. Sentenced September 7, 2018, 14 days in prison, $9,500 fine, probation.

General Michael Flynn, Trump National Security Adviser, pleaded guilty of lying to the F.B.I. about conversations with the Russian ambassador. Awaiting sentencing in September 2018. He is now a witness for the prosecution.

Paul Manafort, Trump's former campaign chair, was indicted in October 2017 in Washington, DC on charges of conspiracy, money laundering, and false statements — all related to his work for Ukrainian politicians before he joined the Trump campaign. In February 2018, Mueller filed a new case against him in Virginia, with tax, financial, and bank fraud charges. Guilty on 8 of 18 counts on August 21. On September 14 he pled guilty to all charges in return for leniency. He is now a witness for the prosecution.

12 Russian military officers, all Russian intelligence officers indicted for hacking the Democratic National Committee, the Democratic Congressional Campaign Committee and Hillary Clinton's campaign during the 2016 election. All 12 are members of GRU, the Russian intelligence agency. Guilty but safely in Russia.

Rick Gates, a former Trump campaign aide and Manafort's longtime junior business partner, indicted on similar charges to Manafort. In February he agreed pled guilty to just one false statements charge and one conspiracy charge. He pled guilty in August 2018. He is a witness for the prosecution.

13 Russian nationals and three Russian companies, all indicted on conspiracy charges, with some also being accused of identity theft. The charges related to a Russian propaganda effort designed to interfere with the 2016 campaign. The companies involved are the Internet Research Agency, often described as a "Russian troll farm," and two other companies that helped finance it. The Russian nationals indicted include 12 of the agency's employees and its alleged financier, Yevgeny Prigozhin. Guilty but safely in Russia.

Richard Pinedo: A California man pleaded guilty to an identity theft charge in connection with the Russian indictments, and has agreed to cooperate with Mueller.

Alex van der Zwaan: A London lawyer pleaded guilty to making false statements to the FBI about his contacts with Rick Gates and another unnamed person. He pleaded guilty and was sentenced to 30 days in prison and given a $20,000 fine on April 3, 2018.

Konstantin Kilimnik: Business associate of Manafort and Gates, based in Russia, charged with Manafort attempting to obstruct justice by tampering with witnesses in Manafort's pending case this year.

May 2017, fires Comey, meets w/Russians Mueller probe and other probes

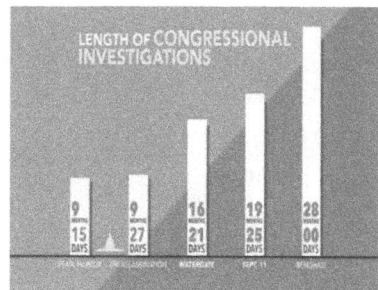

Witness to Treason

How It All Came Down, Post-Election

Jan. 26, Acting Attorney General Sally Gates meets White House (WH) Counsel Don McGahn to warn him that Lt. Gen. Flynn, Trump's pending National Security Advisor, met with Russian Ambassador Sergei Kislyak and discussed US-led sanctions already in place from Obama presidency prior to Trump's inauguration, possibly, before election. McGahn's reply was "why does the DOJ care if the WH staff lie to one another? Hmmm. Well, I guess, you can lie about what you ate for breakfast, or who you had sex with in college, but there should be reasonable concern on topics that impact national affairs.

Jan 27, Trump invites FBI Director Comey to a private dinner alone at the White House. He asks Comey for a pledge of 'personal loyalty'. Comey says he can 'pledge honesty'.

Jan 30, Yates is fired by because she would not implement the Muslim Ban.

Feb 13, Lt. General Michael Flynn, is accused of lying to the FBI regarding meetings with Russian officials, resigns after three weeks as Trump's National Security Advisor.

Feb 14, Trump has a private meeting in the Oval Office with Comey and asks Comey to halt the investigation of Lt. Gen. Michael Flynn. Trump says, "I hope you can see your way clear to letting this go, to letting Flynn go."

May 3, Comey testifies before the Senate Judiciary Committee on Russian investigation

May 7, Comey requests more resources from Department of Justice for the Russian Collusion investigation

May 9, Yates testifies before a senate panel and says that she met with WH counsel Don McGahn to tell him that Lt. Gen. Flynn would be in a compromising position whereby Russia could blackmail him on this information. Republicans were more interested in why Yates would not implement Trump's Dixiecrats, and whether she was responsible for leaking classified information.

May 9, Trump fires FBI Director James Comey! Why? Pick one: a) because Sessions and Rosenstein told him to do so, b) because Trump wasn't pleased with his performance as FBI head, c) because Trump wasn't pleased how Comey treated Clinton, d) because he wasn't pleased that Comey wouldn't pledge loyalty, leave Flynn alone, stop Russian investigation. The firing takes place days after Comey asked the Department of Justice for more resources to perform the growing Russian-collusion probe.

May 10, the day after he fired FBI Director Comey, Trump meets in the Oval Office with Russian Foreign Minister Sergey Lavrov and Russian Ambassador Sergey Kislak, with only the Russian media in attendance, no US press allowed. TASS, the Russian news agency, publishes the only photos allowed to be taken. US news photographers and news correspondents are refused entry into the meeting. Trump shares sensitive intelligence about ISIS with the Russians. This is info not even given to America's allies. US Intelligence agencies move fast to safeguard any exposed sources. Trump says he has an "absolute right to share the information" and Flynn's replacement as National Security Adviser, H.R. McMaster, agrees that the President has "an absolute right" to share the info with Russia. McMaster forgot that Russia is our long-term, primary adversary, not ISIS or Al Qaeda. Trump also boasts to his Russian friends, "I just fired the head of the FBI. He was crazy; a real nut job." He adds, "I faced great pressure because of Russia. That's taken off."

May 11, In a TV interview, NBC's Lester Holt asked Trump about the White House's initial story that he fired Comey because of a recommendation by Deputy Attorney General Rod Rosenstein, Trump said, "I was gonna fire him regardless of the recommendation." In explaining how he made up his mind, the President said, "When I decided to do it (fire Comey), I said to myself, I said, 'You know, this Russia thing with Trump and Russia is a made up story, it's an excuse." He [Rosenstein] made a recommendation, he's highly respected, very good guy, very smart guy. But regardless of [the] recommendation, I was going to fire Comey."

May 12, Trump tweets, "Comey better hope there are no tapes of our conversation before he starts leaking to the press." Weeks later Trump confirms that says there are no tapes. They must've been "fake tapes."

May 17, Comey says that in a February meeting at the White House, Trump asked him to drop the FBI probe into Flynn after Flynn resigned, saying "I hope you can let this go." Comey wrote a highly-detailed, two-page account only hours after he left the meeting with Trump.

May 17, Deputy Attorney General Rod Rosenstein appoints Robert Mueller as Special Counsel for the Russian Collusion investigation.

More Russian collusion

General Michael Flynn, then an adviser to Trump's presidential campaign, met state Rep. Dana Rohrabacher, R-CA in Washington, DC on Sept. 20, 2016. (Note: Rohrabacher, a staunch advocate of policies that would help Russia, and who pushed for better relations with Russia, had traveled to Moscow in June 2013 to meet with Russian officials. Thereafter, he advocated overturning the Magnitsky Act, a 2012 congressional bill that froze assets of Russian investigators and oligarchs). No one has confirmed whether Rohrabacher and Flynn discussed U.S. policy towards Russia in the September 2016 meeting. Mueller's interest in the nature of Flynn and Rohrabacher's discussion marked the introduction of any member of Congress, other than those on the Trump campaign team, into the Russian investigation.

Rohrabacher surfaced in another appearance on behalf of foreign interests. The Wall Street Journal reported in 2016 that Rohrabacher offered Trump a deal. If Trump (once he became president) would agree to not prosecute Assange, the creator of WikiLeaks, and the person behind the released of emails damaging to Hillary Clinton before the 2016 election, for Assange's 2010 leak of State Department emails, Assange would allegedly provide proof that Russia was not the source of the hacked Democratic emails. (Note: The US intelligence community had pointed to Russia as the secret provider of the email trove to WikiLeaks.) This revelation of Rohrabacher's involvement makes Fox News' Sean Hannity's later visit to London to get that same evidence from Assange more interesting.

Most of what had been reported previously about Mueller's questioning of Flynn's lobbying work had been concentrated on his efforts on behalf of Turkey. Federal investigators did investigate

Flynn's lobbying efforts on behalf of Turkey, including an alleged meeting with senior Turkish officials in December 2016 where he was offered millions of dollars to secure the return of the Turkish president's chief rival to Turkey, and additionally, to advocate that a U.S. case against a Turkish national be dismissed. Less was known about his lobbying ties to Russia, though he was paid $45,000 plus expenses for attending a gala in Moscow in December 2015 and being interviewed by RT, the Kremlin-financed cable TV news channel. Flynn did plead guilty to one count of making false statements to FBI agents and is awaiting sentencing pending any further developments in the ongoing investigation. He faces a sentence of zero to five years in prison, but he may avoid imprisonment depending on his cooperation with the special counsel. The prosecution likely agreed to charge him with only one offense in exchange for his agreement to be a cooperative witness for the special counsel prosecution. Gen. Flynn may not get his day or several days in court, but recorded history will allow Americans to see his face and hear his voice shamefully encouraging Trump's campaign mobs to call out in unison, "Lock her up!" The words were prescient, for they would come to apply perfectly to Gen. Flynn, and to the men who surrounded Trump, the man who would be king.

Chapter Twelve
Freedom of the Press

"To announce that there must be no criticism of the President, or that we are to stand by the President, right or wrong, is not only unpatriotic and servile, but is morally treasonable to the American public." — *Theodore Roosevelt*

The Final Barriers to Tyranny

History and literature are full of the tragedies and triumphs of real and fictional men and women, of small towns and large nations that have battled against the tyranny of a single despot or a sinister empire to secure for themselves the freedom of self-government and self-expression. Even before the printing press, written messages were critical to sharing a call for action to others to reject the tyrant and to energize resistance to tyranny. Such stories are plentiful, both old and new, because tyranny is never out-of-fashion. It is found daily in the dark side of humanity where it is nurtured by greed and a vain obsession for power. America is now in the throes of a battle against a growing tyranny – a President and his friends, aided by a submissive Republican Party and emotionally-blinded constituents, who want total control of America, its people and its riches. How can this impending tyranny be stopped? How did the heroes and heroines from history and literature fare so long ago? Most of them succeeded, at least those who inspired us. I recall a lyric from a popular tune sung by the Bee Gees, "How can you stop the rain from falling down." Impossible? The lyric poses for me another question I ask myself. How can this impending tyranny be stopped?

The Freedom of the Press

The founding fathers were men from different colonies, backgrounds, ancestries but they were all familiar with persecution, intolerance, and pettiness that can descend from any authority that rules for its own pleasure, whims, and greed. That is why they or their families fled to America: to flee from tyranny. They wanted individual freedoms to be installed as the foundation blocks of the new nation. These freedoms were highlighted in the Bill of Rights that is front and center and included in the formal Constitution of the United States. The men who penned these ten amendments were proud of the Bill of Rights. They were most pleased that the sentiments in the First Amendment took prominence among all of the amendments.

First Amendment

Congress shall make no law respecting an establishment of religion, or prohibiting the free exercise thereof; or abridging the freedom of speech, or of the press, or the right of the people peaceably to assemble, and to petition the Government for a redress of grievances.

The founding fathers regarded freedom of expression as a fundamental human right. The right to speak your mind freely on important issues in society, to access information, and to hold those in power accountable. These rights all play a vital role in any society. The freedom to be able to speak out publicly about our political opinions without fear of retaliation is powerful in itself. The first amendment emphasizes the importance of the freedom of speech, press, and assembly.

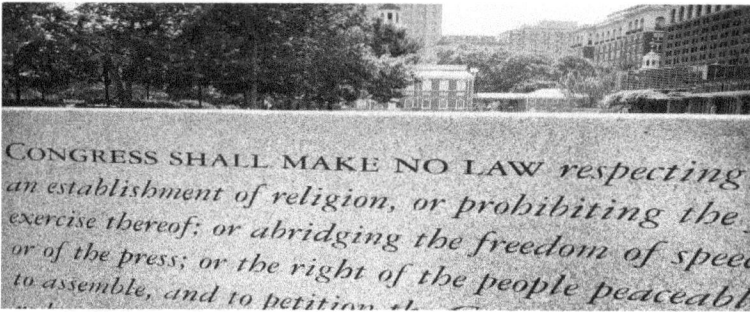

"Freedom of speech" etched in stone outside Independence Hall, Phila., PA

In this climate of lies and deceit continuously generated by the Trump administration, the founding fathers' foresight in establishing the First Amendment provided America with a barrier to stop Trump's first wave of tyranny from steamrolling across the country. (Note: It isn't like Trump would've settled on installing restrictions on just one group, and stopping there; all Americans would soon have a turn in the barrel.) The Fourth Estate, the free press, continues to reinforce itself as a barrier of truth against lies. The fight against this tyranny of lies, chaos, and misinformation was slow to begin. However, the battle began in earnest when Trump, barely seated in the Oval Office, launched his onerous decrees that threatened American freedoms. The national press spoke out against them. When questioned about his actions, Trump and his attack dogs targeted what they considered to be a soft target. But as we used to say in the old neighborhood, they picked on the wrong guy (gal). America's press corps, national news journalists, its print, internet, and cable outlets all rose tall (Fox News excluded), and they have not waivered since the battle began. Kudos go out to all those men and women, seen and unseen, who kept "the presses rolling": who kept America informed: who spoke out to clear away the confusion; removed the smoke and mirrors from the Trump administration. They enabled the truth to come through the thick fog surrounding the White House, a once proud landmark of American democracy, now captive to tyranny.

Candidates for Profiles in Courage

In Chapter 6, there was a search for GOP legislators who might qualify as examples of courage amidst the current crisis of leadership. The search ended poorly. I wasn't surprised. It is the mettle of the men who flourish in today's GOP Party: they lack courage. So, let's look elsewhere. Let's look at the newspapers, cable and network newscasts, and the 24/7, 365 internet news organizations who have fought the battle for everyone else.

I'm not in a position to make cash awards, so I created the *Poor Richard's Almanac Awards* to acknowledge those persons and institutions who have displayed courage during this crisis of leadership from the White House and the Republican Party. These are my personal choices for recognition and they are not in any particular order. These women and men, and news organizations and networks span news journalism across America and reach into some foreign countries. (Russia, Breitbart News, and Fox News do not qualify as real news outlets). We are thankful for the free press in America and for the legions that report facts, and most importantly challenge, and deny the liars. When people are denied the truth, there is a parallel universe, and it is a universe where lies are cheered and goodness and truth are shouted down. It is difficult enough to live in one world without trying to manage a second one, especially an alternate world where up is down, and down is up.

So, as they say in Hollywood ...the *Poor Ricard Almanac Award* winners are...

- The New York Times: owners, executives, journalists, and staff – print and online
- The Washington Post owners, executives, journalists, and staff – print and online
- CNN- Anderson Cooper, Wolf Blitzer, Jake Tapper, Don Lemon, Erin Burnett, Jim Acosta, Brooke Baldwin, Chris Cuomo, and their many colleagues and staff
- TV Network News: ABC, NBC, CBS, George Stephanopoulus, Martha Radditz, Cokie Roberts, Matthew Dowd, Jonathan Karl
- MSN- Rachel Maddow
- The Washington, DC, Press Corps who knew a lie when they heard one - April Ryan and so many others
- The Philadelphia Inquirer, Will Bunch, Trudy Rubin; and my local paper, the Delaware County Times, Jodine Mayberry
- The Daily Kos, Reuters, and numerous other vigilant news services
- Social media warriors such as Resist Trump
- Attorney General Rod Rosenstein
- Special Counsel Robert Mueller, and his entire staff
- U.S. Intelligence Agencies, and Christopher Steele
- Members of Congress who stood tall when they were needed most. The loyal opposition Party, led by Adam Schiff, Chuck Schumer, and other Democratic legislators; and the few GOP members tired of the lies and the hate: Jeff Flake and John McCain
- Professor Christine Blasey Ford
- And the 65 million voters in 2016 who were not fooled

Witness to Treason

A Profile in Courage Award Winner

Forgotten among the daily announcements of one indictment after
another, and the steady stream of reluctant admissions by Trump
associates of meetings and phone calls with Russians that they are "just
now recalling", there was one sacrifice made by a young woman,
Reality Winner. On August 23, 2018, (Ms. Reality Winner, a former Air
Force linguist who was honorably discharged in 2016, pleaded guilty
to one count of violating the Espionage Act. Winner has been the only
person caught and prosecuted by the U.S. government, the Department
of Justice, for leaking information to the media. After two years of
media leaks rumored to have come from inside, outside, and above
and beneath Washington, DC, a 26 year old Air Force veteran, and an
employee of a NSA contractor is the only person they have been able to
find and prosecute.

Ms. Winner was sentenced to 63 months in prison for leaking classified
documents to the Intercept last year. (The Intercept is an online news
publication dedicated to what it describes as "adversarial journalism",
dedicated to making the powerful accountable.) Winner received the
longest-ever prison sentence for someone convicted of leaking
government information to the media. She was arrested in June 2017
after leaking a report that detailed an attempt by Russian intelligence
to hack into voting machine software in the days before the 2016
election. As the government continued to insist that the Russians had
no success in penetrating any U.S. electronic voting systems, Winner
became aware that the government had proof that Russian hacking
occurred, and that Russia used information from the hacking to target
computers in Florida before the election. She printed the classified
report, smuggled it out of her office, and mailed it to the Intercept,
which published its story on the report on June 5. In a statement,

Assistant Attorney General for National Security John Demers praised the Justice Department for prosecuting Winner, adding, "I hope their success will deter others from similar unlawful action in the future." Others have defended Winner for what they see as a noble act. "Reality Winner is a whistleblower who alerted the public about a critical threat to election security," Freedom of the Press Foundation executive director Trevor Timm said in a statement. "Winner performed a public service by alerting the public and state officials to dangerous vulnerabilities in election infrastructure, and it's shameful the Justice Department would seek any prison time for her doing so — let alone the longest sentence for such an act in history." He added, "Far from a criminal, she should be considered a hero." Nevertheless, the DOJ is proud of its success rate on finding and successfully prosecuting a leaker. They are a perfect one for one. Let's see how successful they are in catching another one of the twenty or so they walk by every day in the White House and in the halls of Congress.

Reality Winner chose a path of resistance to a government which was keeping secret the truth that Russian agents attacked the U.S. election process in 2016, and succeeded. The information was likely with-held from the public because it embarrassed the Trump administration and lent credence to Russian collusion. It's possible that Winner may have known how serious a risk she was taking divulging information to the American public that Russia attacked our election. After all, she served in the U.S. Air Force, as Senior Airman, (SrA), and she received an Air Force Commendation Medal for identifying "high-value targets" for American drone strikes. This doesn't sound like someone who doesn't love her country. Reality Winner took a desperate action, a brave action, to serve her country out of uniform just as she pledged to do so while in uniform. My appreciation is sent to her for her courage, and the Profiles in Courage winner for 2018 goes to Reality Winner.

Witness to Treason

In Memory of the Capital Gazette

The price of telling the truth in gun-saturated America increased on June 28, 2018 when a gunman walked into the Capital Gazette newsroom in Annapolis, Md, and shot and killed 5 people. The gunman was arrested and taken into custody at the Capital Gazette newsroom in Annapolis, after he was caught hiding under a desk. "This was a targeted attack on the Capital Gazette," Anne Arundel County acting police chief Bill Krampf said. "This person was prepared to shoot people. His intent was to cause harm." Police said surveillance video recorded the attack, which began with a shotgun blast that shattered the glass entrance to the open newsroom. Journalists crawled under desks and sought other hiding places, describing agonizing minutes of terror as they heard his footsteps and the repeated blasts of the weapon. Officers swiftly responded and arrested him without firing a shot, police said. They recovered a gun and said he also carried smoke grenades.

The shooter had a well-documented history of harassing the paper's journalists, a feud that apparently began over a column about him pleading guilty to harassing a woman. He filed a defamation suit against the paper in 2012 that was thrown out as groundless, and he repeatedly railed against its staff members in profanity-laced tweets. Authorities identified the victims killed in the shooting as 61-year-old Gerald Fischman, 56-year-old John McNamara, 34-year-old Rebecca Smith, 65-year-old Wendi Winter and 59-year-old Rob Hiaasen.

https://www.cbsnews.com/news/jarod-ramos-capital-gazette-shooting-suspect-annapolis-maryland-suspect-indicted-23-charges-today-2018-07-20/

Baseball Ambush in Washington, DC

A year earlier, on June 14, 2017, just across the bay from Annapolis, rifle shots rang out across a baseball field in Alexandria, VA. Six men, including two members of a Capitol Police security detail, were shot. Among them was Steve Scalise, the majority whip of the House of Representatives. All of the wounded civilians were members of a Republican congressional baseball team gathering at a practice field in this Washington suburb.

A man, reportedly distraught over President Trump's election, opened fire on members of the team showering the field with bullets that struck four people. The two wounded police officers were wounded as they exchanged fire with the gunman. The gunman was killed in exchange of gunfire. Representative Jeff Duncan of South Carolina, who left the practice just before the shooting, said afterward that he encountered a man in the parking lot — later identified as the gunman — who "asked me if the team practicing was a Democrat or a Republican team." "I told him they were Republicans," the lawmaker recalled. "He said, 'O.K., thanks,' turned around."

https://www.nytimes.com/2017/06/14/us/steve-scalise-congress-shot-alexandria-virginia.html

C-SPAN Reports Threats against CNN Anchors to FBI

The threat of physical violence entered the TV newsroom on August 7, 2018 when C-SPAN said Monday afternoon that it notified the FBI after a caller said on-air on Friday morning that if he came across CNN anchors Don Lemon and Brian Stelter, "I'm going to shoot them." "Specific threats of violence made on C-SPAN are reported to the appropriate authorities," the network said in a statement. "On Friday, C-SPAN reported the incident and all relevant information to the FBI."

Witness to Treason

The public affairs network also said that it "cooperated fully with CNN Security officials" responding to the threat. The caller falsely asserted that Stelter and Lemon called all Trump supporters "racist." Stelter aired video of the threat during his *Reliable Sources* show on Sunday morning, during a segment about threats to reporters. "I'm not asking for sympathy," he said. "I don't think I'm in extreme danger. I know some of my colleagues get much worse threats than I do."

The security of CNN employees has been an issue for months. In late January, about a week after a Michigan man was arrested for calling in threats to CNN, network president Jeff Zucker told employees during a town hall meeting "that at no time did CNN feel their people were in jeopardy." Stelter and Lemon have been favored punching bags of the Right. On a Friday night, Donald Trump again called Lemon "the dumbest man on television," one of his regular insults.

"Friday's threatening phone call on C-SPAN is just a tiny illustration of the threats that are out there," Stelter said on his show. The press cannot say it but it must be said. If anyone still supports Trump after three years of the harm Trump has done to America, that person is avoiding their responsibility to protect their country from any threats to America's freedoms and to the welfare of all its citizens. They should all feel bad about themselves.   *Jeremy Barr, The Hollywood Reporter, online, August 7, 2018 https://www.msn.com/en-us/news/us/c span-reports-threats-against-cnn-anchors-to-fbi/ar-BBLA59Z?ocid=spartandhp*

One for All, All for One

On Thursday August 16, 2018, American newspapers responded to the Boston Globe's call to jointly defend a pillar of democracy: the freedom of the press. The Philadelphia Inquirer Editorial board joined more

404

than 350 newspapers across America in an effort coordinated by the Boston Globe Editorial Board. The Globe called for editorial boards to push back against Trump's "dirty war on the free press." They wrote, "The impact of Trump's assault on journalism looks different in Boise than it does in Boston. Our words will differ. But at least we can agree that such attacks are alarming."

Philadelphia Inquirer's Editorial August 16

The editorials were noticed. President Trump tweeted that morning, "the Globe is in COLLUSION with other papers on free press." Newspapers throughout the country wrote about the importance of the press as though their freedom to speak freely depended on it. It does.

http://www2.philly.com/philly/opinion/editorials/editorial-free-press-donald-trump-20180816.html

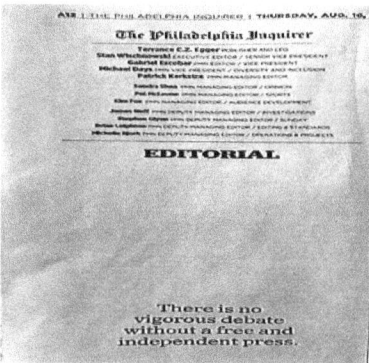

FORMER STAFFER SAYS SHE SAW TRUMP EATING DOCUMENT IN THE OVAL OFFICE

Where Not to Get Your News

Lest we forget. There are examples of what happens to nations where public protest, even conversations with a family member or a friend are potentially dangerous, result in incarceration, or worse. Knowing what is true, or seeking the truth, is nearly impossible. Where are these countries? They are all around us. Their leaders are friends of our President, the people he admires. Russia, Turkey, Philippines, North Korea, China, and Iran are across an ocean; Fox News and Robert Mercer's Breitbart News are inside our own borders.

Their news organizations, are mouthpieces for the government propaganda, more precisely they are lies from the dictator who tightly controls the information that is fed to his counties citizens. Inside their borders, Trump's "good leaders" do not need to defend lies and attack the truth because there is no opposition news. Whoever controls the communication in a village or an empire wields it as a weapon used to tell lies, repeat lies, spin out more lies, deny the truth, and lie some more. This is a brainwashing technique that works over time. Saying a lie often enough, and loud enough, wearies both the hearer and the truth itself. In time, the lie and the liar will believe it is the truth.

Call to Action

Chapter Thirteen
Call to Action

"It is left only to God and to the angels to be lookers on." Sir Francis Bacon

Do Something

Hopefully, after reading the previous chapters, you've seen the damage that Donald Trump has done to our nation in just the sliver of time since he and his friends hijacked America's cultural soundstage in 2015 and launched chaos and division into our nation's political discourse. The Trump presidency is not ended so there is possibly more mayhem to witness. I hope and pray that will not happen. This chapter will show you a few things that you and I can do to stop the mayhem. The most important action to take to effect change (in 2018 that means to restore sanity) is to VOTE. Vote, and take a friend or two with you. That individual action still works in America. Vote. Simply stated, "Use it or lose it."

I wrote this book because I was fearful that I would begin to forget all the outrageous madness that was occurring. So much was being piled up, day after day. The insanity and crudeness was becoming normalized and accepted as routine, threatening to replace civility and decency of manners in public discourse. Trump's way of doing things was fast becoming the new level of normalcy. As Trump said himself, "I will be a different kind of President." So, I decided to keep a record of the "unprecedented" events playing out in newscast and television, I created my first journal. It wasn't as easy as I thought it would be. Hell, it wasn't easy to watch any of this live, then writing it all down. That's why all the circus acts may not be here, but there is enough to look back on now, and again later, and remember it was all true, not fake news. It was outrageous and unprecedented. Here in September 2018, it is not yet over. Trump, the new GOP, Trump's friends, and greed are still dangers to all of us: to our freedoms, our families, our friends, our neighbors. And, lest we forget, we must remember that in this globally-connected world, our neighbors can now live one door away, or an ocean away.

During my many hours of research for this book, I happened to discover Matthew West, a singer/songwriter who communicates his faith and his feelings through music. He says in his notes for his CD, <u>In the Light of Day</u> that he is "wary of sending out a song that calls for action if it doesn't start with calling me to action first." I feel the same way. Matthew begins with talking to God about what he sees going on around him, and he asks God if he is going to fix it. He recalls "that his "aha" moment happens with God responding by saying, "Matthew, I did something; I created you. You go out and change the world and make it a better place." Though God hasn't prodded me directly, Matthew's comment rings true for me, also, and he says it clearly in a track on the CD titled, "Do Something." Lastly, I would paraphrase a Jewish scholar, Rabbi Hillel, who has been speechless for 2,000 years, but whose words echo today, "If not me, then who?"

First Things First

Let's begin this call to action with a list of things you don't want to do. Please feel comfortable with adding your own "Don'ts" and share those with others. I will leave space at the end of the list so you can write in a few "don'ts" of your own.

The list is not in order of importance. They are all important.

Don't hide your head in the sand.

Don't wait for someone else to do something first.

Don't give up!

Don't cry over spilled milk.

Don't accept or excuse racism, misogyny, bigotry, or hatred.

Don't compromise with tyranny, or the devil.

Don't ask someone to do something you wouldn't do yourself.

Don't befriend or defend an unrepentant enemy.

Don't confuse lies with the truth.

Don't be fearful or too timid to ask questions.

Don't be fearful or too timid to challenge authority.

What You Can Do Now

Vote

Register to vote and take a friend or two with you, and encourage them to also register to vote. Then you can share in the singularly most powerful expression of democracy and self-importance in any civil society, the opportunity to have your voice, your vote, counted among the many votes that will decide your town or country's direction. Your candidate may not win, your cause may not be cheered, not at that time, but you will be heard, and you will be remembered. I am hopeful you and those around you understand that the threat to a free and just American history requires and needs your vote in 2018, and in every election thereafter. Note: Thomas Edison knew the importance of every single vote. His first U.S. patent, Patent No.1, was his invention for an automatic vote counter in 1869. It worked but it wasn't financially successful because congressmen in Washington, DC were not interested in it. Some things never change.

Support your candidates

Several old adages apply here. "Put your money where your mouth is", "Put up or shut up", "Don't just say something, do something". Candidates, causes need support in every manner. If you are willing and able, you can make a difference and increase the chances for your candidate's or cause's success. How you can provide support is many-fold. Money is the most popular but time and skills are the bedrock of any successful campaign. Visit a candidate's headquarters, answer a request for political support, and join a friend at a campaign function to test your interest. There is much that you can do: you can lend your skills and enthusiasm to national groups that share your interests such as the Organization for Action; better yet, organize locally, take someone with you and canvas your neighborhood, knock on doors, encourage people to vote for your candidate. Assist at campaign rallies, work at the campaign headquarters on Election Day and assist with rides to the polls. You can introduce your candidate's ideas, strengths, and solutions to others in public conversation; help to educate and energize voters on the issues that benefit or harm them. Someone out there will be thankful you did something. You will be thankful you did too.

Seven takeaways on contributing:

1. Look around your own community to see what needs fixing or improvement. Inform yourself what, how, who. Then ask and listen, then join with others of like mind.
2. Vote, but first educate yourself on issues, learn facts, be ready to work and win.
3. Join with like-minded persons, that makes your voice louder, and your actions stronger, build consensus.
4. Communicate ideas, movements with public, media, etc; focus, be clear, be persistent.
5. Contribute to the cause, money, time, and energy. Put your funds where your heart is.
6. Run for office yourself to ensure you get what you and your group wants.
7. Above all, SHOW UP. At meetings, at workshops, at rallies, at the voting booth.

Support the free press

In the past two years, the free press, neither aligned nor controlled by the government, has protected America from the daily attacks and threats of domestic tyranny. In the United States, the three branches of government given the responsibility to do that are the legislative, executive, and judicial institutions created for that purpose by the U.S. Constitution. None of them have stepped forward to do so. All three are compromised by their relationship to the source of the tyranny threatening America. Fortunately, there is an unofficial fourth branch with significant influence in America: the free press. In England and America, the press is recognized as the Fourth Estate, a segment of society that wields an indirect but significant influence even though it is not formally recognized as part of the political system. Without the guardians, and the men and women among the press corps, the once-gathering storm of dissent and unrest might have been more damaging.

You can speak out to support the truth when you hear it. Stay alert to lies and rumors; challenge them openly. If you see something, say something: political bullying and harassment are enemies of liberty. If you're frustrated with a political system that feels broken or leaders who don't represent your values, speak up. Whenever possible, join others who want to make a difference.

Eliminate gerrymandering

You can help to make gerrymandering become a "dead" strategy. The concept for redistricting must be sensible and consider the human ebb and flow in communities. Permanently drawn grids are a huge simplification and don't reflect the real world where people don't live in neatly-ordered grids sorted by an equal amount of people belonging to different political parties. The easiest way to solve this issue, of course, is to stop party-biased redistricting that creates clusters of communities where a single political party has a built-in advantage for always winning that district, and stop racial gerrymandering which silences the voices of minorities. You can become active in a local group of like-minded people and work to institute "fair districting". Several ways to do that are:

- Educate voters on the importance of bipartisan redistricting; assist with the circulation of petitions for signature, and have the group's legal representative present them to local courts for review and acceptance.
- Support bi-partisan redistricting, recommend the appointment of a-political entities, not affiliated with any political party, to serve on a redistricting commission.
- Consider asking the courts to take the redistricting process out of human hands entirely. There is software capable of doing that now.
- Consider having open primaries. Join action teams to learn how open primaries are done, and what benefits they provide to the election process when all voters can vote for candidates across party lines in a primary election.

Support voting rights

It is still difficult to accept that in 2018, the United States of America must maintain a large staff of investigators, lawyers, and field personnel in the Department of Justice to ensure that American citizens are able to vote in their own hometown. The Voting Rights Act of 1965 was passed by Congress more than a half-century ago (53 years) after white racists in the South brazenly killed black men, and white men and women, and its state troopers attacked a peaceful march in Selma, AL. The murders, and the assault on the Edmund Pettis Bridge were all part of the Southern resistance to prevent blacks from voting. State disfranchisement of minority voters has been the Southern way to keep control of their "white America" since the 15th amendment was passed that gave black Americans the right to vote in America. The problem has always been that parts of the South are not American. The Voting Rights Act of 1965 has been amended three times, and each amendment has been fiercely opposed by state officials in Southern states. The federal government must be vigilante and always ready to provide critical protections for minorities when they go to the voting booth in the South.

What can you do? You can support in any way possible an end to voter suppression. Voter suppression doesn't stop at the Mason-Dixon Line as you travel from the South to the northern states. In Ohio and in other backward Mid-west states, local laws are being invoked that are similar to the former Jim Crow laws in the South, laws that were designed to disenfranchise and dispirit black men and women. These new Jim Crow laws are a product of the growing presence of a large influx of campaign money, and the subsequent increasing number of conservative legislators that have taken office in the region over the past twenty years.

Here some actions that you can do to lessen voter suppression.

- Share this information to other voters
- Support voter registration on-line
- Support voting on-line
- Support simplifying absentee voting rules, making the rules uniform across states, i.e. an absentee ballot should be accepted right up to the poll is closed, avoiding some votes being uncounted because it arrived late by rule, but not later than election day

Support campaign finance reform

Former President Jimmy Carter is leading a national movement to have every candidate in every election at every level be equally eligible for public campaign financing. There are many discussions to be held but it is an idea that deserves attention. All political contributions from individuals, businesses, for-profit or nonprofit charities, and all miscellaneous social groups whether for campaign or other reasons must be limited in amount, and all recipients must disclose the source of such funds who contributed to its campaign.

End Citizens United

Earlier in Chapter 8, the history of *Citizens United was* discussed and lamented. Every day, the tragedy of the court's ruling is visible as it races unrestricted across our nation like a plague in a post-apocalyptical B-rated movie. The Supreme Court's 2010 *Citizens United* ruling is a tragedy for American democracy because it created an "open market" where domestic billionaires, foreign billionaires, foreign countries, and other high-rollers can openly or secretly bid for any U.S. political office they wish to control. The libertarian and conservative politicos talk nobly but money is the engine that drives them, not ideology. All other interests come later. Campaign reform must begin with an end to unregulated "donations" from special interests.

Stop Citizens United

All across the country, there are movements to end *Citizens United*. Presently billionaires and overt organizations funnel obscene amounts of money into political campaigns and political strategies through secondary sources and nonprofit institutions chartered as charitable and educational. This is the 'fault line' that lies beneath the Supreme Court's lame ruling in <u>Citizens United vs FEC</u>. Supreme Court Justice Steven's dissenting opinion makes his view clear that the money is used to focus on a specific political philosophy, cause, and/or candidate, thus corrupting the integrity of one person/one vote in our constitution, i.e., one dollar equals one vote, one hundred dollars equals one vote, but one million dollars obliterates all the other votes.

Five Ways to Fight Citizens United

- **Party for the Cause,** Hold a house party to screen the *The Story of Citizens United v. FEC* and invite others to join the campaign. Invite friends, neighbors, family members over to your place for an evening of democracy in action!
- **Sign on,** Sign Public Citizen's petition calling for a Constitutional Amendment clarifying that free speech is for people, not corporations. A lot of signatures are needed to launch this ambitious campaign. Help to collect signatures and tell others about the campaign. Check online, you can sign electronically.
- **Get National,** Join a national organization working on restoring our democracy. This way your local efforts can be magnified and it'll be a lot easier to track an issue and identify opportunities to get involved locally and nationally. Check out Public Citizen, Free Speech for People, People for the American Way and Move to Amend.
- **Democracy: Use it or Lose it,** One reason corporations have been able to hijack our democracy is that many of us haven't engaged much in it ourselves lately. If we want policy makers who prioritize public good, healthy jobs, and a sustainable environment, we need to get involved, hold them accountable, and engage as active citizens every day—not just on voting day. Join a local organization working on an issue you care about, host a community event to share information, write letters to

your congress people and local newspapers to share your opinion. There are an infinite number of ways to get involved and once enough of us do, we can have a government we want that is really by the people, for the people. Then, we can get to work solving today's pressing problems with a government working for us, instead of big business.

Election 2018

There is one goal in November 2018. Vote in Democrats, and vote out Republicans. This will improve the chances that fairer election maps will get drawn across the nation following the 2020 census. The offices needed to win in 2018 are below.

- **The U.S. Senate.** Keep every Democratic-held seat and pick up two Republican seats to reverse the GOP's 51-49 edge. The benefit to American democracy would be enormous.
- **The U.S. House.** Send Trump and his GOP friends home, and stop the GOP Congress from conducting their "One-Percenter" benefit program, its actions and policies. A Democratic House would be able to block GOP legislation, and continue the Russia investigation and carry it to its conclusion. Take at least 23 Republican seats, and keep all Democratic seats.
- **Governorships & State Legislatures:** Democrats must win back power in several states to gain control of redistricting following the 2020 census, and block the extreme Republican gerrymander maps that they have drawn and are ready to implement. More equitable district maps will ensure that Democrats will have a fair shot at winning the House for the next 10 years.

Witness to Treason

- **Secretaries of State**: The Secretaries of State in the 50 states have tremendous power to protect and expand voting rights. Democrats have the chance to win this important post from Republicans in a number of states this year.
- **State Attorneys General**: Since the 2016 elections, we have seen Democratic attorneys general stand at the front lines of the resistance movement. They have the power to bring lawsuits against Trump and his White House and halt his worst policies.
- **State Supreme Courts**: The GOP-packed Supreme Court means that state supreme courts are even more important to reversing conservative policies of all kinds.

A Student's Essay on Voting

My grandson, Vinny, wrote the following article in 2017 as part of an assignment in his sophomore Speech class. He was 15 then and in the speech he shines a light on our voting apathy. He sourced the cartoon.

It's Important to Vote

There was once a point in time where people were excited to vote. There was excitement to decide who would be leading you. However, it seems now, like many things, that excitement is gone and people think of it as a chore. People forget throughout history how we got to this point, now we are throwing it away. For example, for three weeks in 1917, women suffragettes were beaten and force-fed just like rabid animals. Why was that? Because they wanted the right to vote. Now we can't even get 50% of the eligible voters in America to vote. Why did the 45 civil rights activists get killed in the Sixties? Because they wanted the right to vote. Surely we can vote for their sacrifice. We were one of the first countries with a republic yet we have one of the lowest voting rates for developed countries.

Today, voting participation is a joke! Only about 57% of the people that are eligible voted this year. But 2012 was worse with 53%. We rank 35th in the world for voting out of all developed countries. There are 36 countries on that list. What example do we show when we support democracy overseas, and we can barely get 50% of our population to vote? We are spitting on the advantages we got 242 years ago. Well some of us are.

Over the past 65 years the voting for 18-24 range has gone down significantly. Now only about 18% of that group votes. Voting is important for many reasons. You are given this right to decide who is going to lead your country. There is nothing more patriotic than that. It is one of your biggest responsibilities as a citizen of a republic. Another important reason is people have risked their lives, and some have died so we can keep our republic. In the Revolutionary War, 75,000 people died so we could get this country. We should vote to show our gratitude to our founding fathers like John Adams, George Washington, and many more. Benjamin Franklin once said "it's only a republic if the people keep it that way". This one quote should encourage us to remember why we broke away from Great Britain. The English parliament unlawfully discriminated against American colonists so they broke away so they could have their own voice, and now 43% of our country's men and women threw away their own voice.

People complain about the candidates when frankly they are voting for both of them by not voting at all. Bad politicians don't get voted in by bad people, they get voted in by absent voters. The way you fix this problem is simple: go out there and vote. Regain your voice if you lost it along the way. Your vote matters more than you know, it can make a difference in an election. It is just the right thing to do. You have this ability to speak out, so be thankful for the opportunity to do this. You can vote if you're 18 or older, so go to vote.gov and select a State, in our case Pennsylvania. There are 13 things you have to put in like Name, Email, Address etc., and after that you have legally become a registered voter. Now remember your vote matters. Go register, then vote!

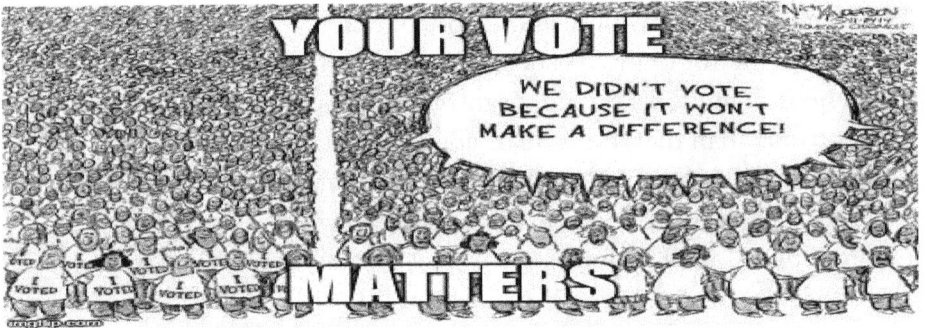

Voters on the left; slackers on the right. (*Nick Anderson, Houston Chronicle*)

Why are we resisting?

Here is an excerpt from the Daily Kos in July 2018. The author's sentiment is smartly expressed and, for me, a reminder of why I am resisting Trump and the army of libertarian, conservative, and Christian fundamentalists whose single-mindedness and bigotry threatens the freedoms of all Americans.

The essay below is excerpted from _Thousands of Red Caps on Capitol Hill_, by Russ Weingold, July 2018

There is something new that I have noticed increasingly cropping up on the Mall, in front of the Capitol, and, yes, in the Food Court at Union Station. There are groups after groups of people many of whom are wearing the same type of red baseball cap with the words "Make America Great Again" emblazoned on it. Now every one of us who was lucky enough to visit Washington DC in our youth wanted to come home with a souvenir or two: maybe a t-shirt saying "Ask not what your country can do for you" or a mug with the words "Mr. Gorbachev, tear down this wall!" What I have never seen before, however, is the uniformity of the people wearing one souvenir, this one type of baseball cap. There may be isolated exceptions, but almost invariably, the student groups in which so many are wearing one of these red caps are composed of teenagers, all white and virtually all male. When I see groups of people including African-Americans, Latinos, or a mixture of different ethnic and racial identities, there are no red hats, at least not Donald Trump's trademark cap.

So assuming each of these kids is wearing the cap of his own free will (one can only hope), why do they like it enough to buy it and wear it? Maybe it is nothing but the latest fad, understandably so given the underdog, unexpected, and unconventional nature of the Trump victory. I certainly recall the appeal of standing up to authority or conventional wisdom at that age and each generation is prone to and even entitled to such attractions. But I fear this phenomenon goes beyond this.

What do the words "Make America Great Again" mean to these young people? Not only is there the implicit assumption that America is no longer "great" in some sense that it once was, there is the underlying question of what made or makes America great. Is it superior natural resources, the strongest military, the biggest economy? We have to hope that these hat-wearers understand the foundational principles that also make this country great—free speech to be sure, but also aspirations for equal opportunity, non-discrimination, and justice for all, along with a spirit that we are all, regardless of our background or how we look, in this together. These principles seem woefully and intentionally lacking from Donald Trump's appeal. Whether it be blatant encouragement of racist groups, ruthless exploitation of anti-immigrant sentiment, reckless disregard for our federal law enforcement agencies, flippant disrespect for carefully nurtured international relationships, or simply rude and relentlessly self-centered conduct, displaying his slogan glorifies things that do anything but make us great.

After the impeachment and resignation of President Nixon, President Gerald R. Ford declared that "Our long national nightmare is over." If Trumpmania takes permanent root among so many of our new generation, our current national nightmare may have just begun. Trump and his cruel and divisive politics must be clearly repudiated both electorally and culturally. Having lived through Watergate and Richard Nixon's desecration of the White House, I note that no teenagers over the years have been touring the Hill with "Nixon's the One" baseball caps. That's because bi-partisan and non-partisan consensus developed to terminate a Presidency that threatened the rule of law and diminished our greatness. At that moment, our system showed how it could respond to a genuine internal threat. At this moment, it must again so that these thousands of red caps will be voluntarily but steadily removed as the country comes to its senses. There is a place on Capitol Hill at the Smithsonian National Museum of American History for a few of them, however, so future generations can learn of how a serious threat to our true greatness was stopped in its tracks and consigned to the past. *Source: https://www.dailykos.com/stories/2018/7/25/1783434/-Thousands-of-Red-Caps-on-Capitol-Hill*

What can you do? How can you save America? Where do you begin? Is it worth your time?

I hope this book and the contributions herein from so many good people across America have helped you answer the questions above. If you've gotten this far, you are someone who can make a difference for your community without having to wear a uniform, be elected to office, discover a better mousetrap, or snag your own cable talk show. I hope you do any one of those things if you wish to do so but what America needs every day in every town and city are people like you who are interested and concerned about our daily lives and the world we live in. Go do something. You will make a difference.

In closing, I learned at his passing that John McCain told everyone his favorite movie was "For Whom the Bell Tolls", a 1939 film with Gary Cooper and Ingrid Bergman. It is a story about courage and the hero, John Jordan, an American who wishes to live a meaningful and committed live, however short or long. The book and John Jordan's character inspired John McCain in his life journey. McCain's favorite quote in the book seems significantly fitting in the challenges that our personal integrity are confronted with today. John Jordan says, "Today

Witness to Treason

is only one day in all the days of the world that will ever be, but what will happen in all the days that will follow will depend on what you do today." Likewise, in your lifetime, you will come upon days where your actions will influence the days that will follow. One such day will come on November 6, 2018. It will be your choice to use that day wisely.

<u>VOTE</u>

Epilogue

Dateline: October 6, 2018

Trump, the GOP, and Christine Blasey Ford

The old men's club within the Republican Party has little respect for women, especially for women who resist any man's automatic presumption of dominance over them. Trump's history of disrespect for women is even more reprehensible, and visible to the world. They all showed it on September 27, when the GOP Senate conducted a kangaroo hearing in Washington, DC on the sexual assault charges brought by Professor Christine Blasey Ford against Supreme Court nominee Brett Kavanaugh. The proceedings were another example of men intimidating women. In summary, they set the time and place, made the rules. They hired a woman to do their dirty work, handing the mercenary the questions and hoping to trap Professor Ford. At the end of the day, the GOP senators left the hearing, dismissed what they heard, and announced they would vote the next day to advance Kavanaugh to a full vote by the Senate the following week. The GOP's open animosity for less than subservient women was alive and well. However, the next day the vote to advance Kavanaugh went as predicted, 11-10 in his favor, but the vote was preceded by even more drama. The GOP-dominated committee was forced to agree to a one week delay on a full Senate vote until after a FBI investigation was completed. Arizona Sen. Jeff Flake's vote was the key to the voting delay. A restricted 3-day FBI investigation was conducted under the control of Trump and the GOP. On October 6, Brett, aka Bart,

Witness to Treason

Kavanaugh was shamefully appointed to the Supreme Court of the U.S.

Trump's 2-year "Rain"

Trump's tortuous 2-year "rain" of shame on America continues to elicit analysis from all sides. A few political pundits still preface their remarks by suggesting that his, and his White House administrators, behavior are creating a new normal. No. Neither Trump nor his administration behaviors are normal. Trump's actions are both singularly moronic and spiteful, and include at least all of the following: executive pardons for friends, threats to fire federal prosecutors, demands for personal loyalty, meeting enemy leaders in private without a record of discussions, defaming his sexual accusers, committing financial crimes, and profiting personally by having his private businesses accept business that is related to government functions (identified as emoluments in the U.S. Constitution).

Trump continues to wear down the American people, one lie at a time. He knows his lies will bury the truth, and in our noble search to find the truth and prove the lie, we will divert energy away from stopping him and the conservative party's billionaires from wreaking havoc on America's individual liberties. Trump's handlers orchestrate daily crises to confuse the truth; to weary the crowds of people in the streets; and intimidate the solitary person in their isolation. Their goal is to make even the outrageous and most criminal offenses become 'numbly' acceptable so the people will shrug and yawn, and say, with a dismissive voice, "but that's normal now."

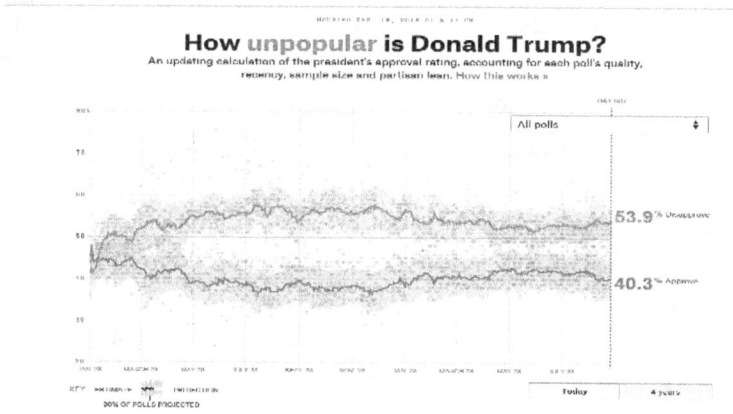

Trump's unpopularity Jan 2017 to Sept 2018, 40% approval Sept 15, 2018

Senator John McCain, August 25, 2018

There was a time, about 25 years ago, when party only mattered at election time. After the campaigns were over, everyone went back to work, to get things done. Senator John McCain was a part of that time. In his final hours as a true patriot, he showed America how things got done 25 years ago.

Senator McCain died on August 25, 2018 a year after being diagnosed with a brain tumor in July 2017. McCain's largeness of spirit, and his sense of duty to his God and his country were strengthened by his constant self-reminder to maintain "unity under stress". In the past two years, John McCain witnessed an unbalanced President who demands loyalty and respect from others but does not respect the truth or other men and women. John showed his American spirit when he completed his last mission for America and voted against the President's Trumpcare bill. McCain said the bill was less than fair to the citizens of America, and he knew the country could do better. So, he voted against a bad bill. It was an important moment that put a crack in Trump and McConnell's petty hold on Congress. McCain interrupted his courageous battle with cancer to walk into the Senate chamber to signal his independence and strength of purpose for all to see. He stood face to face with the architect of the GOP Party of No, Mitch McConnell, extended his right hand outward, then he turned his thumb down towards the floor, sending a bad healthcare bill into oblivion. It was Senator McCain's final vote on the Senate floor. Near death he extolled by his example, principles over politics. The senator recognized that the rule of law, the separation of powers, and freedom of speech are American traits, gifted in citizenship, and nurtured in a common belief in equality.

The final message that John McCain wanted to impress on Americans in our time of political strain and chaos was shown in his request to ask his biggest foes for political office to speak at his funeral. Presidents Bush and Obama presented eulogies, but their presence was more visible as a sign of "unity under stress" in these fractious days. The final echo we are left with is the Senator's insistence that even amidst our differences and many discordant voices, we are Americans, and "we can be better than this."

Trump's Economy

The GOP and Trump point proudly to the Stock Market and see remarkable positive activity. They are proud of the market growth, low unemployment, job growth. Trump and the GOP are giddy with the magic they have done with the domestic economy in two years. What no one in his cabinet wants to tell the emperor is that he had nothing to do with this growth and financial wellness. Just as no one would tell the emperor that he is naked, no cabinet member or aide will tell Trump that his turn to accept credit or blame will come next year and the year after when his administration's policies will bear fruit or not in 2019 and 2020. The lingering financial uptick in 2017-2018 are the residual gains from President Obama's policies from 2008-2016. Trump does get credit for the stock market boom because even the fox will rejoice with the other foxes when there are an abundance of chickens. Who will get the blame after all of Obama's chickens have been taken?

Trump's ranting about cutting costs for regulations and wanting to cut Social Security and Medicare, and reducing funding for programs for the poorest of Americans, is in sharp contrast to his cavalier addition of $1.9 trillion dollars to the national debt primarily caused by his lavish tax cut gift to the wealthy. All of Trump's economic actions are focused on immediate reward to his financial backers. Trump and the GOP want frugal fiscal spending on programs that benefit other Americans, basic things that the rich already have plenty of – food, health benefits, education, and housing. They are increasing spending for those that makes them and their masters happy. In turn, the $1.9 trillion dollars in debt will be paid by all of us, those who voted for them and against them.

Trump's emphasis on tariffs on Mexico, Canada, Japan, may make his voting base cheer, and that is all his base will get to cheer about, but the tariffs will certainly enrich his donors. In two years, Trump has battled with everyone, using tariffs, trade wars, rude behavior, nasty tweets, and a promise of fire and fury. He is willing to risk nearly $600 billion in trade with China, too. His personal trade war with China will make everyone at his table richer, but working Americans will pay the bill. Consumer prices will rise when Trump's tariffs are placed on goods imported from overseas. Additionally, tariffs imposed by foreign countries on American products exported overseas will make

American goods and services cost more overseas, resulting in less American goods. The worm turns, and soon less American goods sold will mean less goods made, then layoffs and business closures. The cycle is complete. We've been there before. Trickle down and supply side economics and the Republican Party platform. The rich get richer, and the poor get poorer.

Russian Collusion Update

The Special Counsel's investigation into collusion between Russia and the Trump Campaign officials completed its first year of activity in May 2018. As this book goes to print, Michael Cohen, Trump's personal lawyer, and Paul Manafort, the Trump Campaign manager at the time of the June 7 Trump Tower meeting, pleaded guilty on federal charges and began to cooperate with the Special Counsel. Additionally, two close friends of Trump were granted immunity by the Special Counsel for their cooperation in sharing information related to the Trump's business activities during the campaign. The two close friends - David Pecker, CEO of National Enquirer and American Media, Inc., and Allen Weisselberg, Trump Organization chief finance officer - agreed to cooperate with the Special Counsel investigation. They are expected to provide details on any background business arrangements during Trump 2016 presidential campaign. It is likely that a line of plea petitioners could start forming in front of the Special Counsel office, all seeking a chance to tell their story.

After, 15 months, the Mueller investigation still has several key persons to interview, least of whom is the President himself. Attorney Jeff

Sessions, Jared Kushner, Don Trump, Jr., and assorted Trump staff members may also be invited to appear before the special counsel.

Special Counsel –Russia and Trump Campaign collusion to date

- Thirty-two people and 3 Russian companies have been charged. Six persons have pleaded guilty.
- Roger Stone, long-time confident of President Trump, is under investigation by a grand jury.
- The President's legal team continues negotiating with Mueller. Will the President testify?
- Paul Manafort's lawyers announced on September 14 that Manafort will plead guilty to defrauding the U.S. and to obstruction of justice related to unreported income received from business dealings with foreign governments. In return, he will cooperate with the special counsel and share all that he knows about the Trump campaign and Russian contacts and activities in 2016. Manafort was Trump's campaign manager in the spring of 2016, and was closely connected to Vladimir Putin. What can Manafort share with investigators?
  a. Information on interactions between Trump campaign and Russia while Manafort was campaign chairman in 2016.
  b. Information and details on the June 7 Trump Tower meeting and any follow-up actions, if any. Manafort was present at the Trump Tower meeting.
  c. Information on what he knows about how changes in the Republican Party platform evolved at the Republican Party Convention in July 2016, and why the changes favored Russian interests.

Climate Control

There was another "fake news" report released on June 13, 2018 by 80 scientists who announced that the Antarctic ice sheet is melting at an increasing rate, pouring 200 billion tons of ice into the ocean every year and causing the sea levels to rise a half millimeter every year. The scientists agreed that this rate of ice melt has tripled in the last decade. They warned that if the acceleration continues at the same rate), low lying cities around the world will suffer disasters. (Note: Sea level can rise by two different mechanisms with respect to climate change. First, as the oceans warm due to an increasing global temperature, seawater expands—taking up more space in the ocean basin and causing a rise in water level. The second mechanism is the melting of ice over land, which then adds water to the ocean.)

Time range	Amount melting
1992-1997	49 billion tons average per year,
2000- 2011	73 billion tons average per year,
2012- 2017	219 billion tons average per year

Notice the increase in tons melted over the past 6 years? The scientists' report shows the acceleration began in 2002. The glaciers are melted from below by warm ocean waters threatening the Pine Island Glacier.

Elsewhere in LaLa Land, Michael Catanzarro, Trump's top energy and environmental adviser (and Charles Koch protégé) was asked to answer the scientists position that Climate Change was real and threatening the environment. He offered nebulous options for combatting climate control and ignored the evidence that climate control is needed. The Trump position of denying climate change is to promote a business plan developed by coal and energy power brokers:

mine the land for coal, ore, and minerals until the land and its labor force are exhausted or dead, and simultaneously drill the land and the oceans for oil and gas until the oceans are exhausted and polluted, and fish are something you take your children to see at the Zoo. When the worst is over, Trump's friends will find something else to plunder. They are looking for it now because their pockets are never too full of cash.

Trumpcare. Has he got a deal for you?

Trump failed to accomplish his first order of business after he became the 45th President. He and his Party of No were unable to remove Obamacare from the face of the earth and so Obamacare still thrives in America. Trump and the GOP hate Obamacare. At the same time, Trump suffered another public defeat when Sen. McCain's thumbs down vote sent Trumpcare to the trash heap. In response, the Trump administration and the zombie-legislators in the GOP Party continue to do whatever is possible and sleazy and deceptive to sabotage Obamacare, the only fair and reasonable health program affordable for all Americans. Trump and his GOP legislators, who by the way have top-shelf health benefits funded by taxpaying citizens like you and I, expanded the availability of their new, streamlined, snazzy, "limited" health plans. That's not good news. The adjective "limited" is the 'fly in the ointment'. These GOP plans that only Trump and the GOP are "excited about" (though they are not excited enough about them to trade in their government health plans for them), take several forms. All of them are a re-hash of the plans that the GOP has tried to stick down the throats of less-than-wealthy Americans for the past twenty years. They are the same plans that they could not agree to among themselves and pass when the GOP had a voting edge over the Democrats only eight months earlier. Trump in his trademark disdain for both the truth and his audience, said in late July 2018, "You are going to save massive amounts of money and have much better health care. It's going to be fantastic. You are going to save a fortune." To give fair time for the truth to be heard, I will paraphrase Sen. Chuck Schumer, D-NY who said, the announcement of these bogus health plans are a sham and they are deceitful tools used to sabotage a health plan that is in place and working (Obamacare). The hoopla from the Republicans supporting these plans is further evidence that the Trump administration is opening a backdoor to allow junk insurance plans to be sold to the most vulnerable and needy citizens in our country. They cost more than they provide. Worse than that, they promise everything and deliver nearly nothing. A simple rhetorical question is why should Americans pay more for canned milk when the legislators who are paid by taxpayers drink fresh whole milk? Where is the justice in that? The congressman at state and federal levels already receive free lunches, great health benefits, and weeks of paid personal time off from work.

Here is a brief description of Trump's "fantastic" healthcare plans for 2018/2019. The first plan is the GOP "short-term plan" that doesn't require the insurer to accept anyone with pre-existing conditions. The insurer also doesn't have to provide basic coverage like maternity, prescription drugs, mental care, etc. They provide the coverage for one year, and it can be renewed for up to three years. What do you think happens in the fourth year? Most likely, the price goes up, if they let you back in the plan. The premiums for this short-term plan are lower than some Obamacare policies (of course they are, the purchaser gets less), but the Obamacare policies include the "10 essential" kinds of coverage. Overall, the Obamacare plans have more medical coverage than the Trumpcare policies. The second, more expensive plan is the GOP "associated health plan" that has to accept persons with pre-existing medical conditions. They also have to cover the "10 essential" kinds of health coverage. They are more expensive and there is a strong likelihood they will increase exponentially.

The GOP Trumpcare plan choices are like new car sales pitches: get a shiny new health plan, pay less per month, for less care, get less preventive maintenance, and pay more maintenance cost per year. In three years or less, you will need a new plan, and like a new car, you will pay more. Wanna deal? Stop by at your local GOP legislator's office. Oh, keep your wagon of coal, and your hurricane flood boots outside.

NRA, under the gun

Approaching 2019, Sante Fe, TX, Parkland, TX, and Antioch, TN are trying to settle back into some measure of normalcy, but they will never be the same. Never. The tragedies that occurred on these quiet towns will never be understood and will never be forgotten. But some things don't change. The NRA continues to sell memberships and get commissions on guns sold from gun manufacturers and affiliated businesses. There are no longer any moments, or words, of regret from the NRA leadership. On the contrary, any crooked look in their direction elicits murderous stares and aggressive words and verbal attacks from their own stable of media attack wolves. The NRA's standard response to criticism, or to anything less than a smile or "howdy", is to sour-up and fight back. The coming year will possibly find the NRA in an even more defensive position. After all, accepting money from Russia for any reason isn't very American. Here are a few things that will keep the heat on the NRA in 2019.

- Public insistence nationwide for Gun Control legislation, and consumer boycotts on products and services connected to the NRA. (goods, food, services)
- Parkland Gun Control Lobby, David Hogg and others lobbying legislators for sensible gun laws legislation: increasing the age for assault rifle purchases, gun owner registration, and background checks for everyone, and extending liability laws onto to gun manufacturers, and boycotting the NRA
- Did the NRA accept money from Russian, and use it to support Trump's 2016 campaign.

Immigration

Right now, it isn't good to be an immigrant in America. It's not even good to look like an immigrant in America. Next year it maybe the Muslims who are targeted. The year after that, black people will move back into their traditional position as the No. 1 targets for discrimination and overt persecution. If the GOP has their way in Congress, everyone will get a chance to be targeted for one reason or another. That's how tyranny works and how freedoms disappear. Immigration is first, everything else is next, the others will just be slower and one at a time. Sinclair Lewis was wrong, "It can happen here." It did happen here in 2016.

Immigration roundups continued while press coverage was lessened. News articles in September during the newest hurricane season reported ICE has received tens of millions of added funds transferred earlier from FEMA to cover cost of adding so many new officers and administrative persons to support Trump's aggressive "zero tolerance" program. This added cash enabled Federal, State, and local police officers, sheriffs, and immigration officers throughout the U.S. to target people with dark eyes, dark hair, and Spanish surnames who spoke with "accents". Once found, illegal and legal persons were arrested and handed over "gestapo-like" to ICE. At the same time, America's shock at seeing children isolated in cages had lessened as Trump aides knew would occur. The Zero Tolerance Program at the border used to terrorize children, and to spite immigrants coming to America continued unabated. Additionally, the Department of Justice under AG Jeff Sessions still threatened all of the states who didn't cooperate with ICE. The DOJ instructions from Trump was simple: no catching immigrants, no federal funding for city services. In America 2018, it was hard to believe what was happening. It was like getting paid to catch slaves.

Trump's Wall

Trump also failed at his second most important promise to his base – he promised to build a wall, Trump's Wall, across the entire southern border between the United States and Mexico, and during his campaign he said, "Mexico will pay for the wall." As early as February 2018, it was clear that Mexico was not going to build a wall, and Mexico was not going pay the United States to build a wall. Instead, Trump's lack of diplomacy insulted Mexico, its President, and its people. Soon, the second most important piece of Trump's promises was temporarily shelved and has been dormant, placed in a basket with his other large wish toys. He has pulled it out of the basket on several occasions over the past nineteen months to dangle it in front of the Democrats, and even Mexico. However, Trump's negotiation style wears thin quickly. After one negotiation with him about anything, no one trusts him.

Witness to Treason

On September 26, 2018, just after Congress voted to extend the fiscal budget for another 90 days in order to continue funding the federal government through Dec. 7 (even the GOP is not dumb enough to shut down the government just before the November mid-term elections), Trump waved his big beautiful Wall at the Democrats. Seeking again to get his Wall funded, he said he would not sign any request to fund the government after December 7 unless he got a full commitment from Congress to build his Wall. Otherwise, he would welcome a "shutdown". Trump is on record for saying that he believes "government shutdowns are good for the country". Whenever he and his GOP Party of No are unable to get their own way on anything, they don't compromise or govern, they shut down the government. Therefore, Trump will stop the federal government from working for the nation and its citizens until he gets a full commitment from Congress to build his Trump Wall across the U.S. southwestern border with Mexico. That's how they do things in Russia, China, Turkey, Iran, and Iraq.

Three Supreme Court Rulings, and worse to come

Trump wants to change the direction of the Supreme Court from protecting all U.S. citizens' rights to championing only the interests of the wealthiest men and most powerful corporations in America. But he isn't interested in politics. He is simply paying back his country club members for their services rendered. Remember quid pro quo? In fact, the increase in the Supreme Court's judicial rulings favoring these interests began before Trump donned his red hat in 2015. The full credit belongs to the political strategists hired by the family patriarchs who we saw gather at Indian Wells in Chapter 7, the men who purchased the Republican Party 25 year ago.

A quick look at recent Supreme Court rulings shows the path of the "limited liberty" that the conservative king-makers envision in America in the imminent future with rulings like *Citizens United* vs FEC, *Gill vs Whitford*, and *Bradley vs West Chester University*. The rulings, in order of appearance above, support unlimited and undisclosed campaign spending, extreme partisan gerrymandering, and restrictions on corporate and government whistleblowers. Other cases recently reviewed or scheduled to be heard by the Court include voter suppression and rights of labor to organize. Now the majority of conservative judges on the Supreme Court gives it massive control of the direction of law through the rest of the 21st century. The direction will not be forward. The nation and its citizens will be pushed back further into the past, both economically and socially. And the rich and the powerful will rejoice that America is great again.

Another example of the Supreme Court's bold abuse of its power is the ruling on Shelby v. Holder where the court struck down the most effective clause in the Voting Act of 1965. The clause 5 required all states to submit voting regulations, etc. to the federal government before making it a local or state requirement. The reason for clause 5 was to prevent new Jim Crow laws (regional laws that prevented black citizens from voting in southern states) from being resurrected in the South. Responsible members of the U.S. Congress in 1965 knew the South would impose new bogus restrictions if the federal law was left unenforced in the states. During the subsequent 50 years, few voter restriction laws were passed in the states, and were nearly non-existent, until now. In Shelby v Holder, 570 U.S. 2 (2013), the new partisan Supreme Court struck down the constitutionality of clause 5. They ruled it was no longer needed. These learned conservative minds defied commonsense and said that because there were fewer complaints since 1965, the clause was no longer needed. So they removed only that clause. Of course, the only reason the Jim Crow laws did not surface in 50 years was due to clause 5 which prevented it, and when such state rules surfaced, the federal government ruled against them. Now, remove the cat, and the rats will play. Since the Shelby v Holder ruling, voter restrictive laws are increasing in the southern states and in the western and southern states where the new GOP has legislative dominance. This is the law that Trump and the GOP want returned to America.

Women's rights and sexual discrimination will soon be on the Court's dockets. The addition of two more "boys from Brazil" to the Court will not make America more democratic. Their goal is to take America back to the "good old days" when old white men made all the rules: good ones for them, bad ones for you. What can be done after the Court is filled with such men? Vote out the men and women who chose them, starting at every election, at every level of government. Don't wait for someone else to take the lead. Lead with your vote.

It's not far-fetched that two more years of Trump's megalomaniac behavior will bring America in close alignment with Trump's Rat Pack tyrants overseas. It is possible that after a second term with the ruinous trifecta of Trump/GOP/Supreme Court in control of our nation, our citizen rights will be eroded and the country's spirit weakened by the daily stress we encounter. Nevertheless, you and I mustn't let any of this insanity become "the new normal" in America. Stay alert. Resist. Vote. And take a friend or two with you.

It's your country.

Bibliography

Dark Money. The Hidden History of the Billionaires Behind the Rise of the Radical Right.
Jane Meyer, 2016, Anchor Books, ISBN 978-0-307-94790-1

The Plot to Hack America: How Putin's Cyberspies and WikiLeaks Tried to Steal the 2016 Election. Malcolm Nance, 2016, Skyhorse Publishing, ISBN 978-1-510-72332-0

It Can't Happen Here
Sinclair Lewis, edit. Michael Meyer, 2014, reprint Signet Classics, ISBN 978-0-451-46564-1

The New Tsar: The Rise and Reign of Vladimir Putin.
Steven Lee Myers, 2016, Vintage, ISBN 978-0-345-80279-8

Index

Bob McLaughlin was born and raised in Chester, PA. He is a graduate of St. James High School and Widener University both in Chester, PA and he is a life-long resident of Delaware County. He and his wife Dorothy live in Ridley Park. He has three children and ten grandchildren.

Bob retired in 2012 from a career as a Purchasing and Construction Manager for several international engineering companies and he was one of a three-person American management team hired to support the establishment and growth of the new Aker-Kvaerner Shipyard inside the former Philadelphia Shipyard in South Philadelphia.

Naturally he is an avid Philadelphia sports fan who supports all local teams. He only rooted one time for a team outside the city. That was the 1960 Pittsburgh Pirates, the subject of first book, *Danny and Mickey, Ordinary Heroes,* available on Amazon and other retail book websites.

More information for *Danny and Mickey* is to be found at
dannyandmickey.com.

www.ingramcontent.com/pod-product-compliance
Lightning Source LLC
Chambersburg PA
CBHW030233030426
42336CB00009B/82